William
Burroughs
and the
Secret of
Fascination

William Burroughs and the Secret of Fascination

Oliver Harris

Southern Illinois University Press
Carbondale and Edwardsville

Copyright © 2003 by the Board of Trustees,
Southern Illinois University
All rights reserved
Printed in the United States of America
06 05 04 03 4 3 2 1

Frontispiece: William Burroughs beside sphinx, Metropolitan Museum of Art, fall 1953.
© Allen Ginsberg Trust.

Library of Congress Cataloging-in-Publication Data

Harris, Oliver (Oliver C. G.)
    William Burroughs and the secret of fascination / Oliver Harris.
        p. cm.
    Includes bibliographical references (p.) and index.
        1. Burroughs, William S., 1914—Criticism and interpretation.
    2. Beat generation in literature. I. Title.

    PS3552.U75 Z69 2003
    813'.54—dc21
    ISBN 0-8093-2484-9 (alk. paper)   2002004723

Printed on recycled paper. ♻

The paper used in this publication meets the minimum requirements of American
National Standard for Information Sciences—Permanence of Paper for Printed Library
Materials, ANSI Z39.48-1992. ∞

A certain great and powerful king once asked a poet: "What can I give you of all that I have?" He wisely replied: "Anything sir . . . except your secret."

—Orson Welles, *Mister Arkadin*

Contents

Preface

B ehind the visible story of William Burroughs' writing, there lies another, secret history, and the aim of this book is to show both the high stakes and the paradoxical difficulties of trying to reveal the truth about his development as a writer. Since the first chapter maps out and models what the rest of the book does, here I just want to acknowledge some of the many things that I don't do. I only deal with Burroughs' writing of the 1950s, the first of four decades. I don't make grand claims for his importance or consider in any detail the great range of his themes or treat Burroughs as a "man of ideas." I don't make an easy, linear story out of the twisting, difficult material of my subject, and most of all, I don't try to do his humor. Twenty-five years ago, a reviewer of the first major critical study, Eric Mottram's *The Algebra of Need,* claimed that Burroughs had perfidiously denied his own gifts, which were "comic and exuberant rather than admonitory and bleak." He concluded: "It may be his just reward, then, to be studied by people who don't find him funny." I half agree with the first part but would like to put on record that the conclusion is wrong. More than anything, I remember the loud laughter of Mottram, who was the examiner for my doctoral thesis in 1988, and I think we shared the same sense that Burroughs is comic the way that Kafka is, laughing at what is not supposed to be funny, laughing not lightly but in the face of fear and horror. The Burroughs I write about is a serious Burroughs, taken seriously, but if I didn't find him funny as well as frightening, I would never have found him so *fascinating.*

This book has been a long time in the writing and rewriting. I started my doctorate in 1984 mainly because of the way Peter Conrad, then my most inspirational professor at Oxford, reacted to the idea. In so many words, he told me it was a dead end, Burroughs was not just a waste of my time and a poor career move but bad news. I have a picture of him in the act of crossing himself to make the point, but this is probably apocryphal.

In any case, since I was ambivalent about staying in academia, that decided it for me. I put aside the thesis years ago, and this book is driven by different needs and desires, but without Peter Conrad, my work on Burroughs might not have begun, so my first thanks go to him.

I must also give thanks to the many Burroughs critics whose work I have used in making my own. For reasons that will become apparent, not all of them will like the use I have put them to, but I hope they will respect my motives. For giving me their time, support, or advice, I also want to thank Ian Finlayson, Robin Lydenberg, Jennie Skerl, David Stanford, John Tytell, and Terry Wilson. Special thanks go to James Grauerholz and of course, if with a certain ambiguity, to Burroughs himself, who generously gave me a little of his time and who has taken up so much of mine.

For institutional support, I thank Keele University and all my colleagues. I am also grateful to the special collections staff at: Green Library, Stanford University; Butler Library, Columbia University; Kenneth Spencer Research Library, University of Kansas; Bancroft Library, University of California; Hayden Library, Arizona State University; Northwestern University Library; and Humanities Research Center, University of Texas. Thanks to Peter Hale of the Allen Ginsberg Trust for permission to use the photograph of Burroughs, to John Wilson for his painstaking copyediting of my manuscript, and to the editorial staff at Southern Illinois University Press.

For generously granting permission to quote from unpublished materials, thanks go to: James Grauerholz, Trustee, the William S. Burroughs Trust; to Bob Rosenthal and the Allen Ginsberg Trust; and to Robert H. Jackson.

I also acknowledge that sections of chapter 3 were previously published as "'Can You See a Virus?': The Queer Cold War of William Burroughs," in the *Journal of American Studies* 33.2 (1999), and parts of chapter 2 were previously published as "Queer Shoulders, Queer Wheel: Homosexuality and Beat Textual Politics," in *Beat Culture: The 1950s and Beyond* (Amsterdam: VU, 1999), and as "Cold War Correspondents: Ginsberg, Kerouac, and Cassady and the Political Economy of Beat Letters," in *Twentieth Century Literature* 46.2 (Summer 2000).

Unique thanks go to Ian MacFadyen, a truly Burroughsian friend.

I wish to dedicate this book to my three girls, Nina, Mia, and Ella, to Jenny, to my mother, and to the memory of my father.

Finally, I have to acknowledge someone I don't really know and who could easily be another apocryphal memory. Several years ago, I found myself in a crowded room, full of postgraduate students discussing Burroughs. I became aware that a man was crossing the room towards me. I don't recall what he looked like or the exact words he said to me. I wasn't paying much attention, just enjoying the atmosphere after giving a paper. It was about Burroughs as an iconoclast mistaken for an icon, and it seemed to have gone down well. When the man was right in front of me, I realized he wanted to ask a question. He mumbled something rather vaguely, and I only caught his last words, which he whispered. It went something like this: "Since you—since you know Burroughs—and—what I mean is, *what is his secret?*" I don't remember the reply I mumbled back, and since I didn't have an answer, it hardly matters. But I have an answer to give now, because now I realize that this man had just given it to me.

Abbreviations

The following abbreviations are used in citations for frequently cited works by William Burroughs.

I	*Interzone*
J	*Junky*
L	*The Letters of William S. Burroughs, 1945–1959*
LG	*Letters to Allen Ginsberg, 1953–1957*
NL	*Naked Lunch*
Q	*Queer*
WL	*The Western Lands*
WV	*Word Virus*
YL	*The Yage Letters*

William
Burroughs
and the
Secret of
Fascination

1

The Secret of Fascination

If one wishes to deceive a man, what one presents to him is the painting of a
veil, that is to say, something that incites him to ask what is behind it.
—Jacques Lacan, *The Four Fundamental Concepts*

A MALICIOUS-LOOKING SMILE

SHADOWY UNKNOWN GENIUS

The fascination of William Burroughs, which somehow always precedes the writing that yet produces it, is a paradox already at work
in his first appearance. This debut is not his first publication, a school
newspaper essay from 1929 called "Personal Magnetism," nor the
abortive novel he worked on with Jack Kerouac in 1945, entitled "And the
Hippos Were Boiled in Their Tanks," although each of these would make
convenient points of departure. The debut I have in mind is far more paradoxical and much more fascinating. It is a "malicious-looking smile" that
appears in Kerouac's own debut novel, *The Town and the City*, published
in March 1950 (373). Looming at the dead center of the twentieth century,
this enigmatic smile that is at once sinister and comic, intensely material
and weirdly spectral, is an image that initiates and seems to predict Burroughs' equivocal presence across the next fifty years. To adapt a line of
hyperbole from the better-known character sketch in *On the Road*, you
might say all of Burroughs is in that smile.

What enables us to read a condensed history of Burroughs' future in a smile? Most obviously, it is the way that he first appears as a character imaged in another writer's novel. From the very beginning, the appearance of his identity had the quality of a fiction, a fantasy projected by others, or a simulation, a copy behind which there was no original. For what is so singular about the iconic figure is not just its cultural proliferation but that the image has always been replicated as much by those under its influence as by Burroughs himself. The smile is a sign of fascination, because it acts out the image's power of mimetic magic and inaugurates Burroughs' distinct iconicity, infectious now across five decades. In this sense, a direct line runs from the 1950s to the 1990s, from Jack Kerouac's fictionalizations to David Cronenberg's filmmaking, Keith Haring's painting, Kurt Cobain's recording, and the whole A to Z of Burroughs' fertilizing influence on contemporary culture from Kathy Acker to Frank Zappa, as it becomes ever harder to separate Burroughs' oeuvre from a generalized production of his image.

This is what makes the first sighting of Burroughs in *The Town and the City* so remarkable, because it predicts precisely the unique form of artistic mediation that would shadow Burroughs' career. For Kerouac presents an extraordinary *double* displacement, an uncannily *twice*-mediated representation, since it is not actually Burroughs' own persona, Will Dennison, who sports his "malicious-looking smile" but Levinsky, the character based on Allen Ginsberg. More curious still, this imitated smile, this spectral grin without a material Cheshire cat, is present not only in Dennison's absence but ahead of his first appearance proper in the novel. Burroughs' reputation during the decade that followed *The Town and the City* was almost entirely mediated by Kerouac and Ginsberg, given the neglect of *Junkie* (1953), the nonappearances of both *Queer* (1985; written 1952) and "In Search of Yage" (in *The Yage Letters* [1963]; written 1953), and the publication of *The Naked Lunch* (1959) outside America.[1] It is easy to grasp therefore how Kerouac's scene marks the creation of Burroughs as a legendary persona *of* the Beats *by* the Beats, as well as being more broadly symptomatic of the way his identity has been constructed and mediated in advance of his own work.

The Town and the City's drama of ambiguous anticipation was a compelling prototype, the first of a script written out again and again during the Beat decade: in John Clellon Holmes's *Go* (1952), a roman à clef that simply borrowed "Will Dennison" directly from *The Town and the City*; in Ginsberg's dedication to "Howl" (1956), where the unwritten *Naked Lunch* was promised as an "endless novel which will drive everybody mad" (*Collected Poems* 159); in Kerouac's *On the Road* (1957), where "Old Bull Lee" is endowed with "phenomenal fires and mysteries" and appears like "something out of an old evil dream" (131, 137); in articles such as that cowritten by Ginsberg and Gregory Corso at the height of Beat media attention, which advertised Burroughs as "the shadowy unknown genius behind the more publicized figures of Kerouac and Ginsberg" (166); and in Corso's own novel, *The American Express* (1961), where he appears as the "spectral" Mr. D, who "stands for danger! disaster! death!" (17, 57). Such dramatic promotion in, outside, and on the margins of fiction inevitably generated a kind of phantom figure. Those images, vivid yet ghostly, seductive but ambivalent, constituted the spectacular substance of Burroughs ahead of his own work, so that his texts were liable to be read as the products of a superimposed Burroughs-Dennison-Lee, a "simulacral" identity preceding and canceling the "real."

The usurping force of Beat mythmaking and fictionalized biography significantly affected how Burroughs has been critically received and popularly imagined. Of course, Burroughs has always been tangential to the movement—its elder statesman, godfather, mentor, or tutelary spook— while his work has tied critics imposing a Beat definition in knots of self-contradiction. But this is precisely the point: the image of Burroughs has remained central to the cultural popularity of the Beats for the paradoxical reason that its presence was always essentially marginal, equivocal, phantasmic. He was never completely there or quite belonged but always marked a limit, a point of excess, a kind of strange inner extremity. This position returns in Burroughs' place within "Beat Studies," where the politics of Beat canon-formation has demanded that he find no exit—Burroughs may not fit, but his name is still needed to add steel and weight— so that he remains neither in nor out but is left dancing a kind of critical hokey-pokey.

It is tempting to free Burroughs from the Beat Generation altogether, to quite simply disregard the context, and this is what certain Burroughs critics have tried to do. The two best studies, Robin Lydenberg's *Word Cultures* (1987) and Timothy Murphy's *Wising Up the Marks* (1997), don't even *mention* Kerouac. But there are good reasons not to yield to this temptation, and those who think that Burroughs' early texts can now be read outside the Beat context, taken out like a picture from an old frame, should think again. For contemporary readers, each of his four texts written during the 1950s comes framed in some way by Beat reference, none of which actually dates from that decade: the reedited *Junkie,* now retitled *Junky* (1977) features Ginsberg's long introduction; the belated publication of *Queer* sports back-flap comments by Ginsberg or (in the first British edition) by Kerouac; *The Yage Letters* combines "In Search of Yage" with Ginsberg's "replies" from 1960; and all editions of *Naked Lunch* after 1962 begin with Burroughs' introduction that credits the book's title to Kerouac. The intrusion of such an array of accessory texts, which have never been reckoned with for their often complex consequences, means that Burroughs remains bound by and to the Beats. And finally, what is true for how these texts are received is also true for how they were written: the effects of the association are too material and too enduring to be ignored, and it is impossible to advance a serious case for Burroughs' development without understanding those effects. Indeed, one reason why the ambiguities of his evolving identity as a writer so troubled Burroughs in the 1950s is that the legendizing of the Beats shaped not only the reception of his early writing but its *production.*

Since even the most conventional literary reputations are what John Rodden calls "radically contingent"—made by "a constant interaction of images and information" (x, xi)—it is not surprising that Burroughs' active participation in the making of his own image has always remained in doubt. In 1953, Ginsberg quotes Burroughs' saying that he is "trading on one of the most appealing characters in literature, the incorrigible old reprobate" (*As Ever* 156). In 1956, Burroughs writes in his journal: "I'll maintain this International Sophistico-criminal Mahatma con no longer. It was more or less shoved on me anyway" (*I* 130). In 1959, he reassures his mother that "sensational publicity" is now "the only way to sell books" and jokes, "I may have to start drinking my tea from a skull since this is the only vice remaining to me" (qtd. in Morgan 320). And in the same year, Paul Bowles claimed that "the legend existed in spite of him, and not because of him: he didn't give a damn about it" ("Burroughs" 15). The ambiguity and the indeterminacy remain, leaving Burroughs somewhere between the Wizard of Oz, stage-managing special effects from behind a curtain, and the Magician's Apprentice, a victim of conjured forces long out of his own control.

In the Beat context, Burroughs therefore occupies that indeterminate space "somewhere between" Ginsberg and Kerouac: which is to say that he neither embraced the self-marketing strategy of Ginsberg, whose genius, according to Ron Sukenick, was to "seize the means of promotion" (14), nor suffered Kerouac's illusory faith that a published writer could escape the reach of the reifying commodity image. In this sense, those like Dennis Cooper, who in 1988 accused Burroughs of "betrayal" because he had become "less a literary threat than a celebrity" (70), are quite mistaken. To read the packaged stardom of his persona as the sign of surrendering control in his "dotage," so that his final publications are no more than impoverished "career moves," naively presumes a past of idealistic motives when he *did* exercise control. On the contrary, Burroughs always ran such risks, to begin with because he had little choice, as should be clear from the compromises and contingencies of his early publication history, and later on because he actively surrendered control through collaborative uses of his work and image. There can be no true "betrayal" of self when there is no false "fidelity" to it either.

If, as Jennie Skerl claimed, Burroughs' "most important 'work' may be his legend, which exists somewhere between the realms of fact and fiction" (2), then it was there from the start. In March 1950, Burroughs had settled into Mexico City and was just beginning work on what became *Junkie,* crossing national and creative borders to venture simultaneously into the twinned territories of expatriate existence and the writing life. Soon after *The Town and the City* arrived in the mail, on 10 March, he wrote a letter back that began by praising Kerouac's novel and ended by revealing he had started his own. And so, at the very moment he was embarking on his own mature writing, Burroughs must have looked into Kerouac's fictionalizing mirror and seen this impersonation of his "own" persona's smile smiling enigmatically back. For cultural impact, the image of Burroughs from *The Town and the City* does not compare to the far more widely read *On the Road,* but it is plausible to suggest that no representation affected Burroughs *himself* more deeply. In his letter to Kerouac, he failed to comment on the portrait of Dennison, but we should not forget that the name Burroughs used for his persona throughout the writing of his own novel, *Junkie,* was not William Lee—a late substitution—but none other than Will Dennison. This was, in turn, the name he had used when cowriting "Hippos" with Kerouac five years earlier, which meant that he was using for his own authorial identity the nom de plume that Kerouac had just transformed into the name of a fictional character. It is only a mild exaggeration to conclude that Burroughs' career as a fiction writer began not at the moment of Kerouac's inspiring success but at the moment Burroughs recognized himself as a fictional character, and a character of a very particular kind; one whose potency to affect others coincides with a disturbing power of autonomy from its real-life author.

WILL HOLLYWOOD NEVER LEARN?

We might ask, did Kerouac "read" Burroughs with prophetic knowledge or did he "write" the Burroughs we know into being? The question raises the fundamental issue of his image. This identity, which conflates producer with his product and strips history of its specificity, is not something we can wish away. Like Dennison's ghost of a smile, it persists and lingers on for the very reason that it seems a text without an accessible and material author, a signifier without any signified. This is the significance of Burroughs to the Beats: they already conjure him as the name of a peculiar kind of secret, an *empty secret,* in the sense that this shadowy figure, hidden "behind the more publicized figures," serves as a *master* precisely because he is never really there at all. The effect depends on a certain distance, one rendered literally through Burroughs' geographic removal from America and figuratively through the enigmatic quality of Beat representations. And if, as John Lardas says, the inscriptions of Burroughs in "Howl" and *On the Road* generated a "disembodied notoriety" (223), then this would be the governing trope, the template for understanding his future appearance. From Barry Miles's allusion to his "strong, though invisible presence" in the London Arts Lab scene of 1960s London (*William Burroughs* 11), to Geoff Ward's general characterization of a "suppression of presence so ghostly as to become its own powerful identity" ("Mutations" 112), Burroughs is typically recognized as "a formidable *absence*" (Craig Karpel qtd. in Hibbard xi).

What then does it mean for Graham Caveney to claim that "there is nothing hidden in Burroughs' image, no secret to be decoded" (19), or for Timothy Murphy to say that since "he hides nothing, he has no secrets which can be revealed" (*Wising Up* 231)? Taking up the myth of transparency that *el hombre invisible* has himself promoted, they approach Burroughs as another Andy Warhol, the great American icon of blank ambiguity. "Warhol," writes Steven Shaviro, "is mysterious and charismatic not because he is so good at keeping his inner life secret, but because he has no secrets to keep" (*Cinematic Body* 206). Does this direct challenge to hermeneutics, to the deciphering of any deep meaning, apply to Burroughs, let alone fit Warhol? Or might we say of Burroughs what Hal Foster says of Warhol, that "the fascination is that one is never certain about this subject 'behind': is anybody home, inside the automaton?" ("Death" 41). Foster's open question preserves a vital ambiguity and allows him to read Warhol's images as both deep and shallow, both referential and simulacral. The alternative is a situation that combines a certain philosophical integrity with a radical short circuit of any grounding whatsoever. When an interviewer asked, "How do you see the relationship between your public image—there's a William S. Burroughs archetype—your body of work, and yourself, the actual man?" to his total consternation, Burroughs replied: "There is no actual man" (Bernstein 707). The identity of Burroughs may be a mythic abstraction, and there may be no unproblematic "objective" truth behind it, but it still has material origins and equally material consequences; and what's more, Burroughs is fully implicated in sustaining its construction. When he says that all his "books are one book" (qtd. in Malanga 94), we should recognize how this makes art into "consciousness" and biography into "legend," as Skerl puts it (18), at the cost of taking Burroughs out of history altogether. Or again, when he says that the "past only exists in some record of it," so that "there are no facts" (qtd. in Malanga 111), we should suspect the tactical convenience, the inevitable temptations of a position that sees truth only in the falsity of claims to truth. The problem with the approaches of Caveney and Murphy then is that in taking Burroughs on his own terms, they risk eliding all doubts and contradictions, dematerializing the historical Burroughs with a credulity that forestalls any suspicion.

An anecdote will illustrate. When he was interviewed for *Paris Review* in 1965 and asked to confirm an account of the genesis of *Naked Lunch,* Burroughs parried the question with carefully chosen words of warning: "Excuse me," he replied, "there is no accurate description of the creation of a book, or an event" (qtd. in Knickerbocker 160). The counsel to distrust historiographic authority sounds salutary, good advice for interviewers and literary biographers. But not, apparently, for Burroughs himself: "Actually," he continues, that book

> was written mainly in Tangier, after I had taken the cure with Dr. Dent in London in 1957. I came back to Tangier and I started working on a lot of notes that I had made over a period of years. [. . .] I went to Paris about 1959, and I had a great pile of manuscripts.

But actually, the famous cure took place in May 1956, the move to Paris in January 1958, and as he later had to admit, much of the book was written before the cure and not only in the form of notes. As we will see, such mistakes are neither isolated nor incidental, so that Burroughs' principled skepticism must be made to apply to all genetic accounts, especially his own. Of course, an incorrect or incomplete account is not necessarily a *falsified* one, but nevertheless some accounts are not only more accurate than others but can only be made by unmaking the inaccurate.

Making such epistemological trouble, Burroughs has not helped critics narrate his literary development with any precision or coherence. More than that, the material failings have had specific interpretative effects across the full range of critical approaches. This is not to say that all readings are predetermined, designed and directed by Burroughs' sinister hand; but rather to insist that we seek, in the past according to Burroughs, a way of accounting for certain features of Burroughs criticism that should not be seen in isolation or as separable from the work itself. If I give so much attention to the state of critical play in what follows, it is because the measure of my own reading has to be its ability to account for prior misreadings.

Since we can neither take Burroughs' word on trust nor simply ignore it, we are forced to adopt a critical method whose generic paradigm *par excellence* is the detective's mission—trawling for clues and throwing back the epistemological red herrings. It is surely no coincidence that during the 1950s Burroughs inscribed his attitude towards knowledge of the past most consistently through this very narrative model, while pressing it towards a point of *ontological* crisis. Hence, his proposed Interpol "Tanger film script" of August 1957: "But the story I want to tell you is not a story of crime and detection, but of a man who made a complete break with everything he had ever known and been—so complete he lost the way back" (*LG* 190). What this script suggests is that to solve the crime—"the creation of a book, or an event"—is either beside the point or risks missing it. What Burroughs is getting at here on the level of theme would become much clearer soon afterwards at the level of method.

Shortly after publication of *The Naked Lunch*, in October 1959 Burroughs wrote to Ginsberg announcing that he had a "new method of writing" and added: "In this game the point is to lose what you have, and not wind up with someone else's rusty load of continuity" (*L* 434). Quite simply, Burroughs' cut-up project of the 1960s began as a way to systematize the drive to lose the undesired past, to cut his way out of an old identity, if not out of identity itself. In his previous letter, he had spoken of discovering another new methodology, the therapeutic "method of Scientology," that would replay the past "until the trauma is wiped off" (431); an attached "Biographical note" begins with the stark declaration: "I have no past life at all" (433). This ambition to make a complete break, to cut off history and dispossess the self, to kick the habit of what Walter Benjamin once called "that most terrible drug—ourselves—which we take in solitude" (*Reflections* 190), this ambition demands discontinuity as a *historical* as well as a formal principle. This is the meaning of the cinematic term that Burroughs chooses to express the "point" of his game: against the "continuity editing" of classical Hollywood film, a system designed to create the illusion of transparency and consistency for the audience's comfort, he proposes narrative cuts that can't be smoothed over, "sudden space shifts" that will not, as he put it in *Naked Lunch*, keep his reader "Gentle" (218). The disjunctive and metamorphic juxtapositions that mark his cut-up texts of the 1960s undo the illusion of fixed identity, and this sabotage coincided, fully and quite deliberately, with the introduction of a radical discontinuity in the narrative of his own biographical and literary history. Intensely personal as well as ideological, the first and deepest cut of all was the one that divided Burroughs' first two decades either side of *Naked Lunch*. The paradoxical upshot of such an assault on narrative continuity is that a critic who narrates with any success the chronology of Burroughs' development across these two decades is, on Burroughs' terms, doomed like a gentle reader of *Naked Lunch* to have missed the point.

If Burroughs was acting out "the death of the author" in advance of Roland Barthes's famous thesis, then like Barthes, we still have to qualify this by saying, yes, as the sole ground and guarantor of meaning the writer has died *but not his chronology*. However difficult it may be to give the Burroughs oeuvre its chronology, to disentangle and reconstruct the histories of writing and reception, it is impossible to make a rigorous reading of his texts without knowing how they relate one to another. Burroughs' mythic identity must *not* be "considered another of his texts" (Savran, *Taking It* 86), except insofar as this one also has its material origins and effects and has helped mystify the production histories and original circumstances of his *other* texts.

KEEPING AN EYE ON HIM

When an interviewer asked Burroughs, "Do you have a lot of secrets?" the significant answer was not in the first phrase but in the second: "No writer has any secrets. It's all in his work" (qtd. in Malanga 111). The secret *of* the work—the crime that is "the creation of a book"—is intimate with the secret *in* it: the material genesis of the text's production is tied to its specific form and to the material effects of its consumption, which is why the possibility of an "accurate account" matters. But the detective who sets out to solve the secret faces an essential paradox: *the fascination of the secret is itself the secret of fascination*. This riddle is succinctly narrated in Antonioni's film *Blow-Up* (1966). As the David Hemmings character enlarges his photographs and develops what Fredric Jameson terms "a lateral engagement or secondary, peripheral focus" (195), sure enough, at last he finds himself gazing at the object—a corpse—that accounts for his obsession. But then the solution literally *dissolves*: having found its trace on the margins of the image, in the scene itself the corpse is not there. From this point on, we need a working definition of this riddle called fascination: a powerful but profoundly ambivalent relation between subject and object in which there is a meaningful blindness at the very heart of vision.

The secret, like the body, disappears when its meaning outside or behind the work is discovered, only to leave behind another secret more enigmatic still: what in the original image it is that causes me to look for what is, in the process of finding, always lost. In *Caravaggio's Secrets,* Leo Bersani and Ulysse Dutoit grasp this vital dimension to the enigma of secrecy at work also in Burroughs:

> The very suggestion of a secret operates less as a barrier to communication than as part of a familiar code that defines communications as erotic. What the secret is—or whether a secret even exists—is irrelevant to the intelligibility given to a relation by the mere appearance of a secret. (16)

It might seem that such an approach is too insistently subjective, but paradoxically, it insists most exactly there where I try to refuse it, where I insist on producing meaning outside a relation of fascination, where, that is, I take up not a materialist approach but an "objective" one and say: here is the secret hidden behind Burroughs' seven veils of fascination . . .

From the very beginning, I have not only been fascinated by Burroughs but conscious of the fact and aware of its ambivalence. I was curious to know whether he held me in a state of inane illusion or whether I was proving, as Ackbar Abbas puts it, "a willingness to be drawn to phenomena that attract our attention yet do not submit entirely to our understanding" (51). Is fascination the necessary subject of an approach to Burroughs, because it is a deliberate theme and a calculated effect of his work? Or is that reading only a ruse on my part, just an alibi to support an otherwise aberrant relation to it? Perhaps the urge to communicate fascination, to say that this or that *is* fascinating, is no more than a way to displace a condition of being fascinated onto some particular object. Because Burroughs is hardly unique in exercising fascination—and equally, since far from everyone finds him fascinating—I am left asking, what does it mean to be fascinated by a writer, any writer, in this way? In her work on Sylvia Plath as an object of popular fascination, Jacqueline Rose reveals an investment of desire that might suggest a kind of common structural imperative: "If Plath is a ghost of the culture, one thing that will be clear in everything that follows is the extent to which she haunts me" (10). There is clearly something secretly possessive in such hyperbolic claims to being dispossessed, while the line between private and public fantasy effectively disappears. Cynthia Sugars is therefore right to argue that if we read Plath's texts as fantasy, then we must "read the critical/biographical accounts of Plath in this mode as well" (1). In short, as a screen for our desire, an object of fascination produces excessive identifications that are obviously singular, even as we seem compelled to insist on their wider cultural recognition. This in turn suggests why we can never say exactly *where* fascination is located, point to its source in a particular book, a page, a word. For we find ourselves rather in the position of Alice through the looking-glass, when exploring a shop that "seemed to be full of all manner of curious things—but the oddest part of it all was that, whenever she looked hard at any shelf, to make out exactly what it had on it, that particular shelf was always quite empty" (Carroll 178). Haunted by an enigma that we ourselves have courted, we begin to see that at the heart of fascination there is no thing, no single and static material object, but a complex and mobile *relation*.

This relation is, or must always appear to be, two-way. That is why it is often less the artwork than the figure of the artist who holds the most potent allure, less the writing than the writer *behind* the words. This is the conclusion Dennis Foster reaches in his analysis of the motives driving Samuel Beckett's readers and critics. Most of them, Foster claims, pursue "the enigmatic genius behind the text":

> despite the evident hollowness of the Beckettian subject, the web of the Beckettian text must, they assume, contain its priceless reward, the master himself. It would be too cruel to conclude that the text is part of a seduction, that its effect is not to reveal the authorial consciousness but to oblige subsequent readers to attempt to represent the writer. (*Confession* 133)

If Burroughs' readers and critics are similarly seduced, is there any way out of the trap? Am I more rather than less of a dupe for imagining there is? On the one hand, I want to reveal and decode a secret history that Burroughs denies exists; I *know* it is there, that it is absolutely material and meaningful, and that after two decades of looking, I have the enlargements to prove it. On the other hand, I also know that it is my own fascination with Burroughs that forces me to do this, that this materialist insistence is the only way I have of acquitting myself, of settling my own score, and that it solves nothing so long as it wants to solve—really, dissolve—too much. "This is what demystification is all about," as Michael Taussig says; "wanting the power of the mystery but without the mystery" (*Defacement* 159).

In retrospect, I see there is a very familiar structure to all this, one set out most elegantly by the biographer Mark Polizzotti in an essay entitled, ubiquitously, "In Search of André Breton." "In a way, I'd been looking for André Breton most of my adult life," he begins, intuiting the logic of uncanny recognition at work as he finds himself ushered "into a world that seemed absolutely and inexplicably *right,* like the confirmation of something never seen but always known" (77). From this point of initial, immediate seduction, Polizzotti describes three phases in a process of biographical pursuit. At first, everything about his subject supports his *particular* attraction: Breton's "entire approach to writing was one of enticement, a beacon sent out to the like-minded few rather than an appeal to mass admiration" (78). In time, he sees through this invitation, recognizing that it "held one at a distance rather than in proximity," as if his subject's "private reality were only another facet of his larger-than-life public persona" (78). In short, the biographer is led towards unmasking and demystifying, to seeking out the hidden keys to a secret story. "*So,* I thought, here's the truth at last; this is what it really comes down to. *This* was the real Breton who hid behind all those fancy verbal curtains" (81). Finally, Polizzotti pulls up short and realizes that it is not only Breton who has changed but himself, that he has moved beyond "unconditional admiration" and the "brief euphoria" of "piercing the mask," too (81). He recognizes the impossible limit to his task: "an attempt to see the subject *simultaneously* from without and from within" (82). Substituting Burroughs for Breton, I see myself in Polizzotti's footsteps, finding myself in the similarly paradoxical position so well expressed by film theorist Christian Metz, who counters cinematic fascination by proposing an ideal critic who should "no longer love the cinema and yet still love it," should not "have forgotten what the cinephile one used to be was like [...] and yet no longer be invaded by him: not to have lost sight of him, but be keeping an eye on him" (15).

What Polizzotti and Metz suggest is the double movement that has driven this book: towards clarifying something vital that was formerly mystified, establishing some emphatically solid ground on which others might build; and towards arriving at something commensurate with the very perplexity that captured my interest in the first place. When we think in terms of the writer and the secret, naturally enough we assume that we are looking for what the writer is hiding; but it is also the case that the writer himself may be looking, and that we too may have something to hide. This hall of mirrors, where we intuit that our search is also his, his concealment also ours, is surely one source of Burroughs' fascination. What must persist in tension with the materialist approach is therefore the "erotic," or more generally intersubjective, relation, a dimension described beautifully in Walter Benjamin's claim that only a *lover* "can bear witness to the fact that truth is not a process of exposure which destroys the secret, but a revelation which does justice to it" (*Origins* 31).

SO THE CUSTOMERS COME IN ON *SMILES*

Since questions of Burroughs' seductive image, influence, and authority are at the heart of Kerouac's scenario in *The Town and the City,* it will be worth returning to it to see the ways in which fascination in the form of a smile can work. And if it seems that I stake too much on a mere detail, my answer would be that the reading that follows is both rigorous and visibly opportunistic; as a material instance, it provides a base that I can depart from and return to and therefore a structure to allow the satisfaction of competing drives towards the revelation of meaning and the experience of fascination.

The scene has Peter Martin, Kerouac's chief alter ego in the novel, arguing against Levinsky's belief in a spreading "atomic disease" or "universal cancer" that he dubs "Virus X" (*Town* 370, 371). "Everybody's trying to be decent," Peter insists:

> Levinsky was aroused with interest. "Let them *try!*" he brought out with an imitation of a snarl, and a malicious-looking smile—a smile he had learned from Dennison.
> "There you go imitating Will Dennison again!" Peter taunted.
> "Nonsense, my days of sitting at Dennison's feet are over—the position is almost reversed, in a sense. He listens to my ideas now with great respect, where it used to be just the other way around." (373)

Here, in absentia, Dennison is cast in the role of guru and located at the key point in a triangular drama of ideas and influence. The striking and complex ambiguity of this casting should suggest something quite different from what is still the portrait of Burroughs from this period: the revered master of the Beats, "an oracular source of the wisdom of experience" for his willing students (Tytell, *Naked Angels* 14). Skerl, for example, begins her critical study very astutely by noting the fictional mediation of Burroughs' biography, but she refers to "the homage" of Kerouac and Ginsberg and singles out the figure of Old Bull Lee in *On the Road,* "who fascinated his friends with his stories and theories" (1). In all the term's ambivalence, the experience of being fascinated is very much to the point. For Kerouac's representations of Burroughs as a teacher figure are fully conscious efforts to dramatize fascination as a profoundly equivocal experience. Pedagogy here is all about power, the power of fascination. "He spent all his time talking and teaching others," Kerouac writes of Old Bull Lee. "Jane sat at his feet: so did I; so did Dean; and so had Carlo Marx" (*On the Road* 131). Since Carlo Marx is, like Levinsky in *The Town and the City,* another version of Ginsberg, that "had" establishes the continuity of the scenes across the two novels; he is the one who ceases to sit at his master's feet. And since Kerouac is at pains to parody or undermine the majority of Old Bull's ideas—like his plan to build a shelf that will "last a *thousand years*" out of a "piece of rotten wood" (135)—his sketch sustains Carlo's changed position. Kerouac appears to offer a simple choice: the blind devotion of homage or detached vision; fascination or freedom.

Kerouac's first two novels feature portraits of Burroughs that may or may not fascinate the reader but that are certainly *about* exercising the power of fascination. While Kerouac dramatizes this sinister power in relation to his portraits of Ginsberg, at the same time we can understand this drama as a displacement, a way of working through his *own* enduring fascination with Burroughs. As early as March 1945, Kerouac wrote that "nobody can actually *like* Burroughs. I think he studied occult yoga magic with which he could throw a cold curse on everybody around him" (*Selected Letters 1940–1956* 89). Three years later, Kerouac admitted in another letter that, even if Burroughs had "lost most of his human qualities" and refused to pay him any attention, paradoxically this actually "makes him even more fascinating" (163). These ambivalent biographical relations feed directly into Kerouac's fictional representations, but more importantly, they carry over into Burroughs' cultural and critical reception: does not the fascination of his image lie in the perverse appeal of someone we imagine *fully* capable of throwing a cold curse on us—to Geoff Ward, a similar scenario is "pure Burroughs" ("William Burroughs" 342)—and that Burroughs appears to *want* us to imagine that? What has been missing to date is any attempt to go back to Kerouac as a crucial point of origin, to see how, from the precise point that Burroughs started to write, Kerouac so exactly and astutely inscribed Burroughs' participation in what might be called an economy of fascination.

It is significant that even when critics momentarily address the Burroughs image's power of fascination directly, as Allen Hibbard and Graham Caveney have done, they appear to be working without so much as a dictionary definition of the term. In cultural and political theory, in philosophy and psychoanalysis, *fascination* has a rich range of meanings that might, for example, have helped answer questions raised only rhetorically by Caveney, when he asks of Burroughs "why it is that he invites us to wonder whether or not he actually" has an "authentic personality" behind the image, or when he asks outright, "what is the nature of its fascination?" (12). For contrasting accounts of how the image fascinates, how it obscures and reveals, seduces and signifies, we might turn to Walter Benjamin or Theodore Adorno or Jean Baudrillard, and in particular to Jacques Lacan and Maurice Blanchot, two great philosophers of fascination. Without losing touch with the material instance, they can help theorize the psychology and politics of the smile as a parable of fascination.

Kerouac says that Levinsky has "learned" this smile from Dennison; Peter accuses Levinsky of "imitating" him. If learning is imitation, then education is a form of mimesis, or possession. It is less that Levinsky has copied Dennison than that the student becomes a copy *of* his master: a kind of clone. Once this is pointed out to him, Levinsky immediately denies it, in a swift about-face that actually suggests the contrary forces simultaneously at work in fascination: seduction and shame, attraction and repulsion. The point about Levinsky's denial, with its tell-tale qualifiers—"almost reversed, in a sense"—is that it goes too far, suggesting that it is mere wishful thinking while implying an awareness that, as Jane Miller says, "there can be no seduction which does not implicate the one who is seduced" (21). Far from reproducing authority or mastery, by imitating his master Levinsky puts himself in the opposite condition of inauthenticity and service. Peter's charge that Levinsky is imitating Dennison *again* confirms that his idiosyncratic ideas about an "atomic disease" called "Virus X" only recycle what Dennison has told him; in resisting Levinsky's "continual attempt to convert him to his, Levinsky's, point of view" (*Town* 366), Peter is also resisting Dennison.

Dennison's actual identity in this scene is immaterial. Rather, his name is the sign of a deeply ambiguous force, a certain attitude towards the world that manifests as a physical symptom its ideological or phantasmic hold over those under its sway. Smiling ought to be a natural reflex, but this smile, as a copy, becomes a reminder of what those who fall under its sign must cast off in order to reclaim their own identities. The very spontaneity of Levinsky's reflex imitation gives the lie to his claim for a role reversal: the fact of his seduction is as clear as the smile on his face. In this way, the smile materializes both the content and the form of Dennison's ideas, as the precisely contrived context makes clear. In what Levinsky thinks is his own thesis, Virus X represents the "early symptoms" of "the real physical disease," a full-blown, explicitly Spenglerian, historical collapse, for which he gives two symbolic examples (*Town* 371). The first concerns Dennison's "close friend," Waldo Meister, "an evil magician surrounded by the decline of the West on all sides [. . .] despised like Philoctetes, avoided, yet hypnotic and compelling" (368, 369). The second features the Nickel-O amusement center in Times Square, where the "castoffs of bourgeois society" provide a spectacle that can only be watched with "the sightless stare that comes from too much horror" (369). Each of Levinsky's symptomatic cases are therefore scenes of fascination, defined as a compelling corruption that invites the traumatic and paralyzed "sightless stare." Such blindness within vision has another side, however, which is the vision of what blinds us; that is, paranoid knowledge of the hidden hand of conspiracy. Levinsky speaks of "people who let themselves be told what to do and what to think by charlatans" (375): "Everyone feels like a Zombie, and somewhere at the ends of the night [. . .] the wise genius behind it all, the Devil if you will, is running the whole thing with his string of oaths and his hexes" (370). In this context, the smile on Levinsky's face is the mark of Dennison's fascinating hex, and the off-stage Dennison corresponds to the charlatans and invisible dark powers who pull the strings and call the tune. In *Naked Lunch:* "I know this one pusher walks around humming a tune and everybody he passes takes it up. He is so grey and spectral and anonymous they don't see him and think it is their own mind humming the tune. So the customers come in on *Smiles*" (6).

VIRUS X

On another level, Kerouac dramatizes a battle of wills, literally between "Will" Dennison and the "will-less," because fascinated, Levinsky. Fictionalizing the Ginsberg-Burroughs relationship in terms of autonomy and control has particular biographical accuracy, but this conflict is also a precise illustration in advance of other interpersonal creative dynamics. The definitive instance and the best known is Cronenberg's pursuit of artistic independence. William Beard begins his article on their relationship by calling "the fascination and influence of the writings of William S. Burroughs on the films of David Cronenberg" a "truism" (823). The filmmaker's production of *Naked Lunch* is readily interpreted by another as an "antidote" to the "infection" of Burroughs' "colonizing influence" (Rodley, "So Deep" 111, 112)—an influence whose power therefore resembles its own thematic substance: call it Virus X. And second, as a ruthless rewriting of Burroughs' original text, Cronenberg's production signifies the "ultimate vindication" of his own artistic authority (Beard 828); a way of no longer sitting at his master's feet. Or rather, in Cronenberg's famous reverie, a way of reversing roles to the point of thinking, "if Burroughs dies, I'll write his next book" (qtd. in Rodley, *Cronenberg* 162). Like Levinsky, he dreams of replacing his master by becoming him and so, ironically, remains no more than his dummy. The final irony, as most critics have noted, is that the film of *Naked Lunch* is not only much weaker but far less Burroughsian than the rest of Cronenberg's work: either the antidote doesn't work or it works too well.

Such dynamics of possession and exorcism, trauma and paranoia, mastery and resistance describe a central thematic core within the Burroughs oeuvre and a major effect of it. Kerouac's scene therefore foretells the radically divided responses that Burroughs has typically received and, in a sense, always demanded. As Adorno said of Benjamin, the "fascination of the person and of his work allowed no alternative other than that of magnetic attraction or horrified rejection" (229). Polarities become the only available responses: there is no middle ground, any more than there are neutrals in the war zone of Burroughs' texts. But fascination is also perverse, a call to *internally* divided reactions, so that, to rework Adorno, we might say that Burroughs commands magnetic rejection and horrified attraction; or less paradoxically, that what attracts us is secretly repulsive, and what we secretly reject is his magnetism. Either way, a more measured academic response may subtract as much as it adds to our understanding, because it is impossible to make meaning coincide with fascination: one always obscures the other. Adorno opposed fascination as a form of ideological mystification, but he grasped its *positive* potential in his commentary on Benjamin: "Misunderstandings," writes Adorno, "are the medium in which the noncommunicable is communicated" (232).

Benjamin's notion of the image that fascinates is in fact fiercely material and historical. For Benjamin, the opacity and cryptic ambivalence of the fascinating image carries out a critique of the reasonable: it resists the tendency of reason to explain the world so reasonably that it explains the world *away*. What fascinates us always calls us back for more. At the same time, this "more" remains forever beyond the meanings or narratives we can produce, because it is a materiality we can recognize but whose content escapes narrative knowledge. This is why when Hibbard asks of Burroughs, "what is it about this writer that has fascinated and held the attention of so many?" (ix), his list of answers is entirely plausible—all the biographical legends, the outlaw mystique, scandalous nature of his work, and so on—and also wholly inadequate, even though I cannot say exactly what is missing from it. In the simplest sense, the "more" that calls me back to Burroughs marks my lack of "proper" critical distance, so that what I really seek in returning is not new meaning nor some definitive objectivity but only this very experience of failing to see and know properly. It is a perverse return but also salutary, a constant reminder of all that I know I would rather forget, a negativity that I need positively: as though, if I no longer suffered this compulsion to repeat, I would succumb to the illusion of freedom. I am tempted to say that if Burroughs did not exist, I would need to invent him, but of course, I *have*, as the name for some hyperbolically indefinable "it." Or rather, this is the fantasy position he occupies within the culture, as the face that does not fit. *"He is different,"* Alfred Kazin insists, "and he writes out of his difference" (264).

Structurally, this indefinable "it" resembles what Lacan calls the traumatic "thing" that marks the unattainable "Real" of desire; that which escapes symbolization absolutely and so is a kind of nothingness, a necessary blind spot within vision itself, and that can be represented only negatively and inferred by its repetitious effects. Blanchot's account of fascination approaches this logic quite deliberately in its very form, his prose style never more opaque and repetitious than when describing the "fascinating realm" of literature that exists in what he calls "time's absence" (*Space* 30):

> It comes already and forever past, so that my relation to it is not one of cognition, but of recognition, and this recognition ruins in me the power of knowing, the right to grasp. It makes what is ungraspable inescapable; it never lets me cease reaching what I cannot attain. And that which I cannot take, I must take up again, never to let go. (31)

Blanchot's construction of fascination as "the absence one sees because it is blinding" (*Space* 33) extends philosophically the description of Burroughs as a "formidable *absence,*" one who suggests "the proximity of Elsewhere" (Craig Karpel qtd. in Hibbard xi). But of course, the price paid for such a reading is the loss of more conventionally recognizable features, more traditional claims for meaning and reference. It would take what Kazin refers to as Burroughs' essential "difference" to an absolute limit. Certainly, conventional literary-historical approaches have tended to denature Burroughs, homogenizing his work by embedding it in a tradition that always misses some vital dimension and that fails to account for his peculiar cultural status. The most common critical solution has been to see the divided response to Burroughs as culturally symptomatic. In their critical overview, Skerl and Lydenberg refer to the "extreme emotional responses that have often prevented critics from looking at the work itself [. . .] Burroughs' work acts almost as a litmus test of a reader's response to the contemporary avant garde" (3). Or again, for David Savran, Burroughs "functions as a kind of Rorschach test for critics" (*Taking It* 85). In the same vein, I propose another model for (the difficulty of) representing Burroughs, courtesy of Lacan's analysis of *anamorphosis* as it operates in Holbein's *The Ambassadors.*

At the bottom of the painting, in front of the two assured and sumptuously adorned figures, there lies a "strange, suspended, oblique object in the foreground" (Lacan, *Four Fundamental* 88). What is this *thing?* Viewed directly, we see only an unaccountable and meaningless distortion, nothing but a ghastly stain. And so, as Lacan says, "you turn away, thus escaping the fascination of the picture [...] It is then that, turning round as you leave" (88), that is, reaching the point where in our sideways glance the rest of the painting now appears distorted, the repulsive object appears in its true form—a skull—to disclose the secret meaning of the picture *(vanitas)*. In short, Burroughs functions as an anamorphic stain on the group portrait of American literature. Looked at directly, "objectively," alongside the canonical writers, his work seems nothing but a formless mess, a repulsive and pointless blot: "the texture of grey porridge [...] disgusting," in the words of the famous "UGH ..." review: "unplanned dribbling and splashing [...] without the shocks and the stench there would be nothing much left" (Willett 41). But when viewed from an oblique angle that renders Burroughs sharp and clear, the position is inverted, and now it is all the rest that appears a confused and stupid mass. In other words, this is his fantasy position within literary culture: whether "different" or "disgusting," Burroughs operates as an inner extremity around which everything else is structured. Paradoxically, he is therefore needed by canonical literary history and criticism the most when he is entirely passed over or dismissed out of hand. In this sense, his foes are doomed to serve Burroughs better than his friends, since in their rejection they keep faith with the structure of a truly traumatic encounter. Literary histories that elide his name therefore testify, unconsciously, to the traumatizing effects of his work, validating Burroughs as the Lacanian Real of American literature and reflecting back the very fantasy identity projected in his work and image; as the irredeemably other, forever unassimilable and always out of place.

The upshot is that to view Burroughs "properly" demands giving up the straight-on point of view, the disinterested critical gaze that would only see nothing worth seeing. Instead, we have to take an *interested* view, one that assumes Bersani and Dutoit's erotic relation to the secret or one at an angle distorted by desire, as expressed in Lacan's notion of the *objet petit a:* "the object *a* is an object that can be perceived only by a gaze 'distorted' by desire, an object that *does not exist* for an 'objective' gaze," explains Slavoj Žižek, "since it is *nothing but* the embodiment, the materialization of this very distortion" (*Looking Awry* 12). As we will see, a similar structure is at work in the heart of Kerouac's tale of Dennison and the fascination of his smile.

Clearly, Lacan demands philosophical rigor rather than selective quotation, and some Lacanian critics might object to my easy appropriations here and perhaps in the following chapters also. But I have no desire to make a Lacanian reading of Burroughs[2] and would rather keep my use of theory local and opportunistic, even *rhetorical* at the level of style, and reserve a rigorous reading for Burroughs' texts and their material history. More narrowly, the above may help simply to identify certain repetitive and disturbing effects characteristic of Burroughs' writing—including the disturbing effects of repetition and recognition. These uncanny effects, redolent of nostalgia but also of trauma, are in turn central to the experience of fascination; they are clues to our intuition that what produces the fascinating text and is in turn produced by it, is a compulsion to repeat tied to a primal psychic economy. If we universalized this notion by conflating psychology with anthropology, we might then claim, like Allen Weiss, that art "has its origin in, and remains, a matter of fascination" ("An Eye" 88). But I am not proposing a general theory of fascination, as if all the different approaches, and often different uses of the term, could be reconciled. In any event, there would be little practical point. For while everything in Burroughs' work arises from and communicates the experience, with the limited exception of *Queer* there is no naturalistic representation of fascination to analyze, no *mise-en-scène* of its operation involving characters caught up in gazes of desire or mastery. This absence, which makes Kerouac's scene in *The Town and the City* so useful by default, may even be a cause rather than a consequence of the kind of writer Burroughs became. Certainly, it means that the approach taken by Michel Gresset, using Sartre and Lacan to study fascination in William Faulkner's fiction, would not work in the case of Burroughs.[3] But if the above neither adds up to a new theory nor permits a critical reading, it may yet suggest why the partisan, fragmentary, *inadequate* state of Burroughs criticism measures by default the radical power of his work, a power at its maximum in *Naked Lunch,* and one that, to adapt Blanchot's account of fascination, I would call its "immediate proximity"; an overpoweringly material affect that seizes and ceaselessly draws me close, even though it leaves me absolutely at a distance (*Space* 33). The attempt to explain such an irresistible and ambiguous power is necessarily fated to end up explaining it away, which is why to "recover" the meaning of *Naked Lunch* is to cure the text of the very sickness that makes it what it is. "Interpretation," as Steven Shaviro says, "is a means for mastering trauma. We 'make sense' by discovering meanings, or by producing them" (*Passion* 3). Cronenberg's response to Burroughs' influence becomes fully understandable in these terms and should stand as a cautionary tale alerting us to the temptations of a certain kind of trap. In effect, his film explains away *Naked Lunch* by fabricating a narrative of its genesis understood entirely in terms of Burroughs' own personal trauma. The point then is not only Cronenberg's reductionism, the naïveté of visualizing the real cause behind the fiction, but that his discovery of Burroughs' secret trauma enables him to get rid of the text and so invert its real secret, which is nothing other than its effect on him, its traumatizing power of fascination, as if to say: "*I'm* not traumatized; *you* are!" The position, as Levinsky says, is almost reversed, in a sense.

PERSONAL MAGNETISM

Burroughs' school newspaper review confirms in a lighthearted way his own early fascination with fascination itself. "Here is how it is done: I must look my victim squarely in the eye, say in a low, severe voice, 'I am talking and you must listen,' then, intensify my gaze and say, 'You cannot escape me'" (*WV* 23). The book that Burroughs read in 1929 turns out to have been Edmund Shaftesbury's *Personal Magnetism*, a weird mix of self-improvement platitudes and pseudoscientific exercises that was the most popular of the many practical guides to the art of fascination in vogue at that time.[4] Emphasizing the power of the gaze to control others as the secret source of power, Burroughs' review describes an essentially nineteenth-century understanding, as identified by Steven Connor: "The power of the mesmerist to fascinate or entrance his subjects was most commonly explained as the effect of magnetic or electrical forces originating in the body of the mesmerist and passing across to his subjects" ("Fascination" 12). This is in marked contrast to Baudrillard's postmodern, seductive world of the simulacra, which describes an intransitive and universal state of compulsive arrest and arousal. Rather, "Personal Magnetism" conceives fascination as a transitive and compelling power, exercised by lone, enigmatic individuals bearing the hypnotic eye. This power recalls Kerouac's fear of Burroughs throwing a cold curse and finds its definitive literary embodiment in Coleridge's Ancient Mariner. Far from coincidentally, the relation of Mariner to Wedding Guest is invoked in Kerouac's scene of the smile: when Levinsky tries to convert Peter to his ideas, or rather to the ideas to which Dennison has converted *him*, Kerouac observes repeatedly the "glittering eyes" with which he "fixed Peter" (*Town* 366, 367). The importance of this relation for Burroughs has long been recognized, and in 1980 Anthony Hilfer analyzed expertly the way it models the ambivalent writer-reader relation in *Naked Lunch*, concluding: "It is probably a psychological contradiction for a writer to say, 'Avoid this *glamorous* and *fascinating* experience,' even if the glamor and fascination are in the mode of horror" (258). In which case, it is tempting to see Levinsky as a kind of Wedding

Guest turned Ancient Mariner and Kerouac's cautionary tale of seduction and rejection as the urtext for Hilfer's paradox.

However, "Personal Magnetism" is really about a different power of seduction: the point is that the young Burroughs wastes his two dollars on a "mass of scientific drivel designed to befuddle the reader, and keep him from realizing what a fake it was" (*WV* 23). The occult how-to book reveals nothing but the money to be made from the desire for occult how-to books. Similarly, the desire to exercise power over others reveals only the actual experience of powerlessness *before* others: if Burroughs was from an early age interested in fascinating other people, there is ample biographical evidence to suggest that this is because he experienced the same force passively, as a helpless victim, not a master, and so knew its shameful secret of need and complicity. Conversely, if we can be seduced by the desire for power and secret knowledge, so too, in what may be the other side of the same equation, can we be seduced by the desire for attributing power and secrets to the other. Indeed, Kerouac is especially interesting for hinting at this very force of fantasy that inclines us to embrace fascination. The clue to this suggestion is the entirely unexpected contrast between what Dennison makes present in his absence and what is absent when he is made present.

WHATEVER WAS BEHIND IT

The subtlety of Kerouac's narrative lies in the way it sets up a series of expectations about Dennison as an enigmatic figure: friends sit at his feet, repeat his strange apocalyptic ideas, and mimic his cynical expressions. And of course, since the smile Levinsky imitates only *looks* malicious, it is a sign less of definite malice than of the undecidable, the mysterious. It may conceal as much as it reveals or, like Levinsky's "imitation of a snarl," blur the line between real and copy. And so when Dennison finally appears in person, Kerouac presents us with an unexpected paradox: having witnessed the compelling, enigmatic presence of the man in his absence, now when Dennison himself appears in full view, the enigma is *not there*. Far from being a seductive source of fascinating ideas, he talks only about the dull practicalities of his drug habit and pays "no attention whatever" to Peter, and when he smiles, he does so "charmingly" (*Town* 400, 401). The reader is entitled, if not invited to ask, what is going on?

On a banal level, Kerouac seems to have staged a deliberate anticlimax: he builds up to a spectacle that never happens, rather like the baffling contrast between the mysterious reputation and mundane reality of Gatsby in F. Scott Fitzgerald's novel. In fact, the parallel is not entirely gratuitous, since Gatsby too is defined by his potent and inscrutable smile and by his relation to the world of the advertised image. So too, Kerouac seems to have intuitively doubled and divided Burroughs, by taking the fictional representation of him as a character in his novel and splitting this into an original preceded and displaced by a disembodied image. We are then provoked into asking what relation ties one to the other. Since Dennison seems so harmless and disinterested, and the smile so vivid and sinister, does the smile figure some essence of the man hidden in his everyday appearance? Or does the image materialize the *effect* that he has on others, an effect that is precisely the urge to imitate the image? At this point, it is useful to take up Ronna Johnson's analysis of Kerouac as a victim to "the hyperreal effects of his iconic fame" (23). Johnson's case is that Kerouac belonged to the first generation of writers to become image celebrities of the modern mass media and to have suffered the wholesale displacement of the real by the image: using Baudrillard's terminology, she writes, "the sign (the author Kerouac and his art) is negated by the simulacrum (the 'image of Kerouac') that consumes and annuls its source in the real" (25).

In *The Town and the City,* the fictionalization includes *within itself* such a structural confusion of real and model. Since we encounter Dennison's image in advance, the priority of origins is lost together with any chance of an "objective" viewpoint, so that Dennison is doomed to appear in terms of loss: he falls short of the image of himself and is less impressive than it because his *impression* is visible as an already circulating image. In Baudrillard's terms, the image no longer reflects a reality, or either masks or denatures one, but has ceased to belong to the order of appearances; it has become its own pure simulation (Baudrillard 6). If so, then what Johnson says of Kerouac's writing—that it "is 'secret' because his immense cultural visibility foregrounds only itself" (24)—is not simply just as true for Burroughs. For what Kerouac's scene establishes is that this fate, whereby the image stands in for the writer and is contingently related to him, was one that Kerouac himself set in motion for Burroughs at the very point he began to write.

Dennison's failure to live up to his advance billing also suggests something about Levinsky and, insofar as it makes sense to read this scene as a parable for reading Burroughs, Levinsky can stand in for our desires and needs in the way that he appears caught between the desire for mystification and the need for demystification. Kerouac prompts this suggestion quite brilliantly through a telling detail about Dennison's apartment: "in the moldy doorway hung a moth-eaten green drape that concealed whatever was behind it" (*Town* 400). Of course, now we are forced to ask, what is the secret behind the green drape?

The short answer is: nothing. To put this another way, the drape is what it appears to be, and it is only our desire to discover something hidden that turns appearance into mystery and a moth-eaten green drape into the veil hiding a secret. In an essay subtitled "The Fascination of Secrecy," the sociologist George Simmell warns of a general tendency to overvalue the unknown: "From secrecy, which shades all that is profound and significant, grows the typical error according to which everything mysterious is something important and essential" (333). A useful warning, but surely something more than this is going on here, as indicated by the specific details in Kerouac's description. These suggest that Kerouac had in mind two particular scenes of cinematic fascination and demystification. Initially, the green drape evokes the familiar scene of the curtain in *The Wizard of Oz* (1939). This drape of course conceals the fact that the Great Oz is no more than an ordinary man, a mere charlatan from Kansas pulling levers to create special effects. However inviting, there is a more resonant parallel text, one that Kerouac (and Ginsberg) would both later associate explicitly with Burroughs: Fritz Lang's *The Testament of Dr Mabuse* (1933).[5] This remarkable film, which is nothing less than a meditation on the power of fascination in modernity, stages its central drama in a series of bizarre encounters with an unseen criminal mastermind known only as "the man behind the curtain." What makes Lang's scenario so interesting is that the great secret concealed behind the curtain is that there *is* no man behind the curtain. The curtain doesn't conceal then but rather stages the illusion that there *is* something to conceal.

The parallel text that completes this exploratory reading is Kafka's parable in *The Trial* of the man who dies waiting to discover the secret truth behind the Door of the Law. From a Lacanian viewpoint, Slavoj Žižek has invented a new ending to this story that brings Kafka somewhat closer to Kerouac and so to Burroughs. He has the man shout at the doorkeeper:

> "You dirty rascal, why do you pretend to guard the entrance to some enormous secret, when you know very well that there is no secret beyond the door, that this door is intended only for me, to capture my desire!" and the door-keeper (if he were an analyst) would answer him calmly: "You see, now you've discovered the real secret: beyond the door is only what your desire introduces there ...". (*Sublime Object* 66)

In terms of Kerouac's scenario, Dennison's drape suggests the illusory quality of the fascinating image; the gap between his spectral and physical appearances in the novel is therefore crucial, since what fascinates Levinsky is not a property of Dennison. However, as Žižek writes in another context, "we must, by structural necessity, fall prey to the illusion that the power of fascination belongs to the object as such" (*Looking Awry* 33). In other words, Kerouac allows us to glimpse the element of fantasy involved in being fascinated, since Dennison serves as the screen that invites Levinsky to project his own secret desire: Dennison is, in Lacan's terms, nothing but the embodiment of a gaze distorted by desire. That is why Dennison is not demystified by his actual appearance, by his anonymity and indifference, but, as Kerouac wrote of Burroughs, is rendered "even more fascinating." Levinsky has not yet grasped what Žižek calls "the real secret."

BROTHER SPHINX

Recalling the first time that he and Kerouac paid a formal visit in 1944, Ginsberg observed that Burroughs already "seemed like some sort of international spiritual man of distinction to us. But we couldn't figure out what his secret mystery was, so we decided to go find out" (Gifford and Lee 36). Almost a decade later, in fall 1953, Ginsberg and Burroughs went together to the Metropolitan Museum of Art and recorded for posterity the definitive image of this secret mystery. From one point of view, the scene appears too self-conscious to take seriously. Standing in the Egyptian wing of the museum beside a huge sphinx, here is Burroughs posing as an authority on ancient secrets, a master of inscrutable wisdom who is himself inscrutable: a "brother Sphinx," as Ginsberg's caption has it (*Photographs* n. pag.). But although it is so obviously staged, or maybe precisely because of it, there's a haunting, tragic quality to the picture, a disturbing poignancy that deepens as you look at it.

Fall 1953 was a crucial period in Burroughs' life, in the development of his writing, and in the relation of both to Ginsberg, and the intensity of this moment informs the photograph's dark beauty. According to Ginsberg, "recording certain moments in eternity" had been his motive for taking such "sacramental" snapshots (*Photographs* n. pag.); but isn't it just as plausible that he was colluding with Burroughs' fantasy self-image, that Ginsberg let himself be seduced into fashioning an icon whose power was itself directed at his own seduction? Indeed, when we take into account the ghastly drama of Burroughs' sexual desire for Ginsberg, about to reach crisis point, then the force of the picture appears suddenly legible: by standing next to the mythical hybrid creature that is the archetypal embodiment of gender confusion, Burroughs presents a precise image, almost a direct statement, about his equivocal sexual identity; the secret of homosexual desire is therefore displayed on the very surface of an image that at the same time encrypts this desire as an unfathomable enigma. And Burroughs, with his long-standing interest in Egyptology, must surely have realised how this conundrum was in fact redoubled in this particular instance. For the red granite statue that lies in the Met once stood on the West Bank at Thebes and turns out to be the Sphinx of Hatshepsut, a Pharaoh from the eighteenth dynasty famous for being a woman who posed and dressed as a man.[6]

However, what makes this image so fascinating is that its symbolic potency inevitably runs out of control and resists definitive motivation: the meaning of the image that Burroughs and Ginsberg so clearly staged together is in fact *unstable* and *unclear,* open to multiple and contrary readings. Burroughs might, for example, have been drawn by a more general historical and mythic reference: the inescapably fateful aura of the *curse,* invoked by the figure of the Egyptologist, and, of course, by the story of Oedipus. The image is capable of conjuring entirely different scenarios—of Burroughs the heroic solver of riddles or the deadly possessor of one—scenarios whose only relation is the same paradoxical destiny: self-destruction and immortality. And so there is a pathos in the parallel gazes, as the two figures stare fixedly ahead. But the really key feature must be precisely the one these uncanny doubles do *not* share, the one missing from Burroughs' face: the enigmatic smile. Because of this absence, the picture reproduces the very gap of fantasy that structures Kerouac's scenario in *The Town and the City.* We are therefore invited to see Burroughs and the Sphinx not as brothers in mystery but as the visualization, side-by-side, of the mundane body and its immortal specter, the empty screen and the projected image, the sign and the simulacrum. This is why the direct, face-on appeal to the viewer is so important. The effect would be entirely different if the faces were aligned in profile, as in a famous publicity shot of Alfred Hitchcock posing with the Great Sphinx at Giza: as Peter Conrad observes, "Hitchcock upstages the monument" and arrogantly trumps its power to mystify (231). In contrast, Burroughs appears vulnerable and perplexed, as if looking not just *at* us but *to* us, in order to account for his presence. This look should therefore make us realize that it always takes two to stage such a scene, so that if Ginsberg's desire was necessary to it, so too, half a century later, is ours.

Burroughs has always been both a secret figure or possessor of secrets for others and also interested in secret knowledge himself. This interest runs through all his writing, as it does throughout his life: from seeking the power of personal magnetism to trying to enlist in Bill Donovan's OSS, the wartime forerunner of the CIA, from pursuing the "top secret" drug *yagé* in the early 1950s (*L* 104), to investigating the Scientology cult in the

1960s, and so on. A central question, therefore, is in what ways does Burroughs' interest in the secret, which is both political and psychoanalytical and always has to do with systems of control, relate to that of his readers? And while it is natural to locate his interest within a specifically American context of cultural paranoia, we should not miss the global dimension mapped out, to give just one example, by Guy Debord in his *Comments on the Society of the Spectacle* (1988). Here, Debord identifies secrecy as a vital support of the spectacle, while insisting that the nature of "our unfortunate times" means that those writing to contest the conspiracy of power must not "give too much information to just anybody [...] Some elements will be intentionally omitted; and the plan will have to remain rather unclear. Readers will encounter certain decoys, like the very hallmark of the era" (1, 2). Paradoxically, to resist the conspiracy of secrecy itself demands a secretive strategy. What Debord calls "lateral critiques" therefore "resemble those facsimiles of famous weapons, which only lack the firing-pin" (76). Burroughs, who was familiar with Debord from the Situationist group, proposed exactly such a strategy in the early 1970s for his own analysis of control systems, succeeding what he had called the "Open Bank" policy of his cut-up project: "Oh I will publish but always hold back the essential ingredient. [...] Like I give a blue print for an internal combustion engine [but] leave out of my blue print the whole concept of *oil*."[7] A decade later, in *The Place of Dead Roads* (1983), Burroughs would include his strategic paradox quite self-consciously within the fiction, describing how he "concealed and revealed the knowledge in fictional form [...] Only those for whom the knowledge is intended will find it" (115). At this point, we have to wonder whether this is a master's promise of real occult truth or just a shallow fictional lure. Is Burroughs being playful or not playing at all? Is he trying to wise his readers up or to take them in, or is he perhaps taken in by his *own* game?

If we track Burroughs' strategy back to his first two novels, what is most striking is how he appears to withhold or deny secret knowledge as a matter of principle. In *Junkie*: "There is no key, no secret someone else has that he can give you" (*J* xvi). In *Queer*: "The Westerner thinks there is some secret he can discover. The East says, 'How the fuck should I know?'" (82). Burroughs' investment in the psychology and politics of secrecy, only hinted at here, will underlie my approach to *Junkie* and *Queer* in the following chapters. In relation to Kerouac's scenario and its extension into Kafka, the key phase of Burroughs' interest in the secret began in early 1955. At this time, he saw *Naked Lunch* in terms of "vast Kafkian conspiracies" fighting out a "basic conflict" between forms of knowledge and power whose symbolic poles are East and West (*L* 269). Significantly, the story he was starting to write at precisely this moment was "The Conspiracy," which plays quite explicitly on Žižek's theme of true and false secrets.

The narrator of "The Conspiracy," Bill Lee, concludes: "I decided it was an error to think in terms of some secret or key or formula: the secret is that there is no secret" (*I* 110). The moral appears clear: to learn to resist the paranoid Westerner's quest for final, hidden knowledge. Case closed. But then, having buried the corpse—of "plot" in its double sense, as narrative and as conspiracy—the next sentence of the narrative entitled "The Conspiracy" digs it up again: "But I was wrong. There *is* a secret" (111). In the final twist, Burroughs moves back to the "false" secret—the elusive formula that is the secret meaning *behind the form,* beyond the door or hidden by the drape, and abandons the "true" secret, which is the secret of the form itself. The false secret presumes some final revelation; the true secret is already there but hidden precisely because it appears on the surface, as the form, not a content.

At one point, Lee seems to have grasped that the real secret at the end of his quest is, as in "Personal Magnetism," no more than his own desire, "as sterile and misdirected as the alchemists' search for the philosopher's stone" (*I* 110). It is at this point that he might have developed the logic of *The Trial* as fulfilled by Orson Welles's film, which also invents a new ending for Kafka's parable of the Door of the Law. Žižek comments: "as K. puts it in Welles's version of his final outburst, the true conspiracy of power resides in the very notion of conspiracy, in the notion of some mysterious agency that 'pulls the strings' and effectively runs the show" ("I Hear You" 76). In this scenario, the "political lesson" is that the hegemony of power is socially effective because of its entirely phantasmic hold: it is a spell over us that can be broken rather than a secret key to be discovered. The fact that Burroughs decided to leave "The Conspiracy" out of *Naked Lunch* may be the sign that he reversed which secret and which political and psychological lesson he wanted to embrace: the meaning obscured by fascination, which is the false secret behind the form, gives way to the fascination obscured by meaning, the true secret in the form. The text's final phrase— "No glot—C'lom Fliday" (*NL* 235)—economically repeats the final twist of "The Conspiracy" but in a way that is meant to leave no doubt as to Burroughs' political lesson: if you want to know the secret, ask again.

MIMETIC SMILE

The final approach to what is going on between Levinsky and Dennison in Kerouac's scenario turns on the nature of the smile itself.

It is surprising how little has been written on the subject. In the literature of social psychology, there is a certain amount of semiotic and clinical analysis; but what neurologists call the "mimetic smile" turns out to be a distinction between spontaneous smiling produced by the hypothalamus and limbic system and the posed facial expressions that originate in the motor cortex (Husain 144)—not much help in this context. In fact, as Daniel McNeill notes, while there are "over one hundred theories of laughter" and other basic expressions, there are "few grand unified theories of smiling" (209).

The most relevant psychological enquiry remains Freud's essay on Leonardo da Vinci, where he analyzes the most famous and enigmatic smile of all time, that of the *Mona Lisa*. Freud addresses the meaning of the smile explicitly in terms of fascination, which he reads as a defense against loss, specifically of the mother: Leonardo is fascinated by the Florentine lady because she bears the maternal smile that he has lost. The relevance of this psychoanalytic case turns on the way in which Leonardo masters loss by an obsession that ironically resembles slavery. As Adam Phillips comments: "When we are fascinated by someone or something, we can acknowledge that it may have a cause, but it rarely feels like a choice" (184). The key point to Freud's analysis of Leonardo, however, is simply the extraordinary circuit of fascination itself: the painter fascinated by a smile paints the most fascinating of smiles; the biographer of a fascinated artist is himself fascinated by the life; the critic of fascination is drawn to scene after scene of fascination . . .

Is fascination infectious, and are those who study it unable to escape its hex? It is surely no coincidence that there is only one case of the smile in Burroughs' fiction prominent enough to have attracted critical attention, which is the dreamy and deadly smile that reproduces itself like a disease in *The Wild Boys* (1971). As Jennie Skerl observes, "the image of a smiling boy becomes a popular icon that subverts the social order by recruiting more wild boys" (83). While this entire text is, in fact, structured from first to last by images of the enigmatic smile, the defining instance occurs in a short story, written at the same time as *The Wild Boys,* entitled "Ali's Smile." Here, the smile is firmly tied to homosexual desire and compulsory mimesis, so that fascination names a perverse pleasure or pleasurable perversity: Ali loses control of his own body by becoming, for a crowd of mocking women, "a *Latah,* that is a condition where the victim must imitate every movement"; then he exacts revenge by running *Amok,* a state of lethal possession; finally, Ali is transformed into the haunting image that ends the story with an enigmatic ellipsis: "Against the icy blackness of space, the ghost face of Ali . . . smiles" (*Exterminator!* 75, 84). Murphy's comment in relation to the murderous wild boys, that "they smile in invitation to the reader" (*Wising Up* 167), captures nicely the threat they pose within and beyond their Book of the Dead: mimetic smiles, fatally so.[8]

What we are looking at in *The Town and the City*, where one character bears the smile of another, is an expression in the sense of an articulated *communication:* a cybernetic smile. Maybe then the paradox of the smile's presence on Levinsky's face and its absence from Dennison's can make a different sense. There would be no contradiction: Dennison lacks the smile not despite but *because* Levinsky now has it. That is, Levinsky has not just copied the expression but rather materially received it from Dennison, who is now relieved of it: hence, the paradox that the copy ceases to resemble the model, because the original no longer resembles itself. Communication as a form of control, or an act of sympathetic magic, becomes a means of catharsis: the smile has the "communicability" of a disease. And so finally we approach the *autonomy* of the smile, the smile that transmits itself, the smile that needs a face the way a ghost wants a body, and we might imagine some unwritten scene in Kerouac's novel where the smile passes from Dennison to Levinsky like a specter or a parasitic virus moving from one host to another.

MIND PARASITE

Kerouac's twice-mediated fictional representation of Burroughs' fascinating image finds its counterpart in twice-mediated critical representations of his equally fascinating voice. Robin Lydenberg begins her article on Burroughs' tape experiments (1992) by going back nearly thirty years to cite Joan Didion's praise for the power of Burroughs' voice: "the point is not what the voice says but the voice itself, a voice so direct and original and versatile as to disarm close scrutiny of what it is saying" ("Sound Identity" 409). So too, Robert Sobieszek begins his artwork catalog *Ports of Entry* (1996) by going back twenty years to cite French critic Philippe Mikriammos: "It's Burroughs' voice. It's that elemental cadence—labelled by one critic as 'vox Williami, vox monstrorum'—which ultimately seduces the listener" (17). A voice that disarms scrutiny. A voice that seduces. To the degree that these critics are right, their repetitions only confirm the degree to which Blanchot's construction of fascination matches the Burroughs effect: "Whoever is fascinated doesn't see, properly speaking, what he sees" (*Space* 33). The point is not the eclipse of meaning, the way these critics risk losing the thematic or referential content of what the voice says, but rather the loss of the content in the form, in the grain of the voice itself.

Instead of resisting seduction and practicing scrutiny, they pass their knowledge on, like a chain letter or a game of round-robin, and so confirm that when criticism deals with the fascination of Burroughs, the only alternative to negation is repetition.

The logic of fascinated replication is apparent even when it is itself the subject of criticism, as in the closing lines of Timothy Murphy's *Wising Up the Marks*. Naming Burroughs "an effect that propagates itself from medium to medium by the force of difference," he concludes: "Even when Burroughs is no longer able to serve as the focus for this force, it will continue to reverberate, indefatigably sounding its critical imperative: listen to my last words everywhere" (232). We are back to "Personal Magnetism" and the occult fantasy of "I am talking and you must listen." The irony is that even Burroughs' most astute critics find themselves in the most uncritical position: that of reproducing the fascinating voice and negating its imperative content, which is nothing other than a warning against fascination itself. When Sobieszek observes that Burroughs' texts and ideas have "insinuated" themselves into the cultural fabric like an "unobserved virus that continually replicates itself" (158), what is extraordinary is the failure to confront the paradox he makes so visible. As Blanchot would put it, Sobieszek does not see what he sees: that is, how completely Burroughs reproduces the ideological and affective power of the seductive image world, and how clearly his words insinuate themselves through critical and cultural reproduction. But to recognize this is still not enough, and it will be my case that complicity in all he opposes is the very *condition* of Burroughs' work, its *material ground* as well as its material effect.

For this reason, it is vital that we grasp the profound difference between the contradiction Anthony Hilfer identified in *Naked Lunch* via the Ancient Mariner and Ron Loewinsohn's version of it: "This," he writes, "is the major paradox in Burroughs's program: 'wising up the marks,' he finds, involves him and his narrators in precisely the sort of mind control that he's trying to warn the marks about" (576). This paradox—a "theoretical dilemma" for John Lardas (178)—might explain the self-reflective vertigo of certain writers of metafiction, but it doesn't work for the Burroughs of *Naked Lunch*. There is nothing metaphoric or theoretical or even reflective about it: his complicity in exercising power coincides absolutely with his writing, because it marks the material point of origin. The traumatized, traumatizing dimension of Burroughs' unique brinkmanship would collapse into no more than affected bad faith if all he had was a "program" in which, retrospectively, he "finds" himself pinched in a paradox. To put this another way, when Ann Douglas says that Burroughs is revolutionary because "only the enemy within can lay hands on top-secret information" ("Punching" xix), she hints at the corollary: that Burroughs, as the "enemy within" the power structure, gains access to information about the structure of power only through the "enemy within" *him*.

In the critical context, to approach Burroughs disarmed and seduced has meant taking him on his own terms—and being taken in by him. Burroughs resists power to the extent that he also exercises it, understands power so well precisely because he has always worked from its deep insides. From the outset, this WASP scion of American big business (public relations on his mother's side, adding machines on his father's) was born to live out power's painful contradictions. His life as addict, homosexual, and writer literalized that undesired inheritance with a perverse vengeance, queering the legacy of "Poison Ivy" Lee and Burroughs Computers by reincarnating it as a pathogenic cultural virus. And so, Burroughs dedicated himself to immortality by becoming what Richard Dawkins in *The Selfish Gene* called a "meme." This is a notion more truly Burroughsian than any of his own pseudoscientific theories, and Dawkins's best-seller spawned other books with fully Burroughsian titles: Richard Brodie's *Virus of the Mind* and Aaron Lynch's *Thought Contagion* (both 1996), as well as Susan Blackmore's *The Meme Machine* (1999). Defined as a "unit of cultural transmission, or a unit of *imitation*," whose "survival value" is their "infective power," memes such as catchy tunes or potent ideas "propagate themselves" analogously to the genetic code and the virus: "When you plant a fertile meme in my mind you literally parasitize my brain" (Dawkins, *Selfish* 206–7). And so, reciprocally, can the mind survive through parasitic self-replication: the viral program "simply says 'Copy me and spread me around'" (Dawkins, *Climbing* 249).

In short, the "malicious-looking smile" that spreads from Burroughs to Kerouac and from Dennison to Levinsky and that embodies Virus X is the very model of a meme. It has the infective power of the Burroughs text that takes like a dye or, in Hilfer's fine phrasing, that "*stains* the imagination" with "images that are imaginatively shocking and obsessively memorable" (259). If this is one of the perverse pleasures of the Burroughs reading experience, to be possessed by one irradiated image after another, one haunting phrase after another, then as he insists in *The Place of Dead Roads*, "the immortality of a writer is to be taken literally. Whenever anyone reads his words the writer is there. He lives in his readers" (42). And what goes for Burroughs' images goes finally for his ideas too: *in the last analysis*, they are no more or less than material provocations, special effects, as all questions of content and reference come down to the irreducible fascination of a form.

This is what Burroughs says: "all poets worthy of the name are mind parasites, and their words ought to get into your head and live there, repeating and repeating and repeating" ("Voices" 6). He could scarcely be more explicit. Given his insistence that "the point is to lose what you have," to wind up with *Burroughs'* rusty load of continuity would indeed be to have lost the point. It may well be those who would gladly burn Burroughs who have best understood the unique force of his work. And so to exempt Burroughs from the terms of his own critique is to miss the whole point of what I will be calling his "textual politics"; that is, not only his texts' analysis of power *but their own relation to it.* The final value of Dennison's mimetic smile is precisely this issue of Burroughs' textual politics and how it came about.

THE SECRET OF THE INVISIBLE MAN

MONSTROUS PERVERSITY

When Burroughs began writing *Junkie* in March 1950 with the example of *The Town and the City* before him, he was returning to the New York City of 1945, so that in terms of period, place, and personalities, his novel began exactly where Kerouac's ended. However, the sinister image of Dennison's smile is strikingly absent from *Junkie* and seems a world away from Burroughs' narrating persona William Lee, née Will Dennison. If anything, Lee in *Junkie* resembles Dennison *without* the smile, since he is defined largely by his anonymity, indifference, and detachment from those around him. There is a very particular history to this identity, since it represents a choice between the two potential aesthetic identities that emerged from Burroughs' collaborations with Kerouac back in 1945.

The first identity that Burroughs and Kerouac acted out was captured by Ginsberg's ever-opportune photographic lens (Charters, *Kerouac* 148). The two figures stand in profile, Burroughs in a double-breasted topcoat, winter sunlight catching one rimless spectacle as he peers over a newspaper grasped in gloved hands. Beside him stands Kerouac, fists thrust deep into overcoat pockets, collar turned up, with Dick Tracy jaw and eyes trained in the same direction. As the caption says, they are playing out a scene from Dashiell Hammett. Hammett was valued—with a good deal of license—for the tough, native masculinity and journalistic objectivity of his prose, a stylization well suited to a work of underworld reportage such as "Hippos," based on the Lucien Carr–Dave Kammerer murder case. And of course, Hammett is routinely given—with no less license—as *Junkie's* dominant style of writing.

But in 1945, Burroughs and Kerouac also staged a second identity of a different national and aesthetic order when they acted out scenes from André Gide's novel *The Counterfeiters*. If Hammett stood for an indigenous realist mode—populist, detached, documentary—then Gide represented the extreme of narcissistic literary autobiography. Five years on, Gide's novel is discussed at length in *The Town and the City*, where his name represents "monstrous perversity" for Kerouac (154). And this unnatural "corrupter" of youth and artist of "falsity" is specifically associated with the image of Burroughs (153). "Dennison," it is said, "is a first-rate fabricator of Gidean romances" (393). In other words, that malicious-looking smile—seductive, ambiguous, suspect—identified Burroughs negatively in moral, intellectual, and class terms; together with Waldo Meister (based on Kammerer), Dennison is for Levinsky one of the "evil figures of decayed families" that index the zeitgeist (367), and for Kenny Wood (based on Carr), he is one of the city's sinister "faggot spooks" (414). By tying Burroughs to the Carr-Kammerer murder case, Kerouac fixes Dennison's name to a scandal of predatory homosexuality that resonates with national, not just local, significance. In the broader historical context, a time when American culture was so politicized that in 1951 NBC had to take *The Adventures of Sam Spade* off the air due to Hammett's communist links, Dennison signifies Burroughs as dangerously "queer" in every sense: homosexual, corrupt, counterfeit, criminal, decadent. Not only corrupt but *corrupting*—seeking to "convert" others—the ominous smile fits seamlessly into the cold war's governing pathological figure of deviance as contagion. Just as cold war rhetoric worked according to a logic of guilt-by-association, so too, through references to Gide and resemblances to other characters, Kerouac cast Dennison as un-American.

The point is that a highly suspect identity was firmly established for Burroughs through *The Town and the City* and that in 1950 he did not take it up. On the contrary, he refused it. In many ways, *Junkie* is the most seductive of all Burroughs' texts, but as a *sign* of seduction to be resisted, Dennison's malicious-looking smile simply does not fit the William Lee of *Junkie*. Indeed, Burroughs defines his faceless narrating protagonist in part through the recurrent smiling of Lee's partner in pushing, Bill Gains. His smile is the sign of precisely that corruption that is itself corrupting signified by Dennison's smile in *The Town and the City*:

> Gains had a malicious childlike smile [. . .] Gains was one of the few junkies who really took a special pleasure in seeing non-users get a habit. Many junky-pushers are glad to see a new addict for economic

reasons. [...] But Gains liked to invite young kids up to his room and give them a shot [...] Gains would look at these converts and smile, a prelate of junk. (*J* 42)

As an "American upper-middle-class citizen" who is "positively invisible" (41), Gains resembles Lee in key respects. But there is no ambiguity about Gains; his smile is genuinely malicious, not malicious-*looking,* and his desire to make "converts" out of young kids marks his categorical difference from Lee.

In *Queer,* Burroughs again contemplates in some detail the smile of a specific character, repeating the word six times in as many lines when describing the terminal narcissist, Winston Moor, who has a "malicious bitch smile" (5–6, 63). Again, Burroughs carries over the resonant adjective from *The Town and the City,* again it loses the ambiguity of appearances, and once again it signifies in relation to Lee. But in *Queer,* the difference is much more ambiguous. For here Lee resembles the Gidean figure of Dennison, being precisely an unnatural "corrupter" of youth and an artist of "falsity," a first-rate fabricator of the dark romances that Burroughs called "routines." In fact, Kerouac himself explicitly reconfirmed the association in *Doctor Sax,* which he wrote when staying in Mexico City with Burroughs as he worked on *Queer.* Clearly inspired by Burroughs and his new manuscript, Kerouac endows Sax with "a malignant smile" and "malevolent humour," describes "an evil Gidean" speaking what sounds like the "Slave Trader" routine from *Queer,* and observes that "you'll be simply fascinated" by him (128, 124, 125). Lee in *Queer* therefore reprises Dennison from *The Town and the City* and resembles Bill Gains in *Junkie* insofar as the fantasy he plays out is that of a predator who tries to "convert" a young kid. Or rather, what we begin to see is not reprise or resemblance but a complex and specifically literary process of imitation, as Burroughs himself took up the imitative smile from Kerouac.[9]

While it is important to establish how fully Burroughs' own creativity was shaped by the material impact of Kerouac's, we should not lose sight of the specific thematic continuity traced through the smile as it returns in *Junkie* and *Queer.* The difference between the two novels suggests how precisely Burroughs first rejected and then, two years later, embraced the sinister and suspect identity Kerouac scripted him in 1950. Since the entire narrative of *Queer* consists of Lee's ugly and desperate attempts to disarm, seduce, control, and ultimately possess his victim, it is clear that *Queer* is about exercising, and exorcising, the power of fascination in a way that *Junkie* simply is not.

35

In the general economy of *Junkie,* the difference between Lee and Gains is absolutely central: Lee has "economic reasons" for needing customers, but he is not a predator in the world of addiction, seducing converts, propagating contagion, feeding his fantasies of control. In fact, one of the most surprising things about *Junkie* is that it includes only one, brief scene where the relationship of pusher to addict is described in terms of power—the "power to give or withhold" (*J* 140). Since the pusher-addict relation is inherently asymmetrical, a ready model for the dialectic of master and slave, Burroughs' virtual refusal to represent it as such in *Junkie* is significant. Equally significant, however, is criticism's failure to see it. And the reason why critics have overlooked what is not there is that they already see junk addiction as the paradigm of control in Burroughs' oeuvre. It is time to shift this paradigm.

BEFORE AND AFTER

The literary criticism and popular reception of Burroughs have long been determined by an undisputed assumption about his work, its master trope and driving force, an assumption grounded in his first decade as a writer. "Heroin addiction," writes David Ayers, "provides Burroughs with the metabolic model of control which structurally informs other models of control which he will subsequently deploy" (225). This critical commonplace accepts that the key subject of Burroughs' work—control—is rooted in and shaped by the "literal addiction" documented in *Junkie* (Watson 306). This is the stencil through which his early texts have been read and his iconic identity has been constructed, and of course, Burroughs has played the part of the junkie in and beyond his own work as well as lived the life of one. This binding identification of Burroughs with junk has generated a convenient paradigm that for thirty years has been largely followed, occasionally sidestepped, but never interrogated; never, that is, questioned for its adequacy or effects. For criticism, the autobiographical paradigm produces the neat diptych of *before* and *after* offered in 1970 by Tony Tanner, when dubbing Burroughs "an addict turned diagnostician, a victim of sickness now devoted to the analysis of diseases": here, pointing to *Junkie,* Tanner announced, is "the actual in which his vision is grounded"[10] (110).

The side effects of the junk paradigm have been catastrophic, because it scores as abstract all Burroughs' models of control and disease. As Ayers puts it, after junk "it will always be an abstract notion of control" that powers later models—including Burroughs' central technology of control, language itself (224). *Abstract* is the key word, and it rings false. Nothing

Burroughsian is abstract: the force of his ideas cannot be separated from the effects of his words. That is why his work can be so potent and so extraordinary, stamped with a strictly literal, overpoweringly *visceral* force: whether it compels or repels, attracts or disgusts, when Burroughs' writing is Burroughsian, it bears the stamp of power and achieves the force of Blanchot's "immediate proximity." For reasons that will become clear, my understanding of what is "Burroughsian" about Burroughs does not dwell on either stylistic features of writing—a typical array of images, a certain cadence, trademark structures, and so on—or on a specific range of themes or representations. Rather, it turns on the textual politics manifest in *Naked Lunch,* as the central point to which his first trilogy leads and from which the second trilogy develops. Control and its terrors are *present* rather than represented in this writing, *produced by* as much as reproduced in it. We grasp these terrors by the experience of being grasped by them.

The junk paradigm does not work adequately, because it produces abstraction at odds with the insistent materiality of this reading experience. It mediates the relation of control to language as an *allegorical* relation, just as Tanner's diptych locates a force outside language and prior to writing that elides the central action of Burroughs' texts. Now, addiction is an important biographical matrix and "master metaphor" (Loewinsohn 564), but this still doesn't make it the *ground* of his writing any more than it makes *Junkie* a "blueprint for all of Burroughs' work" (Tytell, *Naked Angels* 125) or a text that lays the "groundwork for the later novels"[11] (Skerl 21).

The "transformation of junk from fact to symbol" (Stull 16) in turn produces a second stage of metaphor. Franca Bellarsi writes: "Besides addiction, the virus image represents the other metaphor that informs all of Burroughs's work. This second metaphor is of course directly derived from the first" (48). Of course, even more now depends on the original and extratextual facts of addiction, an experience Bellarsi describes in unilateral terms when claiming that "Burroughs surrendered the power to rule his own life to the dealer and his merchandise" (46). Leaving aside the issue of biographical accuracy, the junk paradigm is inadequate to Burroughs' understanding of language as a virus, just as it cannot account for the material force of writing I name Burroughsian. This force is based not on metaphor, not on figuring language as a viral disease, passively controlling the subject "like junk," but on the *literal practice, active as well as passive,* of it as such. Burroughs always insisted word *is* a virus, but critics have taken his literalism as itself only a figure, as when Kendra Langeteig, in an otherwise outstanding article, speaks of "word and image virus, or its equivalent, junk" (137). To say that the word is a communicative sickness was not, for Burroughs, metaphoric analysis or poststructuralist platitude but an awareness integral and material to the act of writing, and this is what the toxicity of Burroughs' textual politics insists upon, ad nauseam.

According to most accounts, Burroughs adapted preexisting theoretical models of language, specifically Korzybski's General Semantics: Caveney typifies the assumption that Korzybski should "be read as the origin of his ongoing war against the word" (51). This makes sense but not of or for Burroughs. What makes Burroughs so interesting is inseparable from his *failure* to apply or develop theory "properly." His cut-up project of the 1960s is a case in point: the priority Burroughs gave to experimental and material practices has been lost in the theoretical shuffle, as critics have reread his texts in light of the "linguistic turn" of (post)structuralism, when it was precisely the *lack* of such a theorized context that enabled Burroughs' experimentalism in the first place. It is a major difficulty to deal with a writer so radically contemporary who seems so perversely, and unfashionably, ante- if not antitheoretical. The word-virus relation is neither a theorization nor an allegorization but must always appear to be so as long as Burroughs' textual practices are assumed to *perform* an already well-theorized position. In the simplest of terms, the problem is this: to bridge the gulf between junk as a metaphor, grounded in personal experience of addiction, and language allegorized as junk, grounded in theory—positions that compel critics to overlook the inconvenient absence of either metaphor or theory in the text that ought to initiate each, namely *Junkie*.

The junk paradigm has been convenient, operating as a sign of apparent continuity. It offered to bridge his first decade as a developing, autobiographical writer—the Beat Generation Burroughs—and his second as a radical innovator—the Postmodern, Cybernetic Burroughs. In fact, junk has made it impossible to narrate Burroughs' career with any conviction. Burroughs' critics have failed to historicize his development as a writer for a variety of reasons, but the simplest reason is this: like the old joke where a man who is lost asks a local, "How do you get from here to there?" the answer is that they have started from the wrong place. In short: you cannot get to *Naked Lunch* from *Junkie*. The only way of getting there, of understanding how Burroughs became that writer, requires us to see through the fascinating force of the iconic image—the *gentleman junky* of Caveney's book, *el hombre invisible* of Barry Miles's—and to reverse the priority of his first two novels. This reversal should also apply biographically, because of course Burroughs was a queer long before he became a junkie, but above all it applies creatively, because *Queer* is the true kernel of *Naked Lunch*. This is so in the most symbolic and material of ways: with respect to the book's very tile. Where did it come from? According to the text Burroughs added as an introduction to *Naked Lunch,* "it was suggested by Jack Kerouac" (*NL* ix). When Kerouac himself read this, he wrote Ginsberg to remind him of an "interesting little bit of ltry history": "remember, it was you, reading the ms., mis-read 'naked lust' and only I noticed it" (*Selected Letters 1957–1969* 258). But, since Kerouac didn't name the manuscript in question, the mystery of the title's origin remained unsolved. We can, however, force the sphinx to give up at least this secret, because in fact the scene Kerouac sketches took place in fall 1953, when the manuscript Ginsberg read aloud was none other than that of *Queer* (whose title Kerouac had also suggested to Burroughs). If we enlarge the picture still further, we can even say with some certainty which use of the phrase "naked lust" in *Queer* Kerouac spotted Ginsberg's misreading and so gave rise to the title *Naked Lunch.*[12] This is precise, narrow evidence of a far larger creative significance, however. For *Junkie* and *Queer,* written back-to-back but published thirty years apart, provide two entirely different paradigms for understanding the genesis of Burroughs' writing and the nature of his textual politics.

THE ESSENCE OF SLEIGHT OF HAND

The problem of Burroughs' literary history might appear no more than a matter of publication contingencies, so that with the appearance of previously unpublished early material this might seem a problem solved: the road to *Naked Lunch*—itself once conceived as a triptych of "Junk," "Queer," and "Yage"—ought to run straight and true. But the reconstituted trilogy of *Junky, Queer,* and *The Yage Letters* has an entirely false continuity, because of the significant delays and revisions affecting all three texts. Remarkably, this first trilogy has yet to be read collectively in any detail, so that no critic has even pursued its false continuity.

Because the first trilogy seems to have a clear autobiographical continuity, it looks like we can restore an apparently stable and unified narrative. In fact, over time the very title of Burroughs' first novel falls into doubt. From his original (and preferred) "Junk," it became *Junkie: Confessions of an Unredeemed Drug Addict* when published under the by-line William Lee as an Ace Double Book in 1953 and *Junky* ever since the unexpurgated Penguin edition of 1977, an edition of many changes as well as new material. These mutations of title, authority, and text are significant, as is the historical and factual confusion they have caused.[13] And if there is a trilogy of sorts in Burroughs' first, seemingly most coherent novel, there is another in *The Yage Letters.* Not only has the text been revised over three editions but its content is shared between two authors and divided across two decades. As for *Queer,* the manuscript fragment from 1952 acquired sections of new text, as well as a new context, when published thirty-three years later. It becomes impossible to slot *Queer* (1952/1985) back in between *Junky* (1977) and *The Yage Letters* (1963) *or* between *Junkie* (1953) and "In Search of Yage" (1953). Far from forming "one book," each of these texts is radically plural, a composite of several distinct and often contradictory material histories. The missing pieces have been restored, but the problems of narrating Burroughs' literary history haven't been solved; they have only just begun.

Predictably enough, *Junkie, Queer,* and *The Yage Letters* have been read biographically in relation to Burroughs' mythic Beat identity. More revealing is the entirely overlooked way in which Burroughs has himself sponsored just this kind of blurring between fictional insides and factual outsides. He has done this in the most influential of contexts, namely the introductions added to *Junkie* and *Queer* and indeed *Naked Lunch.* You might even say that the very *absence* of an introduction for *The Yage Letters* becomes meaningful and has had the same effect by default, since one reason why the text has been so neglected is its uncertain fictional status. Certainly, none of Burroughs' introductions give material accounts for how they were written that can stand up under close questioning. The past according to Burroughs has therefore compounded the contingencies of his publication history and blurred his development across decades as well as within them. This has gone unnoticed in part, as later chapters will show, because Burroughs scholarship has been so weak in this area, in part because these introductions always offer something else that draws our attention, some personal disclosure or thematic statement lacking in the texts themselves.

To a truly astonishing degree, Burroughs' introductions have upstaged all his texts of the 1950s and set the terms on which we should read them. They seem to be irresistible; they are *always* quoted, often in lieu of the texts, indeed to the point where lines from Burroughs' various introductions have become the most quoted of all his texts. However, just as we have to interrogate the Beat context rather than disregard it, so too with Burroughs' own contextualizing: from one text to another, we need to take full account of the obfuscations, deceptions, and disclosures, all the false readings that he has invited and all the true readings he has lured us into rejecting. Or to avoid losing not just the *uncertainty* but both the psychological and the political factors in play here, we have to take him at his word when Burroughs says: "Lies are just not in me and neither is the truth" (*My Education* 6).

If there remains something missing in the history of Burroughs' creative development that has allowed it to be misread, then we must not forget that this case of narrative failure and mistaken identity is far from accidental. To recall his *Paris Review* interview, advice to not believe in history has an inevitable convenience for those with pasts they would prefer to forget—witness the case of Paul de Man—and Burroughs is notorious for having such a past and such an attitude towards it. This very question is directly begged in the same interview when, referring to his wife's death, Burroughs briskly dismissed—"Absurd and false"—what is now acknowledged to be the absurd but tragically true account (qtd. in Knickerbocker 167).

And so we come back to the scene of the "secret," as if, to echo Antonioni's *Blow-Up*, trying to locate the body. As with a murder mystery, the questions are always: How did it happen? Who did it? So too with the strange "body" of Burroughs' work, we ask: How did it come about? What happened between the writing of *Junkie* mainly in 1950 and *Queer* in 1952 to account for their dramatic difference? What are we to make of *The Yage Letters*? How did he make the quantum leap to *Naked Lunch*? In particular, if it is true that *Queer* reveals "the secret of the Invisible Man" and "the origin of his writing genius," as Ginsberg's sensational blurb for the book claimed, then what we need is an accurate chronology and a precise investigation into the material circumstances of Burroughs' writing.

But surely, this secret—don't we already know its name? Hasn't Burroughs himself confessed where the body is buried, in the very introduction to *Queer,* where he reaches his famous "appalling conclusion": that it was the shooting of his wife, Joan, in September 1951 that "motivated and formulated" his writing by bringing him in contact with Control, aka "the Ugly Spirit" (Q xxii)? But the difference between *Junkie* and *Queer,* let alone the ground of an oeuvre-long war on control, cannot be left to the repercussions of that single gunshot, one evening in Mexico. Psychological speculation inevitably works like grapeshot. As Geoff Ward says, Burroughs' "writing life may or may not have depended" on that fatal moment ("William Burroughs" 346); neither Ward nor anyone else can usefully say more. The more that *has* been said, and its far from useful consequences, we will return to in chapter 3. More immediately, the only certainty is that anyone who has ever heard of Burroughs the writer knows these two "secrets": that he was a junkie who shot and killed his wife. And as Ward has pointed out, the image of the killer would replace the stereotype of the addict as "the image dominating public perception of Burroughs' work" ("Mutations" 111). A skeptic might conclude that if one projected image can conceal as much as it reveals, so too might its replacement.

What is most obviously concealed by Burroughs' introduction to *Queer* is his homosexual identity, the very subject of the text itself. This is a kind of *open secret,* in the sense that it is entirely obvious and yet almost always overlooked. But I am not proposing a "Queer Burroughs," a reading to foreground his sexuality that has been long overdue and only very lately redressed,[14] but something superficially far more modest: a "*Queer* Burroughs." This goes far beyond a queer reading of Burroughs, however, because it assumes such a reading as already taken into account in the revelation, in the performance of unmasking that forces us to ask, what *more* could there be to reveal? Mark Sussman observes: "The reveal that distracts and thereby conceals is the essence of the nothing-up-my-sleeve gesture of the conjuror" (93). But Burroughs does more than perform such acts, because, split by the contradictory psychic pressures of concealment and disclosure that drive the "secrecy system" (Osteen 80), he must also invite us to recognize the fact. This is clearest in *Cities of the Red Night,* where he defines "the essence of sleight of hand" as misdirection: "If someone can be convinced that he has, through his own perspicacity, divined your hidden purposes, he will not look further" (90). Of course the upshot is that Burroughs radiates even more the mystique of hidden knowledge, while we risk losing ourselves, as the detective narrative in *Cities of the Red Night* makes plain, in a black hole of paranoia. We can always "look further" and further, but we can at least say that Burroughs plays the conjuror's game with both sleeves, in which case his confession in the introduction to *Queer* is surely the acme of the genre: a true revelation that all the while conceals by luring us towards one open secret—Burroughs' homosexuality—the better to preempt suspicion of another, even more disturbing one. The final irony is that *Queer*'s other secret is only the secret of its form and so lies in open view, in the manner of Edgar Allan Poe's "Purloined Letter."

THE BELLES LETTRISTIC CURTAIN

The secret—of the Invisible Man, of the Enemy Within, and of a textual politics that bears the stamp of power—this secret has an absolutely literal existence. In context of those sensational biographical secrets it hides behind—addiction, manslaughter, homosexuality—it has the appearance of the absurd, although from the point of view of literary criticism, which has overlooked it, nothing could be more material. For the irony is that this secret is the very means of production, the technology and economy of writing that in turn is a key engine for the specific form and force of the writing I name *Burroughsian.* It emerges in the course of his first trilogy, culminates as a uniquely fertile contradiction in *Naked Lunch,* and is radicalized by negation in his second trilogy. Burroughs' secret *techné* of writing, all the more surprising and easy to misunderstand for being so mundane, is the letter, and it has been in more or less open view since 1977, when Ginsberg's introduction to *Junky* unveiled Burroughs' creative debt to their correspondence:

> [This] was the method whereby we assembled books not only of *Junky* but also *Yage Letters, Queer* [. . .] and much of *Naked Lunch.* Shamefully, Burroughs has destroyed much of his personal epistles of the mid-50s which I entrusted to his archival care—letters of a more pronouncedly affectionate nature than he usually displays to public—so, alas, that charming aspect of the otherwise Invisible Inspector Lee has been forever obscured behind the Belles Lettristic Curtain. (*Junky* v–vi)

The only thing more extraordinary than this claim is the fact that for twenty-five years it has attracted no critical attention whatsoever. For Ginsberg is saying that Burroughs' first four texts, the work of an entire decade, were all mediated by an intimate epistolary relation between the two men. Even for someone whose work is as uniquely sui generis as Burroughs, this is a remarkable account of a modern writer's practice. It is inconceivable that such a mode of collaborative creative construction could have failed to exercise some shaping influence. Why then, despite publication of two volumes of correspondence in the interim, has Ginsberg's claim passed so long without critical interest? There are perhaps four main reasons.

First, there is academic disregard for the genetic in general and the epistolary in particular. This has served to foreclose the potential for seeing a significant *productive* relation between letters and texts. The second reason is the limited critical attention to Burroughs' first decade, compounded by publication contingencies. Third, there is the very extent of the claim. For if four such formally distinct texts were all composed in such a way, then we must ask, how determining could the effect have been? The claim invites disinterest rather than incredulity or analysis: what could possibly lie hidden behind Burroughs' "Belles Lettristic Curtain"? This is the fourth reason: the importance of the epistolary is inseparable from the history of its concealment, and the fact of its secrecy has not been recognized precisely because it has remained another *open secret*, apparently not concealed at all.

This is the only conclusion I can reach to understand the curious fate of *The Letters of William S. Burroughs, 1945–1959.* For a full decade, Burroughs criticism has used that volume in an entirely conventional way as a biographical resource, rather than building on the evidence for Burroughs' extraordinary investment of creative energy in his correspondence or developing the case I made in its introduction, that an epistolary economy was central to his writing of the 1950s. That was in fact the easy part, which I have come to see takes us only halfway there. What is at issue here—tying Burroughs' textual politics to his creative development—requires a different rigor. It calls for an investigation of Ginsberg's claim text by text across the following chapters. The road to *Naked Lunch* has to go carefully by way of *Junkie, Queer,* and "In Search of Yage," since what is at stake is both a new narrative of Burroughs' development as a writer and a paradigm shift in how to read these texts. Needless to say, what lies behind the epistolary curtain is not "charming" as Ginsberg calls it, unless we restore the literal sense of the word: *fascinating.*

Exactly how the epistolary scene produced a literal economy of writing, how it originated the workings of power within the activity of writing, and how it became an engine for content and form are questions that govern the following chapters. Each chapter responds in distinct ways to the singularity of Burroughs' major texts of the 1950s and to the state of critical play. What they share is a drive to reappraise the material narrative of his writing, reading each text in terms of its history of production and reception and from the point of view of form as well as content. The basis to identifying their textual politics is to materialize the economic relation between two sets of histories: textual and cultural, genetic and formal.

Clearly enough, in fixing on *Naked Lunch* as the central point to which the first trilogy leads and from which the second trilogy develops, my understanding of what is "Burroughsian" about Burroughs is deeply unfashionable. Recent criticism prefers a different story, as in the judgment Ann Douglas passes on Burroughs' literary history: for her, the "first trilogy" denotes *The Soft Machine, The Ticket That Exploded,* and *Nova Express,*[15] while his second trilogy, *Cities of the Red Night* (1981), *The Place of Dead Roads* (1983), and *The Western Lands* (1987), stands as "his greatest work" ("Punching" xx). For me, the crucial decades are his first and second, but greatness is of little interest; although it appears an idiosyncratic novel of private significance, I see *Queer* as the essential text aesthetically and politically, and I focus on it at length accordingly. To make this case, I pay a good deal of attention to existing Burroughs criticism but not because his critics are all a bunch of dupes, whereas I, *I know the secret:* far from it, if the fascination of the secret is itself the secret of fascination. Rather, it is because, in a certain consistency to their misreadings, the critics reveal something. What all the errors "know" without knowing is the other secret of Burroughs' fascination. If the real secret is that there is no secret beyond the appearance, then the letter is the secret that this logic itself hides; the secret in its mundane form, its most material manifestation. And so, while my questions are multiple and various, the answer will stay the same because, in my ambition of doing justice to the secret, it is the limit of what I can reveal.

2

Junkie: The Procedure Here Is More or Less Impersonal

The whole secret is intent.
—Burroughs (quoting Carlos Castaneda), *Painting and Guns*

BEATING *JUNKIE*

TANGLED HISTORY

Surveying the material history of Burroughs' work, in 1989 James Grauerholz observed that the "scattered circumstances of his literary efforts are reflected in the scattered provenance of much of Burroughs' archival material" (*I* ix). This disarray is certainly true for all his writing of the 1950s, and not one of Burroughs' four novels exists as a fully archived or complete manuscript in any one collection. "In the long run, there will be plenty of work for the critics and textual scholars," Grauerholz concluded, "as they begin to unravel the tangled history of Burroughs' works" (x). That "long run" had already begun for me in 1984, as a research student over from England, in the Butler Library at Columbia University. Leafing through folder after folder in the Burroughs and Ginsberg special collections, I didn't really know what I was looking for, nor whether, after a mass of note taking and photocopying, I had found it. One September evening in Palo Alto seventeen years later, now working on an editing project together with Grauerholz, I might have recalled his words as I held miscellaneous pages of the manuscript that, half a century earlier, Burroughs called "Junk." Added to those assembled from special collections at Ohio State and Columbia, these pages photocopied from the archives in Green Library at Stanford were the last pieces needed to unravel the tangled history of the first of those scattered works.

To the manuscript fetishist's private thrill of handling the original objects, those delicate sheets of paper bearing the imprint of typewriter keys and author's pen, was added the satisfaction of being able to prove certain intuitions about Burroughs' early novels that would change how others read them. But the payoff, in literary research as well as in life, is never quite what we expect, and by morning the thrill had gone. I realized that the fiftieth anniversary of the most fateful date in the Burroughs calendar had just passed, yet what I felt was not a sense of historical connection and proximity but of disconnection and distance. Manuscripts are unique, material traces of authorship, unlike paperbacks bought over the counter, and that is why scholars prize them. But they are also highly seductive, holding out the promise of final, hidden knowledge, of some fact outside the published text that is yet essential to it. Now, having found the secret, it felt as if my insights had been stolen from me by the very evidence I had at long last unearthed to confirm them. Far from bringing me closer to Burroughs, all these bits of paper had taken on their own separate reality, and I knew that, somewhere along the way, I had lost sight of the very experience of reading the novels that had inspired my quest to untangle the past in the first place. These are all reasons why the chronology of a novel's production cannot be allowed to come before that of its reception.

TWO BOOKS IN ONE

If *Junkie*'s textual politics are an exception to the rule of the Burroughs oeuvre, then one reason why this singularity has not been fully grasped is that, critically speaking, Burroughs' first novel has never been read; it has only ever been reread, in a series of rearview mirrors. To begin with, *Junkie* has always been seen in the retrospective light cast by two overbearing contexts: the Beat Generation framework of fictionalized biography, and *Naked Lunch* that was published after it. And second, it has been seen in the light of the two mediating texts that have preceded the novel quite literally: the preface added by Burroughs at the request of Ace Books, and Ginsberg's introduction to the reedited *Junky* twenty-five years later. The net result of all these different frames is an identity crisis, one given vivid form in the narrative told by the succession of jacket designs, starting from the lurid Ace Double Book edition of 1953.

The Ace cover showed a busty, peroxide blonde heroin addict in a tight scarlet skirt being wrestled by a man whose determined grip forces syringe, spoon, and dropper to slip from her desperate fingers. This potent moral drama of violent, quasi-erotic action stages a scene that has little to do with *Junkie* and owes more to the phenomenal success of Mickey Spillane, whose hard-boiled sensationalism virtually defined the postwar paperback in all its "two-bit glory" (Server 26). Over the next two decades, this fabricated struggle gave way to more realist images of lonely addicts, striking a grim sociological tone, until in the early 1980s the book was dignified by a "serious" art cover. This was one of Georg Baselitz's painted upside-down figures; quite a contrast to the Ace edition, with its uncredited artwork (actually by a certain Al Rossi, also responsible for the likes of *Loves of a Girl Wrestler*). The transformation from a pseudonymous book of basement thrills packaged by the pulp trade to the work of a named author with full artistic control and status was finally completed by using a painting of Burroughs' own design from the 1990s. This passage from the quantitative to the qualitative—from a mass-market product sold on the newsstand as part of a bargain deal ("Two books in one—35¢") to one valued as a unique artwork—frames rates of exchange and expectation so opposed as to set real problems for interpretation. Even the question "which presentation best fits the text?" can't properly be asked, since title, credited authorship, and—although this has always been overlooked—*content* have all changed along with the covers.[1]

The passage from low-brow to literary status in turn reprises the effect of critical backdating. This has invested *Junkie* with a capital of anticipation, as it is seen both to rehearse in "conventional" form a range of Burroughsian "raw material," motifs, characters, and themes and to possess a wealth of "unacknowledged" formal complexity (Murphy, *Wising Up* 46). Pointing out that the work is not so simple as it seems but is in fact "deceptively complex" (Ward, "William Burroughs" 341) or "complex and ironic" (Skerl 30) is par for the critical course. But there is a difficulty when deep meanings are restored to *Junkie* in such a way. This is the hermeneutic difficulty of the text itself: as strategies of form, deceptiveness and irony presume motivation, whereas the peculiar force of *Junkie* comes from how far William Lee's narrative purpose is pared down to the rhetorical bone along with his character. What is most striking are precisely its refusals and absences, defaults that risk making "recognition" of *Junkie*'s intentions produce unproblematic readings. Is it artful or is it artless? Far from coincidentally, this is the question posed by Burroughs through *Naked Lunch*.

YOU KNOW THE TYPE

Read always in retrospect, the typically flat, terse narrative of *Junkie* has long appeared solid straight rock beside the treacherous whirlpool of *Naked Lunch*. The contrast in reading experience is so extraordinary, so total, as to imply utterly antithetical conceptions as well as practices of writing. It is not enough to call *Junkie* an "uncharacteristically traditional first novel" (Tanner 111) nor to claim that in "*Naked Lunch* Burroughs has achieved his mature voice" (Skerl 45). So dramatic a transformation demands precision. Indeed, Burroughs himself demanded it: this is surely one reason why he returned to his first novel to make the opening narrative passage of *Naked Lunch*. Here, we are invited to witness the transformation not just *from* one text *to* another but *of* one text *into* another. But what exactly is it that we are meant to see?

> I had the stuff in a package of cigarettes and was ready to throw it in the water-filled gutter. Sure enough, there was a burly young man in a white trench coat standing in a doorway. When he saw me he started sauntering up the street ahead of me. Then he turned a corner, waiting for me to walk past so he could fall in behind. I turned and ran back in the other direction. When I reached Sixth Avenue, he was about fifty feet behind me. I vaulted the subway turnstile and shoved the cigarette package into the space at the side of a gum machine. I ran down one level and got a train up to the Square. (*J* 54)

> I can feel the heat closing in, feel them out there making their moves, setting up their devil doll stool pigeons, crooning over my spoon and dropper I throw away at Washington Square Station, vault a turnstile and two flights down the iron stairs, catch an uptown A train . . . Young, good looking, crew cut, Ivy League, advertising exec type fruit holds the door back for me. I am evidently his idea of a character. You know the type comes on with bartenders and cab drivers, talking about right hooks and the Dodgers, call the counterman in Nedick's by his first name. A real asshole. And right on time this narcotics dick in a white trench coat (imagine tailing somebody in a white trench coat—trying to pass as a fag I guess) hit the platform. I can hear the way he would say it holding my outfit in his left hand, right hand on his piece: "I think you dropped something, fella."
>
> But the subway is moving.
>
> "So long flatfoot!" I yell, giving the fruit his B production. (*NL* 1–2)

Critics have given these passages the comparison they invite, but neither the assumption of "the addict-hustler personality" seen by Jennie Skerl (36) nor the "revenge of the inauthentic" traced by Geoff Ward ("William Burroughs" 348) seem to me to grasp the significant within the obvious. For what motivates the rewriting has to be seen as inseparable from the specific features of its key formal transformation: whereas in *Junkie*, William Lee's first person account of past events is simply narrated, in *Naked Lunch*, Burroughs now aggressively incorporates a live audience. Or rather, two audiences: first, the reader, directly and knowingly addressed—"You know the type"—and then the "type" himself, the Ivy League "fruit" or "asshole." Meanwhile, the shift in tense makes the action and its narration equally immediate, so that the "type"—defined with razor sharpness as a 1950s model American—not only coexists but coincides with the reader. The introduction of this audience into the scene works therefore to structure the narrator's relationship with the reader in the same hostile terms of seduction and exploitation as the rest of the section makes uncomfortably clear. In short, the victimized audience is made the central subject.

However, the most significant point is that this aggressive exposure of the reader's presence applies not just to *Naked Lunch* but also, retrospectively, to *Junkie*. This is because the despised "asshole" of the second version *is* the unaddressed "typical" reader of the original made visible. Falling for Lee's "B production," this "square [who] wants to come on hip" (*NL* 2) would surely have lapped up the *Confessions of an Unredeemed Drug Addict* as readily as he will shortly buy the catnip Lee passes off as marijuana. And so, in another gesture back to the book as actually published and read, Burroughs parodies the publisher's notes inserted into *Junkie* by Ace Books with his handy editorial on catnip—"Frequently passed on the incautious or uninstructed" (*J* 4)—presuming that we know no more than the "jerk."

What has happened is that the force of the scene has shifted from factual narrative action to fictional narrating interaction to reveal the latter secretly within the former. Lee's narration no longer pretends to be disinterested, a record of experience in which the facts speak for themselves. On the contrary, it declares itself a nakedly motivated performance, exercising a power of fascination and collecting an economic profit. Therefore, it is not only a question of returning to *Junkie* as published and read but as bought and sold: the relationship between reader and narrator is made visible as a relation between buyer and seller, and what passes between them is a cultural commodity that repays the image-desiring customer with only an image of desire. The catnip, of course, is entirely symbolic for both Lee and the jerk, since the real sale here is the sales talk itself: the object of consumption is nothing other than the narrative performance. Clearly, this seduction is also an act of calculated payback on Lee's part, since any jerk who works for the image and desire factory of capital, advertising, deserves to be taken for all he's worth.

In short, the introductory narrative of *Naked Lunch* is a text in the homiletic sense. It warns the reader against the seductions of narrative and the fascinating image by focusing on exchange, on the consumption of the text as an economic and cultural "B" production. Because the rewritten version sarcastically flaunts its rhetorical double-dealing and exposes its ugly, exploitative motivations, it is the terse authority of the *original* that now stands revealed as counterfeit: *Naked Lunch* lays bare the power relations silent in Burroughs' own earlier prose. This conclusion turns the standard critical reading on its head: the power of control and the personality of the inauthentic are not added in *Naked Lunch* to the scene from *Junkie* but are found there, and this discovery follows from an acute sense of audience, a sense as indeterminate in *Junkie* as it is certain in *Naked Lunch*.

Clearly, this new sense of readership might be understood as Burroughs' awareness of his own work's reception, an economic and cultural awareness he lacked when writing *Junkie*. More than that, because the reader here is identified with (if not also *as*) a reader of his first novel, what makes the rewritten version so unsettling is the way in which this text, unlike the first, meets our own gaze. And as our transparent window onto the text turns into a looking glass, we find the fruit/jerk/asshole looking back.[2] Made to face the ugliness of our voyeurism and its just as ugly economic exploitation, as readers of *Junkie* we are now forced to recognize ourselves in the image of those "charged a sawski" (i.e., ten dollars) by Lee to enter the "room with a one-way whorehouse mirror" (*NL* 2). With this reversibility, what we have lost is any possibility of the protective distance of the unobserved observer. To put this another way, Burroughs forces *Junkie* to confess its secret mythological identity, spelled out in the introduction added to *Naked Lunch*. Here, Burroughs openly offers us our choice, which of course is no choice at all: "Only way to protect yourself against this horrid peril is come over HERE and shack up with Charybdis. . . . Treat you right Kid. . . . Candy and cigarettes" (*NL* xix). Burroughs looks back on *Junkie* and makes us see not straight-talking, fact-telling William Lee but stony-faced Scylla.

In other words, *Naked Lunch* sustains entirely antithetical rereadings of *Junkie:* from one perspective, what is queer about *Junkie* is its "straightness"—its "uncharacteristically traditional" form, its un-Burroughsian "simplicity," and so on; from another, what looked solid and straight now appears in its true light as *queer* (in the everyday sense of strange, false, untrustworthy, crooked). Burroughs therefore transforms a narrative that seemed to be totally motivated as a sign of itself—to be taken at face value and read literally—into a game of duplicity and decipherment where there must be winners and losers. But the point would be lost if we saw in this transformation a simple shift, from directly lived and narrated life in *Junkie* to life and narration as a series of staged spectacles in *Naked Lunch.* If, as Guy Debord argued in *La Société du Spectacle,* the "real consumer becomes a consumer of illusions" (28; my translation), then the greatest illusion of all is consumption without production, as if the spontaneously natural and self-evidently neutral were anything other than the workings of ideology. The other side to *Junkie* as an object whose produced status has been masked is therefore an anonymous consumer, a voyeuristic reader, one who wants the pleasure of looking without being seen.

What does Burroughs' transformation of one text into another tell us then? That *Naked Lunch* knows—and would force us to know—something monstrous about narrative, about the economy of fantasy and power relations, about desire, something that *Junkie* apparently does not know. *Apparently,* because the question of intention still remains open. Unsurprisingly, the demand for an answer, for motivation, has been *Junkie*'s fate in the Beat context. Here, recourse to biography has worked against the grain of the text, managing to skew both the political force of the novel in its historical moment and its place in Burroughs' aesthetic development.

WHAT I WAS LOOKING FOR

Treated as a roman à clef, as "Burroughs' autobiography" (George and Starr 193, 202), and as one of the works "that defined Beat literature" (Charters, *Portable Beat* xxxiii), it is in the periodized Beat narrative that *Junkie* has been most fully dehistoricized. Accordingly, *Junkie* has been described as an "inverted" (Tanner 113), "failed" (Stull 26), or "unfulfilled" quest (Skerl 30). What sustains this "visionary" reading is the Beat Generation itself, widely understood as a biographical narrative of spiritual mission, a fraternity of postwar outcasts united precisely by a "shared sense of quest" (Stephenson 1). And so, because drugs are viewed as "the key to the spiritual world" (Halberstam 301), and because Burroughs is said to have been on a quest through drugs during the 1940s—"it is clear that he chose this fate. Addiction became his spiritual discipline as an artist" (Skerl 12)—it follows that, contrary to all appearances, his protagonist is on a quest too. Almost the only evidence in the novel itself is its evocative ending—"Maybe

I will find in yage what I was looking for in junk and weed and coke" (*J* 152)—which has been applied retrospectively and used to frame the book inside a "quest cycle." In fact, this conclusion was a late addition demanded by Burroughs' editors, who wanted to anticipate the adventures of his sequel, which they also planned to publish.[3] But scholarship only confirms what we can easily intuit. The ending may speak of transcendence, of actively seeking a vision freed from the "claims" of the flesh, but the narrative itself begins by implying Lee's surrender of agency—"Sometimes we don't want to control it," the junkie novice is warned (*J* 6)—and goes on to exhibit chiefly his disturbing passivity before the brute materiality of junk and its "biological necessity" (*Junky* 124). Therefore, despite the self-evident literariness of the subject, addiction brings Lee no more aesthetic pleasure than moral pain, and the last genre to which *Junkie* belongs is that of the *Künstlerroman*.

Significantly, those who animate the cipher that passes for Lee's identity are performing the same maneuver as Burroughs' biographers. For example, Ted Morgan argues that he was hiding his "real motive" for taking drugs—entry into a criminal and liminal fraternity—so that, contrary to its "surface" appearance, *Junkie* is really "about finding a place to belong" (208). A less fraternal community is surely hard to imagine: the mooches, fags, stool pigeons, bums, and thieves who people Lee's world are—to use the relevant terms from Jack Black's *You Can't Win*—not honorable members of the tolerant, quasi-Beat "Johnson Family" but so many disloyal, solitary, and self-serving "Shits." By beginning *in medias res* and by all but shunning reflection, the narrative avoids the expected dualisms—of social identities past or present, lost or found, legal or illegal—along with the expected progressions of plot and moral development of character: although Burroughs had the inspiring example of Kerouac's *The Town and the City* before him, there is nothing of the bildungsroman in *Junkie*.

Whether reading addiction in *Junkie* as a quest for *communitas* or as a spiritual mission, the misuse of biographical speculation is the same: always prone to *horror vacui*, the critic faced by an unnatural absence of motive gratefully discovers in biography the secret but necessary key. No doubt this is why the preface has proved so useful, since it invites us to ground the narrative in a fully autobiographical world. Whereas the narrative starts from Lee's first experience with junk and almost never looks back, the preface starts at birth, a move that motivates Lee's thirty-year passage from 1914 to 1944. From another point of view, of course, what we are looking at is a belated surplus that makes good an original lack, a lack that we would be bound to notice if only we read the text in the order of its composition rather than in the order of its presentation. Certainly, by detecting an assertive ego to match his first name (Will-I-am), we motivate Lee with goals both social and sacred, only at the cost of smoothing out all that is so unnerving in the reading experience. This is because it is not only the protagonist who lacks purpose, who merely drifts into the dead determinism of addiction, and who solipsistically gives only the facts of his experience without ethical regard but his narrative, not only the junkie but *Junkie* that seems to go nowhere and offer nothing.

Junkie may give autobiographical witness to a criminalized subculture, a black economy of undesirable others beneath and inside official urban America during the immediate postwar years, but the novel's critical force is the very negative of any definable as Beat. The hallmarks of Beat writing—its obsessive group mythologizing, an aesthetics of self-expression, the political value of the deviant and defiantly personal, the romance of the marginal, a visionary narrative motivation, and so on—such hallmarks are not only not present in *Junkie,* they are conspicuous by their absence. The Beat reading simply rewrites the novel from an already known script. Its textual politics have therefore been predetermined by the insistent relation of the aesthetic and the autobiographical as advanced by Kerouac and by Ginsberg, as if compensating for *their* conspicuous absence from Burroughs' narrative. Indeed, this is the context imposed on the reedited *Junky* by Ginsberg's introduction. Since 1977, this has mediated the text by setting out two related histories: an account of its genesis, and the story of its initial publication. These histories of origin are related through a complex network of psychological, political, commercial, legal, and aesthetic conditions that taken together motivate the writing of *Junkie* by constructing it within the key terms of Beat literary history. Rather than simply rejecting this context as false, we need to fulfill its logic before turning to reappraise the text itself.

DEEP CORRESPONDENCE

According to Ginsberg's narrative of events, *Junkie* was conceived and developed in a context of mutual psychological support conducted by mail between Mexico City and New Jersey. In "deep correspondence," Ginsberg encouraged Burroughs to write more prose:

> In any case he responded to my letters with chapters of *Junky*. So the bulk of the Ms. arrived sequentially in the mail, some to Paterson, New Jersey. I thought I was encouraging him. It occurs to me that he may have been encouraging me to keep in active contact with the

world, as I was rusticating at my parents' house after 8 months in mental hospital as result of hippie contretemps with law. (*Junky* v)

Because of its location, Ginsberg's account of how, and by implication why, Burroughs wrote his first novel naturally took on the status of an authorized version; it has been often repeated, sometimes ignored, but never really considered. However, this history of *Junkie*'s genesis has two particular significances for its interpretation. First, it gives priority to the material origins of writing by uniting means with motives and writer with reader: if the manuscript was begun "as a series of letters to Ginsberg" (B. Cook 177) and sent "in epistolary fragments" (Server 74) in response to Ginsberg's own, then it assumes the function, if no longer the form, of the letter as an act of private expression and communication.[4] Second, the work is seen as mediated by the psychological needs of both writer and reader in their acute and shared isolation; Ginsberg, just released from the Columbia Psychiatric Institute, and Burroughs, just starting his Mexican exile. But what is truly arresting about Ginsberg's account is the way he massively ups first the aesthetic ante on its method of writing and then the sociopolitical ante on the text as psychological testimony and so locates both scenes at the center of the Beat narrative.

First, Ginsberg goes on to say that the reciprocating structure of their correspondence "was the method whereby we assembled books not only of *Junky* but also *Yage Letters, Queer* [...] and much of *Naked Lunch*" (*Junky* vi). As I have argued, what is called for is an investigation of Ginsberg's claim, text by text, across the following chapters. More immediately, it is his claim for *Junkie*'s epistolary genesis and its contextualization within Beat aesthetics that needs to be put to the test.

And so, to the second raising of the stakes in Ginsberg's introduction. Emphatically, he goes on to frame the psychological needs that Burroughs' writing is said to have addressed inside a wider context of both personal and national crisis as they intersected in the publishing industry circa 1952. He describes unsuccessfully taking the manuscript of *Junkie* to Louis Simpson ("himself recovering from nervous breakdown at Bobbs-Merrill"), and then to Carl Solomon at Ace Books, who accepts it ("'The damn thing almost gave me a nervous breakdown'") but adds a publisher's note "pretending to be the voice of sanity," inserts editorial disclaimers, and solicits from Burroughs a preface (*Junky* vi, vii, viii). Finally, Ginsberg concludes that the manuscripts he was then touting—of *Junkie* and *On the Road*—"indicated we were in the middle of an identity crisis prefiguring nervous breakdown for the whole United States" (vii). The key lies in this insistent relation of the cold war political to the individual psychological and how this operated through the cultural and commercial nexus of the book trade.

Burroughs' and Ginsberg's deep correspondence at this time was dominated by issues of sanity and conformity, individuation and socialization; in Foucault's terms, the ways in which a disciplinary social order produced "madness," which it then demanded legal, medical, and bureaucratic intervention to "control, reform, or prevent" (Connolly, *Politics* 107). Add to that list the liberal university academy. For Ginsberg entered the Psychiatric Institute in 1949 courtesy of his Columbia University mentors, Mark Van Doren and Lionel Trilling, whose testimony freed him from the prison cell by volunteering his confinement to the mental ward. Outraged, Burroughs denounced his professors as liberal "weaklings" and his psychiatrists as a "lot of New Deal Freudians" (*L* 51). This intersection of two Columbias—the university and the psychiatric institute—in turn leads to a third, as the site of one of Ginsberg's most dramatic experiences and the occasion for some of his most astute analysis: the Columbia University Bookstore. The incident took place exactly one year earlier, on the day after Ginsberg's momentous vision of William Blake. Looking back, he describes leafing over a book of Blake's poetry and suddenly returning to "the eternal place" of his original vision, now realizing that the "infinite self" it revealed was not his private madness but a consciousness secretly shared by everybody in the bookstore (Interview 308–9). Suddenly, Ginsberg was made aware of the commodification of literature and its meaning: "in other words the position that everybody was in was *ridiculous,* everybody running around peddling books to each other. Here in the universe!"

This scene clearly articulates the postwar convergence of therapeutic, academic, literary, and commercial institutions and suggests how the Romanticism of Beat aesthetics would insist on imaginative creation as an image of nonalienated labor, as opposed to rationalist and empiricist ideologies enslaved to "fact" (Eagleton 24). It would also insist, against the formalist orthodoxies of the New Criticism, on the inseparability of the writer and his work. What happened in classroom, bookstore, and publishing house reinforced the internalized censorship that took place at the writer's desk. Hence, the drama of "Howl" and *On the Road* turned not only on the acts of behavior they would mythologize but also on the activity of writing, on the physical and mental courage needed "to commit to writing, to *write,* the same way that you . . . are!" (Ginsberg, Interview 288). Ginsberg saw the writing of *Junkie* in exactly the same boldly humanistic terms, inviting it to be read in line with that of "Howl" and *On the Road.*

In 1955, "Howl" could only be begun outside the scope of public institutions demanding harsh self-repression and so defined a readership of *only* the likes of those to whom Ginsberg dedicated his poem: Kerouac, Cassady, Burroughs, Carl Solomon, and Lucien Carr. One of the key resources for Ginsberg's poem, and for Kerouac's novel, was therefore the intense, conversational intimacies that had defined the Beat circle a decade earlier. These shared intimacies had exposed what Ginsberg later called the "hypocrisy of literature": "The problem is to break down that distinction: when you approach the Muse to talk as frankly as you would talk with yourself or with your friends [...] And that was Kerouac's great discovery in *On the Road*" (Interview 289, 288). And it was also Ginsberg's in "Howl for Carl Solomon." The dedication in the title is crucial: more than a traditional dedication, a writing *for,* it is like part 3 of the poem itself, a direct address, a writing *to.* This understanding would elide the difference between the poem as publishable and public property and as a written personal communication—that is, the letter form.

Indeed, Ginsberg had already entered quite literally into a reciprocal economy that makes letters into poems and poems into letters, most directly in 1953 with what he would later describe as his "first breakthrough as a poet": "The Green Automobile" (Miles, *Ginsberg* 153). This poem was addressed, in both senses of the word, as a work-in-progress to Neal Cassady in the course of their own long-distance "deep correspondence." Ginsberg's identification of letter and literature could not be clearer than when in September 1953 he enclosed "a writ copy of the as yet unfinished GREEN AUTOMOBILE, which shows you that though this letter is late I've been writing it, in other forms" (*As Ever* 153). That resonant final phrasing measures his poetry's unacknowledged debt to an epistolary economy of exchange and desire, an intimate economy that underwrites a range of formal features in his later work. More broadly, this context takes us to the core of any articulated Beat aesthetic, and it is here that Ginsberg's account of *Junkie*'s genesis via the intimacy of epistolary address needs to be read.

The letter played a vital role in the Beat narrative, and a sketch of its centrality will prove essential for situating Burroughs' own epistolary practice. At the same time, the very fact that such an account is needed at all is revealing. It shows the extent to which Beat correspondence has remained taken for granted; so familiar as a basic biographical resource that its profound structural and historical importance has been remarkably overlooked. It is almost an embarrassment that it should have taken a critic working *outside* the Beat field—David Savran, in *Taking It Like a Man*—to even begin, however narrowly, the task of precise analysis.

OPEN SECRECY

For Ginsberg and Kerouac especially, the letter represented two key possibilities in the context of postwar America: a technology of self-expression and communication opposed to the superficiality of modern mass media; and an economy of interpersonal intimacy opposed to the impersonal relations of commodity exchange. For them, it wasn't just a matter of personal preference or the kind of writers they already were. It is because epistolary space was one of the few interstices in the cold war's disciplinary regimes of self-regulation that letter writing became vitally important to their creativity. The letter was an old but readily available technology for sharing and preserving newly suspect privacies and otherwise incriminating confidences. Indeed, one of the reasons why Ginsberg and Kerouac in particular came to invest essential energy in their correspondence was that, during the late 1940s and early 1950s, their marginalization was not only social and political but also cultural and economic. It was their position as not just unpublished but, so it must have felt, *unpublishable* writers that made letter writing so uniquely important. Steven Watson's comment that "the intimate circle was both subject matter and audience" (6) succinctly describes the very circularity into which they were forced.

The importance of the epistolary for the Beats is therefore tied to their particular history as a uniquely intimate and isolated circle of "internal exiles" that was then dispersed over time and through space. Correspondence not only maintained camaraderie by bridging the physical distances of this diaspora but embodied dreams of an alternative personal and social space. Out of such private practice came the Beat project of "open secrecy" as Ginsberg called it, by which he meant writing that was addressed initially to "his own soul's ear and a few other golden ears" that would exemplify what their politicized culture and its mass media threatened to blue-pencil ("Notes" 318). And in the early 1950s, the political stakes could not have been any higher. Cold war paranoia demanded the conscription of private selves in the name of national security by motivating the secrecy of everyday life in terms of what David Caute called the Myth of the Vital Secret: the apocalyptic secret of the Bomb (62). As Ginsberg immediately recognized, the true victims of this absolute secret were not just the so-called atom spies Ethel and Julius Rosenberg, executed in 1953, but the candor and spontaneity of everyone.

Although Beat critics have overlooked the key role of the letter in its economy, they have established that the drive to contest the alienation and fear produced by cold war secrecy was central to Beat practice: its aim, as

Ann Douglas puts it, was nothing less than to "*de*classify the secrets of the human body and soul" ("Telepathic Shock" 14). In this sense, Beat correspondence fulfills epistolary tradition, since, as William Decker observes of nineteenth-century practice, "the claiming of confidential, intimate, utopian space figures among the letter's genre-specific themes" (177). The historical vitality of the letter as a form for the Beats, in short, was that it promised to preserve a truly private space, a shared space available for documenting and expressing visions unspeakable in American society, unspoken in American "letters," and unsalable on American markets.

If the defining fiction of the letter sustains "our belief in the immediacy of truth and the communicability of lived experience" (Cousineau 28), then this was especially so for Kerouac and Ginsberg. Historically linked to the Romantic idealization of spontaneity, the letter promised to extend the originally oral, intimate, and mutual confessions of the early Beat circle through a mode of writing inherently concerned with spontaneity, intimacy, orality, and mutuality. A product of absence, the letter symbolically and practically answered to desires for presence: for making present both a subjective logos—what Ginsberg called the "very spark of life" ("When the Mode" 329) and Kerouac, referring to the method of spontaneous composition he named "sketching," called "the thing itself" (*Selected Letters, 1940–1956* 356)—and an intersubjective relation with another, equally committed self. For this reason, Beat aesthetics share fundamental epistolary ideals, while certain Beat texts have to be understood not only in terms of the close interpersonal relations they *represent* but just as importantly in terms of those mediated by the material activity of their writing.

Kerouac's debt to the example of Neal Cassady's long, autobiographical letters is the most familiar instance. Just three months before the marathon writing of *On the Road,* Kerouac vowed to "write the confession of my entire life to you, Neal Cassady, and send, by mail, in installments three thousand two hundred miles across the continent we know so well"— which meant he had "renounced fiction and fear" (*Selected Letters, 1940–1956* 246, 249) and found in the confessional letter a means to sidestep both the demands of a public literature and damnation by publishers' dollars. It is no coincidence that the epistolary bond that weds the first person "I" to a second person "you" accords so precisely with the central relationships in so many of Kerouac's novels, most visibly in *On the Road* and *Visions of Cody.* The intersubjective frame of the Kerouac-Cassady correspondence affirms that the Beats' autobiographical impulse of self-expression coincided with and was sustained by the epistolary dynamic of close communication.

Put briefly, it must be reductive, but the major aesthetic breakthroughs of Kerouac and Ginsberg during the early 1950s—the period of *Junkie*'s writing—coincided with creative investment in the singularly private and interpersonal at the expense of the public and impersonal. The result was autobiographical writing that privileged "honesty, clarity, spontaneity, and improvisation" (Skerl 18), that was "de-academised, visionary, performative" (Lee 2)—key terms for any epistolary aesthetic—and also ironically vulnerable to commodification to the very extent that it was conceived in innocence of the commodity's relations. For if Ginsberg and Kerouac looked to the letter as an exemplary countereconomy of writing, one that escaped the very formal economic and professional systems from which they were excluded, then we have also to grasp the intractable historical contradictions of their vision.

In an age of modern mass media and telecommunications, such practices become archaic, willful anachronisms informed by a certain nostalgia. Ginsberg and Kerouac knew that they were resurrecting a philosophy and a practice from the era of Emerson, who also dreamed of an epistolary "colloquy divine" (qtd. in Decker 110). In an era that politicized privacy "in the name of protecting it" (Rogin 245) and that inaugurated a *totalization* of economy and communication, the likes of Ginsberg and Kerouac were simply unable to liberate a truly private and utopian space as the binary alternative to a well-policed public dystopia. Letter exchanges always implicate, and are complicit with, technologies and economies of communication and desire at work in the wider social body. To put this another way, privacy itself becomes a fiction delivered by the post and so becomes doubly vulnerable.

From the outside, the letter exchange is open to incriminating interception and authoritarian state censorship: this liability, as Wilhelm Reich argued in *The Mass Psychology of Fascism,* makes the postal system an emblematic site for the "arbitrary practices" of a bureaucratic apparatus exercising power (307). And of course the Beat circle didn't need to read Reich to know this (although, for other reasons, they did read him); they experienced this scene of violation firsthand and in numerous ways. In one month, April 1949, *both* Burroughs and Ginsberg were arrested on separate charges and implicated through their correspondence; one of these scenes sent Ginsberg to the Columbia Psychiatric Institute, and Burroughs dramatized the other in *Junkie* (*J* 84–86, 90–91), making a rather different connection between correspondences than the one Ginsberg would offer in his introduction to the novel twenty-five years later. Burroughs' description of how the cops read Lee's personal letters in turn stands in for other disciplinary violations: for example, Herbert Huncke, fictionalized as Herman in *Junkie,* was already in prison when FBI agents grilled him by reading out letters to and from Burroughs and Ginsberg (Huncke 263). Burroughs well understood the *political* importance of criminalizing private communication.

The second form of the letter's vulnerability is the very mirror image of the first: secrecy tempts deceit as well as surveillance, spontaneity turns strategic, and desire is found to be complicit with the power it would escape. Which is to say that the letter writing of Ginsberg and Kerouac often betrayed or falsified the brotherly bonds they celebrated, so that the public world of cold war America and the private world of the Beat Generation were far from mutually exclusive: to an uneasy degree, they corresponded. The material consequences are clearest in the case of Kerouac, since his sense of destiny as a writer is bound up with the question of his writing's *destination.* Despite his pledge to "renounce all fiction," he can never really be rid of "the mysterious outside reader," a tormenting revenant who reminds Kerouac of his writing's public, that is to say, *economic* destiny (*Selected Letters, 1940–1956* 246, 248). His letter of 29 December 1950 structures this contradiction quite openly, first demanding Cassady "burn these things" and then giving him precise instructions on how to hand them "personally, to Giroux the editor of Harcourt-Brace" (246). To nominate Cassady his literary agent admits that the private economy of their letter exchange exists as capital for public consumption. There was no uncontaminated binary to the "hypocrisy of literature," and Ginsberg's vision of Beat communion might be seen as a nostalgic myth of togetherness and spontaneity, a fantasy of accessing what Lacan would call the impossible Real of desire: a dream of primal unity and plenitude manufactured in the medium and from the viewpoint of separation and loss. In short, it was less a utopian vision than an epistolary fiction.

Kerouac saw himself suffering "the curse of Melville" (*Selected Letters, 1940–1956* 239)—neglect—but he ended up a victim to Thoreau's "curse of trade"; he should have known that real huckleberries, let alone "messages from heaven," never reach market (Thoreau 47, 117). In fact, if the American Renaissance held for the Beats an exemplary text, it would have to be "Bartleby, the Scrivener," where the alienation of labor and the failure of communication reach Melville's dark postal terminus: the Dead Letter Office.

Ginsberg's claim for the mediation of Burroughs' writing via an intimate and reciprocal epistolary relationship locates *Junkie*—and its sequels—within such a context. Clearly, given this contextualization—with its Romantic valorization of the subjective and communal, the spiritual and irrational, with its expressivist aesthetic of singing the self and soliciting an audience, and with its dissent from writing grounded in the economic and formal necessities of literary publication—we are left with only one way of reading *Junkie:* ironically.

DO YOU WANT TO SCORE?

SHIRTS THIRTY-ONE CENTS

"Deviant society," so Jennie Skerl argues, "mirrors the dominant society, exposing a predatory, amoral social order and individuals without 'character' or free will whose identities are wholly formed by needs and social functions" (28). This is a persuasive reading that understands *Junkie* as an ironic critique of capitalist relations. As Greil Marcus claims, *Junkie* would indeed be a twentieth-century "Bartleby" (203). Certainly, the preface emphasizes that it is the *anomie* of Lee's economic freedom that determines his descent into addiction. The turning point is reached during the war, when he still "did not have to have money": "It was at this time and under these circumstances that I came in contact with junk, became an addict, and thereby gained the motivation, the real need for money I had never had before" (*J* xiv–xv). Perversely, addiction becomes a positive gain because it teaches the dilettante the "real" necessity and value of money—which slyly accepts that *only* the need for money is real and of value, that this is the *only* meaningful economy, the *only* source of motivation and satisfaction. So far from contesting social norms through deviance, the addict simply sees no legal or moral difference in the life cycle of capital. Junk represents simply another business economy with its "wholesaler" and "customers," its "credit" and "profits" (53), where spiritual needs are translated into material forms that can be satisfied by the consumption of commodities.

Far from romancing a utopian alternative space of desire and community, *Junkie* presents a dead society, a corpse-cold, one-dimensional realm as reduced to meaningless materiality as junkies are to their motiveless somatic needs, a realm that is the impoverished worldview of objective empiricism and capitalist rationality thrown back in its faceless face. In Murphy's astute formulation: "Not only is capitalist society haunted by the junky, its phantom double, but also capitalist society haunts the junky" (*Wising Up* 55). Or to put this another way, Burroughs closes any gap between Lee's private self and his junkie identity: there is no personality behind or outside, since a junkie is made simply of junk, and "they all looked alike somehow. They all looked like junk" (*J* 30). The addict simplifies economy to the point where all needs are reduced to one need and so lit-eralizes capital's principle of equivalence and interchangeability. As Edward Halsey Foster observes, in *Junkie* "the only important contacts between people involve buying and selling" (155). The irony bites therefore when Lee mocks the rhetorical duplicity of the marijuana trade—"a peddler should not come right out and say he is a peddler"—compared to the straight deal-ings of the addict who "hands you the money, takes his junk and cuts" (*J* 17). The junkie has the integrity to call an economic spade a spade.

But there is another side to Foster's coin, because it is exactly the *un*-important contacts between people that are most significant in *Junkie;* that is, the social relations conducted both within and through the narrative. Bearing in mind Ginsberg's account of the novel's genesis and its relation to the expressive and communicative ideals of Beat aesthetics, the most striking formal feature of *Junkie* in the Burroughs oeuvre is its unique and consistent use of both first and second persons: the very "I" and "you" of the intimate epistolary bond. And yet, the unnerving effect of the book, and the cutting edge of its textual politics, derives from its *lack* of either identifiable origin, motive, or address, its *lack* of necessity as a narration. The force of the novel lies, in equal but opposite measure to that of *Naked Lunch,* not in its limited narrative action but in its zero-degree narrating *inter*action. Take the scene early on where Lee goes to an apartment to look up Jack but instead finds Mary.

The scene lasts some four pages. Mary introduces herself, asks Lee in-side, and describes the unusual decorations on the walls and ceiling. She takes Lee to Times Square to find a connection, picks up someone named Peter, and during the next thirty hours in the apartment details the way to treat "Johns," "suckers," and "chicks." After taking Benzedrine, Lee reports that he "began talking very fast" (*J* 15), but what he says is not reported for us to hear. During the entire scene, Lee records only three words of speech, inspired by the "Chinese character in red lacquer" painted on Mary's apartment wall:

> "We don't know what it means," she said.
> "Shirts thirty-one cents," I suggested. (13)

The economy of this comically dead-pan exchange is absurdly literal: meaning is reduced to money, sense converted into cents. But the point is that this is not a case of social interaction reduced by or to the level of a drug transaction. The relation between Lee and Mary does not involve buying and selling, only telling and listening, and this is not a relation of exchange or even of value. Several times Mary asks Lee questions, but there are never any replies, as if the questions were only rhetorical. The bizarre climax of Lee's scene with Mary indicates the full significance of his ghostly absence as a subject within the narrative:

> Mary was describing the techniques she used to get money from the "Johns" who formed her principal source of revenue.
> "Always build a John up. If he has any sort of body at all say, 'Oh, don't ever hurt me.'" [. . .]
> "If you want to really bring a man down, light a cigarette in the middle of intercourse. [. . .] Say, this is sort of a fireside kick," she said, pointing to the radio which was the only light in the room. (15–16)

Mary's monologue is presented as an advice column or tutorial, setting out her tricks of the trade as if holding a business class for aspiring whores. But her audience here consists of Lee and Peter. What are they meant to do— take notes? Mary's instructive anecdotes are related to an audience, and yet they mediate no human relationships, so that her illuminated radio points up the unbridgeable distance between even people in the same room via the strictly one-way character of her speech.

This pattern typifies what passes for social interaction within *Junkie* and applies to storytelling as well as to advice-giving, but its importance lies in what it reveals about the narrative address, the storytelling and infor-mation-giving, of Lee himself. Whether Lee's preferred narrative voice shows that he has listened to and learned from other addicts or whether their delivery reproduces his own, the effect is to create a world in that style. This world wears a face like Mary's, which has a callous "blank, cold smile" and features strange, solipsistic, clearly inhuman "cold fish eyes that looked at you through a viscous medium she carried about her" (*J* 13, 16). In such eyes, to borrow terms from Emmanuel Levinas, courtesy of Jeffrey Nealon, "the call or face of the other counts for nothing" (61), to the point of a shocking, comic banality, beyond ethical response, as when Pat tells Lee that Don has cancer: "'Well,' I said, 'I guess he'll die soon.' He did" (*J* 76). This is the world into which the reader is taken—and *taken in,* as a confidant. Addressed directly and yet anonymously, the reader is invited to share a narrative relationship with Lee modeled on that between Lee and Mary. This relationship is a kind of dream to the familiar waking world of social and human experience. Someone has to be there when Mary speaks, but Lee, as an individual, might as well not be. A qualitatively valuable rela-tionship is simply not desired or, since in *Junkie* desire is always converted into need, *not necessary.* The story Lee relates so impersonally is less a story without meaningful personal relations than one without meaningful need for them, and that includes need for the reader. And so if the only functional relation is economic, then it is not just the social order it represents that conforms to the one-dimensional world of impersonal capital but *Junkie* itself. For all the notes and prefaces and blue-penciling, Ace Books' key act of censorship was the shift in emphasis and meaning that went with the change of title: reading *Junkie: Confessions of an Unredeemed Drug Addict,* they knew, begged fewer questions than buying "Junk."

DO YOU WANT TO SCORE?

As *Junkie*'s first critic, Alan Ansen, observed, "the use of the first person is almost a mockery" (20)—to which we can add, so too is its use of the second person. Here lies the rub of *Junkie*'s irony. Consider one of the "factual lectures" that intersperse the narrative:[5]

> In 1937, weed was placed under the Harrison Narcotics Act. Narcotics authorities claim it is a habit-forming drug, that its use is injurious to mind and body, and that it causes the people who use it to commit crime. Here are the facts: Weed is positively not habit-forming. You can smoke weed for years and you will experience no discomfort if your supply is suddenly cut off. (*J* 18)

The passage balances uneasily on an edge as the "you" modulates silently from a use equivalent to the German *Mann* or French *on* into a direct vocative address. This "you" seems to mean "us": *we* can smoke weed for years, and *we* will not become addicted. Ambiguous instances like this abound in *Junkie,* flickering between impersonal observation and pearls from the advice manual: "You need a good bedside manner with doctors or you will get nowhere" (*J* 21); "If you want to push, the first step is to find a wholesale connection" (*J* 41); and so on. The irony here seems double: targeting not only the medical profession or the legal business economy but also the reader. So long as the second person remains anonymous, it is unproblematic, but once this "you" is taken to imply a communicative circuit, once "anyone" becomes a specific "someone"—say, *you*—then the ground shifts: now, it is no longer the motive for Lee's actions as a junkie and for his narration of them as *Junkie* that is at issue but the reader's legitimate interest in both; what is it that *we* are looking for?

The effect of this slippage is, as *Naked Lunch* forces us to see, to rob us of our safe position as unobserved observers of the junk world: we become suddenly aware of the point from which we look. In other words, the seeming neutrality of Lee as a narrator of facts, as a virtually disembodied witness to events, slyly solicits an equally neutral and invisible reader, and this cunning pact is simultaneously exposed and broken at those points where "you" becomes *you,* at which point it reveals nothing about the narrator but something about the reader. The question of our own desire is answered therefore by the sight that holds our attention: the junkie realizes the repressed truth of our own desire. In what was originally the manuscript's final line, an old-time junkie poses the book's ultimate rhetorical question: "Do you want to score?"[6] (*Junky* 115).

It is one thing to be told "the facts" in order to demystify the state's misrepresentation of certain illegal activities but quite another to be implicated as accomplices in the need to know them. As with Mary's monologue, the flat, guidebook pragmatism here and throughout the novel seems to mime the crude, utilitarian values of the culture, stripped of legal distinctions: as a manual of material self-help in the vein of the decade's most popular nonfiction book, the Reverend Norman Vincent Peale's *Power of Positive Thinking* (1952), what's missing is the reassuring rhetoric of spirituality and morality. This is the significance of Carl Solomon's publisher's note for the original Ace edition, which recognized this incriminating mode of address by denying it. Like the "voyeuristic rather than decorative" covers of the hardboiled pulp trade (O'Brien 3), it promised vicarious pleasure at a safe moral distance. By emphasizing the first person plural ("We follow them [...] We watch [...] we see [...] We see [...] We witness the sordidness of every crevice of their lives"), Ace's note sought to reaffirm through reader voyeurism the otherness of the junkie and of *Junkie.* Allaying anxieties by restoring clear demarcation lines between "us" and "them" and identifying difference with deviance, the note patriotically falls in line as part of the larger cold war narrative of demonization and containment. Or as Ginsberg put it, this was (Carl Solomon pretending to be) the "voice of sanity."

If Burroughs uses the critical possibilities of the second person—Baudelaire's "You! hypocrite lecteur"—then the way he does so begs the question of ironic intention. The more ambiguous, the more potent irony is as a strategy. Yet, as a strategy, it requires intentionality and precision, and this determinate level of purpose is what *Junkie* frustrates most rigorously. Perhaps this is what makes *Junkie* so seductive: since we assume that seduction entails involvement rather than detachment, we are blinded to the way in which our attention is arrested precisely by *not* being addressed directly. That is why the undecidable neutrality of the second person is so important to *Junkie.* All it would take is one instance of pointed self-reference, one clear moment when the plain informational surface vanishes to reveal that everything is artfully staged to catch the reader's desire—but in *Junkie* there is no such moment. And so, to see the novel as a "Trojan-horse narrative" (Self 6)—a phrase that deftly performs an ambush of its own (*horse* means heroin)—is to invest its style with the subversive political force of an ironic double bluff. This may work retrospectively, in terms of effects. But when it presumes intention, such a reading is not only much more problematic but liable to miss the point.

By motivating *Junkie,* critical irony naturalizes it and so loses the very uncertainty that gives the work its distinctive edge and historical meaning. The maneuver is the precise mirror image of that staged in the original publisher's note, where expedience also required specifying the calculation of intentions and effects. Ace claimed for this "criminal confession" the status of a moral health warning "calculated to discourage imitation by thrill-hungry teen-agers" (*Junkie* n. pag.). And of course, the other side to the moral coin consisted of the "unredeemed" author's "unsubstantiated statements" made "in an effort to justify his actions." It is no coincidence that Ace presented the book in exactly the terms that Burroughs himself denied when informing Ginsberg of the philosophical code he called "factualism." When Ginsberg made the charge that *Junkie* was intended as a moral apologia, it was on his "principles as a factualist" that Burroughs stood (*L* 85). He appeared outraged at the very *idea* of motivation and defended himself from the accusation: "As a matter of fact the book is the only accurate account I ever read of the real horror of junk. But I don't mean it as justification or deterrent or anything but an accurate account of what I experienced during the time I was on the junk" (83). There, repeated, is the key phrase: "accurate account." Burroughs asserts an utterly empirical historiography: presenting himself as a positivist, a disinterested historian carrying out the documentary task of recording the facts, producing not an authored novel but what he thought of as authoritative and referred to as a "record."[7] And that is why, of all the genres investigated by David Lenson in his "pharmacography," *On Drugs,* it is the least likely—the "objective" clinical study—that approximates *Junkie*[8] (ix). Over the years, Burroughs would take every opportunity to dismiss *Junkie* as artless, to insist on the simplicity and modesty of his ambition, that he was just "sticking close to the facts and using, as Wordsworth put it, 'the language actually used by men'" ("My Purpose" 265).

But of course, it would be a mistake to read *Junkie* as only a dispassionate account, nothing more than a report filed on the unvarnished and mundane real. The text is shot through with unaccountable moments, hauntings of memory and hallucination, glimpses of lost pasts and imagined futures, sightings of the spectral and uncanny. There are visions of horror that come when Lee shuts his eyes and sees giant centipedes crawl through ruined cities or Oriental faces that melt into hieroglyphs (*J* 28, 133) and instants of supernatural wonder, such as the "dream feeling when you find money" or when "your wishes have a dream power" (*J* 102, 114). Such moments of subjectivity and spirituality are ghosts in the machine of Lee's disciplined, dismal reportage: that they shouldn't be there but are suggests their potency. In fact, they reveal the unspoken underside to Burroughs' claim for a Wordsworthian aesthetic, since they function precisely as "spots of time," those magical moments that punctuate the prosaic flatness of *The Prelude*. Such instances draw attention in effect to the repression of some vital and unaccountable quality, some fact that points beyond "the facts": they would mark the site of Lacan's unrepresentable Real, as opposed to what we know as "reality," in a text that is otherwise not Lacanian. The implication of these exceptional moments will become clear from the point of view of *Queer*, since this is virtually "textbook" Lacan. But the point remains that they *are* exceptions, and the rule of factualism in *Junkie* has clear implications for any reading that depends on irony. The writer's subjective motives and his writing's subjective effects on the reader are just what it would deny.

Where does this leave the claims made by Ginsberg in his introduction to *Junky* and recycled by so many critics? They turn out to be misleading not just in broad terms of aesthetic context and value but in precise matters of fact. For the writing of *Junkie* at least, his account of its intimate epistolary genesis is mistaken; the evidence simply contradicts it. By the time Burroughs first told Ginsberg of the work in May 1950—some seven weeks after informing Kerouac—it was to say that the book was "about finished now" (*L* 70). This was premature, but nevertheless, by reconstructing the manuscript history of *Junkie*, a clear picture emerges of Ginsberg's precise but limited role in it. Burroughs worked on the manuscript he called "Junk" over a period of two-and-a-half years and only added the final forty pages, the last quarter of the published novel, as late as July 1952. There were also two main phases of revision, first in spring 1951 and then spring 1952, when he made a half-dozen smaller additions and two significant cuts.[9] All of this he discussed with Ginsberg, especially in summer 1952. Nevertheless, from the chronology of the manuscript, it is clear that almost three-quarters of the text we now have was effectively complete by the end of 1950, and up to this point, Ginsberg's role had been strictly secondary. On 1 January 1951, Burroughs wrote Ginsberg: "I have sent the finished MS. of my book along to Lucien [Carr] and told him to peddle it for the best price he can get" (*L* 75). Although Ginsberg would eventually clinch the publication deal with Ace Books in April 1952, it is still the case that during the majority of its writing Burroughs directed his material more to Kerouac, as a fellow-novelist, and to Carr, as a potential agent, than to Ginsberg, as a friend who gave or needed emotional support.

If the material facts fail to support Ginsberg's claim for the epistolary construction of *Junkie,* we need to recognize that this failure is not the reason why some critics have ignored his claim and preferred to recycle a completely different genetic account. According to this, Burroughs wrote the narrative like a diary at the prompting of his old friend Kells Elvins. This version of events better matches the facts of the manuscript history (at least, up to December 1950) and the evidence of the text, but the real point here is the irreconcilable contradiction between accounts itself. Trusting the truth of *one or the other* of these versions, critics have signally failed to use either as a way to interpret *Junkie.* But recognizing this contradiction clarifies the need to establish an accurate genetic history, which in turn makes it possible to see the significance of a false as well as a true genetic account for an interpretation of the novel. This is why it is important to show the factual inaccuracy of Ginsberg's claim as a way to remove *Junkie* from the Beat context and from a deep correspondence between the letter and literature. For Burroughs' manuscript was not privately addressed—in either sense of the word—to a specific reader as it was written, and the narrating voice of *Junkie,* like its narrative world, shows no signs of an interpersonal epistolary aesthetic. When Lee checks into Lexington, and the doctor tells him that "the procedure here is more or less impersonal" (*J* 61), it is to Lee's unspoken but no less evident satisfaction.

EVEN GIDE

The stylistic choice of *Junkie* defined the narrative's identity as "straight," in nearly every sense of the word: candid, moving in one direction, uncomplicated, trustworthy, readable. In style and motivation, this was to be, as Burroughs insisted to Ginsberg in May 1951, a "straight narrative" (*L* 83). But the "straightness" of *Junkie* is, aesthetically and historically, thoroughly perverse, a matter of refusals, absences, negations. The most fundamental of these refusals concerns Burroughs' presentation of the literary identity of his narrative.

The narrative itself has no literary reference at all, a refusal that does more than make a cultural philistine of Lee: it blocks off all direct connection between Lee's experience and any *tradition* of aesthetic or spiritual dimensions. But there is one scene in *Junkie* that might have grounded those odd, unaccountable, and uncanny moments scattered through the text that perforate its positivist surface like mysterious black holes. This is the scene of Lee's haunting nostalgia for the innocence of a lost maternal union, a return of the repressed that prompts his decision to quit junk:

> I remembered a long time ago when I lay in bed beside my mother, watching lights from the street move across the ceiling and down the walls. I felt the sharp nostalgia of train whistles, piano music down a city street, burning leaves.
>
> A mild degree of junk sickness always brought me the magic of childhood. "It never fails," I thought. "Just like a shot. I wonder if all junkies score for this wonderful stuff." (*J* 126)

Lee's "wonderful stuff" *is* the eternal quality of Romantic wonder, an aesthetic and psychological quality, like magic and childhood, to which the quantitative, habitual world of *Junkie* is dead. The scene returns to the preface's account of the child's encounters with a parallel spirit world, his hypnagogic hallucinations that bring "no fear, only a feeling of stillness and wonder" (*J* xi). And since the magic *always* comes, *never* fails, the single moment given here stands in for a recurrent experience. Lee then gives himself "an injection of death," and "the dream was gone."

Like the scene as a whole, there is something disconcerting in this last phrase, a troubling resonance that is hard to place. Maybe it is because in the passage itself Lee doesn't refer to a dream, so all that is present is the trace of its passing, the "dream was gone." But what has disappeared from the narrative *was* once there, and in the manuscript reading room of Columbia University, one day in 1984 long before its significance became clear to me, I came across this missing dream. The underlined words cut from Burroughs' yellowed manuscript couldn't help but catch the eye: after the phrase "magic of childhood," "The glory and the freshness of a dream."[10] Now, we can see how precise and large is the irony to Burroughs' invocation of Wordsworth. The particular phrase cut from his manuscript, taken from *Ode: Intimations of Immortality from Recollections of Early Childhood*, draws its energy from the very barrenness of *Junkie*. And this, of course, is a spiritual vacancy given meaning by Wordsworth's *Ode*.[11] Invoking nostalgia for the aesthetic and political project of Romanticism, as well as nostalgia for a pre-oedipal mother world, Wordsworth's dream stands as a negation of the negation embodied by the world of junk, which is precisely why Burroughs had to cut the literary association.

In contrast to the narrative, the preface does set out a literary context for *Junkie* but not of the kind we might expect. In an account of suggestive juxtapositions, it describes the formative reading habits of Lee's adolescence:

I read more than was usual for an American boy of that time and place: Oscar Wilde, Anatole France, Baudelaire, even Gide. I formed a romantic attachment for another boy and we spent our Saturdays exploring old quarries, riding around on bicycles and fishing in ponds and rivers.

At this time, I was greatly impressed by an autobiography of a burglar, called *You Can't Win*. [. . .] It sounded good to me compared with the dullness of a Midwest suburb where all contact with life was shut out. I saw my friend as an ally, a partner in crime. (*J* xii)

That "even Gide" is very precise: it implies a potential limit for the future writer's aesthetics by invoking the arch, European, self-reflexive modernist, the seductive sign of "monstrous perversity" in *The Town and the City*. But Burroughs moves swiftly on to the autobiography of an American criminal, so that he has no sooner identified with a suspect sophistication than asked us to ignore it, like inadmissible evidence to be struck from the record. If *Junkie* is "straight," then its preface says so perversely by denying that it is "queer."

There is another maneuver here too, one that concerns the crime of writing itself. Consider the literary references that Burroughs *fails* to cite in his preface. The roll call of an entire tradition from Coleridge to De Quincey, from Poe to Cocteau, all the writers of addiction—Burroughs names none of them. To be sure, their absence marks another refusal of Romantic tradition. *Junkie* is certainly no "meditation on the mechanism of the imagination" as is De Quincey's *Confessions of an English Opium Eater* (Hayter 7). Its "nightmare flatness" (*J* 139) is likewise a world away from *Opium*'s elegantly aphoristic notes, illustrated by the stylized fantasies of Cocteau's line drawings: no surprise that, unlike Burroughs, Lee never refers to opium as "Cocteau's kick" (*L* 77, 80). Something else is going on here, or rather *not* going on, because the absence runs deeper than a rejection of high literariness. This is clear from Burroughs' equal failure to mention that *You Can't Win* documents in detail the addict's struggle with "Opium, the Judas of drugs, that kisses and betrays" (Black 371), so that this was his first contact via books with the drug world. In later contexts, Burroughs would repeatedly signal his adolescent "romantic/literary" interest in drugs (qtd. in Ploog 136); but not here, in the preface to *Junkie*. And the other side to Lee's interest is equally missing. There is no record of his prehistory as an author, of how *Junkie* grew out of his earlier literary efforts or how he was inspired or influenced by his reading, any more than there is an account of how he came to write the novel. What we get instead are the curious juxtapositions that make Lee's reading habits appear to determine both his sexual and criminal behavior. For just as a homosexual romantic attachment is formed immediately after reading Gide, so Lee sees his friend as a partner in crime straight after reading *You Can't Win*. Books may have seduced the lonely youth by turning Lee into a homosexual thief, but this correspondence between reading and behavior only draws attention to the influence that is avoided, namely the actual subject and activity of Burroughs' own writing.[12]

The point, clearly, is that *any* reference in the preface to the literature of addiction would have invited a loop of questions: What effect did this reading have on Lee's addiction? What is the motive of his own narrative? And so finally, what is the effect of Burroughs' writing? In short, had he been drawn to addiction by reading about it, then *Junkie* must either repeat or break the cycle of contagion, either infect or protect, fascinate or repel the reader.

The issue is less whether *Junkie* should practice or resist power but that it *could* do so, that writing might smile and seduce, and that this power is negated. This is why the precise historical context and the circumstances of writing and publication are so important. Burroughs' preface was, after all, solicited by his pulp publishers as a response in advance to specific anxieties about the corrupting power of the word. In 1952, the paperback industry came under investigation by the House Select Committee on Current Pornographic Materials. Responding to fears that softcover books were propagating perversion, the so-called Gathings Committee attacked those that "dwell on narcotics and in such a way as to present inducements for susceptible readers to become addicts out of sheer curiosity" (qtd. in O'Brien 133). Of one book, *Marijuana Girl*, the committee observed: "A more appropriate title would be: 'A Manual of Instructions for Potential Narcotic Addicts.'" Little wonder that Ace Books took no chances with *Junkie* and not only handcuffed Burroughs' novel to a reprint of *Narcotic Agent* but spelled the point out by representing a handcuffed addict on the cover. Ace knew that in the symbolic economy of cold war America, every little detail counted. Their packaging of *Junkie*—from the choice of title and subtitle, from the cover design to the inserted editorial disclaimers, from the publisher's note to the preface they demanded—all this becomes by default, in denial, an exact measure of its textual politics. In a way, the Ace original is the *least* contingent edition of the novel, since it is the *most* historically precise "answer" to it.

This context makes all the more striking Burroughs' failure to identify addiction as a *communicable* disease and to develop the analogy with writing. His refusal to apply the toxicity of junk to *Junkie* follows, however, the book's own logic, where addiction cancels communication and forecloses desire. "Junk short-circuits sex," Lee observes. "The drive to non-sexual sociability comes from the same place sex comes from, so when I have an H or M shooting habit I am non-sociable" (*J* 124). If junk suspends desire and the word, then its toxicity is actually a kind of withdrawal; a withdrawal from the will to communicate and from political or libidinal economy. It is as if to avoid the social and sexual perils of Charybdis, Burroughs had indeed first shacked up with Scylla.

But there is a strictly historical dimension to all this that must be reckoned with too. In March 1950, Burroughs started *Junkie* as "virtually a Mexican citizen." "What a relief to be rid of the U.S. for good and all, and to be in this fine free country!" (*L* 65). That is, he put behind him an America that was no land of the free but a nation rapidly organizing itself into a disciplinary social order of behavioral repressions and material rewards, of McCarthyite sticks and Madison Avenue carrots, of patriotic moral mission and Un-American Activities. At such a time of partisan side-taking, it isn't Lee's late, overt politicizing of both addiction and his expatriation—the latter described as a response to the "police-state legislation" used to deal with the former (*J* 142)—that constituted an act of subversive disloyalty. On the contrary, it was the stylistic neutrality of *Junkie*'s decriminalized narrative, its absolute refusal to recognize or romanticize its own deviance or need to confess, its indifference to a moral discourse of motives and effects, of imitation and deterrence; in short, its very objective, authoritative straightness. "Here are the facts." This straight-faced narrative turns queer, however, and breaks into what looks like a malicious-looking smile in that part of *Junkie* that was written last but destined to be read first—its preface.

ACTUALLY

"I was born in 1914 in a solid, three-story, brick house in a large Midwest city. My parents were comfortable" (*J* xi). The first line seems as solid and upright as the family home, but the prose deceives. Lee "could put down one of those nostalgic routines about the old German doctor who lived next door," but he doesn't, because "comfortable" describes financial security on the outside, hiding psychological trauma within: "Actually my earliest memories are colored by a fear of nightmares." The sudden and surprising shift is given insistent emphasis: four times in as many lines he repeats the word "afraid" to depict the "supernatural horror [that] seemed always on the point of taking shape." Most disturbingly, the child's fear— of the dark, the invisible, the unknown—comes from the wrong side of the high wooden fence around the solid brick house, comes from within not without. Yet, there is no diagnosis, only a palliative prescribed by the boy's maid to bring "sweet dreams." "I said: 'I will smoke opium when I grow up.'" The causality is brazenly reductive, but what shocks is the overturning of expectations: rather than representing a tragic fall from childhood, from a Midwestern idyll worthy of nostalgia, the adult's addiction and the narrative to follow are grounded in that time of supposed innocence and safety. Life as a drug addict is foreseen as an escape from, not into, an American nightmare, since the addict world serves in effect to repress and replace the child's bad dreams and the infantile trauma that inspired them.[13]

A sentimental domestic narrative has been offered and then blue-penciled as mere rhetorical convention. An upright, middle-class, middle-American household has been found to harbor specters too terrible to name. What appears familiar and homely in the first account, but turns out to be fictional, gives way to the unhomely, the *unheimlich,* or uncanny, and this appears to be factual. In short, the ideological rock upon which cold war American internal security stood is unpatriotically libeled by turning the wholesome material and spiritual comforts of the family into a Gothic house of horrors. However autobiographically accurate, the details here are tactically deployed: alert to historical and literary contexts, these opening ironies confront a series of implicit desires and dependencies, held both by loyal American citizens and by readers accustomed to the confessional genre, and then gives them a calculated twist.

Something significant is going on here at the level of form as well as content. For inevitably, the effect of giving *two* versions of the past, presenting one as glib falsification, the other as factual, is to demonstrate Lee's potential for abusing his authority and therefore for abusing us. Once we know that he could satisfy readerly expectations by passing off as autobiographical truth what is a comforting domestic myth, the result must be skeptical self-awareness of Lee's credibility per se.

The crucial point, however, is that these subtle but perverse contradictions and self-subversions do *not* indicate the ironic strategy of *Junkie.* On the contrary, they indicate a major strategic *shift* from the narrative as a whole. When Lee states, "Here are the facts," the accuracy of the information and his own trustworthiness as a narrator is not put in question. Lee does not trade knowledge for attention, satisfying his own needs by stimulating the desires of others. He claims the authority of disinterested knowledge, of a pedagogy that does not need to advocate. The shift in strategy is even clearer when the published preface to *Junkie* is contrasted with Burroughs' original introduction, which dates from late 1950.[14]

Two differences are basic. First, the introduction is marked by a complete absence of autobiographical material, while Burroughs clearly separates himself as the author from the following narrative as a "fiction" that is "based on facts" of his experience. Second, he focuses on exposing anti-narcotic "propaganda" and "officially sponsored myth" that has prevented any "accurate" writing on the subject. Itemizing this myth, point by numbered point, he sets it against "facts" stamped with the authority of actual knowledge; when Burroughs begins his counterstatements with "Actually"—which he does three times—he insists unequivocally on empirical truths. The contrast with the published preface, written in the summer of 1952, is telling. When using "Actually" here, he does so ambiguously, correcting a biographical "myth" that he has himself sponsored. The preface not only shifts attention to the writer's life but does so in a way that questions, rather than asserts, his own authority, integrity, and purpose. The effect of the preface is not to authorize the straight-dealing narrative that follows, therefore, but to expose claims to truth as contingent and rhetorical, by revealing the author's own manipulations and the manipulations of authorship. Written in retrospect yet serving as a guide, the preface anticipates *Naked Lunch* by visibly exposing the supposedly disinterested factualism of an "accurate account."[15]

THERE IS NO SECRET

What marks the preface to *Junkie* is more than an authorial self-consciousness and an awareness of audience that are strikingly absent from the narrative. The key point is how this consciousness coincides with the simultaneous exercise and demystification of narrative power. The distinction between preface and narrative is therefore of absolute importance. When Lee states that he could put down a *nostalgic routine,* something basic has changed. The book's glossary spells out what the key phrase implies: "To give someone a story, to persuade, or con someone" (*J* 157). It is with this potential to tell stories equated with manipulative confidence tricks that the Lee of *Junkie* metamorphoses from a disinterested narrator of facts into an author of fictions, one firmly inside a verbal economy of need and exploitation, seduction and coercion.

What is materially significant about the routine Lee could put down is exactly that; he *could* put one down here in the preface, written in summer 1952, whereas in the narrative, largely completed by December 1950, he could not. This is the measure of a basic shift in power relations: a pusher of junk within the narrative, Lee is never a pusher *of* the junk narrative. When Lee refers to the role of peddler as a "public service" with a rotating "term of office" (*J* 29), the irony only goes so far. What cuts it short is the signal absence in *Junkie* of any absolute relation between peddling and power; if it is meant to be the basis to an ironic critique, Lee's own behavior as a peddler hardly indicts official, social, or economic institutions as monstrous or predatory. On the contrary, the force of *Junkie* depends on normalizing narcotics—"If you have a commodity you naturally want customers" (*J* 42)—rather than on offering addiction as a model to expose capital's perverse system of artificial desire. Such a direct analogy is precisely what the representation excludes, and must exclude, if the address to the reader is to function neutrally. Therefore, when critics speak of "the irresistible opportunities for manipulation and control created by the gulf between the addict's abject dependence and the supplier's predatory power" (Beard 842), we must recognize that this *never* describes Lee's situation in *Junkie,* either as a character within it or, by analogy, as the narrator of it. Numerous critics have equated junk with capitalism as "the ultimate control system" on which "all others are modelled" (Savran, *Taking It* 100), and they always repeat Burroughs' own definition of junk as "the ideal product" and "ultimate merchandise" (*NL* xi); what they always overlook is its failure to fit the novel Burroughs himself called "Junk." The one exception—Bill Gains, the malicious pusher—is the exception that proves the rule. And so the published text remains true to its original introduction, which dismisses as "myths" the claims that "Addicts never get enough" and "Addicts want to get others on the stuff." Since these are the very principles of the "algebra of need" defined in the introduction to *Naked Lunch,* it becomes even clearer that *Junkie* does not inaugurate the junk paradigm but completely contradicts it.

There is just one point in the narrative where Lee does exercise power as a relation of control, but that is precisely when he is forced to relate socially rather than economically, when communication and desire displace consumption and junk. Indeed, this is a key moment because it exemplifies the paradox of power in Burroughs: the drive to control others coincides with losing the power of self-control. Lee quits junk and records its agonizing results:

> My emotions spilled out everywhere. I was uncontrollably sociable and would talk to anybody I could pin down. I forced distastefully intimate confidences on perfect strangers. Several times I made the crudest sexual propositions to people who had given no hint of reciprocity. (*J* 127–28)

What Lee as a protagonist describes doing in speech is, however, exactly what Lee as a tight-lipped narrator does *not* do in writing. We do not get to hear his compulsive personal confidences and homosexual propositions. *That* we do not get to hear them confirms the contradiction they pose. This striking contradiction not only resembles that between narrative and preface, it comes out of the same essential transformation.

At the end of the preface, we are told that there "is no key, no secret someone else has that he can give you" (*J* xvi); but in describing the precise difference between need and desire, this advice appears totally out of place in *Junkie,* where Lee never looks to another for a secret. To bridge the gap between the Lee who narrates *Junkie* and the Lee who prefaces that narration, and between the Lee who states the facts and the Lee who is driven by desire, is to recognize the gulf between the writing of 1950–51 and of 1952. The only Burroughs critic to have considered the manuscript history, Barry Miles, has speculated about the effect on Burroughs' work of his wife's death in September 1951 and lamented the loss of the manuscript written before it (*William Burroughs* 48). In fact, the original draft *has* survived, and what it reveals is a very precise transformation tied to another act of writing. The investigation into chronology now shifts from a contradiction within Burroughs' first novel to one between that and his second. For if the Lee who loses control and verbally assaults perfect strangers seems to belong to another narrative altogether, that is because he does: he belongs to *Queer.*

This is the material secret revealed by finally piecing together a definitive history of the "Junk" manuscript. The key decisions took place during summer 1952, when Ace Books demanded a further forty pages of new material to complete Burroughs' lightly revised one-hundred-fifty-page manuscript of December 1950. For the middle eighteen pages of this new material (125–42 in *Junky*), Burroughs turned to the opening sections of his *Queer* manuscript, transposing from third person narrative into first person, and making—quite literally, with the use of scissors and paste—numerous small cuts.[16] It was originally the Lee of *Queer* who "forced distastefully intimate confidences on perfect strangers" (128) and who observed the "power to give or withhold" (140), not the Lee of "Junk." In July 1952, Burroughs cut and adapted the material from *Queer* that he knew would best fit in with and complete the narrative of *Junkie;* even so, it was absolutely inevitable that he would introduce such signs of a fundamental contradiction, because Burroughs' second novel bears the stamp of an entirely different textual politics.

3

Queer: Welcome to Your Destiny

It is truth which is hidden, not the letter.

—Jacques Lacan, *The Purloined Letter*

THE APPALLING CONCLUSION

OUT OF PLACE

When Burroughs began *Queer* in March 1952, he told Ginsberg that it "could be part II of *Junk*" but that it was, "however, complete in itself" (*L* 105). Seven months later, he stopped work on the novel, reckoning that it "was out of place according to any frequent viewpoint": in fact, he couldn't see himself "writing any sequel to *Queer* or writing anything more at all at this point" (138). In other words, while the problem for Burroughs when he started to write *Queer* was the continuity from one novel to the next, it would soon turn into a full-scale crisis of writing itself. This development gives added urgency to the most material of problems that has remained unresolved for fifty years: simply how to understand and grasp the significance of the fundamental difference between Burroughs' first two novels, a difference only magnified by the fact that he began one as an immediate sequel to the other. This mystery can't be solved by manuscript research alone but neither can there be any solution without it. A number of critics have claimed that *Queer* is a "transitional" work,[1] but it seems to me that they have answered too quickly the wrong question; namely, how does *Queer* fit into Burroughs' oeuvre? The real challenge is to ask: how does it *change* the oeuvre?

INDECISIVE FIENDS

Of course, it isn't easy to argue the centrality of *Queer* and not just because of the novella's embarrassing slightness next to *Junkie*. The first problem is that the published text can barely conceal its exceptional contingency, which must qualify any attempt to rehistoricize either the text or its production. It is exceptional because the compromises and exigencies are historically *doubled*. The letters from the period of *Queer*'s writing reveal a grimly pragmatic Burroughs. He is under no illusions about his impotence as a "completely unknown" author dealing with commercial publishers, always having to accommodate his desires to "whatever they prefer" (*L* 113). In April 1952, he knew that the month-old manuscript was already at the mercy of Ace Books, subject to their "not only highly irritating but contradictory demands" for a novel "neither joined nor separate to *Junk*." "I feel," he joked, "as if I was being sawed in half by indecisive fiends who periodically attempted to shove me back together" (113, 119). More is at stake here than simple matters of editing and economics, as the psychological dimension to Burroughs' comedy of cuts and recombinations suggests, but the bottom line is to recognize to what extent the integrity of *Queer* was compromised from the very start of writing.

Thirty years later, where once Burroughs had relied on Ginsberg as his amateur literary agent to negotiate with a pulp publisher, now New York's top agent, Andrew Wylie, was including *Queer* as part of a six-figure, multi-book contract with Viking-Penguin. But in 1984, brute commercial factors again played a major part in creating *Queer*. For "this long-rumored and much-anticipated publication," as James Grauerholz called it (*WV* 45), the recently rediscovered manuscript was disturbingly short and visibly incomplete.[2] This was the context in which Grauerholz, in his own words, "cobbled together a broader Introduction" than Burroughs' initial "handful of notes," and (in an inspired move) gave "the book a better ending" by adding on the epilogue, which was in fact an unused part of the quite separate "Yage" manuscript. These new frames, together with unannounced insertions in the narrative taken from Burroughs' contemporary letters and a series of editorial corrections and expansions, add up to a full *quarter* of the actual publication. Finally and most significantly, just as Burroughs was forced to oblige Ace Books when they solicited a preface for *Junkie* in 1952, so thirty years later, it turns out that writing the introduction to *Queer* was one of the preconditions of a publication he didn't even fully endorse: "It wasn't really my decision," he insisted in an interview (Weinreich 615). If the Viking contract of 1984 was a measure of Burroughs' new commercial clout and status as a writer, when it came to *Queer* it was as if nothing had changed.

The contingencies of *Queer* are not only historically doubled but *related*. That is to say, the editorial interventions of 1985 were a direct consequence of the history of the manuscript's editing in 1952. It is not just that Burroughs' original draft was poorly revised as well as incomplete. The editors also had to respond to Burroughs' own earlier gutting of almost a quarter of the manuscript as he looted the opening chapters of his second novel to help make his first up to the length demanded by his publishers. Three decades later, almost exactly the same process was required to make *Queer* up to a length more suitable for publication. Clearly, this history has crucial consequences for understanding and interpreting the relation between *Junkie* and *Queer,* since the continuity of such major manuscript surgery across decades is tied to the essential discontinuity between the two novels we now have and of course to the very content of both.

In July 1952, Burroughs cut from *Queer* all the material that *could* be cut and transposed with only minor changes. On 6 July, he wrote Ginsberg that he was "starting work immediately on the additional 40 pages of JUNK" and, clearly indicating his intentions, asked whether Ace objected "to QUEER in toto": "I can of course omit references to queerness and concentrate on the subject of junk. But I would normally use *some* of the material covered in the first part of QUEER."[3] Burroughs went on to do exactly what he suggested. What remained of the *Queer* manuscript was therefore all material that could never, even with extensive revision, have been added on to the end of "Junk," because this was something other than its sequel, "part II." Paradoxically, then, Burroughs' solution to the problem of his novels' discontinuity had the effect of creating—or perhaps, revealing—a more dramatic discontinuity still.

BIENVENIDO A TU DESTINO

Such a fraught textual history, none of it acknowledged at the time of *Queer*'s publication or considered since, makes the task of historical recovery troublesome. Then again, the main reason for *Queer*'s peculiar critical status is not the absence of a genetic account but the massive attention given to one that is so highly problematic. Indeed, if we needed to reappraise *Junkie* because it has been seen largely in the light cast by overbearing contexts and additional texts, then this is true for *Queer* on a grand scale. This is because Burroughs' second novel was completely neglected by criticism for over a decade and has since been read in very limited ways, due almost entirely to Burroughs' endlessly quoted introduction of 1985, whose momentous autobiographical confession completely upstaged the text of 1952. Before he reaches the shooting of his wife, Burroughs himself raises the two key genetic questions—why he came to write *Queer,* and why it differs so much from *Junkie*—so that the critical reception of *Queer* is intimately bound up with and determined by claims about its production. And so the approach to *Queer* must broadly follow the same path as that to *Junkie;* first considering its reception, then examining its key formal and thematic features in historical and cultural context, and finally establishing its full and proper genetic history. The main difference is one of *scale: Queer* demands far more attention than *Junkie* both because its neglect has been worse while its importance is greater and because the story of its genesis is far more complicated and has consequences that are much more far-reaching.

While *Queer* had no critical presence until Timothy Murphy's reading of it in 1997, it did quickly gain a very high profile within popular and critical biography. Cued by the introduction, its narrative was almost immediately appropriated to reconstruct the events of Burroughs' life during 1951, passing over *Queer* as a text written in 1952. Barry Miles, for example, has a chapter entitled "Queer" and quotes from the introduction at length, but he never once refers to the narrative itself as a text. Such unquestioned biographical assimilation is true also of the detailed study made by Jorge García-Robles in *La Bala Perdida: Williams S. Burroughs en Mexico (1949–1952),* a full-length treatment devoted to a single period and place. Like most others, this account is driven by a relentless predestination, summed up by the section title *Bienvenido a tu destino,* so that the narrative is motivated and its perceptions framed by the inexorable "missing" conclusion, the one given—physically in advance of the text but thirty years belatedly—by Burroughs himself. For *Queer,* the effect of García-Robles's insistence on "Joan's death, the great absence in the novel," is clearly stated: "The drama of *Queer* was less in the text itself than in the author who wrote it" (91, 86; my translations). Joan's death, he argues, brought Burroughs in contact with the "Ugly Spirit" and turned him into an *escritor fatal,* a writer who must write to live: at the instant of firing, "the addiction for writing penetrated his body" (78). Likewise, the French biographer, Christian Vila: "From that moment" Burroughs "consecrated his art to a struggle against all forms of possession and control" (46; my translation). Or again, for John Tytell this was "the wound that finally precipitated his art": "Suddenly [. . .] he was able to write" (*Paradise Outlaws* 104, 12).

Recycling *Queer*'s introduction, such accounts demonstrate something more than uncritical acceptance. For one thing, Burroughs' dramatic claims suddenly sound like biographical melodrama of the most sensationalist kind, their causality reductive to the point of *Weekly World News* headline absurdity: *Evil Spirit Shot Wife and Launched Literary Career Says Famous Writer*. Repeated like this, "the appalling conclusion" Burroughs reached now appears appalling *as a conclusion*, in its would-be sufficiency as an explanation. Here, the introduction's effect is most dramatic: for the fatal shooting has simultaneously framed both ends of *Queer*, providing not only its traumatic point of creative origin but also its tragic narrative destination, so that the instant of the fatal shot elides the text out of existence.

OVERLOOKING THE OBVIOUS

Whether the introduction's accounts have been repeated wholesale and naively, accepted selectively, or analyzed critically, they have never been interrogated *as* accounts, which is to say, *materially* and *strategically*. No one seems to have noticed that, before mentioning the psychological trauma of the shooting, Burroughs offers another equally determinist, entirely separate, and finally contradictory explanation for *Queer*. He explains the radical difference between his first two novels—or rather explains it away: "The difference of course is simple"—according to the drastic physiological effects of withdrawal, insisting: "Unless the reader keeps this in mind, the metamorphosis of Lee's character will appear as inexplicable or psychotic" (Q xii–xiii). This is the argument from physiology repeated at length by Timothy Murphy, who pointedly avoids the traumatic scenario of the shooting. Where Murphy shuns psyche to embrace soma, David Savran has taken precisely the opposite tack, ignoring junk to focus on Joan. Ironically, it is because their approaches are entirely different that each critic overlooks the multiple contradictions within and across accounts that is the clue to their *strategic* effect.

Murphy's tacit refusal to be seduced by the endlessly recycled story of Joan's death seems only to incline him to embrace and recycle the junk story rather than to resist or question it. He therefore "keeps in mind" the context of a withdrawing addict that Burroughs himself insists upon but fails to ask *why* this context might be forgotten by a reader of the novel. The simple answer is that *Queer* does not say until the seventh of nine chapters that "Lee was a little junk sick"[4] (Q 79). The more subtle answer is that Murphy ignores the thoroughgoing blurring of fictional and autobiographical borders that pervades the introduction. At stake here is the very basis to his case for the "important formal difference" between *Junkie* and *Queer,* specifically the development of the routine form (*Wising Up* 58). The logic of this case collapses when the claimed transformation— "from confessing addict to communicating writer" (63)—is understood in terms of *Lee*'s addiction. For if we understand the routines of *Queer* as a by-product of Lee's withdrawing from junk, we can't *also* understand them as a response to Burroughs' shooting Joan: logically, as well as chronologically, these events are simply incompatible. By repeating Burroughs' own ontological contradictions—as when speaking of "Lee" as "*he* develops as a writer" (*Q* xv)—Murphy repeats his foreclosing of historical accuracy or reference and the introduction's refusal to distinguish character from author, 1951 from 1952, text from context, product from production.[5]

On the face of it, Savran's approach to *Queer* via its introduction could not appear more different, since his point of departure is a detailed inter-rogation and interpretation of "Burroughs' mythologization" of the shoot-ing (*Taking It* 42). However, the point is *not* his skepticism about Joan's death as "the primal scene of writing" but rather his very insistence that he must "revisit the scene of the crime" (43). The telltale line is when Savran observes of Joan that "as Burroughs himself later suggests, her presence/ absence is decisive to his autobiographical narratives of those years" (44). *As Burroughs himself later suggests.* In short, Savran takes Burroughs on his own terms and accepts what he gives retrospectively as the untold, secret story, the true object of analysis. However astute or trenchant Savran's re-interpretation, it remains a reading *invited* by Burroughs. As countless de-tective novels or movies demonstrate, crime scenes exercise an inherent fascination: they become sites of a compulsive revisiting because, structur-ally speaking, that is their purpose. The point in the case of Burroughs' "crime scene" is not any particular response, any final solution, but the formal or strategic function of drawing such attention in the first place— which is to say, *distracting* attention away from something else that is there/ not there. For to the extent that there was any public expectation of dis-covering a secret, it could only have lain in publication of the "long-ru-mored and much-anticipated" text itself. But according to the introduc-tion, this is precisely where the secret turns out *not* to be, since Burroughs' revelation accounts for *Queer*'s long absence in terms of something entirely absent from the text, something that was not looked for and could not even have been guessed otherwise. Primed by either of Burroughs' two accounts, let alone by both at once, reading *Queer* must be a baffling experience, while the only relation between the spectacular interest created by the introduc-tion and the interest of *Queer* itself seems to be that the one has been at the expense of the other.

The true significance to Burroughs' strategy of concealment rests how-ever on the paradox that the belated critical interest in *Queer* does not in itself change anything. This is for two reasons. First, because of the need to take into account the complex play of secrecy and revelation itself; for without recognizing that the convoluted story of *Queer*'s reception is itself meaning-ful, criticism remains unable to grasp the significance of its own response.[6] Second, because we need to see that the content of the distraction that leads our attention astray in the introduction is far from arbitrary or dishonest: rather, it gives us all the key terms but in displaced form. To begin with, Burroughs introduces and dwells on the mystery of his writing's genesis: the motivation for *Junkie* "was comparatively simple," but it was "not clear" and "more complex" for *Queer;* finally, he faces the hidden truth that Joan's death "motivated and formulated" his writing (Q xiv, xxii). In this way, the introduction stages a drama of detection whose unexpected solution so far exceeds the initial genetic mystery as to conceal it by hypervisibility. Bur-roughs' story of *Queer*'s genesis becomes hidden in plain view and with it all its self-contradictions. In short, the dialectic of "absence/presence" ap-plies to the fact and strategy of the introduction *itself.*

If Savran identifies himself as a literary detective, returning to the scene of the crime with a critical magnifying glass, then he might have consulted Inspector Dupin of Poe's "The Purloined Letter" as an expert in how con-cealment can work through "hyperobtrusive" display (221). The secret is that there is no secret, or as Ross Chambers observes: "The 'secret' is in the form of the words, writ large there, not somewhere behind that screen" (64). Or better still, recall the Hercule Poirot of Agatha Christie's *The ABC Murders.* When Poirot receives the first in a series of incriminating letters, it causes him an intuitive but unaccountable anxiety; he worries that his very skill as a detective may lead him into an unforgivable error. To the question "What do you call the unforgivable error?" Poirot replies: "Over-looking the obvious." Explaining his ingenious solution at the novel's end, Christie's detective finally returns to his original intuition: "What I had to discover was: the motive of the crime, the motive of the letter" (12, 176). The point, he now realizes, turns on the *intended effect* of the text rather than on some fact beyond it. The duplicitous strategy of Burroughs' in-troduction now becomes clearer. It speaks the genetic truth about *Queer* but hides this truth by displacing it onto a sensational extratextual "fact." As William Beard says of the relation between *Queer* and Joan's death, without the introduction no one "could arrive at such an analysis of it" (826). Equally, I would say that *with* the introduction, no one is likely to consider, let alone arrive at, some other analysis of its genesis.

At this point, conveniently primed by references to "The Purloined Letter" and *The ABC Murders,* it is tempting to announce: *Bienvenido a tu destino!* To agree—this time—with the claims made by Ginsberg in his introduction to *Junky* and to declare that the "true scene" behind all the false ones, the genetic destination to which we have all along been inexorably driven, grounding the discontinuity between *Junkie* and *Queer's* textual politics, is nothing other than the letter itself. However, this case must be resisted—or at least deferred until the following chapter—because it would only mean repeating the false lesson learned by David Cronenberg. As the story of how Burroughs supposedly wrote *Naked Lunch,* Cronenberg's version draws on his "letters, prefaces and other things" in an effort "to see beyond, to the reality of the situation" (qtd. in Rodley, *Cronenberg* 163). Since the result is to get rid of the text itself, the moral is all too clear. If there is a determining secret to *Queer* other than the one given by Burroughs himself, then it must also be materially "obvious," not in some reality beyond it.

Burroughs claimed that a writer has no secrets, because it is all "in his work." Rather than dismissing this, I think we must take it literally, reversing García-Robles's conclusion to say that the drama of *Queer* is indeed in *Queer* itself. This move helps us to see that this novel is in fact *about secrecy* and that it makes perfectly good psychoanalytical and political sense to say that it is the work that knows the "secret." Genetic accounts need apply, therefore, only according to their *material* correspondence with the text, since far from being an extratextual or pretextual fact beyond the text, the "crime" and "letter" of *Queer* are fully textual, being no more nor less than the form and content of Burroughs' narrative of desire. As so often with Burroughs, the secret is to read *à la lettre.*

QUEERS AND HIPSTERS

INCARCERATE ALL UNDESIRABLES

Significantly, when Burroughs first mentioned his "queer novel" to Ginsberg in March 1952, he ended his letter by discussing Donald Webster Cory's *The Homosexual in America* (1951).[7] The treatment of same-sex desire in early Beat culture was, as Richard Dellamora has argued, severely constrained by "the absence of public modes of expression that could have provided alternative narratives of personal experience" (150), but Burroughs still dismissed Cory's social model and its message of tolerant liberalism out of hand: "I hate the stupid bastards who won't mind their own business," he snaps, "which is why I never could be a liberal" (*L* 106). From the vantage of Mexico and the particular license it afforded him as an expatriate, an ethnic minoritarian or civil rights model of same-sex identity held little appeal for Burroughs, even though he consistently related social environment to psychological conditioning in general and sexual behavior in particular, especially when writing to Ginsberg.

From the outset then, from his very first reference to writing *Queer,* it is apparent that Burroughs began his second novel in the context of a direct engagement with contemporary public discourses about homosexuality. He was quite literally writing to Ginsberg with Cory's recently published book before him (open to page 152), while this letter was itself part of a sustained, private dialogue with Ginsberg about their sexuality and about its determination in different national cultures. Refusing to accept compulsory heterosexuality in the figure of "the woman with the official federal stamp of approval" (*L* 129), Burroughs certainly understood that his narrative of undesired sexual identity would, of necessity, contest the binary politics of desirable national identity in force over the border. In an earlier letter from Mexico, Burroughs had challenged Ginsberg for avoiding "any experience that goes beyond arbitrary boundaries (and boundaries set by others)" (68)—a challenge directed to the self-disciplining of consciousness, to the self-colonization of the body, and to the voluntary border-patrolling of sexual identity in cold war America.[8]

On the other side of the Mexican border, a highly politicized psychopathology of sexual identity was being constructed, operating as a central rhetorical tactic in the postwar strategy of domestic containment and the consolidation of consensus. Working through a series of guilt-by-association equations that sought to naturalize a duality of health and disease mapped onto one of patriotism and treason, the paranoid style of American politics represented political dissent as unnatural and sexual deviance as un-American. The Kinsey Report of 1948 was crucial in this respect, since its immediate effect was to "magnify suddenly the proportions of the danger" posed by the homosexual menace (D'Emilio 37) and so make private behavior—the *most* private behavior—a matter of pressing national concern. For homosexual desire offered the very image of subversion from within: corrupt and corrupting drives that could not be controlled, only hidden.

The secret of homosexual desire therefore provided an ideal model for searching out secreted political desires, for fostering self-examination, and for scrutinizing signs of un-American activities, even in one's own unconscious. The paranoid rhetoric of public health at risk from contagion— "One homosexual can pollute a Government office" (qtd. in D'Emilio 37), a key Senate report stated flatly in 1950—was especially potent, since the unspeakable and unnatural were figured as virtually undetectable, viral threats to the integrity of national and individual immune systems. This added up to what Andrew Ross memorably calls "the Cold War culture of germophobia" (45). And so, when homosexuality was linked to national security, federal departments and the military responded by purging thousands classified simply as "undesirable."

Over the border, in May 1952, Burroughs was himself reporting a purge of "queers and hipsters" that had taken place at Mexico City College, describing it as "Un-Mexican" but typically American and concluding: "They aim to incarcerate all undesirables, that is anyone who does not function as an interchangeable part in their anti-human Social Economic set-up" (*L* 124, 125). By definition, the queer and the hipster should represent, as Murphy claims, "points of departure for an exacting critique of the social organization of late capital" ("William Burroughs" 118). Together with the editorial compromises imposed on *Junkie*, Burroughs' failure to get *Queer* published comes to express the political potency of his first works: the marginalized and outlawed social identities of the addict and the homosexual are embodied in the publication histories of the texts themselves, equally marginalized and literally outlawed.

PROBLEM NUMBER ONE

From a certain distance then, what we see is the historical alertness and natural continuity of Burroughs' writing from *Junkie* to *Queer* as he progressed from documenting one of his socially marginalized and politically demonized identities to the other. However, if cold war discourses of national security had an economic bottom line, so that, as Robert Corber has argued, they "marginalized forms of male identity that were not conducive to Fordism's needs and aims" by representing them as deviant, if not potentially homosexual (*Homosexuality* 104), then it must be clear *which* identity in Burroughs' 1952 blast against the social economic order should pose the more pressing threat.

Corber's case for the "centrality of the politicization" of homosexuality to postwar American culture (*In the Name* 9) echoes and confirms Jonathan Dollimore's claim that, historically and culturally, "the negation of homosexuality has been in direct proportion to its symbolic centrality" (*Sexual Dissidence* 29). It also clarifies the historical potency of *Queer* over and above that of *Junkie* at the moment of Burroughs' writing. While there were points of intersection between antinarcotic practices and anticommunism, the figure of the junkie was neither a sufficient symbol nor a sufficient sociological reality to radiate the threat posed rhetorically by the queer. As Gary Indiana has remarked, Burroughs was ahead of the times, prophetic indeed, with respect to junk: "drug hysteria" may have become a "major implement of state terror" in the 1980s and 1990s, but it was a "relatively minor tool of social repression in the 1940s and 1950s" (124). In sharp contrast, homophobic panic not only "dominated the national agenda" of those years (Savran, *Communists* 5) but, tied so closely to the red scare and to fears of social disease and economic disorder, was instrumental in authorizing an unprecedented surveillance of the American body politic.

Cultural historians like Corber make very clear the contemporary political stakes of *Queer.* They suggest in turn the extent to which Burroughs criticism has overlooked or downplayed those stakes throughout his work and why redressing this neglect must take into account the reasons for it. Why, for instance, should Murphy refer to the House Un-American Activities Committee and the cold war "drive to criminalize un-American activities" with reference to addiction, not homosexuality (*Wising Up* 52)? Perhaps because, taking his cue from the introduction to *Queer,* he follows Burroughs' example in disregarding the novel's thematic referent and historical context. The point about Murphy's historical reading of *Junkie,* but not *Queer,* is that it is so characteristic, so fully consistent with the dominant junk paradigm. To speak of "American society's desperate anti-junk paranoia" (57) but to pass over its much *more* desperate and politically charged homophobia is to follow that paradigm against the historical grain.

69'D

When *Junkie: Confessions of an Unredeemed Drug Addict* appeared in 1953, Burroughs' paperback publishers not only chose the title but policed his text by packaging it with *Narcotic Agent.* This other half of the Double Book was put there, as Geoffrey O'Brien notes, "to set things straight" (133). Ironically, when Ginsberg added his introduction to the reedited *Junky* in 1977, he spoke of these books being "69'd" (ix); which is doubly ironic, since it begs the question what text might have policed and straightened out *Queer,* while the answer turns out to be Burroughs' own introduction. For the effect of Burroughs' 1985 introduction to his 1952 manuscript is to depoliticize the title and the text of *Queer.* The term itself passes without comment, although its deployment not only anticipated more radical usage—even before the advent of identity politics and the "queer theory" that rose to contest it—but was very deliberately adopted at the time of writing.[9] When Carl Solomon, editor at Ace Books, suggested "Fag" as an alternative, Burroughs was outraged, his reaction leaving no doubt as to the degree of his disgust for stereotyped effeminacy: he would see Solomon "castrated first," because a masculinized identity was precisely the distinction he was "trying to put down uh I mean *over*" (*L* 119). But in *Queer*'s introduction, there is no attempt to historicize desire by, for example, charting the precise historical shifts in the terms *queer, homosexual,* and *gay.* Burroughs might, at the very least, have repeated his previous claim about the novel's suppression, that it was rejected by Ace because in the early 1950s it would have endangered any American publisher—but that too is a story that goes untold.

Queerer still, when Burroughs turns to the narrative itself, he actually argues *against* a sexual reading of its central relationship, the agonizing courtship by William Lee of Eugene Allerton. "Also bear in mind," he insists, that Lee's "inexplicable or psychotic" behavior is the result of a "withdrawal syndrome" that lasts "no more than a month" (*Q* xiii). In an interview shortly after publication, Burroughs was even more insistent that "*Queer* is about a very specific phenomenon—the phenomenon of withdrawal. That's what the book's about, about a month of withdrawal" (Ziegesar 161). But Burroughs didn't entitle his text "Withdrawal," and surely he protests too much. Not enough, though, for those who bear his words in mind and obligingly read *Queer* as not-*Junkie,* so that the novel is "less about the presence of sex and more about the absence of junk," as if homosexual identity were no more than a temporary chemical side effect (Caveney 160). In fact, it would make more sense to argue exactly the opposite, that *Junkie* is not-*Queer,* that *Junkie* is less about the presence of junk and more about keeping at bay the trauma of being queer, that Burroughs' first novel is really his second. Indeed, there is an enticing parallel between the way in which heroin appears to displace Lee's crisis of sexual identity and the way in which the junkie image has conveniently displaced Burroughs' queer identity.

Since it is the sustained, realist representation of a sexual relationship—indeed of *any* intersubjective relation—that makes *Queer* absolutely unique within the Burroughs oeuvre, his flat denial of what constitutes the narrative is truly remarkable. In effect, he asks us not to see what is before our eyes. Rather, what Lee "clearly" seeks in Allerton is, Burroughs explains

> an audience, the acknowledgement of his performance, which of course is a mask, to cover a shocking disintegration. So he invents a frantic attention-getting format which he calls the Routine: shocking, funny, riveting. "It is an Ancient Mariner, and he stoppeth one of three. . . ." (*Q* xv)

Having passed over both the subject of homosexual identity and the pressing national history that was *Queer*'s original context, Burroughs completes the process of political foreclosure by abstracting and aestheticizing his own personal history. Cut off from history in this way, *Queer* ceases to be a story of human, let alone homosexual, relations at all. Queer indeed.

Above all, the emphasis on Burroughs' *private* history not only isolates *Queer* from its wider national history but insists on a historically false choice, since it was precisely the politicization of the personal that defined cold war culture, especially in terms of sexual identity and of homosexual desire in particular. Indeed, one way to recognize the transformation of Burroughs' writing from *Junkie* to *Queer* is to borrow from Timothy Murphy the terminology of Gilles Deleuze and Félix Guattari and say that the negative force of *Junkie* might be reduced to this: in its commitment to objective reality, it refuses the flows and productions of desire and fantasy and so refuses *"the unconscious of social productions"* (Seem xviii; my emphasis). Significantly, the clearest sign of this detachment of political economy from an economy of the libido is the moment late in the novel when Lee overtly politicizes addiction, denouncing "police-state legislation penalizing a state of being" (*J* 142). Burroughs likens the state's fascistic scapegoating of the addict to "anti-Semitism under the Nazis," a simile that Murphy says is not made "idly," because it is based on and represents Burroughs' "first-hand experience" in prewar Austria (*Wising Up* 54).

However, Murphy misses two key points. First, while this political scenario forces Lee into permanent exile, it otherwise has little bearing on the narrative or relation to Lee's own actions as an addict. *Junkie* may document sociologically the cold war state's disciplinary institutions of control—law court, prison cell, and hospital ward—but is the *unilateral* and *institutional,* or what Jennie Skerl terms the "totalitarian" and "sadistic" power relationship between the authorities and addicts," really the "basis for Burroughs' analysis of power in the later novels" (26)? I suspect that Murphy would agree with Michel Foucault, who insists that the strategic adversary is "not only historical fascism, the fascism of Hitler and Mussolini [. . .] but also the fascism in us all, in our heads and in our everyday behavior, the fascism that causes us to love power, to desire the very thing that dominates and exploits us" (viii). In this light, the second key point that Murphy passes over is the precise and absolute inversion of *Junkie* performed in *Queer.* Here, in a gesture that typifies how in this text the object of power is at the same time its subject, the victim of power also its lover, Lee's routines repeatedly feature tasteless Jew jokes, at one point concluding: "I must be careful not to lay myself open to a charge of anti-Semitism" (*Q* 51). However we understand this troubling inversion, it is a fundamental one because, as David Savran argues, the main source of critical "dis-

may" with Burroughs continues to be "the absence of clear signals of meaning in a body of fiction that, at first glance, is so flamboyantly misogynist,
racist, homophobic, and anti-Semitic" (*Taking It* 85). Together with the
routine form, this dismay begins in *Queer.*

What we might call the *fantasmatic fascism* of Lee's routines in *Queer*
marks a definitive formal shift from *Junkie,* a transformed *economy* of
writing, that in turn marks an entirely different engagement with history
and power.[10] This is why its place in the oeuvre as a whole is far more than
"transitional." Central to my case is the way in which Lee's routines connect private desire with public communication and bind his personal fantasy with a national imaginary. They show that a libidinal economy of
communication and a cybernetic economy of desire are two sides of the
same queer coin. And so, when Murphy observes that "nothing in the early
texts prepares the reader for the barrage of mass-media control technology" from *Naked Lunch* onward (*Wising Up* 89), he is only half right, as
bound by the priority of *Junkie* and the junk paradigm as any previous
critic. The historical recovery of *Queer* therefore enables two essential
outcomes: first, to secure *Queer*'s centrality to Burroughs' writing and its
relation to the cold war 1950s; and second, to reconfigure the relationship
between his two crucial decades of development and experiment. The
stakes are high, because Burroughs' second novel shatters the junk-virus
paradigm by encoding the essential queerness of *Naked Lunch* and the cut-
up trilogy, even as it frames the queer identity in viral and cybernetic terms,
and so *does* prepare for the works that follow. To recognize how *Queer* in
fact redefines Burroughs' textual politics, we will have to materialize its two
histories—one textual and cultural, the other genetic and formal—and finally, their economic relation.

Since the book's publication in 1985, only a brief essay by Vince Passaro
in *Harper's Magazine* seems to understand the real necessity of reading
Queer, recognizing that it "can be read as a key to the work that follows
it" (73). Indeed, the specific ways in which it reappears in later texts establishes that Burroughs kept returning to *Queer:* several of its major routines
were reworked for *Naked Lunch;* an allusion to Lee's "phantom" partner,
Allerton, appeared in the original (1961) edition of *The Soft Machine* (173),
only to be cut for later editions;[11] most significantly, he reprised the Lee-
Allerton relation to form the opening narrative of the revised *Ticket That
Exploded* (1967); and finally, in *The Western Lands,* written after the publication of *Queer,* the character of Allerton appears again, now "with an air
of arrested age" (23), as well he might. We begin to see the inexorable return *of* this text, which, like a familiar revenant or unlaid ghost, wouldn't

go away but drew Burroughs back to it, and in this sense too, *Queer* is a key. And so, if, as Thomas Newhouse says, "*Queer* is a far more fascinating and complex book than *Junkie*" (85), perhaps unsurprisingly I find that despite my best efforts to make an exhaustive critical reading of its complexity, the fascination still remains.

THE UGLY SPIRIT

QUIEN ES?

As a term, *queer* readily takes on meaning through a well-ordered set of oppositions: unnatural/natural; counterfeit/genuine; spurious/honest; inexplicable/understandable. In *Queer,* these binaries lose their normative and hierarchic reassurance, and it is in this sense, as an enigmatic disturbance of systems of knowledge and classification, rather than in the vein of contemporary queer theory, that the term needs to be used here. In this light, the terrain of the text becomes one of constant ideological conflict, making problematic what ideology would have us take for granted by making possible mutually contradictory readings; contradictions that cannot be resolved if the text is to remain true to its title. And what is true at the level of meaning is equally so at the level of form: short as it is, the text is remarkably hard to pin down, because its structure and narrative voice are so inconsistent and unstable. From an objective perspective, from any "frequent viewpoint," *Queer* may not be a satisfying or successful novel, and its lack of "finish" is obvious compared to *Junkie,* but there is something about it that remains irreducibly disturbing.

To begin with, the narrative details a social scene, carefully distinguishing certain types of restaurants and bars according to their homosexual habitués. Based on an actual queer bar Burroughs visited in Mexico City, *La Linterna Verde,* for example, the "Green Lantern boys" are classed as "screaming fags who would not have been welcome at the Ship Ahoy" (Q 35). But even here, the realist dimension is unstable as the text becomes increasingly preoccupied with "borderline" sexual identity and repeated disputes as to who is or is not queer. When Lee is accused of "pretending" to be queer in order "to get in on the act" (34), this not only inverts the logic of the closet but traps identity in theatricality. Thus, Lee's courtship of Allerton is troubling not just because *en passant* Lee identifies himself as a married man and his partner appears heterosexual but because the third point of this odd love triangle, Allerton's friend Mary, is described in exactly the same ambiguous and artificial terms as Allerton. She has "dyed red hair and carefully applied makeup," and he has hair "bleached by the sun like a sloppy dyeing job" and an "equivocal face" that conveys "an impression of makeup" (19, 16). Twinned by falsity, the characterizations queer the presumed authenticity, integrity, and normativity of heterosexual identities.

Lee's pursuit of Allerton aggravates the site of pressing cultural and political fears post-Kinsey by showing sexual categories as not stable and mutually exclusive but, in Jennifer Terry's gloss, "permeable and highly contingent" ("Anxious Slippages" 159). In this sense, Lee in particular embodies the alarming dissolution of distinct boundaries. But Lee is himself alarmed by this instability, a fact that attests to the force of the binary, its power to secure identity, however falsely. Equally, his alarm makes it clear that, rather than resolutely going beyond a net of controls, he is quite unable to assert a coherent self-definition. Under the propulsion of desire, Lee runs ever faster out of control and into a zone of disassociated fragmentation, a state at times of schizophrenia, of ontological crisis and breakdown. It is not only the characters who are "borderline" (*Q* 7) but the world in which they move, and this is the case not just geographically and nationally but physically and metaphysically, as the narrative becomes increasingly visited by visions of a dreamworld, spectral encounters beyond the level of Lee's fleshly desires. A year before his drug-induced vision of the "Composite City" in "In Search of Yage," *Queer* presents an early version of Interzone and defines it in queer terms as a global no-man's land in excess of symbolic stability or systematic classification. The true capital of this queer zone is therefore Guayaquil, with its "curiously mixed populace: Negro, Chinese, Indian, European, Arab, characters difficult to classify" (93).

Caveney observes that "'queer' functions as an adjective rather than as a noun" (160). This is a significant distinction: First, there is Burroughs' general stance on the "hugely important" principle of "infinite differentiation" "overlooked by social planners," the substance of one of his lectures in semantics to Ginsberg in 1950: "Human, Allen, is an adjective, and its use as a noun is in itself regrettable" (*L* 68). Second, there is the historically specific "mania for category-making" of the cold war era, described by Carla Kaplan as a "passion for creating and identifying human types, rooting out undesirables, marking the limits of national desirability" (151). Typecasting is of the essence. Allerton's failure to recognize Lee as queer— since he "associated queerness with at least some degree of overt effeminacy" (*Q* 27)—establishes that the queer is not a fixed and recognizable type. A brief but crucial exchange between Allerton and Mary early on begs the essential question: "Who is he?" asks Mary, speaking the only three words voiced directly by a female in the novel, to which Allerton replies, "I have no idea" (23).

The deep problem posed by the queer identity then is that it fails to identify anything, and it was such failure to match a classification mark, to wear a fixed label, that incurred the mania of McCarthyism. At the very time Burroughs was working on *Queer,* the senator was insisting: "I feel strongly about labelling products for what they are. Poison should be labelled as poison; treason should be labelled as treason; lies should be labelled as lies" (qtd. in Glazer 248). Since Burroughs was labelled by the Mexican authorities an "undesirable alien" in May 1951—the period fictionalized in *Queer*—and "classified as a 'pernicious foreigner'" in March 1952—the time he began to write it—he could only have been acutely aware of how such labelling operated to define desirable national identities (*L* 90, 107). However, Burroughs does not contest the prevailing medical and national models of homosexuality—as poison, treason, lie—by downplaying difference, by promoting the integrationist policies of Cory and of contemporary homophile movements, such as the Mattachine Society. In sharp contrast to the era's typical forms of homosexual fiction, Burroughs refuses the status of tragic victim or romantic rebel, let alone an "egalitarian presence crying out for status as a human being" (Newhouse 72). On the contrary, he presents Lee in terms of a radical failure to conform to type or class. To borrow from Mary Douglass's well-known anthropological analysis of purity and danger, the end result of such a failure to fit his classification would be to "confound the general scheme of the world" (55).

Putting knowledge into doubt is a source of subversive potency, as is embodying such indeterminacy. "Danger lies in transitional states," as Douglass put it, while recognizing the double-edged implications: "The person who must pass from one to another is himself in danger and emanates danger to others" (96). In *Queer,* Lee's disintegration is overwhelmingly negative and regressive—*pain* is his dominant feeling, always tied to images of betrayed childhood and so to lost psychic wholeness—but it also promises an alternative horizon; positive dis-integration. That is, not "falling apart" but extrication from an integrated system (Bredbeck 492); Lee's state of trauma has itself the potential to traumatize, his horrified individual disintegration the potential to disintegrate the system with the powers of horror. Repeatedly "depressed and shattered," separated from life by "a glass wall," and so constantly feeling "the tearing ache of limitless desire" (*Q* 58, 94, 96), Lee experiences the kind of masochistic abjection that, for Leo Bersani, might "shatter" identity itself (*Freudian Body* 39).

THE THING ITSELF

Perhaps then, *Queer* gestures towards "the positivity of horror and abjection" associated by Judith Halberstam and Ira Livingston with another "queer" form, the so-called posthuman body. Indeed, Halberstam and Livingston offer a useful version of disintegration understood in terms of "functional dysfunctions that make other things happen" (14). Even so, *Queer* starts off as straight narrative, and you might say the text only becomes itself through its own narrative disintegration, its steady collapse into a series of barely connected episodes. Indeed, the main reason why Ace Books rejected *Queer* in 1952 was surely not the moral and legal controversy of its subject matter but rather the way it falls apart so rapidly as a coherent narrative; as Carl Solomon recalled, Ace Books "didn't feel it was up to *Junkie*" (Tytell, "John Tytell" 252). *Queer*'s rapid disintegration should remind us of *Junkie*'s uniqueness as a (relatively) continuous narrative.[12] For two decades, nothing that Burroughs wrote would achieve anything like such sustained coherence or, by default, such commercial viability. And so, while in March 1952 he saw his manuscript as "a queer novel using the same straight narrative as [he] used in *Junk*" (*L* 107), the fact that he didn't finish the sequel as "straight"—did not, in fact, finish it at all—only emphasizes the problematic, crisis-riven nature of this writing and of the writing that was to follow.

If Burroughs recognized that *Queer* was "out of place according to any frequent viewpoint"—which implies that the place of *Junkie* was known or that *Junkie* knew its place—it is because, as Bruce Fink puts it, "something only has a place within an ordered system—space-time coordinates or a Dewey decimal book classification, for example—in other words, within some sort of symbolic structure" (52). The title therefore does double duty. First, it signals the riddling status of *Queer* itself and its anomalous place in the Burroughs oeuvre. Or rather, it marks a point where the very notion of an order to authorship and writing begins to break down: its belated publication becomes a useful reminder and renewal therefore of its disruptive effect in the decade of its initial composition. The title also signifies the historical position of the queer, who not only fails to fit within the existing social order but causes massive epistemological trouble. It was on such a note that Burroughs ended the "refresher course in Semantics" he gave Ginsberg in May 1950, observing that while "psychiatrists will claim to understand anything," queerness defined a limit and a lack in understanding itself: "Some essential fact is missing" (*L* 67, 69). The queer constitutes therefore an enigma, or what the Lacanian analyst

Jean Laplanche has called an "enigmatic signifier": a question "posed by someone who is not conscious of the essential, and who does not have any solutions" (11).

To the extent that *Junkie* embraced factualism as an empirical method, a positivist model where language represents reality, the queerness of *Queer* turns on the degree to which the correspondence of word to label is disrupted by the enigmatic force of something that *can't* be symbolized. This is the difference between writing an "accurate account," as Burroughs thought of *Junkie* in May 1951 (*L* 83), and his sense of *Queer*, exactly a year later, as *in*accurate writing in the face of the *un*accountable: "Writing must always remain an *attempt*," he insists, because "The Thing itself, the process on sub-verbal level always eludes the writer" (126). The crucial phrase here—*The Thing itself*—we have encountered before, in Kerouac's May 1952 description of the spontaneous method of writing he termed "sketching" and what it promised to achieve (*Selected Letters 1940–1956* 356). Kerouac was writing in the very same month as Burroughs, indeed while sharing his apartment in Mexico City and working on *Doctor Sax,* which further insists on the entirely opposite approaches the two writers took to the same "Thing." Where for Kerouac spontaneous self-expression and rendering of reality never fails, for Burroughs its object *always* eludes the writer and words *must* fall short. Although Burroughs did not have *"das Ding"* of Jacques Lacan in mind (or that of Freud or Kant before him), his comments on *Queer* do invite a Lacanian reading, even an opportunistic one, since both their "Things" define the Real in terms of a constitutional resistance to representation. And as that which *is,* but must not be known, Reality is for both Burroughs and Lacan defined precisely as a *secret.*[13]

Lacan's terms are notoriously hard to grasp, but Slavoj Žižek, who in the past decade has done the most to "popularize" them, clarifies the key point that the "Real *qua* Thing is not 'repressed,' it is foreclosed" (*Metastases* 199). That is, it stands not for taboo material or a mystical beyond but for an impossible otherness that marks an internal limit inherent to any appearance of closure, a point where we lose a coherent sense of "reality": there always remains "some strange, traumatic element which cannot be symbolized, integrated into the symbolic order—The Thing" (*Sublime Object* 132). Although, in Judith Butler's gloss, the Lacanian Real is precisely what "any account of 'reality' fails to include" (192), it is, as Žižek goes on to observe, "precisely through this failure that we can in a way encircle, locate the empty place of the Real" (*Sublime Object* 172). In other words, dysfunction can become functional. Or as Lacan himself put it, all art is "characterised by a certain mode of organisation around this emptiness"

(*Ethics* 130). In which case, one way to grasp the vital, paradigmatic difference between *Junkie* and *Queer* is through their differing "mode[s] of organisation around this emptiness."

To put it crudely, when Lee in *Junkie* says, "Here are the facts" (*J* 18), he supports the illusory fullness, adequacy, and rational consistency of the symbolic order and of his self. This is the language of self-possession, of someone who knows what he knows and has the words to represent his intentions. The irony here, and the political point, is that a heroin addict should model the rational self, the conscious ego that takes itself "to be master of its own thoughts and whose thoughts are believed to correspond to 'external reality'" (Fink 43). In Burroughs' own precise description, Lee "comes across as integrated and self-contained, sure of himself and where he is going" (*Q* xii). Lee *comes across* as integrated. Read: he represses knowledge that would break his one-dimensional self and world into pieces. In this sense, Lee resists "knowledge of the unconscious, to protect the ego's illusion of objectivity and its identification with 'reality'" (Ragland 32). This traumatic and therefore impossible knowledge surfaces in the preface to *Junkie*, in the form of Lee's terrifying childhood dreams, "where a supernatural horror seemed always on the point of taking shape" (*J* xi).

The exact nature of the traumatic Real encountered here, that the child can neither grasp nor escape, might motivate the quest of psychoanalytical biographers; in itself, it is of no value or interest here. What matters is the absolute structural contradiction it exposes between the neutral, "objective" knowledge that is the content of Lee's narration—"Here are the facts"—and the truth of his subjective position: as an exercise in discursive fixing, the controlled, "impersonal" words of the first person narrator try to exclude or cover over, and so are secretly motivated by, the fascinating horror of the Real Thing and the inner chaos of the traumatized subject. This contradiction in turn finds its absolute inverse in *Queer*. Here, with no pretense at factualist disinterest, Lee is always letting slip the truth of his desire in the form of fictions, his comic-horror routines that aren't "supposed to be fair"—that is, reasonable, objective, accurate—but do contain a typically unwelcome "modicum of truth" (*Q* 103).

In terms of the emergence of another agency, a foreign voice within, Burroughs' slip of the tongue between "Queer" and "Fag" as book titles is exemplary. For the routine form itself is a kind of Freudian slip, an impossibly extended parapraxis, that ends up exposing as a con—putting *down*—precisely what it is intended to communicate—to put *over*.[14] In fact, the routine form acts out the return of the repressed in all its characteristic guises—slips of the tongue, jokes, puns, repetition compulsion, fantasy work—because, in Freud's terms, "a thing which has not been understood inevitably reappears: like an unlaid ghost, it cannot rest until the mystery has been solved and the spell broken" (*Two Case Histories* 122). In its primal form, this "thing" is the traumatic enigma of desire itself, precisely an "enigmatic signifier," because Lee *poses* as a riddle to another that to which he himself has no solution.

The routines Lee tells Allerton clearly invite a psychoanalytical reading. But more than that, we begin to recognize that their relationship is *itself* the playing out of an analytic encounter. Mladen Dolar's description applies exactly to Allerton: "The Other to whom this flow of words is addressed is present as the figure of the analyst, as the supposed addressee of the messages of the unconscious, the symptoms, the dreams [. . .] the 'subject supposed to know' what they mean" ("At First Sight" 147). This is how Lee presents himself to Allerton; as someone who "seemed to mean more than what he said," someone who gives "a special emphasis to a word" and appears "somehow familiar," as though "Lee were saying, '*You* know what I mean. *You* remember'" (Q 23). Their relationship structures a classic scene of transference—one that Burroughs knew well from experience—where Lee mistakes one prepared to listen for one that is loved and loves in return. Allerton's attraction for Lee is therefore suitably contradictory in terms of communication as well as queerness. On the one hand, there is his presumed cryptanalytical skills as a veteran of Counter Intelligence Corps service[15] (24). This ought to make Allerton an ideal psychoanalyst, since encounters with the unconscious necessarily require a deciphering of language. In fact, this is the secret logic to Lee's choice of Allerton, his expertise in the field of secrecy. This in turn motivates his routines, since they insistently encode the intimate world of Lee's secret desire in a global language of political conspiracy. On the other hand, there is Allerton's supposed "pellagra" (16), which Lee interprets as if it meant deafness (but is actually a form of eczema; "rough skin"). His contrary qualities are precisely chosen since Lee's routines always say more *and* less than he means, are both obscenely explicit *and* heavily encrypted, making present knowledge that is too traumatic to *either* repress *or* find direct representation. In effect, Lee chooses a *deaf analyst* to decipher his secrets for him and so provides a model of short-circuited communication that enables us to recognize a crucial dimension of Burroughs' textual politics.[16]

Finally, if Lee's routines are symptomatic disturbances, ciphers of some repressed meaning that decenters the subject and calls for interpretation from the other—"*You* know what I mean"—they are not to be mistaken for the fascinating secret that separates *Queer* from *Junkie*. Here, where the fantasy dimension has finally taken over reality, any secret will be in the secret of the form, in the "dream-work." In the terms of Lacan's paradox, while "[w]hat one finds in *das Ding* is the true secret," this cannot appear as a signifier that can be deciphered and given a determinate meaning (*Ethics* 46). Laura Mulvey makes the distinction between two orders of secrecy: "A secret thing may be hidden away, in a concealed place, but a secret meaning must be transformed into a code" (53). But Lacan goes one further, in what he called the *sinthome*. Here, the secret of the "Thing" comes in an insistently material but meaningless form: not as a coded message to decipher, a symptom to dissolve, but, in Žižek's gloss, as a compulsively repeated "fragment of the signifier permeated with idiotic enjoyment" (*Looking Awry* 128). It is a matter of *affect* rather than *interpretation,* of truth rather than meaning, of recognition rather than cognition, and so points to the particular fascination *Queer* exercises, to the uncanny Burroughsian force that is the other side to knowing what it means: "*You* remember."

The meaningless materiality of the sinthome appears in *Queer* through an always overlooked feature of the text: its recycling of recurrent words and phrases. One of the quintessential trademarks of the Burroughs oeuvre, this disturbing repetitive textuality, entirely absent in *Junkie,* is inaugurated in *Queer*. Because these seemingly arbitrary repetitions are distributed on a formal level independent of Lee's subjective experience, they can't be naturalized. Subtle but crucial supports of the increasingly dreamlike mood of the novel, culminating in Lee's metamorphosis into the phantomatic Skip Tracer, these formal patterns create an effect that is indeed *uncanny* in Freud's strict sense: a "constant recurrence of the same thing" that reminds us of our inner "compulsion to repeat" (*Art* 356, 361).

Far from coincidentally, this uncanny textuality appears most forcibly in Lee's dream of the Skip Tracer. Restaging the relationship of Lee to Allerton as a psychic encounter and borrowing from F. Scott Fitzgerald's story of evil possession, "A Short Trip Home,"[17] the scene (*Q* 133) derives its disturbing effect from the way it materially recycles resonant bits and pieces of the preceding text: the persistent color yellow (19, 29, 85, 89, 98, 119), a "warm Spring wind" (3, 52), the sound of "humming" (12, 23, 48, 65), a spectrally "blank" face (13), and so on. Tracing such textual patterns within and across Burroughs' texts to their conclusion promises to reveal a definite psychic structure, to disclose a final secret of desire. This would be his sinthome, glossed by Dennis Foster as "the fantasy that founds the subject, some moment of arrested enjoyment to which he will always return" (*Sublime* 14). However, while the Skip Tracer is about a settling of psychic accounts, any final settlement, any final accounting, is impossible, a dead end, so that to trace these patterns only reproduces the selfsame "idiotic enjoyment" their repetition designates. When Burroughs says, "No writer has any secrets. It's all in his work" (qtd. in Malanga 111), I take this to mean that the work knows secrets unknown to the writer, that the secret is in the form itself, so that the writer is unable to say what it is, precisely because any secret that *could* be said is already *not the secret.*

Like the political cryptanalysis of counterintelligence, the activity of decoding meanings is therefore best attempted on the level of Mulvey's second form of secrecy, a more pragmatically productive level. This means resisting the promise of the final secret and going back to my point of departure; namely, the possibility that Lee's psychic disintegration in *Queer* is subversive, that it advances a politics based on the "positivity of horror and abjection."

UGLY AMERICAN

The short answer is: no. As David Savran argues, it would be a mistake to assume that Lee's disintegration possesses a subversive power that matches the liberating fragmentation of the subject valorized by poststructuralists (*Taking It* 36–37). Certainly, if self-humiliation marks the beginnings of self-overcoming, then this is not how it looks to Lee. Rather, what makes *Queer* so disturbing politically as well as psychologically is the massive violence unleashed and directed outwards by a subject in the process of internal collapse.

As Allerton's association of queerness with effeminacy suggests, Lee as American homosexual fails to conform to type. But as homophobic American, he conforms all too readily to type because, like the desirable national identity, he too demands an abject other, indeed the *same* abject other: the detestable, effeminate, "screaming fag." In this way, as the straight/queer binary is replayed in the binary queer/fag, the queer aligns itself with the straight in its most pathological and potentially fascist dimension. It is hard to imagine a contemporary readership—homophile or homophobic—that would not have been appalled by this alignment.

In *Queer,* the catastrophic effects of desire on identity are tied ever more tightly to the economic, racial, and ideological through Lee's routines. In these performances, Burroughs articulates a pathological and progressively *politicized* psychology. To begin with, his routines appear as bizarre, self-conscious allegorical fantasies, manic monologues seeking to dispel the impression of being "a peculiar and undesirable character" (Q 22). His first, the saga of the Texas Oil-Man, is the polyphonic performance of a shaggy dog story that encodes, if Allerton can decipher it, the strategy of Lee's intended courtship. Lee's second routine openly confesses his "uh, proclivities":

> "I thought of the painted, simpering female impersonators I had seen in a Baltimore night club. Could it be possible that I was one of those subhuman things? I walked the streets in a daze, like a man with a light concussion—just a minute, Doctor Kildare, this isn't your script." (39)

What seems clear is the routine's strategy: the arch, melodramatic tone exaggerates homosexuality as the *peccatum contra naturam* so that Lee can mock his own anxiety and disarm any residue of abhorrence or resistance in Allerton. Lee then introduces the character of Bobo, whose lesson to conquer prejudice with love—clearly modeled on Cory's derided book— is rewarded by a "ghastly shlup," a disemboweling and strangulation Isadora Duncan–style. It is at this point, as Lee glosses Bobo's words of wisdom, that his routines turn sinister:

> "'No one is ever really alone. You are part of everything alive.' The difficulty is to convince someone else he is really part of you, so what the hell? Us parts ought to work together. Reet? [. . .] What I mean is, Allerton, we are all parts of a tremendous whole. No use fighting it." Lee was getting tired of the routine. He looked around restlessly for some place to put it down. (40)

Simultaneously, his "script" takes on an unwanted, rather than parodied, momentum of its own and declares a purpose that has less to do with overcoming another's prejudices than with overcoming the other altogether. Needing not only to deposit but to depose the routine, Lee finds himself a victim of his own libidinal and authoritarian intentions towards Allerton as the tension between parody and sincerity collapses. Lee may adopt Bobo's rhetoric of physical and spiritual democracy—"we are all parts of a tremendous whole"—but he lets slip an aggressive will—"No use fighting it"—entirely at odds with the tenor of a tradition that runs from Wordsworth and Whitman down to Ginsberg. If he wants to follow Ginsberg in pursuit of Whitman's "great Camerado, the lover true" (117), a model of adhesive American democracy, then Lee is traveling in the wrong direction. If anything, there is a trace of Melville's Captain Ahab here, another great monologist and monomaniac, seeking wholeness by absorbing the other into the self and enslaving other bodies to his imperial will.[18]

For all its heightened autobiographical intimacy, *Queer* not only has far more direct political reference and commentary than *Junkie* but makes that political engagement, through Lee, integral to its narrative—and to his *narrating*—action. *Junkie* reduces meaningful interpersonal relations to a virtual degree zero. As Avital Ronell argues, the apparent libidinal autonomy of the addict unhooks him from an "effective circuit" to mark what she calls "the constitutive adestination of the addict's address" ("Our Narcotic" 64, 71). *Queer* moves in the opposite direction, its routines polarizing into mastery and subordination the effects of power by turning interpersonal relations into a zero-sum game. Unlike *Junkie,* from first to last *Queer* is almost textbook Lacan. From *Junkie* to *Queer,* Lee has passed from need, which has a fixed object that can be fulfilled organically—"fixed" in the junkie's sense: "Junk is a biological necessity" (*J* 124)—to desire, which has no object and can never be satisfied—"He felt the tearing ache of limitless desire" (*Q* 96). Lee's "gnawing emptiness" cannot be "relieved" by Allerton (77), and this inner void propels "a frenzied search, a recurrent nightmare," where he is doomed to find only "an empty room" (84). *Queer* therefore fulfills the Hegelian lesson of Lacan, demonstrating how the dialectic of master and slave is rooted in desire, where the other person is valued only as an object to make good a lack, and there is no room for ethics but also no possible chance of success.[19]

That Lee does not see himself and Allerton as equal "parts" who can "work together" is apparent from the explicitly political episode that follows. The episode begins outside the Russian restaurant featured in the previous scene, with Lee's promise of a Napoleon brandy that does not appeal "to the mass tongue" (*Q* 41). The episode ends in Lee's apartment where he seduces Allerton into bed. It is the action in between these two moments and locations that charges the personal relations with political significance. Lee calls a cab:

> "Three pesos to Insurgentes and Monterrey," Lee said to the driver in his atrocious Spanish. The driver said four. Lee waved him on. The driver muttered something, and opened the door.
>
> Inside, Lee turned to Allerton. "The man plainly harbors subversive thoughts. You know, when I was at Princeton, Communism was the thing. To come out flat for private property and a class society, you marked yourself a stupid lout or suspect to be a High Episcopalian pederast. But I held out against the infection—of Communism I mean, of course." (41–42)

Lee's characterization of political conditions during the New Deal years, where capitalism is queer and communism the norm, perverts the historical record in line with the cold war climate two decades later. At the same time, that Lee is himself a pederast and is en route to the "infection" of a straight American—a national security nightmare, given Allerton's service in the Counter Intelligence Corps—clearly problematizes his status as an upholder of American capital against the infectious perversion of communism. If Lee's encoded gags test Allerton's presumed code-breaking skills, the message remains unclear to the reader: is Lee really putting his queer shoulder to the hegemonic wheel of American ideology?

The contradictions are unstable, inflammatory. But Burroughs carefully sets Lee's actual behavior into sharp relief against the ambiguous humor of his exchanges with Allerton. The power of a single peso speaks bluntly: he whose brandy does not appeal to the mass tongue can silence the tongue of the masses with a wave of the hand. When he cuts four pesos down to three, Lee performs in miniature the covert colonialist exploitation of "Point Four," an arm of US foreign policy operating under the guise of a philanthropic "war against disease, poverty, and ignorance" (Whitfield 57). In *The Yage Letters,* which begins as an effective sequel to *Queer,* Burroughs would hammer this particular political point home, making open reference to "all this Point four and good nabor crap and financial aid" (11), while pressing Lee still further into the contradictions of American national identity. Clearly, there is no romance of Spengler's *fellahin* for Lee. Contrast Kerouac's contemporaneous *On the Road,* where Sal Paradise indulges in fantasized identification as a Mexican peasant, a fantasy that Robert Holton scathingly terms a naive and depthless "racial version of cross-dressing" (272). In *Queer,* there is no such temptation to vicarious alignment with other oppressed others, no promotion of the liberal "model of political solidarity" across "multiple axes of difference" celebrated in Robert Corber's *Homosexuality in Cold War America* (4). Corber sees identifications "across racial, class, and gender lines" as "subversive," because they "destabilized the series of binary oppositions that governed the production of the Cold War subject" (7); Burroughs turns this strategy on its head. Romancing the racial other, Kerouac projects Mexico as the paradisial end of the road for Sal, but the further south Lee travels, the more he magnifies, rather than wishes away, his own imperial identity. What goes for race goes for class too, since if Sal's social mobility is headed in the "wrong" direction—down towards the underclass of hoboes and peasants—Lee exaggerates the rigidities and privileges of his own class identity, insisting on hierarchic differences by playing up his aristocratic "old world" manners (*Q* 18, 22).

Whereas Sal's fantasy in *On the Road* "completely—and horrifyingly—ignores the economic and social realities" of the racial other (Savran, *Taking It* 61), Lee in *Queer* completely and horrifyingly *exploits* those realities in the convex mirror of his fantasies of power. He seems to relish the oppression and objectification of others in a psychological maneuver that implicates a national pathology. When Lee jokes of having sex with Mexican boys, "'Taint as if it was being queer" (*Q* 77), he objectifies them to a point of naked excess; embracing the logic of abjection in order to refuse his own identification as "one of those subhuman things" (39), Lee lays bare the ugliness of this very logic. His joke translates an ugly eugenic fantasy applied in fact to queers and Jews, among others—'taint as if they was *human*—that is much more disturbing here than when, in *Naked Lunch*, Clem and Jody repeat the same line; after all, we know these walk-on types are operating as cold war double agents, their mission "to represent the U.S. in an unpopular light" (*NL* 181). In *Queer*, the question of Lee's agency and intention is not so much doubled strategically as *divided* schizophrenically. When a Mexican passerby insults Lee and Allerton in the street, Lee reacts with a blunt display of colonial power, dismissing the Mexican's "little jerkwater country" under the benevolent economic imperium of his "good American dollars" (*Q* 53). On the other hand, Lee's reaction also implies the limits to American foreign policy, exposed as a national fantasy of control, since he has to resort to the threat of force—showing his gun—a threat based on fear: "'Someday they won't walk away.'" National and individual fantasy coincide consistently along a symbolic and sexual axis, so that there is nothing coincidental about the "Napoleonic pose" (73–74) Lee strikes when next using his gun—shooting the head off a mouse in another bravura display of deluded masculine potency—any more than there was in his choice of brandy—one that "Napoleon must have pissed in" (43)—to seduce Allerton.

But Lee does more than magnify the ugliness of the Ugly American, and the episode in the cab has a second function. This is to ally fellow Americans abroad, a tactic that by seeking to resolve the hierarchic play of power between them only underlines its existence. And this is the reason why, despite their overlapping autobiographical narratives, in *Queer* Lee's relationship to Mexicans is entirely different from that in *Junkie*. In *Junkie*, Lee learns the idealist lesson that his worst enemy is "the frightened flesh" of his own body (*J* 152): addiction confers the illusion of self-sufficiency and heroin "trumps" desire (Lenson 33). In *Queer*, Lee's identity is destabilized by desire: he tries to shore up the walls of his psyche by aggressively policing the borders of his national identity, attacking the body politic's enemies without in a defensive reaction designed to deal with an enemy within. It is in the context of relations of power, more particularly the *frustration* of power, that Lee now takes on an identity so emphatically based on class, race, nationality, and money.

PSYCHOANALYZE CAESAR

Queer's insistent interchange between the particulars of Lee's relationship with Allerton and a larger narrative of power reaches its apogee in Guayaquil. Ecuador is another "jerkwater country" to the Ugly American tourist, but what is arresting is Lee's alliance with its internal order of power, its "alarmed" rich people:

> "What they need here is a security department, to keep the underdog under."
> "Yes," said Allerton. "We must secure uniformity of opinion."
> "Opinion! What are we running here, a debating society? Give me one year and the people won't have any opinions." (Q 106)

As a national security expert hired out to the imperial state, Lee asks no questions: he has "not come to psychoanalyze Caesar, but to protect his person" (106). Allerton's repartee plays the game, but Lee drives it to a point of uneasy excess. Our discomfort that this is not parody at all is, as before, borne out by the way Lee's exchange with Allerton is followed by direct and unambiguous action. When his hotel neighbor, overhearing through a ventilation gap, says "something in Spanish to the effect Lee should be quiet," Lee's reaction is fascistic without being funny:

> "Ah, shut up," said Lee, leaping to his feet. "I'll nail a blanket over that slot! I'll cut off your fucking air! You only breathe with my permission. You're the occupant of an inside room, a room without windows. So remember your place and shut your poverty-stricken mouth!" (107)

Again, Lee plays the Ugly American all too convincingly. His malicious performance oddly exceeds narrative necessity, which makes it difficult to motivate as a tactic to make bonds with Allerton by outbidding him, since all the money in the xenophobic pot is Lee's own. His sadistic aggression towards racial others seems to be an act of hysterical compensation for the impotence in his sexual relationship. The aggression is also clearly directed at Allerton himself, fantasizing the power of absolute economic leverage and threatening to act out Lee's suffocating demands. Given the context, it is hard not to read Lee's relationship with Allerton through the lenses of contemporary political power struggles and vice versa. Allerton is made to occupy a number of positions, from fellow American to third-world "underdog" to superpower opponent. And yet—*Queer* is not a political allegory. Rather, it is *about* allegory, in the sense that Lee is possessed by the allegorical impulse, by "a fundamental process of encoding our speech," as Angus Fletcher called it (3), or, in what amounts to the same thing, by a coding of desire that he cannot control and that "speaks" Lee in terms of his imperial class identity.

Indeed, the imperial identity returns throughout Burroughs' writing of this period, and Lee's identification with doomed military emperors from Caesar to Napoleon in *Queer* anticipates "In Search of Yage." Here, he claims to "feel like a Roman exiled from Rome" (*YL* 31) and not just because for the last eighteen months of his time in Mexico City, while writing *Queer,* Burroughs had lived in an apartment in the *Colonia Roma.* Within "In Search of Yage," the significance of his identification appears most clearly in "Roosevelt after Inauguration," where the president appears "dressed in the purple robes of a Roman Emperor" (36). For Burroughs, the "imperial" presidency signifies power exercised to a point of extreme self-contradiction, presaging the fall of empires found in Spengler's *Decline of the West.* No wonder then that Roosevelt seeks "new frontiers" of human depravity by abusing his power over others, in order to "make the cocksuckers glad to mutate" (39). It is as if Burroughs had taken Charles Olson's famous remark that "the American has the Roman feeling about the world" (73) and turned it into a perverse imperative towards abjection.

Lee's masochism towards Allerton is clearly inseparable from his sadism towards racial others, as the racist imperial fantasy compensates for the feminizing implications of homosexual desire. The political lesson of *Queer* turns always on this point of contradiction, whereby the active subject and passive object of power are recto and verso of the same pre-scripted identity. Like Burroughs' manuscript, Lee is a text "sawed in half" by literally contra-dictory demands. Since the fantasmatic, the very blueprint for desire, "is incorporated into the subject from outside" (Silverman 354), the fantasmatic fascism of Lee's routines draws on those very "arbitrary boundaries set by others" that Burroughs had accused Ginsberg of accepting, in all their pathological cold war negativity. Even more alarmingly, Lee's investment in border controls betrays a dread of dissolution that approximates that of the Freikorps militia studied by Klaus Theweleit: like Lee, these protofascist killers also secure their bodily integrity by holding to boundaries given by "the disciplinary agencies of imperialist society" (1: 418). Since Lee identifies so fully with the pathology of cold war power, he invites us, precisely, to "psychoanalyze Caesar," so that we might take up Barbara Ehrenreich's invitation to update the historically specific focus of Theweleit's study and ask, "what do we make of the warrior caste that rules the United States and, in combination with its counterpart in the Soviet Union, rules the world?" (xii).

For Theweleit, the psychic key to the fascist imaginary is that the subject "can only be confirmed in violence against its other, this other that is also 'the female self within'"[20] (Benjamin and Rabinbach xix). In exaggerating to the limit a libidinal aggression against feminized foreign others and the foreign feminine inside, Lee's routines are indeed fascistic. His fantasies of merging with Allerton—"Wouldn't it be booful if we should juth run together into one gweat big blob" (*Q* 100)—project a profoundly narcissistic form of body fusion arising, as Theweleit says of the Freikorps soldier, "out of his own fear of splitting": "And he is split if and when the suppressed 'half' of himself, the worse 'half' to whom he is married, the 'lower half' of the people, the dominated on every level, demand independence" (2: 102). Hence, on the one hand, there is Lee's national security fantasy of "keeping the underdog under" (*Q* 106), and on the other, his erotic fantasy of bodily merger—"shlupping" (40)—that threatens the one thing that Allerton has to lose: "Independence" (72). Hence also not just Lee's identification with military emperors but his particular routine about ancient Rome, when "the Jews rose up" and did "stripteases with Roman intestines" (51).

The anti-Semitic dimension of *Queer* has always been overlooked,[21] but the Jew takes on a key symbolic as well as historical role in the articulation of Lee's position.[22] Each reference to Jews in *Queer* is loaded with a precise and resonant contradiction: from Carl Steinberg, whose "heel-click" and Aryan blond hair evoke the Nazi history of his birthplace, Munich (*Q* 1); to the doctor whose name Lee gets from a café in Quito where "German refugees hung out" (80, 84), who gives Lee a "long, human look" as he refuses to prescribe paregoric (85). The medical allusion prompts a sustained development of the Jew-disease nexus, since Lee enacts a fantasy revenge on the doctor for rejecting his "dysentery routine" (85): he becomes the "old humanist German doctor" forced to reintroduce parasitic malaria in Lee's fascistic routine of supporting Caesar by suppressing the racial "underdog" (106). Dysentery, of course, is an infection of the intestine, which brings us back to the uprising in Rome, imperial capital of the ancient world, as Washington is of the modern.

This is what makes *Queer* such a precise and potent political text: the way Lee gives the lie to what Amy Kaplan has described as the historical "disavowal of American imperialism" (12). Far from showing "American exceptionalism as inherently anti-imperialist," in opposition to the Old World or the totalitarian regimes of the Nazis and Soviets, *Queer* acts out, in the form of sick jokes, a fascist imagination that asserts an unpalatable historical continuity. Noting how some characteristics of fascism were perpetuated in cold war discourses of anticommunism, Suzanne Clark has argued their precise links to anti-Semitism as the very basis to a "ruthless national psyche" that is profoundly unstable: "As the metaphor of disease suggests, the imaginary war would be cast as the struggle of national subjects in crises of identity" (38, 24). And of course, this is exactly the point about *Queer:* that Lee's personal crisis of sexual identity insistently works through explicit political reference and increasingly aggressive politicized metaphors.[23] For *Queer* maps a pathology of the national *imaginary,* its unconscious logic, onto a precisely referenced national *history* to expose and structure a central contradiction: the way Lee acts out to the demonic limit a national foreign policy in the subject position of an imperial identity that would, domestically, place him too in the abject position of the demonized, colonized subject.

The inability to control his own flesh renders it for Lee both feminine and feminizing. It is therefore the "She-Jews" who revolt against Roman rule and eviscerate their oppressors (*Q* 51), so conflating the revolting feminized insides of the imperial body politic with the abject and alien innards of the imperial male subject. The enemy within and the enemy without are in such horribly close material correspondence that the question of whether the political allegorizes the psychic or vice versa simply does not arise: in Lee's routines, there is no easy allegorical separation of form from content, any more than theme is separable from effect. Now, we see why Lee follows his Jew jokes by cracking gags about Baked Alaska—"Hot on the outside and cold inside"—or roasted pig—"still alive and twitching inside" (52)—since each is a queer culinary dish that perverts the relation of form to content. From here, it is a short step to the "Transcendental Cuisine" routine in particular and *Naked Lunch* in general. For the function of the routine as a form of humorous and horrific excess is to make explicit our fantasmatic entrails, pulling them out to a point of nauseous visibility.

THE JACK-BOOTED UNCONSCIOUS

At the time of writing *Queer,* Burroughs claimed his routines were "not intended as inverted parody sketches" (*L* 126), a claim that plays on his own status as a sexual "invert" (98) but that also poses the question of intentionality itself. It is a troubling coincidence, therefore, that when Burroughs reflected on the "routine as art form" in a 1954 letter to Ginsberg, he should first note that "it is subject to shlup over into 'real' action" and then elide any distinction between the realization of personal and historical desire: "In a sense the whole Nazi movement was a great, humorless, evil *routine* on Hitler's part. Do you dig me? I am not sure I dig myself" (216). The question, directed at a Jew of course, suggests Burroughs' level of discomfort with his own sinister analogy; what are we to make of the admission of his uncertainty? What did he *intend?* Clearly, the key word is "humorless," to identify a routine as evil, since it already implies the "unmalicious, unstrained, *pure* laughter that accompanies a good routine" (245). The problem posed by *Queer* is that it seems an entirely false choice to say either that its routines are wildly funny or that they are frighteningly ugly. But precisely because the ethics and effects of humor are so uncertain, Burroughs' alignment of his personal fantasy form with the historical fascism of Nazism is highly suggestive in the context of *Queer.* Never mind his firsthand experience of Nazism in pre-*Anschluss* Austria and how this may underwrite his likening of antijunk hysteria to anti-Semitism in *Junkie.* Let us remember that Burroughs was writing the Jew jokes of *Queer* after the whole world's knowledge of the Holocaust. The second simile is not "made idly" either. It is the comic but profoundly sinister double of the first, the work of Burroughs' left hand, as we might say, is the routine form itself.

Queer acts out not only fantasies of fascism but the fascism of fantasy, of desire turned against itself. If its routines bear the stamp of what Nick Land calls "the jack-booted unconscious" (qtd. in Redding 202), it is in the sense that Lee bares the totalitarian desire of the cold war unconscious, a routine threatening to "shlup" the whole world. What makes Lee so powerful a vehicle for political critique is the fact that the Ugly American, defined so brutally in terms of class and colonial authority and exercising a fascistic elitism, racism, and will to power is a death-driven, near-schizophrenic homosexual. Or to put it another way, when this definitive "enemy within" cold war America (Sinfield 281)[24] exposes the enemy within himself, it turns out to define nothing less than the cold war American.

A BACKWAY OUT

The contradictions of Lee's national identity—abjected un-American at home, abjecting Ugly American abroad—are embodied everywhere throughout the text. They appear quite literally in Lee's physical appearance, since he has the look of a superimposed photograph in "simultaneous double exposure" (Q 18), and even in his alcohol consumption, since whether drinking tequila, martini, or rum coke, he always drinks *doubles* (4, 7, 36, 49, 64). But the text also offers a specific moment when we see all too clearly how, at the very core of his being, the contradictions of ideology coincide with those of desire. This is when Lee's sexual anxiety suddenly prompts "a killing hate for the stupid, ordinary, disapproving people who kept him from doing what he wanted to do," and he projects escape into an idyllic fantasy:

> Lee's plan involved a river. He lived on the river and ran things to please himself. He grew his own weed and poppies and cocaine, and he had a young native boy for an all-purpose servant. (97)

Lee's golden age idyll shows, in its last chilling phrases, just how deep down the colonial dream goes, since it bares the very ground of universal oppression—sexual, racial, economic—in the course of imagining its private transcendence: freedom fetishized at the expense of equality. The dream of personal freedom, of an ideal subjective autonomy, turns out to describe the very nightmare of dehumanizing mastery from which Lee seeks to awake. As Jeffrey Nealon argues in a related context, "subjective imperialism is not the solution but rather the problem of control itself" (62).

Burroughs' vision of individual freedom here is false precisely insofar as it imagines a flight from history and society. Indeed, Lee's fantasy can be seen as a deliberate rewriting of Burroughs' own contemporary plans for such an escape as retold by Kerouac. Writing from Mexico in June 1952, Kerouac's description of these plans emphasizes their specific historical context and their *communal* ambition:

> Bill Burroughs says he's going to found his farm on an Ecuadorian high jungle river not far from coast and invite Hipster Colony of anybody hip come down and found an island in the coming Soviet and Totalitarian invasions of the world . . . so we'll also have a backway out. (*Selected Letters 1940–1956* 363–64)

Substituting a utopian colony of fellow hipsters outside cold war history with a one-master, one-servant colonial state, Burroughs reminds us of Foucault's insistence that the strategic adversary is "not only historical fascism." Far from establishing what Timothy Murphy sees as the embryonic form of a revolutionary community—because Lee comes to "experience other subjectivities and perspectives" (*Wising Up* 85–86)—*Queer* implies that two is not company but the very seed of totalitarianism.

THE FAMILY JEWELS

Does Lee participate in a fascist construction of identity or does his display of entirely antagonistic desires subvert it? Slavoj Žižek has argued that a work is not totalitarian if it "publicly displays the underlying obscene phantasmatic support of 'totalitarianism' in all its inconsistency" (*Plague*

72). In which case, it is Lee's insistent identification with the imperial identity that serves as a strategy of subversion.

Referring to the shooting of his wife, in his introduction to *Queer* Burroughs speaks of the "dead hand" of possession and Control, an "evil" that Lee "tries to escape with frantic flights of fantasy: his routines, which set one's teeth on edge because of the ugly menace just behind or to one side of them" (*Q* xix). What is clear by now is that Burroughs gives all the key terms but in displaced form, since if Lee's routines set the teeth on edge, it is due to the ugly menace they make fully explicit. What makes them disturbing is their fantasmatic mise-en-scène of power, the fascistic intersubjective truth within their fiction, not a hidden fact belonging to Burroughs behind or to one side of them. The "dead hand" of possession is a precise phrase to describe what the novel actually shows in a much more politically significant way. This is the hold of a murderous fantasy over Lee, a hold that becomes untenable for the very reason that Lee *refuses to exempt himself* from it, refuses to claim any absolute distance from his national ideology, as if he could exit from it, or as if it were an inside that he could put simply outside. On the contrary, Lee actively embraces the very self that subjects him in its most extreme and contradictory forms, toting his gun—a "Colt Frontier," of course (63)—and shouting out *Americanus sum* in the name of a queer manifest destiny. It is therefore less that Lee inverts the ideological fantasy, turning it inside out or upside down, than that he shows the invertedness of it as it stands already.

Much of the unnerving force of *Queer* derives from the excessive, visceral embodiment of this basic contradiction in Lee himself as his desire not only seeks to escape authoritarian repressions but in fantasy form itself drives and enforces them. But this contradiction is also fully reversible. Lee points to this conclusion when describing his homosexuality as a "curse" that has been in his family "for generations" (*Q* 39). In its double sense, this curse is what *Queer* is all about: the curse that is generational, and the generational as itself a curse. When he declares, "The Lees have always been perverts," Lee thereby identifies his patrician class and national identity as a perverse curse cast upon him *and* identifies that identity as secretly fueled by a channeling of the very perverse desires they explicitly repress. As Dennis Foster well puts it, this evil lies precisely "in its failure to recognize that perversity is what sustains it" (*Sublime* 134). Burroughs inherited an aggressive, business frontier spirit from both sides of his family, of course: from grandfather Burroughs, who invented the adding machine, a man whose life was "a parable of entrepreneurial capitalism in the land of limitless opportunity" (Morgan 15); and above all from Uncle "Poison Ivy" Lee, a notorious onetime PR man to both Rockefeller and Hitler.[25] These inheritances return in various forms throughout *Queer,* so that Lee's routines mark the switch point between economics and erotics, capital and communication, dramatizing his familial identity as an ugly fantasy structure that writes his cultural and genetic script.

Over the years, Burroughs would gloss this infernal circuit, identified as the Ugly Spirit, in alternatively universal and historical terms. His account in *Ghost of Chance* (1991), for example, would attribute Lee's "killing hate" to "the Ugly Animal," man, who "has killed for the sheer ugliness of the thing. The Thing inside him. The Ugly Spirit who found a worthy vessel in Homo Sap" (48). Most often, he would relate it to the "competitive, acquisitive, success minded spirit that formulated American capitalism" (*Adding Machine* 129) and to "Rockefeller, that whole stratum of American acquisitive evil [. . .] The ugly American at his ugly worst" (qtd. in Ginsberg, "Exorcising" 30). According to Ginsberg, it was "a family thing" (30). The one gloss that the routines of *Queer* do not support is the one Burroughs offers in its introduction having to do with Joan's death. When critics try to generalize from this account, rather than from the text itself, the effect is a simple non sequitur, as when John Lardas concludes: "Burroughs felt that he had confronted the full onslaught of the 'Ugly Spirit' in Mexico, the same one that had invaded America" (182). It is hard to know what Lardas means here—a rise in the national wife-shooting rate?—but had he examined the precise anatomy of evil in the text itself, he would have been able to recognize the perverse power enacted by Lee's routines and its specifically historical and familial forms. Taking the tip from Burroughs' preface to *Junkie,* which begins by describing the House of Lee as a haunted house, we can say that this is Lee's curse: to be inhabited by the Ug-Lee Spirit.

Lee's routines would therefore lay bare an underlying fantasy that governs man in general and the Ugly American in particular but that only becomes visible under conditions of total crisis—a crisis fixed by addiction in *Junkie* and intensified by desire in *Queer.* In the first novel, far more than in the second, Lee passively suffers society's inability to mind its own business; but only in *Queer* does he seek to mind other people's business, seek to *change their mind.* This crucial and highly politicized shift in intersubjective relations coincides with Lee's removal from America and its cold war institutions of control; that is, precisely when he escapes the external machinery of modern power to confront its fantasmatic structure deep within himself. After the social reality of state institutions documented in *Junkie,* Burroughs in *Queer* projects the spectral, dream dimension of atavism and pathology. And this confrontation takes place in Mexico, America's "nearest alien culture" (Gunn 218), which to Burroughs appeared "sinister and gloomy and chaotic with the special chaos of a dream" (*L* 91). An ideal place, in other words, to confront the alien within: no wonder he recommended it to Ginsberg as better than "continued analysis" (89).

If Lee's routines take an antagonistic polyvocal form, it is, therefore, because through them he confronts all the foreign desires that populate the unconscious, the chaos of familiar voices that he has internalized and that won't mind their own business. As both foreign and familiar—and familiar in both senses—they mimic the "enigmatic signifiers" of desire, "the opaque messages transmitted by our parents" (A. Phillips 202) that, as Lacan put it in his 1955 seminar, "The Circuit," we not only can't escape but are "condemned to reproduce": "one can't stop the chain of discourse, and it is precisely my duty to transmit it in its aberrant form to someone else" (*Ego* 89). And if we see this cybernetic generational circuit as a "meme," Richard Dawkins's viral "unit of cultural transmission," then whether it compels destruction or desire, we recognize its inherent threat to notions of agency and autonomy. *Queer* therefore gives historical as well as aesthetic form to the same—strikingly Lacanian—question that Burroughs was still asking at the very end of his writing career: "How long does it take a man to learn that he does not, cannot want what he 'wants'?" (*WL* 257).

ORIENTAL OVERTONES

Lee's unbearable, masochistic dependence on the other, embodied in Allerton, brings into play his own fantasies of an enslaving imperial will, so that Lee dreams the cold war dream of total control. In tune with postwar laboratory and field research, consolidated in the CIA's secret drug-and-mind-control program MK-ULTRA, set up in 1953, Lee becomes obsessed with finding the supposed telepathic drug, *yagé.* Telling the botanist, Dr. Cotter, that "there might be a buck in the deal for both of them" (*Q* 116), Lee locates his quest within a larger imperial mission to exploit third-world resources and colonize new markets: telling Allerton *not* to say, "Dr. Cotter, I presume" (113), affirms an updating of the colonial project.[26] *Yagé* therefore models the ideal of new economic and military opportunities: what better commodity to control than one promising the power to control? By joining the cold war race for power, Lee thoroughly psychopathologizes the dream of control that crosses the cold war divide. He is well placed to offer a precise diagnosis:

"Automatic obedience, synthetic schizophrenia, mass-produced to order. That is the Russian dream, and America is not far behind. The bureaucrats of both countries want the same thing: Control. The superego, the controlling agency, gone cancerous and berserk." (91)

Speaking a common language of technological rationality and social engineering, both sides desire sameness and objectification—"the same thing"—and not only "give orders" but desire order.

Lee's speculations that the Russians and Americans are both following in the steps of the ancient Mayans by experimenting with tools of mass "thought control" (50) are historically alert. There really was a cold war *yagé* race, and the search for the Manchurian Candidate begins presciently here.[27] Condon's novel was set in the Korea and America of 1952 and tells a story of the early cold war that is particular to the historical moment Burroughs was writing. That is, panic news of brainwashing and biomedical warfare are specific to the Korean War. In both 1952 and 1953, there was widespread media coverage of the confessions given by captured US pilots about the American use of germ warfare, and one source dates this precisely as "beginning on February 21, 1952" (Farber, Harlow, and West 272)—just days before Burroughs began *Queer*. These POW confessions were read in turn as evidence of communist "brainwashing," a term first coined in 1950, or what an early historian of "mental seduction" and thought control, Joost Meerloo, termed "menticide." Indeed, Meerloo's study provides near contemporary evidence for how *Queer* plays out a fantasy of conversion narratives and mental enslavement drawn from contemporary cold war phobias while, like *The Manchurian Candidate,* it gives that fantasy of captive minds a specific pathological and racial inflection. On the one hand, "totalitarianism and psychosis" go together, because the schizophrenic's "weird fantasies become more real" than the real world and leave him "like a puppet on a string" (Meerloo 124, 118). On the other, totalitarianism is a "bug," a contagious "disease of inter-human relations" that flourishes in the "Oriental psyche," since the Eastern ideal is "that of oneness": "Man is part of the universe [...] He is not a separate, independent entity" (124, 108, 109). Meerloo's sweeping stereotypes fit *Queer* very well and also suggest a curiously overlooked dimension to the name of William Lee. That is, one half looks West, the other East. As Burroughs himself put it, he liked "the Oriental overtones" of his alter ego's last name[28] to offset the "Anglo-Saxon ring" of his first (*L* 127).

The obvious dimension to the name William Lee is Burroughs' use of the matronym. Lydenberg states the manifest significance of the choice: "In

Junkie Burroughs first identifies himself publicly as a writer by taking on his mother's family name" (*Word Cultures* 170). However, the choice and its significance is not all it seems. First, Burroughs used the name Dennison throughout the writing of "Junk," and second, the choice of Lee demonstrated the most extraordinary self-deception imaginable: since he decided to "drop Dennison because Ma read Kerouac's book" (*L* 111), then what *worse* way to hide his identity from her? Third, although he would spend two months hesitating over the choice of a first name, Burroughs settled on the name Lee in March 1952 specifically for his new novel, *Queer,* and it is no coincidence that references to domineering mothers appear insistently from its opening pages. Far from containing "virtually no female characters and no reflections on women's roles and functions" (Murphy, *Wising Up* 9), *Queer* begins by twice invoking the stereotypical figure of maternal power, the Jewish mother (*Q* 2), and makes numerous significant references to controlling wives (4, 7, 14, 20, 21). Inevitably, the repeated and aggressive association at the outset of the novel of mothers with homosexuality invokes "Freud-traducing clichés which claim that homosexuality is caused by 'momism'" (Caserio 194). The association also takes on a specific political significance in *Queer*'s insistently invoked historical context, a time when homosexuality was aligned with communism as immature forms of heterosexuality, each fixated on the mother and both endangering national security. When Joe Guidry's boy identifies himself as "an Oedipus," the point is that he learns this—in one of the text's many military references—from an *army* psychiatrist (*Q* 54).

Lee is never more vocal than when attacking the emasculating and controlling figure of the maternal woman: "What are you, henpecked?" he taunts Jim Cochan for saying, "I got to go" (*Q* 21). Of course, this aggression is to be understood as the sign of deep ambivalence, and sure enough, it echoes exactly Lee's own passing reference to being married: "I had to go home to my wife" (4). This echoing of the maternal figure's power to command takes on its full meaning, however, only when Lee makes a desperate bid to break up Allerton's relation with Mary by disrupting one of their innumerable games of chess. In silent "lover code," Mary telepathically gives Allerton the order that they "have to go now" (66). The game of chess not only figures the traditional ritual of heterosexual courtship but is a model matriarchy, ruled by a dictatorial queen. Once again, Burroughs anticipates *The Manchurian Candidate,* where the Queen of Diamonds is the control card, figuring a classic cold war conflation of brainwashing, momism, and communism. Lee's routines, like his name, manifest control as a pathology of the maternal superego.

Given all the various attacks on maternal figures, anyone would think that Lee had something to hide, which points to the one obvious omission in *Queer:* direct reference to Lee's own mother. This, we recall, is to be found in an anomalous scene late on in *Junkie:* Lee's incestuous scene of nostalgic reverie and the "magic of childhood," from which Burroughs struck Wordsworth's line "the glory and the freshness of a dream" (*J* 126). Partly because of that significant cut in the manuscript, and the academic pleasure of finding it, I used to wonder what this scene was doing in *Junkie,* unable to agree with Eric Mottram that it was no more than "spurious psychoanalysings" (30). I kept wondering—until the day another manuscript turned up. Despite my intuition, I was still taken aback: this whole scene had in fact been cut from *Queer*—indeed, it turns out to have formed the very beginning of Burroughs' original manuscript.[29] By transposing this material into *Junkie,* Burroughs made his story of homosexual desire start by literally *cutting off the mother's body.*

But research only confirms what should be obvious, since the mother returns like the repressed on every page of *Queer,* embodied in Lee's very name. Far from being silenced, the mother now does all the talking, dictates everything for Lee, because what remains of her is literally his mother tongue. What more potent inscription of maternal power, its fear and fascination for Burroughs—indeed, according to Alice Jardine, for the male American writer at large[30]—than this simultaneous erasure and self-identification?

By cutting Lee's dream of maternal union, Burroughs removed the explicit etiological basis to homosexuality, which would have formed the ground for a familiar developmental narrative. Or to shift from Freud to Lacan, Burroughs cut the "primal cut" itself, that is, the separation of the mother-child dyad, the original loss that is also the point of individuation and entry into the symbolic order. The "magic of childhood" is therefore represented by elegiac images, the "sharp nostalgia of train whistles, piano music down a city street, burning leaves" (*J* 126), melancholic motifs that recur, verbatim and as variations upon a theme, across the whole Burroughs oeuvre as traces of a lost world of the Real.

But this "magical moment" of presymbolic bliss remains fundamentally ambiguous—as traumatic as sublime, as horrific as wondrous—because of the eternal conflict between the drives towards merger and independence. And this is, far from coincidentally, at the core of Wordsworth's "Immortality" ode where, as Daniel Ross observes, the "return of the repressed 'intimation' of unity with the mother traumatizes the speaker" (633). Even so, when "piano music down a city street" returns in the voice of the Skip

Tracer, "like music down a windy street," what was magic is translated into pure menace.

Since it is the mother who seems to the child to demand symbiosis, we recognize Lee's relation to Allerton as a precise playing out of that relation but *in reverse*. That is, Lee plays the suffocating mother to Allerton's reluctant child,[31] forcing him to insist on independence but also, in the guise of the superegoic Skip Tracer, forcing him—and hence himself—to recognize the guilt of an unpayable symbolic debt. Lee's apparent desire to control Allerton aims ambivalently at its own defeat, because he has cast Allerton—whose similarity to Lee includes his "Oriental" features (*Q* 16)—in exactly the position that secretly, guiltily, he himself wants to occupy; that of being autonomous, indifferent to desire, indebted to nobody, self-possessed—free from the possessive mother. If, as René Girard put it, "the slave's admitted desire destroys that of the master and ensures his genuine indifference" (109), then the perverse logic of Lee's routines becomes clearer. They work not to achieve but to *short-circuit* mastery.

Of course, Burroughs also short-circuited something else by removing the original opening to *Queer*. If we recall that the scene of maternal reverie includes and motivates Lee's decision to quit addiction, then the key effect of the deletion is to render Lee's behavior strictly unaccountable. Paradoxically, it is because *Queer* lacks this causal scene, is incomplete from the start as well as to the end, that we are tempted to reconstruct and restore its psychological or physiological motivation. Or to look at it another way, the discovery of this manuscript secret must not be allowed to prove the truth of interpretations that are reductive and false to the text as published. Disregarding what Burroughs says in his introduction to the novel, Lee's character *should* appear "inexplicable." Only in this way, inviting multiple interpretations while foreclosing any final adequacy or accuracy, does the *Queer* text keep faith with its title. "The Westerner thinks there is some secret he can discover," says William Lee, dividing the epistemology of secrecy into cultural hemispheres that match the self-division encoded in his own name. "The East says, 'How the fuck should I know?'" (*Q* 82).

Finally, it should come as no surprise to find the most spectacular recurrence of Burroughs' key maternal motifs in "The Conspiracy," since here too Lee contemplates the "true" and "false" secret. Although it seems unlikely, these are in fact precisely linked texts, since each is about the ciphering of the same primal secrecy. What makes "The Conspiracy" so significant is the emphatically *political* dimension that Burroughs gives to the "fleeting, incalculable" nostalgia experience (*I* 108). The private psychoanalytic truth it discloses, which Oxenhandler claims would locate the genesis of Burroughs' creativity in the "moment of childish reveries" (146), becomes the ground of a war between mythic and world-historical forces of life (coded East) and death (coded West). As in *Queer*—and as I attempt in this reading of *Queer*—Burroughs integrates individual psychology with global politics in a unified structure of quest and conflict. And so, if nostalgia opens a portal to the dream dimension and "artistic faculty," then its elimination produces "an automaton, an interchangeable quantity in the political and economic equation" (*I* 109). In other words, if the secret of "The Conspiracy" is "the nature of power itself," as Mottram says (119), then it consists precisely in the conspiracy to eliminate the secret—or to incarcerate those "undesirables" who fail to "function as an interchangeable part in their anti-human Social Economic set-up." Burroughs concludes: "There *is* a secret, now in the hands of ignorant and evil men, a secret beside which the atomic bomb is a noisy toy" (*I* 111). The germ of this secret lies at the center of *Queer*.

LIKE DICTATION

A GAME FOR THINKING MACHINES

Although at first glance it appears anomalous and therefore inconsequential, the key passage in *Queer* precedes Lee's recognition that he "could not give up" his hopeless pursuit of Allerton:

> Lee was interested in the theory of games and the strategy of random behavior. As he had supposed, the theory of games does not apply to chess, since chess rules out the element of chance and approaches elimination of the unpredictable human factor. If the mechanism of chess were completely understood, the outcome could be predicted after any initial move. "A game for thinking machines," Lee thought. (63–64)

Chess is the game played continually by Allerton and Mary to the exclusion of Lee, but his interest here conflates, with exemplary economy, the intimately personal narrative action of *Queer* and the activities of a larger cultural history of technology and power. For Lee is tuning into an absolutely central understanding of the cold war years as the emergent age of cybernetic systems, an age defined famously by Norbert Wiener as that of "communication and control." And as Burroughs clearly knew, chess was a vital link between the key players in the early development of computer science, cognitive psychology, and information theory: Wiener, John von Neumann, Claude Shannon, and Alan Turing.

The particular figure of a "thinking machine" goes back at least to the 1830s, when visitors to Charles Babbage's London salon used the term to describe the wonders of his Difference Engine, the first (although never completed) modern computer. By the time Burroughs wrote *Queer*, this figure and its avatars—such as "mechanical brain"—had been popularized by recent and rapid developments in American computing technology, driven on by war and then cold war imperatives: from ENIAC (Electronic Numerical Integrator and Computer), one of the first valve-driven, digital machines, completed in 1946, to UDEC (Universal Digital Electronic Computer), installed at Wayne State University in 1953 by none other than the Burroughs Corporation. It's not clear how much of this history Burroughs knew, but he was certainly familiar with at least some of the primary texts, including von Neumann and Morgenstern's *Theory of Games and Economic Behavior*, from which he effectively quotes in his reference to chess.[32] For von Neumann, chess was important as a game of "perfect" information, the ultimate two-player, zero-sum match that fulfilled his grim theorem of "minimax" strategies, a deadlock scenario that is allegorized in the "Chess Master" routine that Lee delivers to Allerton: "When both contestants starved to death it was a stalemate" (*Q* 65). Burroughs' interpersonal scenario hints at the much larger political stakes already grasped by Norbert Wiener, whose *The* Human *Use of Human Beings* (1950) noted that the *Theory of Games* had "made a profound impression on the world, and not least in Washington" (206). In a remarkably bold attack on cold war ideology, Wiener warned of the "very sinister possibilities" implied by such theories and by computerized chess programs in particular, concluding:

> The steps between my original suggestion of the chess-playing machine, Mr Shannon's move to realize it in metal, the use of computing machines to plan the necessities of war, and the colossal state machine [. . .] are clear and terrifying. (203, 209)

If Wiener might be predicting the plot of *The Terminator* (1984) here—or indeed of *The Ticket That Exploded*: "The enemy uses a vast mechanical brain to dictate the use and rotation of weapons" (110)—the contemporary cultural response to computer and cybernetic developments is best represented by Kurt Vonnegut's debut novel, *Player Piano* (1952). Drawing on firsthand experience at a General Electric research lab in Schenectady, Vonnegut depicts future America as a fully cybernetic industrial society, governed by a single giant computer, EPICAC-XIV, clearly modeled on ENIAC, a world where the specter of permanent unemployment caused by automation has become reality. Vonnegut openly names the key names—von Neumann and Wiener—and features a game-playing computer called Checker Charley, while the very figure of a player piano derives from *The* Human *Use of Human Beings,* to which, as David Porush notes, his novel is a direct response (92). Clearly, *Player Piano* is a work of an entirely different kind than *Queer,* different in every possible way, and so raises the by now obvious question: how can Burroughs' single, passing reference to thinking machines and the theory of games support the weight of a cultural history based on cybernetics? Surely, when Porush compares the "earlier works" of Vonnegut and Burroughs and the way they both "create baldly didactic satires on the situation of technological civilization" (85), he is correct to take "early" Burroughs to mean *The Soft Machine* (whose title Porush borrows for his own book) and his other cut-up texts of the 1960s.

From a certain point of view, Burroughs in 1952 is evidently "behind" Vonnegut, who could fictionalize a detailed techtopia where the engineering of social control and industrial production represents the logical application of Wiener's admonitory thesis. However, that point of view assimilates Burroughs to a model that might fit the Vonnegut of *Player Piano* or the Thomas Pynchon of "Entropy" (1957) but that fails to reckon with his characteristic point of departure. Whereas "Vonnegut introduces the machine into his novel both as a metaphor of social functioning and as a relation" (Seed 13), Burroughs takes a minimal turn towards cybernetic theory and computer history but does not work *from* it. Paradoxically, this is why Burroughs is, if anything, "ahead" of Vonnegut. Formally, *Player Piano* is a highly conventional novel: not until 1969, with *Slaughterhouse 5,* would Vonnegut "resist the metaphor of cybernetics *internally*" with respect to language and form (Porush 86). When the president in *Player Piano* is described as a "gorgeous dummy," his speeches scripted by EPICAC, he becomes, as David Seed observes, "a mechanism channelling thoughts originating from invisible agencies" (13). This sounds like Lee in *Queer,* but of course Burroughs doesn't *describe* a mechanical dummy in *Queer* for the purposes of his theme; rather, Lee's ventriloquism is a material instance of the automaton that renders the internal form of the text as a cybernetic system. Burroughs works *from the inside out.* For this reason, we have to reverse the emphasis given by Richard Dellamora, who cites Lee's description of the cold war dream of control and reads it as a cybernetic exercise of power but ignores entirely the central fact of Lee's *own* fantasies of control (146–47): no reading of *Queer*'s political analysis can be made in isolation from its articulation of individual desire without missing the point of the text. For the same reason, we must reverse Porush's analysis of *The Soft Machine* as a war on the cybernetic control system of language: far from taking "his battle from the cosmic, intergalactic scale to that most intimate part of our selves" (100), *Queer* establishes that the intimate preceded the intergalactic.

Unsurprisingly then, *Queer*'s interest in chess is specifically grounded in the autobiographical events fictionalized in the narrative (Allerton's real-life original played chess to Burroughs' distraction) and bears an "internal" significance. Not, as Burroughs later generalized, "that chess is the point": "The point is they don't dig anything *special* about you. Or is it that they *do* dig it and don't want it? Fear and/or hate it?" (*L* 230). This is exactly how chess functions in *Queer:* as a two-player, rule-bound symbolic game of black and white, a cybernetically controlled universe of binary pairs that shuts out Lee and, by implication, disavows his "special" subjectivity, the excessive and unaccountable, out of place secret "Thing" that Burroughs terms the "unpredictable human factor." In this sense, the closed, binary world of the chess board corresponds to cold war policies of sexual and political containment, to the socioeconomic order that Burroughs called a "closed corporation of the desirables" that excluded "strangers" like Lee (*J* xiii), and to the epistemology of cybernetics, a synoptic science that abhorred the random and the irrational. Haunting these cold war games of control with ambiguous "powers of horror,"[33] Lee appears as a "curiously spectral" enigma (*Q* 13), an unlaid queer ghost in the machine.

Chess therefore measures *Queer*'s deliberate engagement with the *other* side of a machinic social structure. Moving away from the field of labor, technology, and production—never a major concern for Burroughs—chess develops the *reciprocal* and philosophical potential to the figure of a "thinking machine." For as Paul Edwards observes, the corollary to "cybernetic machines as thinking minds" was "human minds as cybernetic machines" (239). That is, the machine that thinks "for itself"—like a human—suggests the human that does *not* think "for itself"—like a machine. By 1954, the figure of the "mechanical brain" had prompted Burroughs to recognize the first "stirrings of autonomous activity," and of course *Naked Lunch* is thick with such allusions, including the chess-playing "electronic brain" that goes berserk (37). But significantly, this science fiction scenario didn't really interest him: "Give that one to [Ray] Bradbury" (*L* 202). Likewise in *Queer*, Burroughs originally described the malfunctioning television set in the Rathskeller bar as emitting "horrible guttural squawks *like a frankenstein monster*" (my emphasis), only to edit out the final phrase.[34] More interesting to Burroughs was the other figure, the idea of a determinist mechanism already on the inside, in the very depths of the human, one that all but eliminates the "unpredictable human factor" and so suggests a scenario even more apocalyptic than Vonnegut's total state machine.[35]

Burroughs' interest in determinism should be seen in the light of Alan Turing's prediction in 1950 that by the end of the century, "one will be able to speak of machines thinking without expecting to be contradicted"[36] (qtd. in Edwards 18). What is most relevant and resonant about Turing in the context of *Queer* is the so-called Turing Test for machine intelligence, which he also proposed in 1950, and Turing's own personal history. First, the British mathematician's expertise in cryptanalysis, the code-breaking art of counterintelligence, was the Allies' secret weapon of World War 2. And second, Turing's naive inability to keep secret his homosexual identity led to a public court case in March 1952, the very month Burroughs started work on *Queer.* Forced to accept chemical castration treatment and denied security clearance, Turing committed suicide two years later. As Andrew Hodges put it, Turing fell victim to a cold war double whammy because he combined "the two great unthinkables, cryptanalysis and homosexuality" (510).

What would have fascinated Burroughs about the Turing Test was that Turing invalidated his own theory of digital computers as universal machines "able to solve any problem that could be systematized" (Edwards 114). This is because he showed that it was the irrational and the errant—Sadie Plant's examples are "Slips of the tongue, innuendo, black and white lies" (212)—that distinguished humans from such early mathematical models of artificial intelligence machines. Nevertheless, in promising "a technical control of social processes to equal that achieved in mechanical and electronic systems" (Edwards 114), Turing's universal machine, together with Wiener's cybernetics and Shannon's information theory, formed the historical context for Burroughs' recognition that the atomic bomb was just a noisy toy in comparison. While working on "The Conspiracy" in early 1955 and seeing in it the "theme" of what became *Naked Lunch,* Burroughs feared the invention of an "anti-dream drug" by means of which human "behavior can be controlled and predicted by the scientific methods that have proved so useful in the physical sciences. In short, this drug eliminates the disturbing factor of spontaneous, unpredictable life from the human equation" (*L* 268). The precise echo of *Queer* is unmistakable and is highly revealing about the way in which Burroughs worked: from the germ of an idea in *Queer,* he planned an entire narrative structure based on an explicitly theorized model—and then, at the point where Vonnegut might have gone on to write a three-hundred-page novel, Burroughs abandoned it and wrote *Naked Lunch* instead.

Here again, we see the significance of how Burroughs wrote *Queer*. His point of departure was the relationship between its central characters, which "seems to be the central theme" (*L* 105), while the "ending just hasn't occurred yet" (117), so that his writing stayed quite literally open to the "unpredictable human factor," in the sense that his key phrase defines the human as *that which cannot be said in advance*. The war between contingency and control would stay at the heart of all Burroughs' formal experiments as well as thematic concerns, because his interest in the man-machine interface, glimpsed in *Queer,* confronted a basic fear: the fear that in a world where the stochastic is eliminated, the human is no more than the automaton of von Neumann's dreams—the possibility, in short, that he is only a soft machine, coded and wired so perfectly he doesn't realize that there is no one inside.[37] As Sadie Plant observes of the cyborg: "What makes this figure so tragic is the extent to which he has been programmed to believe in his own autonomy" (99).

At this point, we begin to recognize the precise *historical* relevance of Lacan, who in the early 1950s turned to the field of cybernetics and computing in search of "models for deciphering unconscious mechanisms" (Fink 5). He asked such questions as "Why are we so astonished by these machines?"and "Why has the paradoxical expression *thinking-machine* been created?" (*Ego* 119); and in a comment that echoes Wiener and is so resonant for Burroughs, he spoke of "that most modern of machines, far more dangerous for man than the atom bomb, the adding machine" (88). The answer to the first question, and by extension his others, is "Because cybernetics also stems from a reaction of astonishment at rediscovering that this human language works almost by itself, seemingly to outwit us" (119). Or putting it another way: "The most complicated machines are made only with words" (47).

Now, it becomes only too apparent what lies behind Lee's fantasy of controlling and objectifying Allerton through *yagé,* the very drug that also promises the wordless contact of telepathy:

> "Think of it: thought control. Take anyone apart and rebuild to your taste. Anything about somebody bugs you, you say, 'Yage! I want that routine took clear out of his mind.' I could think of a few changes I might make in you, doll [. . .] you do have those irritating little peculiarities. I mean, you won't do exactly what I want you to do all the time." (*Q* 89)

In Lee's reverie of reconstructing the other towards conditions of absolute predictability, the affectionate "doll" is synonymous with automaton, the "irritating little peculiarities" with "the unpredictable human factor," and his routine a fantasy in miniature of the rending and reassembly of human minds as mechanical brains to suit the specifications of power. But what lies behind Lee's recycling of the totalitarian and technological fantasies of cybernetic power if not the ambivalent specter of his *own* absolute lack of rational autonomy?

Lee's fantasy of fulfilling the brain-as-computer metaphor imperils the very sublime, irrational, and ineffable excess that makes him "special," that which constitutes the "Real of consciousness," in Dennis Foster's terms; "that part of mind and brain that, because the brain is *not* actually a computer, cannot be fully, finally represented" (*Sublime* 17). The real fantasy therefore is not control of the other but *self-control* because, as Žižek insists, "freedom means not only that I am not fully determined by my surroundings but also that I am not fully determined by *myself*" (*Indivisible* 71). The fundamental ambiguity then rests on the fact that it is Lee himself who refuses to do exactly what he wants. When he gives Allerton as an example of "automatic obedience" the command "Stick out your tongue" (*Q* 91), the point is that this is the very imperative driving Lee's routines. These have become interminable soliloquies, barely sustained by the ever more minimal responses of Allerton. Their relationship recalls a scenario given by Roland Barthes in *A Lover's Discourse* where, as the other is stifled and "disfigured by his persistent silence," so too is the soliloquist deformed, made into "a monster: one huge tongue" (165, 166).

GET DIRTY

We come at last to the queerest scene of the novel, which follows directly after Lee's comments on chess and information theory. Interrupting one of Allerton's games of chess with Mary, Lee launches into a routine dramatizing a number of scenarios, each of which ends in stalemate or death. Neither as verbal foreplay, whose goal is contact between bodies, nor as an aesthetic performance, whose goal is audience attention, does Lee succeed. On the contrary, his routine proves irresistibly fascinating not to the listener but to the speaker, so that far from captivating Allerton, it is Lee who is captured in an absolute inversion of ends and means. This is the defining moment in *Queer:*

> Lee paused. The routine was coming to him like dictation. He did not know what he was going to say next, but he suspected the monologue was about to get dirty [. . .] Mary and Allerton left. Lee was alone in the bar. The monologue continued. (66)

How are we meant to understand the undisguised autonomy of the routine that follows, which Burroughs at the time named the "Slave Trader" (*L* 126)? The answer has to be: in relation to its content—or to be more precise, in the relation between what is enunciated and the process of the enunciation. As the name of the routine suggests, the content stages a thoroughly Hegelian drama of trading places: in a suitably colonial setting—which seems to be German West Africa—Lee narrates his involvement in a series of master-slave relations in which the roles are always reversed. Now, all Lee's previous routines to Allerton had been clearly *situated* intersubjectively: that is, the narrations figured allegorically the narrative situation of their own telling, in all its ambivalence. This is still the case at the outset of the Chess Master routine. But in the case of the Slave Trader, a routine that consists largely of dialogue but is told to no audience, a *monologue,* the only intersubjective relation is on the level of the enunciated, *inside* the routine. What has changed is that the appearance of an *active* form of ventriloquism, a power to speak through other voices, has disappeared to reveal ventriloquism in its *passive* form, the powerlessness of being spoken through by other voices, an experience of possession (Connor, *Dumbstruck* 14). In a structuralist reversal of the routine's core fascistic fantasy, the Great Dictator is himself forced to take it "like dictation."

The question then is this: if Lee is scripted here, does he only appear to speak elsewhere, as the dummy only appears to talk? If so, then Lee, a fascist in fantasy, experiences Burroughs' version of the fascism of language, understood in Barthes's dictum, not as a form of inhibiting censorship, not as the prohibition to speak, but rather as the obligation to speak, where speech is always on alien and alienating terms and always an intermingling of "servility and power"[38] (*Barthes Reader* 461). Does *Queer* demonstrate that "power is the parasite of a trans-social organism" inscribed, as Barthes says, in the "necessary expression of language" (460)? Steven Shaviro has argued persuasively that "it's always some *particular* parasite, with its own interests and perspective, that's issuing the orders and collecting the profits" ("Two Lessons" 43; my emphasis). His case illuminates the common ground between two of *Queer*'s most insistent preoccupations—politically, with foreign economic exploitation, and sexually, with images of intestinal activity—that punningly reveals the colonist to be himself colonized, infected in his very guts. Lee's fantasy of colonial domination, of possessing the other as an object, coincides with his own domination, his own possession by the colonial other inside. Lee's contradictory national identity—abjected un-American, abjecting ugly American—is itself subject to an even more profound dialectical subversion: he may speak the language of empire, but what speaks him is the empire of language.

In the absence of the other, of a receiver or destination for the routine, Lee remains a speaker only in the technical sense of a piece of amplifying sound equipment, a transmitter of received messages. As the interpersonal dimension vanishes, Allerton stands revealed as no more than a prop, a pretext for what appears essentially as a sadomasochistic encounter between Lee and an intrapsychic other: not the social other but the Symbolic Other. This Burroughs would name the "Other Half," and in *The Ticket That Exploded* he would explicitly figure the relationship of word to host as a universal colonization: the viral forces of control "infected the human hosts very much in the same way that the early colonizers infected so-called primitive populations" (59). Or even more explicitly still: "The other half is simply an internalization of the oppressive colonizer."[39] What *Queer* demonstrates is the point of exposure of an embodied parasitology: the Other Half as an *organism*. That this was understood by Burroughs from the outset is in fact clear from the very titles of his first two novels, not as they came to be published—*Junkie* and *Queer*—but as he intended: *Junk* and *Queer*. As a sequel to *Junk,* what *Queer* denotes is not an identity but an entity, precisely a parasite as distinct from its human host.

CLAUSE 6(X)

One reason why the Slave Trader routine is so significant, both within *Queer* and beyond it, is that here we can see how the figure of ventriloquism, so recurrent in Burroughs' writing, already points towards the related but far more theoretically potent figure of the virus. How do we reach this point? All along, my case has been that Lee's routines enact a process of making explicit, a process of giving voice that enables Lee to identify the agency and etiology of his own desires, his own speech. As Steven Connor says of ventriloquial possession in its demonic form, so too the routine "gives disease not only a name, but also a tongue, making it possible thereby to converse with the disease itself" (*Dumbstruck* 114). As a theatrical form, the routine is committed to achieving an excessive vocal presence in proportion to the frustrating invisibility of power. The routine exposes the viral to the extent that, as it turns autonomous, its excess of any consciously intended meaning is understood symptomatically, as a sign of the otherwise hidden or naturalized presence of a disease that invisibly dictates Lee's speech and determines his desire. In this sense, what David Punday says about *Cities of the Red Night* applies also to *Queer*: "Burroughs' description of language and power as a 'virus' [. . .] implies a hidden, logically replicating structure that gives rise to everyday relations" (38). The generational determinism encoded in Lee's own last name is genetic—"Genes, the presence of our ancestors in us" (Godbout and Caillé 207)—so can it really be coincidence that his destiny is embodied in the first name of his antagonist—Eugene; or "you gene"?[40]

This pun is fully activated in the epilogue to *Queer,* with its allusions to "degenerative illness" and "recessive genes" (*Q* 123), and most emphatically in Lee's dream of Friendly Finance. It is here that Lee draws Allerton's attention to the sadomasochistic "contract" that binds them together—"Haven't you forgotten something, Gene?"—and in particular to "Clause 6(x) which can only be deciphered with an electron microscope and a virus filter" (132). Lee's point is that, no matter how small, the small print in our historical and biological "contracts" cannot be forgotten. It is a properly viral model of determining encryption since, as theorized explicitly in *The Ticket That Exploded,* "like all virus the past prerecords your 'future'" (188). This is also what Lacan meant by the *letter* as a permanent chain of signifiers, according to Fink: "The unconscious *cannot* forget, composed of 'letters' working, as they do, in an autonomous, automatic way; it preserves in the present what has affected it in the past" (20). Equally, since the relation of Lee to Allerton is also the exteriorization of an *internal* relation, the point is not only how iniquitous is Lee's pursuit of the other for the other but for Lee himself: Allerton has come to embody the identity of Lee insofar as he wants out, while the Skip Tracer visualizes his other half, the obscene power within him that refuses to let him go. The crucial clause in their contract, which identifies the "account" that must be settled, is therefore ciphered materially in its alphanumeric designation: what is "6(x)" if not "sex"?

To measure its impact on the received version of Burroughs' literary history, it is essential to recognize the significance of the emergence of the viral in *Queer.* This is grasped by observing how those Burroughs critics who have best interpreted the virus have done so in terms of its genealogy. What David Ingram, Kendra Langeteig, and Douglas Kahn have in common is the assumption that Burroughs' development of the virus was based on theoretical models—chiefly, works by Korzybski, Reich, and Hubbard—and on his engagement with modern technologies of mass communication. What each overlooks as a result is the *untheorized, material role* that the communication technology of writing itself played in this development—as the following chapters will demonstrate. Here, it is enough to note the negative effects of this shared assumption. In Ingram's case, theory is simply abstracted from Burroughs' texts without sufficient regard for chronology or context. In Langeteig, the toxicity of the viral word is grounded in *Naked Lunch* and equated with junk, ignoring *Queer* entirely, even though her analysis explores precisely the point of intersection between communication and homosexuality: if the "body is consistently portrayed as a 'soft machine' for receiving and transmitting toxic communications" (147), then surely *Queer* is where this starts.

In the case of Kahn, his identification of two distinct historical phases of the virus depends on a theoretical shift, dated 1959, that skews his otherwise excellent analysis when it comes to *Queer*. On the one hand, Kahn disregards the pressing cold war context and so overlooks the specific political stakes to the pathological figure, and on the other hand, he insists on a taxonomic division where, it seems to me, none exists: if the "usurper virus"—that can "render another entity nonexistent by ingestion into one body"—is present in *Queer,* so too, I would argue, is "the mutated virus [that] existed parasitically as another body inside the organism, primarily in the form of Burroughs' well-known figure of the Other Half undetectably controlling a person's thoughts, words, and deeds" (*Noise* 296, 298). Surely Lee's routines give voice to the "irrepressible speech of the Dianetic demon" well in advance of Burroughs' reading Hubbard's *Dianetics*? Surely *Queer* demonstrates *both* the protoplasmic "schlupping" of desiring bodies *and* the language-based model of inscription deployed at the "microbial scale" that Kahn calls "pathography"?

In fact, there is incontrovertible evidence that Burroughs himself recognized in *Queer* the origin and model of this thesis. In her study of his tape experiments, Lydenberg notes his description of the *word virus*

> as a conveyor of predetermined aspects of human life [. . .] an invisible writing that imposes absolute control. He makes both this metaphor and the process it represents concrete and literal in *The Ticket That Exploded,* where the narrator is trapped in an uncomfortable fusion with the anonymous parasitic "other rider." ("Sound Identity" 412, 413)

Her analysis is exactly right; what must be added to it is the absolutely crucial fact that this "concrete and literal" representation of language as "an uncontrollably proliferating infection" is material Burroughs added for the revised *Ticket* by going back to *Queer*. For the passage Lydenberg cites is a deliberate reprise of Lee's relationship with Allerton, featuring all the essential details: the South American location, his "CIA voice," and a "limited intelligence" defined by his chess playing, which Lee subjects to an exemplary cut-up queering "by making completely random moves" (*Ticket*

2). Lydenberg's case needs to be understood in reverse order, because the concrete and the literal preceded the metaphor and produced the theory. In short: *Queer* is the point of viral origin.

BEING WRITTEN

Finally, to gauge its importance, the Slave Trader requires an entirely different kind of approach; an *ethical* reading of Lee's routines. Consider a letter that Burroughs wrote in May 1951, when he catches himself in the act of excusing his behavior during an earlier attempted seduction: "That is one thing I can't abide about psychoanalysts—always the alibi. ~~After all, how could anyone expect me to act any way but crummy, me having all these traumas and complexes?~~" (*L* 85). Since an alibi is the claim to have been *elsewhere* at the time, Burroughs is effectively insisting on the need to take responsibility for one's crimes, even when they appear to be determined at an unconscious level or by traumatic external events. In the context of *Queer,* the point is that Lee *identifies* with his name, with the traumatizing legacy of familial and national identity it embodies, to the very limit. He is as far removed as possible from Bill Gains, the pusher in *Junkie* who smiles his malicious smile when declaring himself "Just a victim of circumstances" (*J* 55). Lee neither claims an alibi nor a false autonomy: he knows that he is a ventriloquist's dummy, a puppet on a string of words, but also that there is no fully external puppet master; hence, his transformation into the phantomatic Skip Tracer, a pure embodiment of the "anti-human Social and Economic set-up" in all its perversity. Lee's transformation recalls the reversal that closes those peculiarly fascinating narratives where the hero, usually a detective, moves into a science fiction or supernatural dimension only to discover that he is *himself* the inhuman alien: the best example being Alan Parker's *Angel Heart* (1987). The twist in Parker's film is particularly resonant, since the hero, Harry Angel, has forgotten to settle his contract with Louis Cyphre—Lucifer, the fallen angel, who doesn't "like missing accounts"—while the encryption of destiny—encryption *as* destiny—is right there all along in their very names.

The ethical dimension manifests itself in *Queer* in two, potentially contrary ways suggested by the Skip Tracer. First, there is the way Lee embraces rather than disavows his destiny. In Lacanian terms, he engages in a process of subjectivization, the "process of making 'one's own' something that was formerly alien," as Bruce Fink puts it:

> One assumes responsibility for the Other's desire, that foreign power that brought one into being. One takes that causal alterity upon oneself, subjectifying what had previously been experienced as an

external, extraneous cause, a foreign roll of the dice at the beginning of one's universe: destiny. (xii–xiii)

The result is what Freud meant by his famous formula *Wo es war, soll Ich werden* ("Where It was, there must I be"): "where the Other pulls the strings (acting as my cause), I must come into being as my own cause."

One value of this reading is to help us see a vital connection between the Slave Trader routine and the dream of the Skip Tracer. In the former, speech has lost both its human destination and point of origin, in the literal absence of any audience and the effective absence of Lee as a speaking subject. At the point where Lee's monologue comes like dictation, the first person voice is displaced by and into that of a third person, the voice of an other. This shift takes place in reverse in the scene of the Skip Tracer. While the entire epilogue shifts from third to first person narration, it switches back again at the point where Lee mutates, within his "dream," from a representative of Friendly Finance into the identity of the Skip Tracer. The true significance of this switch point only becomes fully clear, however, if we restore to this moment the crucial aside cut from the original manuscript: "Shift of tempo. This was written three days later while I was drinking a cupa tea inna quick lunch. *Like taking dictation. I have less and less control over what I write*" (my emphasis).[41] Lee has fulfilled the meaning of Freud's "Where It was, there must I be," which does not mean that the ego displaces the id but that the subject achieves "*identification with the symptom*" (Žižek, *Sublime Object* 75), or in Lacan's gloss, "*Here, in the field of the dream, you are at home*" (*Four Fundamental* 44).

The second ethical aspect follows from the first and is again manifest in the Slave Trader and the Skip Tracer scenes. What is the most startling feature of both the real and the dream scenarios? Simply, that in both situations *Allerton disappears*. If Lee's transformation into a psychic repo man is meant as an answer to the failure of his routines, then the effect in each case is the same: they don't work. He thereby avoids what Steven Shaviro calls "the fascistic, imperative nature of language" that operates whenever and however we react to it ("Two Lessons" 43). In other words, the true ethical dimension to Lee's routines rests on the way in which they work insofar as they *fail* to work. Allerton's failure to be fascinated by them represents the only form of success Lee can achieve, because what this failure preserves is the quality of "independence" whose violation the routines thematize and threaten to communicate. By allowing his fantasies of possessing the other to run their course to a limit point of revolting, naked excess, Lee ensures not so much his interpersonal failure as his failure to coincide fully with the other agency, that of the routine itself. The ethical dimension resides in the short circuit.

What is being played out in *Queer* is not communication *of* a disease—homosexual desire—but *as* a disease. The will to communicate, the human "yen to control, coerce, violate, annihilate [. . .] anybody else's physical or psychical person" that Burroughs called "Pure Evil" (*L* 333, 334), is sabotaged through feedback, defined as "a self-feeding system seeking its own catastrophe" (Weiss, *Phantasmic* 6). In effect, Lee says: "I can't help myself. But if I am compelled to want to possess you, I can at least make obscenely explicit this drive to possession that possesses me. My real message, my true self, emerges in and as this short circuit of the apparent message, the false self, and it is to this that you must reply, by *not replying* . . ." Lee therefore takes upon himself masochistically an abject failure to dictate to Allerton desires that are sadistically dictated to him—and as the ground of Burroughs' textual politics, this short-circuiting of control is exemplary. The point is that Lee's routines fail to fascinate, and Allerton disappears, leaving behind nothing but words on the page.

It now becomes materially apparent why this ethical conclusion must not be confused with the standard critical equation, seemingly prompted by Burroughs himself, with the figure of the Ancient Mariner. There is no "theoretical dilemma" here or a "paradox" in which Burroughs finds himself caught, because the causal sequence here is the very *inverse* of that assumed by John Lardas and by Ron Loewinsohn. It is not the effort to liberate others that causes Burroughs to find himself in a logical trap but the failed attempt to trap others that forces him to see liberation as the short circuit of this economy of fascination and power.

Needless to say, *Queer* still leaves us with an ethical paradox. This is a version of Anthony Hilfer's reading of *Naked Lunch* as the injunction to avoid the "fascinating experience" it presents (258). For paradoxically, there is in this very obscene, sadomasochistic excess of fantasy meant to repel, both a hilarious enjoyment and a horrible attraction, a perverse appeal that realizes some secret of our own desire, one that makes us aware that, despite every possible warning, we continue to return . . . Since Burroughs acts out a sadomasochistic relation with himself, it is unsurprising that his work holds a sadomasochistic attraction-repulsion for his readers. And so, if one ethical response is, like Allerton's, to walk away, to turn a deaf ear, another is to identify with Burroughs and to keep on reading as a reminder of our very inability to learn this lesson, to persist in our fascination until or unless we reach that point where, as the imperial president puts it, we are *glad to mutate.*

Finally, what has remained unsaid in this reading is the simplest but most troubling observation of all concerning Allerton's disappearance. When he walks out of the bar and fades away in the dream, the internal listener vanishes, and the coercive economy of communication appears to stop, to give way to autonomy. But in his absence, both monologue and dream are transformed into another means to deliver Lee from the burden of his message and to disarm, seduce, and fascinate the other—namely, *writing*. This is why, when Burroughs claims that "While it was I who wrote *Junky,* I feel that I was being written in *Queer*" (*Q* xiv), this shift amounts to more than a "critique of subjectivity," as Timothy Murphy sees it (*Wising Up* 58). Murphy's case overlooks the inconsistency in Burroughs' own conclusion: "So the death of Joan brought me in contact with the invader, the Ugly Spirit, and maneuvered me into a lifelong struggle, in which I have had no choice except to write my way out" (*Q* xxii). Surely, the point is the direct relation between Burroughs' experience of "being written" and of his possession by the Ugly Spirit. Say then that writing was the way out because it was also the *way in,* and that it is not really a question of Burroughs' writing his way out but of writing *from out of* that experience. That's destiny.

Thus, Lacan's cybernetic circuit, which condemns Lee to transmit the discourse transmitted to him "in its aberrant form to someone else" like a chain letter,[42] is not broken at all. That someone else, who is not the letter's "literal addressee, nor even whoever possesses it, but whoever is possessed by it" (B. Johnson 144), is now *the reader*. And so, as Lacan says, a letter always does reach its destination.

4

Queer Letters and *Yage Letters*

The demons, especially if they are demons of language (and what else could they be?) are fought by language.

—Roland Barthes, *A Lover's Discourse*

BLACK MAGIC LETTERS

THE TURNING POINT

But how exactly does the letter—the actual, material letter in history, not in Lacanian theory—arrive at its *Queer* destination? The key scene is when Lee's Slave Trader routine takes on a life of its own, because when Allerton walks out at this point, a reader necessarily steps in. The material support for this reading is given by Burroughs at the time of writing, as he told Ginsberg in May 1952:

> The Oil-Man and Slave Trader routines are not intended as inverted parody sketches à la Perelman, but as a *means* to make contact with Allerton and to interest him. The Slave Trader routine came to me like dictated. It was the turning point where my partial success was assured. If I had not achieved the reckless gaiety that charges this fantasy, Marker would have refused to go with me to S.A. The point is these fantasies are vital part of the whole set-up. (*L* 126)

Clearly, in the narrative economy of the published text, the Slave Trader routine does *not* make things happen in this way, can *not* make contact with

Allerton, because Allerton is not there. The clue to this essential contradiction in function lies in the confusion in Burroughs' own letter, as he slips from referring first to the fictional character and then to the "real" Eugene Allerton, Lewis Marker.

Logically enough, critics have assumed that for the routines of *Queer,* Burroughs more or less transcribed oral material spoken to Marker in 1951. However, the line that links Burroughs' slippage from Allerton to Marker in his letter—"The Slave Trader routine came to me like dictated"—suggests a different understanding. If this experience bridges the fictional and real worlds represented by Allerton and Marker, then the "turning point" is the turning of speech into writing represented by this act of dictation. To take dictation is preeminently a matter of *writing,* never of speech, and it is in these terms that we can reread the situation of the routine in *Queer.*

The subtlety of this maneuvering, and the understanding that follows from it, is bound to be obscure so long as we assume that, however minimally, the narrative context continues at this point to frame the Slave Trader routine naturalistically. But the routine's very length goes far beyond the bounds of all naturalistic credibility. Perversely, it is only because the monologue continues without its audience that we are inclined to read the routine as a case of bizarre behavior: if Allerton were present, its absolute implausibility as speech in the presence of a listener would be self-evident. What the polyphonic performance suggests is a *written* attempt to re-create the vocal vitality of routines spoken to a listener—an attempt that exceeds even that excessive economy.[1] In narrative context, we read the routine as speech; we might better hear it as writing. Once recognized, this paradoxical translation of Lee's speech into writing clarifies why his routines, while ostensibly intended to hold Allerton's attention, provoke such minimal responses. In a sense, Lee is always alone, whether in the Ship Ahoy, Bar Cuba, Pat's Steakhouse, Quito, Manta, or Guayaquil, because the routines he tells Allerton function less within the immediately reciprocal realm of the oral than within the inherently more distanced economy of the *epistolary.*

In short, Allerton's disappearance marks the point where Burroughs' material can no longer be seen to represent the written record of a past relationship with a listener conducted through spoken routines but can be seen as part of a present relationship with a reader conducted through routines written in letters. Illogically then, the written routines are not copies but *the originals.*

At this point, what becomes clear is the hidden common denominator to all the biography-based approaches to *Queer;* whether focused on Burroughs' drug addiction, the death of his wife, or his sexual relationship with Marker, the common denominator to these readings is that in them the year 1952 has simply *disappeared*, and with it, the entire time Burroughs actually wrote the novel. Since this process is amply documented in his published letters of this period, for nearly a decade it has been a truly open secret. This is not a matter of individual critics overlooking some local biographical data, however, because in their failure to question the genetic history of *Queer*, they have succumbed to a blind spot that has far-reaching consequences. Encouraged by Burroughs' introduction to *Queer*, which refers only to Allerton and to 1951 and never to Marker and 1952, this blind spot typifies a recurrent critical paradox. Aside from the material difficulty of such an investigation, why is it that no critic has tried to give proper weight to an accurate chronology of Burroughs' writing? Principally, because of a readiness *either* to accept at face value *or* to dismiss the received account. Skepticism has proved no better than gullibility, because it hits the same blind spot by an opposed route, failing to reckon with the effect of this very disbelief, which is once again to foreclose the need for investigation.

That no critic has attempted this task testifies not only to the effects of Burroughs' introduction but to a persistent bias in the way in which criticism reads a writer's letters. The longstanding failure to take up Ginsberg's invitation to investigate the possibility of their importance shows just how little interest or relevance genetic criticism in general and epistolary criticism in particular have held for Burroughs' critics. Then again, this is not entirely surprising, since both these critical traditions have tended to deal with writers belonging to much earlier literary periods. If the "gospel of genetic criticism" is "to understand a work by its history and not just by its final outcome," as Daniel Ferrer notes (224), then this approach itself now strikes us as, well, *historical*. Equally, while epistolary fiction has undergone a "renaissance in the postmodernist era" (Altman 211), this rebirth in fact followed an assumption about its *death* as a meaningful practice for fiction writers during the postwar period.[2] When it comes to Burroughs, there simply hasn't been an established critical context for recognizing the genetic—as distinct from the biographical—importance of letter writing.

For a historical approach to *Queer* to work productively, it must historicize the material circumstances of the *writing*, not just the written. On this basis, we can say that *Queer* is marked by what Janet Altman, in her groundbreaking study of the epistolary genre, calls "epistolarity"; that is, "the use of the letter's formal properties to create meaning" (4). Adapting her term for *Queer*, we can begin to recognize how certain formal features dictate specific thematic effects. More than this, by approaching the epistolary as an *economy* and as a *technology* of writing, giving structure and substance to Burroughs' textual politics of desire and control, we can now grasp the true stakes for reading *Queer* in particular and Burroughs in general. As a practice of writing, the letter has a unique proximity to the written product published as fiction, so that what we are looking at is neither allegory nor speculative recourse to extratextual biography but an absolutely *material correspondence* within the activity of writing. *Queer's* secret debt to the letter in turn underwrites the special place it merits in the Burroughs oeuvre.

This is not to say that the economic relation between *Queer's* genetic history and its formal and thematic features can in every case be settled definitively. Indeed, if the study of manuscripts is necessary "because the final text *does not contain* the whole of its genesis," as Ferrer claims (234), then in the case of *letters,* the uncertain status of these marginal texts is complicated still further by the unique dynamic of the epistolary relation. That is to say, because Burroughs' creative processes and published texts have a secret relation to writing first addressed to the gaze of a specific reader, we not only have to study the traces of the work of writing in progress but a writing in which an other, a textually *absent other,* plays a central role. Since this other represents "an unavoidable relay in its genesis" (Kaufmann, "Valéry's Garbage" 78), then to the already difficult intersubjective economy produced by the Burroughs text, we have also to reckon with that other intersubjective economy that mediated its production.

Nevertheless, the rapid and radical transformation of Burroughs' writing from *Junkie* to *Queer* does make it perhaps uniquely possible to isolate the genetic factor as the hitherto missing determinant. The letter provides therefore a material ground for the otherwise mysterious emergence in *Queer* of that nexus of desire, technology, language, and power so central to the textual politics of *Naked Lunch* and to the cut-up project that was to follow. And so, if we have to reverse the chronology in Robin Lydenberg's claim that Burroughs made his word-virus metaphor "concrete and literal" in *The Ticket That Exploded* ("Sound Identity" 423), this is not just to restore a secret narrative debt to *Queer;* we also need to see the even more secret methodological debt of the cut-up text to that most concrete and literal of textual forms that is the letter.

TO A. L. M.

By bringing together the activities of Burroughs' letter writing to Marker and his writing of *Queer,* we undo the conflation of Burroughs' actual relationship with Marker and the fictional relationship of Lee with Allerton.

But we also need to recognize, while not reproducing, the confusion that at the time visibly confused Burroughs himself.[3] To understand this blurring of borders and identities, and its full significance, we need to establish an accurate chronology of *Queer*'s composition.

Although the history of the *Queer* manuscript is complicated by the removal of material in the 1950s and by additions and changes made in the 1980s, Burroughs' correspondence gives an account of his writing's progress that is well supported by all the available manuscripts. Having started to write his new novel some time before 20 March, by 14 April Burroughs had about ten pages "ready to go" and about sixty more of rough draft (*L* 117), which meant he had probably written up to the middle or end of chapter 3 of the published text.[4] After "working day and night," by 26 April he had a manuscript of twenty-five pages typed, with seventy more in longhand notes that he reckoned would "simmer down" to forty or fifty (122). By 14 May, Burroughs had turned this into a typescript of sixty pages that he mailed Ginsberg (124), and analysis of precise references establishes that this corresponds roughly to the published text to the end of the sixth chapter. After mailing a "corrected M.S" of the same material a month later,[5] Burroughs then started "the S.A. sections of *Queer*" and had completed a twenty-five-page typescript by the first week of July that would approximate the seventh and eighth chapters of the novel.[6] Burroughs sent all this material to Ginsberg and asked his opinion on it, and then, a full year later, they reviewed the manuscript together in New York during the fall of 1953. As he claimed in his introduction to *Junky*, Ginsberg's supportive involvement with *Queer* as a manuscript for publication was therefore concrete and comprehensive. But of course, what his account leaves out is the *other half* to this genetic story; the entirely different epistolary creative relation between Burroughs and Marker.

All existing critical accounts share a biographical assumption summed up by David Savran's reference to "*Queer*, his fictionalized account of the time": "His journey to South America in search of the miracle hallucinogen yage, with Lewis Marker (the Eugene Allerton of *Queer*) whose lover he aspired to be, was a fiasco" (*Taking It* 41). In fact, a careful reading of the correspondence shows that this conclusion is mistaken, while a reading of the novel in light of this correspondence shows why the mistake is so crucial to its interpretation.

There is no available record of the journey Burroughs and Marker took from Mexico to South America in summer 1951, but the first letter written after Burroughs' return, dated 5 November, refers for the first time and in no uncertain terms to the state of their relationship: "The boy I went to

Ecuador with is still around and may return there with me. I like him better on closer acquaintance" (*L* 96). Indeed, five times between November
1951 and March 1952, Burroughs repeated his plan to repeat his journey with
Marker. The "fiasco" assumed by Savran applies to the fictional relation of
Lee and Allerton, but this contradicts the real relationship between Burroughs and Marker, both during their journey and for six months after it.
In many ways their entire relationship *was* a fiasco, but far from having ended
in disaster, it was ongoing at the time Burroughs started to write *Queer*.

On 20 March, he announced: "I have been working on a new novel (with
Marker away and no one around I can talk to I have need of distraction)"
(*L* 105). The immediate context for the writing of *Queer* is clearly established: Burroughs began to write only in Marker's absence, and the writing was seen as in lieu of talking. Since from the outset he identified his
"central theme" as the relationship between himself and Marker, it's quite
possible that he already saw this writing as not only an act of fictionalizing retrospection but as itself a continuation of that real-life relationship.
If Burroughs had no sense of his novel's closure—"Perhaps the ending
just hasn't occurred yet" (117)—then this is only consistent with the general economy of epistolary relations, in which, as Elizabeth MacArthur
notes, "real correspondents generate their narrative forward to an unknown
future" (32).

This then marks an essential difference between the writing of *Junkie*
and that of *Queer*. Burroughs didn't begin his second novel as he had the
first, by disinterestedly documenting a past, but by addressing a present in
which he was still intimately involved. Nevertheless, when he began his
second novel, he could only half grasp its distinction from his first. Burroughs' writing was at a pivotal moment, tilting literally both ways in the
space of the same letter. On one side, there is his plan to use the "same
straightforward method" as before, implying continuity with *Junkie* (*L*
105). On the other, a basic contrast: "Decided to dedicate *Junk* to Phil White
(under his correct name) if it is ever published. Guess A. L. M. (Adelbert
Lewis Marker) is slated for dedication in present work." Whereas his first
novel acquires a dedication in retrospect and to a man now dead, his second is begun already dedicated and to the other half of the book's central
relationship. From start to finish, this writing was transitive and desire-
driven. When in October 1952, Burroughs contemplated giving up on
writing, it would be for the simplest of reasons: "I wrote *Queer* for Marker.
I guess he doesn't think much of it or of me" (138). On the other hand,
dedication—writing *for*—is distinct from address—writing *to*—just as a
finished book is distinct from a personal letter. There is no evidence that

Burroughs began to write having in any sense reconceptualized his writing or that he saw the overlap between his letters and his manuscript as significant. On the contrary, it's clear that he failed to anticipate where this material might take him. *Queer* started out straight.

What happened? Maybe, having begun *Queer* because of Marker's absence, as this absence continued Burroughs found that writing was after all a poor machinery of compensation or sublimation, perhaps even counterproductive. For certain, choosing to write about their past courtship must have become acutely problematic once Burroughs discovered, a month on, that it wasn't only the physical distance between Mexico City and Jacksonville, Florida, that separated him from Marker. The moment of crisis in their relationship was registered in his letter to Ginsberg of 22 April 1952, a letter that marks an extraordinarily sudden and dramatic turning point in Burroughs' writing. Leaving aside for now the details of this crucial context, it's clear that in the midst of a creative breakthrough Burroughs experienced deep despair: "Marker wrote he isn't coming with me to S.A. [. . .] I am deeply hurt and disappointed. I will try to change his mind but I don't know" (*L* 120). The situation on 15 May: "I haven't given up yet on Marker. He may change his mind and come with us to Ecuador or wherever we go" (124). It was one week later that Burroughs corrected Ginsberg's misreading of the Slave Trader by insisting that the fantasy was "a *means* to make contact with Allerton," without which "Marker would have refused to go with me to S.A." (126). The extent and the basis of the confusions become clear. Factual Marker blurs with fictional Allerton because of the absolute structural coincidence between the two periods of Burroughs' relationship. In 1951, Marker's failed resistance and Burroughs' successful persuasion were both oral, face-to-face; in 1952, Marker finally refused, and Burroughs failed to persuade in writing, letter-to-letter.

Marker's initial absence and subsequent desertion have a range of significant psychoanalytical, formal, and thematic consequences for reading *Queer*. To begin with, if Burroughs started to write because he had "need of distraction" (*L* 105), then clearly enough this writing turns on the desire to avoid introspection. First Marker's presence and then the activity of writing seem to have compensated for a definitive and permanent absence, as Burroughs recognized the following month: "How I miss Joan! Also discouraged and hurt, because of Marker and I got no relaxation, nobody to talk to" (123). The effects of the shooting can't be marginalized then, since in any case they bear upon Burroughs' relationship with Marker.[7] However, to conclude that "Allerton is an alibi" fails to grasp the *materiality* of the real-life epistolary relationship, and since I made the claim myself in the introduction to *The Letters of William S. Burroughs, 1945–1959* (xxiii), I know that this failure springs from, and reinforces the overwhelming visibility of, Joan's death. What is now clear to me is that while any psychoanalytical approach is necessarily speculative, because Burroughs' relationship with Marker took on a wholly textual form, it holds a *uniquely proximate* relationship to the writing of *Queer*. "Real letters" can be as productive in their effects on a text as those analyzed by Janet Altman in her strictly formalist study of the fictional genre. "Thematic emphases in letter fiction," observes Altman, "tend to grow out of, rather than to dictate the choice of the form [. . .] it is the structural or syntactic approach that is logically prior to all other approaches" (200). Even so, we can specify how the syntax of Burroughs' epistolary practice is integral to the themes and form of *Queer*.

A BROKEN CONNECTION

One of the clearest indications of the way in which Burroughs' epistolary relation with Marker coincided materially with the writing of *Queer*, how it produced particular formal and thematic effects, comes in his letter of 4 June:

> Marker isn't coming. That is clearer with every day that passes and no letter from him. I have written five or six letters to him with fantasies and routines in my best vein but he doesn't answer [. . .] I told him I didn't expect him to answer all my letters, I just wrote because it was as near as I could come to contact with him like I was talking to him and I hoped at least he would be amused by the letters because they were funny, but he didn't answer that letter. (*L* 129)

Since none of these letters seem to have survived, we can only assume that in part they overlapped Lee's routines in *Queer*. In this context, the timing of Burroughs' 22 April letter, when he first reveals Marker has deserted him, is crucial. In all probability, Burroughs wrote what became the fourth, fifth, and sixth chapters of *Queer* in a period of just over a week, as he worked "day and night" on the novel up to the twenty-sixth of the month. From this, we can tell that Burroughs must have written the Slave Trader routine immediately before or after 22 April. Since this was not only one of his funniest routines but a fantasy dialogue clearly concerned with sexual desertion and possession, it is hard to imagine that Burroughs would not have mailed it to the very person who inspired it. But whatever their specific content, the epistolary fantasies addressed to Marker during April and May 1952 share the identical function that Burroughs specified for the

Oil-Man and Slave Trader fantasies—a "*means* to make contact"—and the function Lee explains to Allerton in *Queer:* "Just a routine for your amusement" (*Q* 103).

If Burroughs only began to write *Queer* in the silence of Marker's absence, then it is understandable why the epistolary should be the medium that gives rise to the routine form. Simon Bischoff, in Deleuzian terms, observes: "In the letter the line of flight which leads away from writing and back to the voice is intensified (signs become bodies!)" (45). Likewise, Linda Kauffman notes how crucial is the speaking voice for the letter "which is written solely because the writer cannot speak to the addressee": "The traditional *je crois te parler* motif informs all epistolary production: writing nurtures the illusion of speaking with one whose absence is intolerable" (*Special Delivery* xix). *Je crois te parler;* or Burroughs' writing as a substitute for the need to "talk to" Marker, simulating vocal contact according to the desperate, compensatory logic of the epistolary. And in that desperation, driven to re-create the illusion of presence and to provoke a response, Burroughs found the letter served him well as a recorder of voices, while encouraging the urge to excess. Bischoff again: "It is a dialogue with an absent partner, potentiated dialogue, an infinite and unhindered stream of monologue. It is dialogue unchecked, fearing no intervention" (45). In the case of Burroughs' letter writing, comments that might seem overheated are only accurate. And suggestive: the birth in *Queer* of Lee's manic oral energies, so extraordinary after his virtual muteness in *Junkie,* less represents the effects of drug withdrawal or of Joan's death in 1951 than it registers the immediate nature of Burroughs' written relationship with Marker in 1952.

The increasingly coercive fantasies of Lee in *Queer* articulate therefore what became a crisis of communication and desire in Burroughs' unreciprocated epistolary relation with Marker at the time of writing, not within his oral relation the year before. Only by insisting on the priority of 1952 over 1951 can we understand why, despite Burroughs' successful seduction of Marker through oral routines, those of Lee fail to succeed with Allerton. More than that, we can also grasp the specific ways in which that failure is represented in the text. Because Lee's routines have turned independent of *Queer*'s internal narrative situation, Allerton is not there for them as a physical listener but as a reader, so that this material takes on the properties of writing and his desire the properties of *texts.* Allerton is "insubstantial as a phantom" (*Q* 110), and Lee is "spectral" (30), for both are paper-thin identities. No wonder then that Lee reaches out to touch him with "ectoplasmic fingers" and "phantom thumbs" (25), for as extensions of desire, these are what his routines have become: if bodies become signs, signs have equally become bodies. Here, we see at work a principle central to the epistolary situation: the way in which the letter writer "fantasizes the beloved and writes to that shadow," as Ruth Perry says (101) but is, as Altman puts it, inevitably "engaged in the impossible task of making his reader present" (135). This spectral reality was, for Kafka, what made writing his letters to Milena "nothing but torture" (*Letters to Milena* 224): "It is truly a communication with spectres, not only with the spectre of the addressee but also with one's own phantom" (qtd. in Altman).[8] If Burroughs joins the great tradition of the letter, his spectral and sinister point of intersection is still recognizably Burroughsian.

An economy of desire as "torture" commences in *Queer* then not only as a result of the shift in subject matter from *Junkie* but as a direct result of a shift in Burroughs' writing practice. To look at it another way, to say that the breakdown of Lee in *Queer* has its origins in neither the effects of soma (withdrawal sickness) nor psyche (the shooting of Joan) but in the traumatic experience of homosexual desire is necessary but not sufficient. To prevent any allegorical separation of form and content, we have to insist that the central narrative action of *Queer*, Lee's desire-driven narration of routines to Allerton, is materially produced by the scene of writing itself. That is why the virtual zero-degree narrating interaction in *Junkie*—inside the novel *and* through it—makes for such a telling contrast to *Queer*. To see the material unity of desire and writing is in turn to recognize that *Queer* is the product of a relationship where desire can *only* pass through the act of writing. And if desire is integral to the economy of letter writing, driving it on, producing fantasy and projecting contact to overcome absence, then the reverse is equally true: in *Queer,* the letter is integral to the economy of desire. And the true horror of desire as an epistolary fiction is the same as that of Virtual Reality: not that the virtual is now mistaken for the real but that we treat real persons as virtual and so become free to act out any fantasy normally repressed in our intersubjective relations.[9]

But a very obvious question arises at this point: if the epistolary relation between spectral desire and material communication was so important, then why doesn't *Queer* represent it? Why does it leave no explicit trace in the text at all? One answer would be that Burroughs himself did not recognize it, that either he didn't see the crossover between letter and novel or that he lacked the kind of metafictional interest we might expect of an altogether different type of writer. In fact, I would go so far as to say that it is precisely *because* of the letter's overwhelming and immediate material importance to Burroughs' development that he would hardly ever represent letters literally or as metaphors within his fiction. There is also another answer, which is that *Queer* does include such representations but in displaced form. They only become visible as such once we recognize the letter as a *technology* for the transmission of voice and mediation of desire, albeit a historically antiquated one. In this sense, the epistolary is displaced most emphatically through *Queer*'s repeated figuration of Lee's desires in terms of telephonic connections and ruptures.

At the very start of the novel, Lee projects a "shadowy line of boys," the last one "so real" in his mind that he replies aloud to a rejection that takes the form of a telephone voice, saying: "Sorry . . . wrong number . . . try again" (Q 3). Undoubtedly, Burroughs knew Lucille Fletcher's hit radio play, *Sorry, Wrong Number* (1943), and its equally famous film version (1948) featuring Barbara Stanwyck as the hysterical, maternally possessive invalid who lives—and dies—on the telephone. Also without a doubt, a contemporary readership would have been able to connect Lee to this paranoid figure and to connect the novel as a whole to a film that, as J. P. Telotte rightly says, "develops a motif of control or possession that sketches a world of human relationships defined by patterns of appropriation and power" (79). The telephone line stands in for the epistolary exchange because of the potential for both technologies of communication to imperil the receiver's whole identity at the hands of a sender and, crucially, *vice versa*. As Telotte adds, the very effort to control others "only reduces the self to an object, subject to another's possessive desires" (79). In line with this reversible logic, Lee both suffers and projects the telephonic voice of a specifically maternal superego, the "voice of a machine of Destiny," as Ford Maddox Ford called it (654). Such a voice has been associated with the telephone throughout its history and has been more recently located in the technology-schizophrenia-desire nexus mapped by Avital Ronell—"There is always a remnant of the persecuting, accusatory mother in the telephone system" (*Telephone Book* 144)—and by Ellis Hansson—"To be queer is to hear strange voices, to answer an obscene call" (53). Both wanting to give and taking it like dictation, Lee finds himself caught up in an infernal circuit of sending and receiving.

Each technology also restages a trauma of crossed lines and missed connections, operating as systems that not only relay messages but can bring about psychotic breakdown when they malfunction. Updating the old *techné*, *Queer* displaces an originally epistolary rupture of failed contact to render the catastrophic effects of losing one's place in the system. And so when Allerton decides to "remove himself from contact," Lee is left in a void: "The effect was like a broken connection. Allerton was not cold or hostile; Lee simply wasn't there so far as he was concerned" (*Q* 19). Likewise, the increasingly manic polyphony of Lee's routines suggests how such a crisis in an epistolary network can reproduce the one that beset the apparatus studied by Hugh Kenner in *The Mechanic Muse,* as when he calls T. S. Eliot's *The Wasteland* "a telephone poem, its multiple voices referable to a massive short-circuit at the central exchange" (36). Above all, like the disembodied telephonic voice, the vocal projections of Burroughs' letter writing, insofar as they are reproduced in Lee's spoken routines, seek to compensate for a material absence by their phantasmic presence, by materializing in the other's head a ghostly speech that would reembody the sender by usurping the inner voice of the receiver.[10]

The displacement throughout *Queer* of the epistolary as a technology is also an *extension* of the letter into the field of more advanced forms of communication and control and so motivates the novel's allusions to radio, television, and film transmission.[11] In this way, the letter cannot represent an alternative medium, a mode of production lying outside or defined against those of the modern mass media, but simply disappears into them to imply their continuity. This implied process of substitution should not, however, distract from what remains *specific* to the letter in general and to Burroughs' practice in particular. As a technology, the letter is a somatic as well as psychic extension of self, operating as a prosthetic displacement of the human body; taken to the limit, this function would, for Norbert Wiener, imperil human individuality itself by eroding the distinction between transmitting information and "transmitting a living organism such as a human being" (Human *Use* 103). The other side to people delivered *"as if they were letters,"* as Timothy Melley puts it (88), is texts that function like life-forms.

When Burroughs saw draft excerpts of Kerouac's *Visions of Cody,* just weeks after starting to write *Queer,* he would identify "this kind of writing more than any other [as] an actual amoeboid-like organism" (*L* 109). The description matches Lee's spectral extensions of desire in *Queer,* specifically the autonomous "amoeboid protoplasmic projection" that reaches towards Allerton when the two watch Cocteau's film, *Orphée* (*Q* 36). The phrasing in turn suggests a typically epistolary investment in the physical body of the love letter, in its prized ability to mediate desire by reaching across space and time to actually touch love's body. This is its metonymic function, as given by Janet Altman: "the letter itself, by virtue of physical contact, stands for the lover" (19). We recall Burroughs' investment in metonymy when he identified himself with *Queer* as a text written for Marker, describing a transfer of self into what Barthes calls the "amorous gift" of the lover's dedication (*Lover's Discourse* 75): "I guess he doesn't think much of *it* or of *me.*" In *Queer,* Lee *dedicates* his routines metonymically, seeking to overcome the distance of a reader experienced as an intolerable severance, as a physical amputation and psychic division of one half from the other; hence, Lee's fantasies of corporeal merger and union, invasion and occupation, control and possession. For we can understand Lee's desire to *correspond with* Allerton, his urge towards the absolute presence of fusion and unity, as an effect of Burroughs' frustrated dependence on *corresponding to* the absent and unresponsive Marker.

The existential fact of isolation and the unbearable emotional trauma of self-inflicted losses—of wife, children, homeland—must surely have become unbearably material for Burroughs, *as a writer,* when separation and loss is measured in terms of letters sent across actual space that elicit no reply, week after week. Taken to new limits, this is the terror of the dead letter: "In the abortive missive is so much lost being, so much death," wrote Emily Dickinson (qtd. in Decker 164). Although this theme is a commonplace for all letter writers, it has a particular resonance for Burroughs; not only because of his immediate personal situation but also in broader cultural terms, insofar as Dickinson's dread represented the dark side to a utopian nineteenth-century discourse of American romanticism, a discourse resurrected in the epistolary idealism of the Beats. For Savran, "no writers before them seem to have textualized their activities as thoroughly and obsessively as the Beats," and what they produced amounted to a radical "textualization of the interconnected self" (*Taking It* 55). But what Ginsberg called the "continuous tissue, continuous fabric" formed by Beat letter exchanges (qtd. in Savran 55) had, as I argued in chapter 2, important *historical* precedents, and these can serve to emphasize how Burroughs' version of epistolarity affirms a fundamental *political* distance from Ginsberg and Kerouac.

If in the early 1950s, Ginsberg and Kerouac dreamed of what Emerson had called a "colloquy divine," a utopia of total intimacy and union for which the intertextuality of letter relations served as a model, then it is no coincidence that such a dream of perfect communion appears in *Queer* in openly satiric form. Bobo comes to a "sticky end" in Lee's routine, because his philosophy of wholeness with fellow man and the natural world is indeed "from the tomb" (Q 40), a posthumous or dead letter. Lee invokes a doctrine of bodily and natural merger that once promised a properly philosophical correspondence with an idealized other, of a kind articulated precisely by Melville a century earlier. Indeed, as Richard Hardack has demonstrated, Melville "could formulate his most deeply held philosophical tenets only in the specifically 'intertextual' genre of letters": letter writing offered Melville "a divine merger with other men in nature, a sacrilized epistolary male fraternity" (127) that would appear in texts like *Pierre* as a "soft social Pantheism," that "rosy melting of all into one" (Melville qtd. in Hardack 139). In Lee's routine, such a dream of absolute, undifferenti- ated union turns promptly into a sinister nightmare, a cellular "shlup" that envisions less a Romantic ecology of interconnection than a cybernetic horror of entropy.

ABSOLUTE END OF WRONG LINE

If the letter can generate both a thematic and a fantasmatic of "correspon- dence," and if that turns in *Queer* into a vision more demonic than divine, then we see here the most literal signature of Burroughs' own immediate epistolary experience, reflected back to him in the abjection of his failed correspondence with Marker. The appalling force of this failure is revealed in his letter of 4 June 1952. A week earlier, Ginsberg had written Burroughs an extraordinary analysis of his quest for love and transcendence, invok- ing Melville's Ahab ("a madman in a rage") and Antonin Artaud ("who also changed fact") before describing *Queer* as "from the inside of the madman" and concluding: "You are attempting to work black magic."[12] This was Burroughs' reply:

> Of course I am attempting black magic. Black magic is always an attempt to force human love, resorted to when there is no other way to score. (Even curse is last attempt at contact with loved one. I do not contemplate any curse, that is absolute end of wrong line. ~~The picture of him slipping further and further away from me, laughing talking thinking of me less and less is intolerable picture of indiffer- ence.~~ The curse is last attempt to regain attention.) (*L* 128)

The struck-through lines are painful enough; but Burroughs made a revi- sion that can't be shown that is more disturbing still: "I do not contem- plate any curse, that is absolute end of wrong line," was itself a line he added, in a shaky hand, on the margins of his typed letter. A telling clarification. When Burroughs spoke of *changing Marker's mind,* here we see what the "absolute end" of that line looks like: the demonic potential of writing to produce effects.

This is where the fantasmatic exercise of and resistance to power in Bur- roughs' writing originates then: in his material experience as a writer of being controlled by the need to control, rather than from either the con- dition of addiction or from the pulling of a gun trigger. If these were violent experiences of "possession" for Burroughs, neither holds any necessary relation to the act of writing itself nor produced the fascistic political or psychopathological fantasies of Burroughs' routines. Burroughs' investment in the routine form and his investment in the epistolary coincided, and together they originated the workings of power within the activity of writing as an exercise of will directed against its reader. And so if, as David Ingram suggests, language is understood as an exogenous, invasive power that "treats the body as a machine for inscription" (103), then for Burroughs the beginning of knowledge is itself the act of inscribing.

Whatever the general force of such self-knowledge, consider what it must have done specifically for his emerging self-identity as a writer. Burroughs' "black magic" is power: whether in the epistolary tradition of seduction as "an attempt of one person to change another's mind, an attempt to enter the consciousness, tamper with it, and reverse the intentions of the will" to the point of "mind-rape" (Perry 129, 135); or in the narratological sense of seduction where "to tell a story is an act, an event, one that has the power to produce change, and first and foremost to change the relationship between narrator and narratee" (Chambers 74). But *Queer* is not "about" the writer/reader relationship. In Burroughs, it must be literal: power relations are only now fully represented in his writing because only now are they invested in it. And crucially, it is based less on an experience or on a theoretical understanding external to writing than discovered within the act of it.

The consequences of this grounding are all-important for shifting the paradigm of drug addiction as Burroughs' determining experience and controlling metaphor. The origin is *not metaphoric,* and because it is integral to the activity of writing, it allows no distance, no sanctuary, no exit. To recall Tony Tanner's neat diptych of *before* and *after,* where Burroughs is "a victim of sickness now devoted to the analysis of diseases" (110), it becomes clear that such an understanding locates a crisis outside of language and prior to writing that elides the victimizing, the sickness, the disease *of* writing that is the central action in Burroughs' work. But this isn't to propose a closed, aestheticized writing, a text without material relations because it never arrives anywhere, trapped in the circuits of language, although this is exactly what Burroughs himself implies in his introduction to *Queer.* Here, he speaks of writing as possession and immunization but as if this defined a closed system in the fictional relation between Lee and Allerton. Once we restore the actual intersubjective economy to this writing of disease and remedy, then we recognize its external social relations and material effects. This writing also therefore meets the necessity of which Nietzsche spoke, of "doctors and nurses *who themselves are sick*" (qtd. in Brown 168). This is a writing whose indelible knowledge of motives and effects will deliver a uniquely literal and lacerating textual politics; a writing that bears the stamp of power.

If the literary text is seen as a technical device intended to "produce certain desired internal states in the reader," as David Porush argues, then "we bring fiction into cybernetic territory" (21). This economy is *unavoidable* for the letter writer who composes "with his or her gaze on the other in order, primarily, *to produce an effect*" (Cousineau 31; my emphasis). This is fully consistent with Burroughs' conception of the writer as a practitioner of magic rather than mimesis, not writing to describe what happened—say, with Marker in 1951—but—say, with Marker in 1952—writing "to *make something happen*" (*Painting and Guns* 32; my emphasis). The logical end would be the colonization of the other in the image of the self, as constructed by Burroughs' definition of a writer's purpose: "He's trying to reproduce in the reader's mind a certain experience, and if he were completely successful in that, the reproduction of the experience would be complete. Perhaps fortunately, they're not that successful" (Palmer 49).

Failure is fortunate. Here, we hit upon the perverse and paradoxical grounding of Burroughs' textual politics. Writing is granted transformative power, but in a complete reversal of the expected logic of oppositional claims, this is a virulently *negative* potency. Burroughs' key tropes—ventriloquism, virus power, possession, and so on—define power relations from which we must not extricate Burroughs himself. Nothing could more denude or falsify his writing than to put him outside the very systems against which he is forced to work from their insides. If "Burroughs projects human subjection in terms of a universal viral incursion," as Dellamora claims (145), then universal it should be seen to be, and not as a theorized project but as a material process, not a thematic subject but a literal practice of writing. It is in this sense that, far from writing his "way out" of Control (*Q* xxii), Burroughs really had no choice except to write *out of* that experience. There is no "way out"—not so long as he is writing. In which case, his Ugly Spirit is most deeply implicated in the black magic at the absolute wrong end of the epistolary line. In Barthes's darkest words: "If we call freedom not only the capacity to escape power but also and especially the capacity to subjugate no one, then freedom can exist only outside language. Unfortunately, human language has no exterior: there is no exit" (*Barthes Reader* 460).

"I do nothing that does not have some interest in seducing you"; so writes Derrida in the epistolary section of *The Post Card* (69)—but again, it might properly be Burroughs. Whatever his tactics of resistance, nothing conceals the fact of complicity, while this in turn becomes the ground of Burroughs' integrity. This is because the engagement with power is mimetic and metonymic rather than metaphoric; since the site of action is within the activity of writing, there is no analytical or allegorical distance between symptom and treatment. To approach this special form of "authenticity" in Slavoj Žižek's dialectical terms, it is a simple but radical question of the *position* of enunciation. That is to say, everything turns on whether Burroughs' position is that of the excluded observer safely exempted from the content of his enunciation or whether he is himself included in the content, inscribed fully into the process. This is the condition so precisely stated twenty-five years ago in the last words of Eric Mottram's pioneering critical study: "Burroughs employs no ideological alibis or false objectivity: his map of his location in history includes himself" (271). To which all I would add is that this is so not just at the level of the *written* but on the plane of the *writing* itself.

Such is the case with *Queer,* where Lee refuses to exempt himself from his national ideology and where we get with an almost visceral force the sense that Burroughs knows—knows inside out—what the "absolute end of wrong line" looks like. In his own account, his writing after *Queer* is the homeopathic creation of "a weakened virus" to "set the record straight" (*Q* xiv), which admits a need to redress the pathogenic force of his queer record and its debt to the writing of black magic letters. And so finally, the point is not that Burroughs' letter writing was the real basis, the true ground, of his emerging critique of universal control systems, including those that implicate the writer, since he could have arrived at such analysis in any number of ways. This is not a matter of source hunting. The point is Burroughs' own *actively material and immediate complicity* in this economy, located in the very act of writing, in the very moment of it.

THIS BIOGRAPHICAL MONSTER

WHAT YA THINK I AM, A HACK?

At this point, we need to go back to deal with what from a genetic viewpoint is without a doubt Burroughs' most important letter. This is his letter of 22 April 1952, which marks a truly radical turning point in his correspondence, in his writing, and in the relationship between the two.

This letter is the first of an entirely new kind. It vibrates with an energy barely glimpsed before, bursting into a fast-paced, comic, and idiomatic inventiveness that inaugurates, in effect, the routine as a written form. This was a key moment, and Burroughs knew it. Even the physical form of the original letter articulates its distinctiveness. For the first time in his correspondence, Burroughs retyped the letter and kept both drafts, which reveal additions and revisions that themselves show an attention to detail he previously reserved for manuscripts. And Ginsberg recognized the difference, making his own typed excerpts on receipt, following the prompt of Burroughs' closing remarks: "Better save my letters, maybe we can get out a book of them later on when I have a rep" (*L* 121). This sudden anticipation of his future as a reputed writer—*when* rather than *if*—clearly coincided with the signing of a book contract with Ace: now, almost two and a half years after starting *Junkie,* Burroughs could for the first time believe in himself as a writer. With a new self-consciousness, he revels in the identity, referring to "we authors" and "Us writers" and finally closes with the telling signature: "Willy Lee—That Junky writin' boy" (120–21). I find that signing off so suggestive because it leaves the impression that Burroughs knew at once that "William Lee," coined only that month, was more than a *nom de plume*—or rather, that it was exactly that: Burroughs' name as a writer, who he was when he wrote.

The context makes Burroughs' investment in the name of the writer resonate, because most of this letter is concerned with the effects of writing and publication on identity. In particular, Burroughs was faced by the request of Carl Solomon for a new kind of preface to *Junkie:* "Now as to this biographical thing, I can't write it." Instead, he improvises an extravagant "routine, like you see on the back flap," packed with absurd parodies. This moment establishes the precise context in which Burroughs thought about what became *Junkie*'s preface:

> Seriously, Sweetheart, I do have to concentrate and I can't be distracted from *Queer* by vaguely menacing Kafkian demands for notes and insertions and biographical indications of unspecified length and subject matter. [. . .] when they ask me to write a "biographical sketch" I feel like a personnel manager just said, "Tell me about yourself." (*L* 120)

To construct his identity in terms of commercialized packaging is more than simply reductive; by invoking Kafka, Burroughs integrates the generic conventions of biography within the larger institutional frame of bureaucratic control. Burroughs evades and resists these demands by offering not a metaphoric whole self but jumbled metonymic parts of himself: "I have worked (but not in the order named) as [. . .]" (119). This logic of fragmentation and multiplication is the germ of a *dis*continuity editing system.

Burroughs' first epistolary routine quickly prompts another, one that itself draws in and on other routines and stories, in an increasingly animated style whose governing logic is to oppose unity and coherence with the fragmentary and excessive:

> For example, I think of the Anderson period (How could I ever have been interested in that?), well I take one incident as indicating setup and wrote a short story (incomplete of course. What ya think I am, a hack?) I enclose story with some mighty sorry biographical material. I have to write specific, Al. They wanta hear about how I cut the end joint off my little finger? [. . .] O.K. I'll tell them. Say, maybe that's an angle. Just hit the highlights in this biographical monster. Talk that up to Sol. (*L* 120)

Now, it is apparent why the preface to *Junkie* shows signs of so marked a division from its narrative and why Burroughs not only *could* now put down "one of those nostalgic routines" but chose to do so. This is less a matter of looking back and reconceptualizing narrative than of a skepticism born from the congress of his new self-consciousness as a writer and his new engagement with autobiography, which took place in the context of the epistolary.

However, the letter's final paragraph—"I simply must get to work. Just squandered three hours writing to you and Marker" (*L* 121)—shows Burroughs still thinking in conventional terms of a clear division between the business of literature and the left-handed labor of the letter—Hemingway: "Any time I can write a good letter it's a sign I'm not working" (qtd. in Baker ix)—even as it hints at the merger to come. Equally, the landmark letter of 22 April signals formal experimentation in the moment of breakthrough. Routines improvised in letters or put down in prefaces and on backflaps of books, independent autobiographical short stories—this is the simultaneous evolution of multiple forms. The range itself marked a significant departure in Burroughs' writing, a turning away from full-length narrative towards the fragment as his working unit.

Directly and indirectly, the narrative progression of *Queer*, or rather its progressive collapse as a narrative, registers the impact of Burroughs' sudden and fraught investment in letter writing. There must have been some crossover of voice and content, as features of his rapidly evolving epistolary style carried over into his writing of the novel, when what he wrote as letters in the morning leaked into what he wrote as fiction in the afternoon—and of course vice versa, in a circuit of cross-fertilization and confusion. For surely, one reason why *Queer* is such an odd text is that, in a novel where the "3rd person is really 1st person" (*L* 111), its narrative point of view is actually so unstable, suggesting Burroughs' technical inability to resolve the question of voice. Little wonder then that in a line deleted from his 22 April letter, he now concluded: "Personally I am so confused I don't know whether to think in 1st or 3rd person at this point."[13] This confusion between narrative voices, between "I" and "Lee," runs in parallel with the confusion between Marker and Allerton as it becomes ever harder for Burroughs to separate the audience inside the fiction from his audience outside it.

Burroughs' decision to try his hand at short stories in 1952 anticipates his inability to finish *Queer* beyond the scale of a novella and predicts the formal crisis ahead, the years when his material and any attempt to structure it as a continuous textual body would be in permanent conflict. But this is to get ahead of ourselves, and at this point, all we can say is that in Burroughs' preference for the short tour de force the epistolary model shows itself already at work. From the very start, the routine is tied to both the morsel of writing that is the letter and to what Deborah Harter terms the "morselization" of the human body in the genre of the fantastic. Forced to reproduce the monstrous body of biography, Burroughs writes a short story—"incomplete of course. What ya think I am, a hack?"—that offers up the end joint of his little finger. In a gesture typical of Burroughs' routines, he therefore literalizes the idiomatic expression *giving the finger* to those publishers who threaten to feminize the homosexual writer by "sticking their nasty old biographical prefaces up her ass" (*L* 120).

The short story Burroughs mentions here, later titled "The Finger," was quickly followed by several others, including those later titled "Driving Lesson" and "Dream of the Penal Colony."[14] These stories—which were all rewritten over the next three years—complicate the formal development and the psychological grounding of Burroughs' writing at this point. Taken together, they check any temptation to oversimplify or indiscriminately generalize the epistolary genesis of the routine as a stable form. What makes these short stories particularly interesting is that, while they arise at this specific mid-1952 turning point and are revealing on account of that particular context, the light they shed falls equally on other pasts and other futures.

COMPOSITIONAL INTENTION

There are significant autobiographical continuities between Burroughs' three short stories and *Queer*. Each scenario is a variation on the same theme: the obsessed figure of Lee is blocked in his attempts to impress a reluctant lover, and the result of frustrated emotional communication and homosexual desire is self-destructive violence, abjection, and failure. The surface similarity to the central drama of *Queer* is clear, so that these stories demonstrate how in writing the novel Burroughs was led to confront repetitive behavioral patterns by going back into his past. Both "The Finger" and "Driving Lesson" have been read as narrative accounts of incidents in Burroughs' relationship with Jack Anderson a decade earlier. The self-destructive other self that appeared in 1940 with Anderson returned in 1951 with Marker and, as we will see in the next chapter, in 1953 with Ginsberg.

Perhaps Burroughs has to be understood as a victim of what Freud termed *Schicksalzwang*, or fate repetition compulsion, a neurosis that Karen Horney linked to masochism in which the subject finds himself again and again the victim of the same scenario, becoming "an object, without a will of his own" (234). I take this to be what Burroughs means in his introduction to *Queer* when he addresses the question of what motivated his writing:

> Why should I wish to chronicle so carefully these extremely painful and unpleasant and lacerating memories? While it was I who wrote *Junky*, I feel that I was being written in *Queer*. I was also taking pains to ensure further writing, so as to set the record straight: writing as inoculation [...] So I achieved some immunity from further perilous ventures along these lines by writing my experience down. (*Q* xiv)

The context here implies that all this has to do with his wife's death, but if we concentrate on what is in *Queer* rather than supposedly missing from it, then the short stories that Burroughs began to write in parallel confirm that what is at stake is a different kind of peril.

"The Finger," "Driving Lesson," and "Penal Colony" are, like *Queer*, palimpsests of memory, case histories of a masochistic psychopathology. If they inscribe experiences of homosexual abjection, they also reveal a further layer of text beneath, one etched from early childhood trauma. This pathological archaeology is most evident in "The Finger," where Lee is revealed to be in analysis when the self-mutilation takes place. At least in its finished form, this "exquisite and macabre" tale, as Kerouac would describe it (*Selected Letters 1940–1956* 530), has a double chronological structure. The first half, a simple narrating of events, is strangely detached from the second. Lee retells the pitiful narrative as a cynically comic, spoken routine and only now gives his infatuation (with a "girl" standing in for Jack Anderson) as the incident's motive: "Did I ever tell you about the time I got on a Van Gogh kick and cut off the end joint of my little finger?" (*I* 17). "Sort of stupid, insincere queer lingo," Burroughs observed, "contrasted with bare horror of the severed finger."[15] The contrast in stylistic registers creates a ghastly effect, but the shift is more than tonal: the structure's effect is to render the given motive secondary, as if Lee's relationship with the girl were itself a deferred effect, not a cause. Here, various local details in the text—details that are recycled repetitively across the other stories and in *Queer*—invite a psychoanalytically primed reader to discover the infantile trauma that surfaces in Lee's disturbed dreams in *Junkie*'s preface. When the boy in "Penal Colony" breaks off relations, Lee is in despair because *"I haven't discovered the Secret"* (*I* 45). The withheld secret that Lee pursues in others—throughout *Queer* but never in *Junkie*—would be, in Lacanian terms, the Real of desire, a missed encounter that cannot be represented and so must be repeated, "determining all that follows" as a round of constant deferrals, an endless return of the past in the present (*Four Fundamental* 55).

If the continuities between Burroughs' three short stories and *Queer* construct an autobiographical path back towards a point of traumatic origin, they also reflect on the material and more immediate situation of writing, and this is what really interests me here. For while these returns to Burroughs' past mark a basic distinction to the writing of *Queer,* the distance in time collapses once we recognize a continuity that is not just thematic but operational in the present. These stories are about the frustration and self-destructive tyranny of homosexual desire because they were written in the context of it: their subjects are active in the situation of writing, returning to the past to articulate the present and implicitly using the past in order to *effect* the present. That is why strict biographical readings of these scenarios as records that offer insights into Burroughs' state of mind in the 1930s and 1940s are incomplete and misleading. As with *Queer,* what motivates them is the present situation and scene of writing. If, to use James Grauerholz's resonant phrase, they show a "compositional intention" towards a particular reader (*I* xvii), then the effects must determine their content, not vice versa.

My point is twofold. First, Marker's failure to reciprocate in the present, which determines the writing of *Queer,* is the exact double of Anderson's in the past, as represented in "The Finger" and "Driving Lesson." Second, no matter how accurate the characterization might be, Anderson is not represented in "The Finger" according to his failure to reciprocate emotionally in April 1940 but according to Marker's failure to do so in April 1952. What counts most here is the moment that Burroughs wrote the stories, a time when Marker's lack of reciprocation was an *epistolary* failure. The girl in "The Finger" and Jack in "Driving Lesson" fail to respond to Lee's desire in the same way that the letter writer fails to reply, in physical terms *cannot* reply, as the endings to each story suggest. In "The Finger," for example, since the girl had "gone to Chicago" by the time Lee is let out of Bellevue, the finger joint he planned to present as a memento would have to be put in an envelope and mailed to her. Isn't this how Burroughs must have sent "The Finger" to Marker?

WRITING IN THE FLESH

What is most interesting about "The Finger" is that it in effect dares rejection by threatening to repeat its scenario in the present. That is to say, if "The Finger" fails to impress its reader, the events narrated within it threaten to stir into life: mimesis risks turning into magic. Its title presents the reader with the same blackmailing gift that Lee fails to give to the object of his desire, the girl whose lack of response drives Lee to literalize the figure of his emotional pain: "It's tearing me all apart. . . . So I hit on this finger joint gimmick" (*I* 17). In this context, the listener internal to the second part of the story plays a crucial role: the audience for Lee's spoken routine is conspicuously absent and so suggests his true identity as a *reader*.

While both "The Finger" and "Driving Lesson" have a formal control that implies psychological mastery, Burroughs thought of these texts in 1955 when defining the routine as "Lee's special form": "It is *not completely symbolic* but subject to slide over into action at any time. (Cutting off finger joint, wrecking the car, etc. [. . .])"[16] (*I* 127). Given their precision and polish, these texts would be atypical routines, but the specifically epistolary scene of Burroughs' writing inserts them back into an economy, one that reintegrates the reader as their receiver. If, as Burroughs observed of this material, "the audience is an integral part of the routine" (127), it is because the routine was an integral part of the epistolary. The economic system of the letter is distinct from a general economy of exchange, however, and has more in common with rituals of the gift. As "gifts," Burroughs' texts become part of an exchange that, as the ethnographer Marcel Mauss established, produces obligation. This is a debt that must be repaid not with money but with symbolic interest. The Skip Tracer looks at the fingernails of his left hand—the hand of profanity, evil, the sinister, the hand also of Burroughs' own mutilation—and mutters, "about your, uh . . . account" (*Q* 134). Like any score, the psychic accounts must be settled, the record set straight, the books balanced, and from *Queer* onwards, this will become one of the refrains that recurs across the Burroughs oeuvre.

In letters to his brother, Vincent van Gogh developed a theory of love as the equilibrium between two dangerous extremes: "in love one must not only give but also take; and, reversing it, one must not only take but also give" (qtd. in Michaud 31). Seven years later (1888) in Arles, he would leave for Gauguin his severed earlobe, a gift of himself that, like Burroughs' finger joint, is specifically unreturnable and repulsive. The point must be that it is also *unforgettable*. Van Gogh intones: "Verily, I say unto you, you will remember me" (qtd. in Dunlop 174). Burroughs tropes him by having Lee offer the "trifling memento" of his "undying affection" in order to make an "impression" (*I* 17). The dis-memberment will leave its undying trace, its indelible record, in the act of re-membering—if not by the girl, who stands in for Jack, then by the listener, who stands in for Marker, who stands in for the reader.

Taking the physical properties of the letter to their logical extreme, Burroughs' texts become acts of self-inscription and self-amputation, the masochistic offerings of inscribed body parts. The metonymic plane of writing here, which insists on the physicality of the word and its traumatic relation to the body, suggests a key material link to Burroughs' methodology of the next decade; is there not some sense in which the slicing of paper bodies performs over and over again similar acts of self-mutilation and rituals of exorcism and conjuration? More immediately, we can recognize the literal behind the metaphor of Burroughs' "lacerating memories": *lacerate,* meaning to tear to pieces, to mangle, to harrow. His claim to "being written" in *Queer* now seems to invoke a definitive literary figure, one very much on Burroughs' mind in the early 1950s. On 5 November 1952, in his last letter before leaving Mexico, Burroughs described the state of his relation with Marker and, before changing his mind so violently that he all but erased his words, asked Ginsberg:

> ~~Do you know Kafka's Penal Colony? Where the officer says after six hours of the script writing in the flesh of the scriptee, we offer him a little rice pap: "And not one in my experience ever refused the rice pap."~~ (*L* 140)

Kafka's lethal inscription machine is not invoked casually here. Burroughs is being very precise in this letter: in Kafka's story, the sixth hour is the turning point, when the victim doesn't swallow the rice but spits it out, grows quiet, and reaches enlightenment because, as the Officer explains, at last "the man begins to understand the inscription" and now "deciphers it with his wounds" (*Collected Stories* 150). As Arnold Weinstein observes, the story's verdict is that "we must learn viscerally, not verbally; the script must be in us, not in front of us" ("Kafka's Writing Machine" 124). But even such knowledge did not set Burroughs free. Indeed, that he should have asked Ginsberg if he knew the Kafka story is eerily predictive; for on 22 April

1954, two years to the very day after first writing "The Finger" in the context of Marker's epistolary rejection, Burroughs, now in Tangier, wrote to complain of friends' dismissing him "as a vampire who tries to buy them with some gift, money, or routines, or cut off fingers"—and the friend who failed to respond was now Ginsberg himself: "The withdrawal symptoms are worse than the Marker habit. One letter would fix me" (*L* 206).

It was during this period in Tangier that the epistolary economy of Burroughs' routines would became fully integrated as a script of addiction. Unsurprisingly, he also rewrote his three Mexican stories and mailed each to Ginsberg, so that their "compositional intentions," their functions as black magic or blackmail, were transferred once more; where Anderson had stood in for Marker, he now stood in for Ginsberg. So much for "writing as inoculation," for achieving "immunity from further perilous ventures along these lines." If Burroughs turned to past failures of communication and control in order to articulate desires in the present, then the threat of repetition extended into the future as a recurrent nightmare of isolation and dependence. Do we not see that inexorable logic of destiny, of the fate repetition compulsion Freud called *Schicksalzwang,* at work in the uncanny confusion not only of fact and fiction but also of past, present, and future, in the very names of the other, as (Jack) ANDERSON, (Eugene) ALLERTON, and ALLEN (Ginsberg) all run and blur together? And since the root etymology of Freud's term links destiny *(Geschick)* with sending *(shicken)* (Derrida 63), is there not a certain inevitability that the text to follow *Queer* should have been the epistolary "In Search of Yage"?

THE LETTER AS LITERATURE

WHERE AM I GOING IN SUCH A HURRY?

The passage from *Junkie* to *Queer* to "In Search of Yage" traces a line of seemingly inexorable flight. Forced to leave the land of his birth and then to abandon his adopted home of Mexico City, in December 1952 Burroughs found himself exiled twice over and following the dictates of a destiny signposted South. Burroughs let the Immortal Bard speak for him on the eve of his departure for Central America: "Let determined things to destiny hold unbewailed their way" (*L* 143). But if we take these determined things to signify the life of Burroughs' books rather than the book of Burroughs' life, then how true does the line of letters towards "Yage" now run?[17] The question is posed on the back of my preceding analysis, which makes possible a complete reversal of this text's position within the trajectory of Burroughs' development. After all, for years "Yage" has been either viewed from a distance, so that *yagé* becomes just a substitute for junk as the goal of identical quests for identical questers, or else it has been passed over as a mere anomaly, a biographical bridge to cross or an irrelevance to circumvent. This fate has much to do with *The Yage Letters*'s unstable hybrid form, its composite construction out of work from two decades and by two authors, and even more to do with the status of the "Yage" section as an autobiographical epistolary novella of undecidable authenticity.

The truly diminutive critical stature of "Yage" has to be addressed in terms of its generic anachronism and the indeterminacy of its literariness. An *epistolary novella* by William Burroughs? *A selection of letters?* But this formal anomaly has itself always been neglected as such. Even those traditional questions basic to the genre have not been asked of it, questions about the ideology of authorship that go back to *Lettres portugaises,* the genre's seventeenth-century *locus classicus:* but if the correspondence is authentic, can it be *art?* The traditionalist belief in what Elizabeth MacArthur calls "an aristocracy of literature" holds that birth determines merit, so that the critic has a right to know unambiguously the origin and type of a text before beginning the work of interpretation (116). Work: the traditionalist critic needs the assurance, the insurance, of responding only to the orderly results of certain, approved sorts of productive labor. And private correspondence doesn't qualify: that's not literature, it's *letter writing!* Such issues used to preoccupy critical discourse about the epistolary. To leap media, they are in one sense reminiscent of the kinds of response that greeted the first modernist collages: that's not painting, it's *gluing!* Was that a real postage stamp, stuck right there on the canvas? Yes, it was: recently mailed by the Italian artist and critic Ardengo Soffici and affixed by Pablo Picasso onto one of his earliest collages, from spring 1912, entitled, of course, "The Letter" (Poggi ix). That's not writing, it's *plumbing!* (Samuel Beckett on Burroughs' cut-up methods). Once the questions are asked, the more obvious it becomes: these issues are not eccentric for Burroughs but seminal.

In fact, as MacArthur argues, while "real correspondences are almost never read as works of literature," all letters are "fictional constructions," and any correspondence may be given a literary reading (117, 118). On the other hand, when the letter is transposed into the literary, it runs the risk not of fusing art with life but of its opposite, making a mere rhetorical figure out of the literal. What is at stake here can be demonstrated by the case of Antonin Artaud, for whom letter writing was absolutely integral to the production of his verse and criticism and was a key reason for the "ambiguous status" of all he wrote (Hayman 11). In 1924, Artaud protested to Jacques Rivière that he would not see their yearlong private correspondence transformed into an epistolary novel, even by so slight a transposition as giving invented names to addressee and signatory:

> Why should we lie, why should we attempt to bring to the level of literature a thing that is the very cry of life, why should we give appearances of fiction to that which is composed of the ineradicable substance of the soul, like the lament of reality? (qtd. in Kaufmann, "Life" 97)

This is a pressing issue here, for two reasons. First, in Burroughs, writing exactly thirty years after Artaud, the cry of life and the level of literature refuse to keep their assigned domains: what division and priority is possible between "original" and "fictional copy" for a letter that bears the signature "Willy Lee" when posted in May 1953 (*L* 162) and the name "Bill" when edited and published in "Yage" (*YL* 34)? Second, the ambiguous status of the letter, intermediate between life and writing, makes it a form of literature designated "minor" by Deleuze and Guattari. The passage from *Junkie* to *Queer* to "Yage" takes on the appearance of a flight from "major" literature, a regress of accelerating pace towards raw metonymic materials, fragments cannibalized, rather than a progress towards works with the professional ambition, scale, and artistry of metaphoric "finish."

Remaindered so long in the margins as anomalous, *The Yage Letters* as a whole and "Yage" in particular might now be seen as absolutely central and inevitable, the entirely logical next step for Burroughs. Having found the phantom fingerprints of epistolarity where they were least suspected—in *Queer*—it isn't even necessary to assert Burroughs' investment in his correspondence as a creative context for "Yage," since epistolary form is the very structure of the text. If Lee's routines in *Queer* can be read as one half of a phantasmic epistolary exchange, then the formal appearance of "Yage" seems to confirm Burroughs' deliberate engagement with the genre to which his compositional practice belongs. Since it is the letter medium that, in a very material sense, produced the distinctive persona of William Lee, then the epistolary mode of "Yage" becomes his natural, because natal, form.

But to speak of genres is to invite, not solve, a series of questions. "Yage" may well be considered *in relation to* epistolary tradition but not as written *within* it. For just as there has been no *critical context* for *reading* Burroughs' work of the 1950s in relation to the epistolary, so too, long before the recent critical revivals and postmodernist experiments first observed by Janet Altman in 1982, there was simply no *creative context* for him as a *writer*: as a fictional form available to Burroughs at this time, let alone as a form based on his material practice of letter writing, the epistolary scarcely existed.[18]

The few near sightings of the epistolary in Burroughs criticism are therefore interesting because, as missed encounters, they make the same points by default. Of most immediate relevance, there is Johnny Payne's analysis of Burroughs, which is revealing because it follows detailed readings of experimental Latin American epistolary fiction but fails to make the link.[19] Payne's oversight is also ironic, because the political and geographic focus of his book makes for a significant prompt in relation to "Yage." If Ovid's letter-writing heroines narrated from exile, Payne brings the conjunction up to date by showing the epistolary as "the consummate mode for understanding the attempt at giving literary expression to the fragmentation lived by a nation of exiles, both internal and external" (102). While his focus is on the very different situation of Argentina in the late 1970s, to see the years of the Process (of National Reorganization) as "epistolary years" for intellectuals because, in Tomas Eloy Martínez's words, exile was "that place from which the letters arrived" (qtd. in Payne 102) enables a *politicized* reading of the genre as used by Burroughs. His prescient remarks on Robert Oppenheimer's fate—"a deviant tolerated for his usefulness" (*YL* 34)—combine with his denunciation of South American dictatorships to identify "Yage" as a document of cold war censorship and control. If Kerouac and Ginsberg saw themselves as belonging to a generation of internal exiles and used correspondence to offset their social and cultural exclusion, then the letter form represents Burroughs' condition as permanent writer-in-exile.

In terms of Burroughs' formal development, however, "Yage" departs dramatically from the first person narrator Lee of *Junkie* and, for the first time, ties voice and agency directly to the activity of writing and the identity of Lee as a writer. To identify more precisely the place of "Yage" within the trajectory of Burroughs' writing and to grasp its textual politics requires relating the specificity of its form to that of its subject matter. In the first instance, we are looking less at epistolary fiction than at *yagé* letters.

REAL DESTINY

To address the letters by way of dealing with *yagé* and the Putumayo jungle that is one of its key habitats enables us to see the scoring of South America into the imagination of Burroughs' fiction, which deepens across his early texts and is a major presence beyond them, especially in *Naked Lunch* and *The Soft Machine.* Burroughs' expedition in 1953 would, as he observed, give him "an awful lot of copy" and bring encounters with "the extra dimensions of character and extremity that make the difference" (qtd. in

Knickerbocker 168). The "difference" of South America, its proximate alterity for Burroughs, would continue to exercise its fascination in recurrent dreams of returning to the site of his "real destiny" throughout the decade (*L* 285).[20] Burroughs' geographic movements south—"Keep on like this I will end up in Tierra del Fuego" (97)—were also regressions in time, a way out that was a way *back* to the past.

It wasn't only the allure of lost worlds and long-closed frontiers that pulled Burroughs back but also the atavistic pull of the ethnographic field itself. Burroughs combines the fascination with the primitive of modernists like Rimbaud and Conrad with that of anthropology as a science. Read in the light of "Yage," *Naked Lunch*, which incorporates large sections of the (then unpublished) text, appears all the more evidently a work of massive encyclopedic reference, from Mau Mau voodoo men to sex rituals among the Eskimos via jokes on "Primitive Man" at the expense of Franz Boas (*NL* 42, 83, 110). Here, in dense juxtaposition with fantasies of science and rituals of postwar Western society, archaic remnants suggest the primeval chaos immanent to capitalism and support Michael Taussig's wry claim that modernity "stimulated primitivism along with wiping out the primitive" (*Mimesis* 231). Within that scenario, "the Putumayo is but a figure for a global stage of development of the commodity fetish" (Taussig, *Shamanism* 129). In this context, there is one figure that carries over from "Yage" of singular significance: the *latah*.

Although it is not named in *Queer*, the *latah's* presence is registered there in Lee's speculative remarks on the ability of *yagé* to induce "automatic obedience" and the "synthetic schizophrenia" he sees at the end of the evil rainbow of cold war dreams (*Q* 91); at least one mid-1950s report made the connection explicit, linking *latah*, as a condition of "hypersuggestibility and automatism," to the Korean War brainwashing scare (Farber, Harlow, and West 275). What makes the *latah*—a condition actually associated with Southeast Asia—so central a figure for Burroughs is that it reproduces *yagé's* fantasized promise of total telepathic control. It also underscores the vampiric logic of postwar colonialism as described by Taussig in terms of modernism and primitivism, a logic that for Burroughs would elide as second order all distinctions between market and command economies. That is, the First World fantasizes a regulated empire of compliant *latahs*, contented citizens remade in the image of their cultural and ideological consumptions, and does so by drawing on figures of compulsory mimesis taken from the Third.

This is at the center of the *latah*—and also of its cousin condition, the *amok*—as defined by cultural psychiatry. To cite a standard authority, *la-*

tah is seen as a by-product of rapid "social change, particularly colonialization," and is a response *in extremis* to the "imposition of the customs and goods of powerful Western nations upon peoples of the Third World" (Kennedy 1160). As acute pathologies produced in a colonial society, the symptomatic imitations of *latah* or *amok* are linked to forced cultural training in general and in particular to what Anna Freud termed "identification with the aggressor" (qtd. in Kennedy 1159). In fact, as "culture-bound syndromes," *latah* and *amok* have a particular socioeconomic history, cultural logic, and therefore political dimension; but clearly, it is not their specificity that interested Burroughs. On the contrary, he appropriates the symptomatic results of colonial trauma without discrimination. This might be seen as a further act of Western consumption, another way to use ethnography to sustain an imperialist hierarchy, rather than as a political act of cross-cultural solidarity. However, what I think "Yage" shows, as an extension of *Queer,* is the visible evidence of a Western pathology of the ego itself. Lee speaks in the master's voice precisely in order to hear an alien colonial language talking—one that, like a *latah,* he is forced to reproduce in order to "be" himself.

Burroughs' insight is to seize upon a figure so resonant and reversible for Lee's involvement with a place and a pharmacology as profoundly ambiguous as the land of *yagé.* On the other hand, whereas Lee's fantasy of controlling the other politicizes the drug so emphatically in *Queer,* in "Yage" itself, where Lee actually takes it, this dimension is entirely lacking. Despite his political engagement and commentary, Lee never once mentions *yagé* as a possible tool of political, let alone personal, control. It is a significant difference, one that despite the continuities between the texts says a good deal about the completely different textual politics of *Queer* and "Yage."

THE LIBERATING FOOL

"Yage" literally begins with last things, the first letter identifying Lee's address in Panama as the Hotel Colon. This image of the ends of the body is perversely double: the colon being a point of exit that serves Lee as a point of entry, both for his letter and his body: "I stopped off here to have my piles out. Wouldn't do to go back among the Indians with piles I figured" (*YL* 3). And so, if for Lee as an American in Panama the Hotel Colon is the residence of colonial occupation, in a contradictory move he prepares himself for offering up his body for sexual colon-ization by the colonized. Since, in Leo Bersani's formula, to *"be penetrated is to abdicate power"* ("Is the Rectum" 252), this contradiction inaugurates the radical ambiguity and reversibility of Lee's position throughout "Yage" and between "Yage" and *Queer.*

When Lee first learns of the hostile Auca Indians, he contemplates capturing one: "You cover both exits of Auca house and shoot everybody you don't wanna fuck" (*YL* 31). In the context of Ecuador's history of oppressive exploitation, Lee envisages literalizing the work of "colonial pederasty" as denounced forty years earlier by another reporter on the Putumayo, the onetime comrade of Joseph Conrad in the Belgian Congo, Sir Roger Casement (Taussig, *Shamanism* 131). It is less than a coincidence then that Burroughs would bring together Belgian Congo ("where they turned in severed black genitals and collected the bounty") and Putumayo (with its "rubber-boom guards and foremen") in a retrospective survey of colonial terror (*WL* 148). Casement's relation to the region has an especially relevant political irony, because the homosexual Irishman could identify with the Indians as victims on the basis of his *own* oppressed national and sexual identity. So too can Lee, but equivocally, as befits his state of undisguised self-contradiction. He knows that he is implicated in the mutual exploitations of colonized and colonist and in the Putumayo's palimpsest of economic, political, and religious oppression that extends from the past into the present to predict a blighted future: from the rubber and cocoa businesses—both now "shot" (*YL* 22)—via Capuchin priests—"advocates of death" who "lead the life of Riley" (12, 18)—on to Texas Oil, which the locals refuse to believe has pulled out, so that mistaking Lee for a company representative, they confirm both *their* colonial dependence and *his* imperial fantasy by treating Lee like "visiting royalty" (22).

Haunted by a grotesque history of colonial genocide and economic exploitation, the Putumayo region was called in one report "The Devil's Paradise" and dubbed the "space of death" by Taussig. Burroughs loathed it. "Especially," he wrote Ginsberg, "I hate the whole Putumayo region" (*L* 174). This is an important kind of hatred for the Western traveler: Burroughs hates it with the horror of the colonist who confronts a fantasmatic mirror, who sees himself in the looking glass of alterity. Lee finds himself therefore bisected by the colonial fantasy. In *Queer*, Lee's dream of libertarian autonomy serviced by "an all-purpose" native boy is followed by his derision of Bolívar, "The Liberating Fool" (*Q* 98). In "Yage," the cynicism vanishes as Lee crosses sides: "What we need is a new Bolivar who will really get the job done" (*YL* 34). But it is not really a matter of crossing sides or even of knowing them, since Lee isn't simply joking in *Queer* any more than he is revealing his true politics in "Yage." For Burroughs, these are contradictions not to resolve but to enlarge. As Ronald Berman comments, if Burroughs "makes Norman O. Brown sound like Matthew Arnold," the politics of "Yage" are "as unthinkable to the liberal as to the conservative" (212).

Burroughs often identified Lee's travels within the genre of the pica-resque, and "Yage" can certainly be located in a tradition that runs from Petronius and Menippean satire through Nashe's *Unfortunate Traveller* to Céline's *Voyage au bout de la nuit*. However, this kind of generic identity endangers the geographic specificity of Lee's presence in the Putumayo and the colonial psychology of loathing and self-loathing it inspired. The same story, set in the same region, is told thirty years later by the German film-maker Werner Herzog during the extraordinary production of *Fitzcarraldo*, and it makes equal sense to relate "Yage" to the making of this movie. Herzog was forced to see in the Putumayo jungle's "overwhelming growth and overwhelming lack of order" (qtd. in Taussig, *Shamanism* 79) a pic-ture of his own activities; forced, that is, to recognize his own cursed cre-ation and his own cursed colonial presence—bringing Caruso to the jungles, bringing Klaus Kinski—in the alien mirror of the accursed land-scape itself. The association is necessary because, unlike *Queer*, "Yage" has an extraordinarily strong sense of *place*, and it is this region of dread and decay, as much as the nomadic picaro figure, that animates Burroughs' text. The Putumayo is Burroughs' Heart of Darkness (Africa would never compete for interest), that signifies a destined rendezvous, a rendezvous *with* destiny.

Lee is pressed through South America by the dictates of an unnamed but relentless psychic malaise, his "stasis horrors" (*YL* 40) manifesting a hatred of being himself as a fear of being *anywhere* at all. This suggests the urgency of Lee's unanswered questions in what were the first edition's fi-nal lines: "Where am I going in such a hurry? Appointment in Talara, Tingo Maria, Pucallpa, Panama, Guatemala, Mexico City? I don't know. Suddenly I have to leave right now" (43). This is a glimpse of the future as death, not left behind but waiting up ahead; hence Burroughs' evocation of "An Ap-pointment in Samarra," that quintessential parable of running backwards into the embrace of Death and Destiny.[21]

HOLD THE PRESSES!

Lee is here because he's "in search of *yagé*," but it is never made clear *why*. The question of motives remains curiously vague, a sign of something ei-ther not understood or not to be communicated, perhaps both. Just how far Burroughs underplays Lee's motivation is visible by comparison of the published text with the "real" correspondence it overlaps, although even here some essential fact is given only in the form of an enigmatic hesita-tion: "There are things of which I can not bring myself to speak" (*L* 160). For the most tangible sign of a potential motive, however, we have to look to a "Yage Article" that Burroughs wrote two years later. This grounds his interest explicitly in claims to serious anthropological, pharmacological, and general scientific research:[22]

> I have a special interest in narcotics. I have taken Peyote with Indians in Mexico, I have smoked hasheish in Morocco [. . .] I have the subjective cellular knowledge of drugs that would enable me to compare, evaluate and classify a narcotic that I had not already experienced. I am interested in telepathy, foresight and clairvoyance, the ESP phenomena studied by Rhine, Warcollier and others, and have experimented with thought transference. So I had two reasons for interesting myself in Yage.

Initially planned in late 1954 as a conventional, "short book on Yage like Huxley's peyote book" ("Positively no schoolboy smut"), this article, finished by the end of 1955, was aimed at "an adventure magazine like *Argosy*" (*LG* 82, 172).[23] Burroughs' reference here to Huxley, who took mescaline for the first time the same month Burroughs took *yagé* and whose *Doors of Perception* was published in 1954, confirms the prescience of his experiments as a novelist with this drug. This was a time when *yagé* (aka Banisteriopsis Caapi, *ayahuasca, natema, pinde*) was only of emerging interest to a few professional ethnobotanists, principally Richard Evans Schultes ("Doc Schindler" in "Yage"), the Russians, and the CIA. Nowadays, any big city bookstore sells ethnopharmacological studies of *yagé,* such as *Vine of the Soul* by Schultes or *Food of the Gods* by Terrence McKenna, and literary-anthropological accounts, such as Taussig's *Shamanism, Colonialism, and the Wild Man;* there is even now an *Ayahuasca Reader* (Luna and White), a large Internet Web site, and a problem with "ayahuasca tourism" (Metzner 38–39) in the region. All of which makes it only too easy to forget that back in 1953 Burroughs was a genuinely pioneering amateur. While *yagé* had been discovered for the West in 1851 by the British botanist Richard Spruce, when Burroughs researched the subject with Ginsberg's help in July 1952, there was almost nothing to find. This was the point he stressed in his "Yage Article," which included a technical bibliography of half a dozen works, including Spruce's *Notes of a Botanist:* that the few references were "vague and contradictory" and that "the informants had not taken Yage themselves." "Obviously," he concluded, "if I was to gather any accurate information it would have to be done at first hand."

The four different trips recounted in "Yage" represent part of a significant *empirical* experiment according to Burroughs' principle of factualism, one that here fulfills the methodology that William James called "radical empiricism": if all knowledge must be based on observation, then this can and must include observed experience of subjective, altered states too. As Ralph Metzner has argued, James points towards an "epistemology for the study of consciousness" that enables and validates *yagé* research (7). Burroughs' accounts of his trips also hold up surprisingly well against more traditional professional fieldwork, such as Michael Harner's research with the Jivaro Indians in 1956–57 and the Shipibo in 1960–61. Not that I'm about to make a claim for "Yage" as a serious ethnographic report. While Metzner may be right that the "shamanic lore of ayahuasca entered most strongly into Western culture initially through *The Yage Letters*" (14), and while Rod Phillips has called it "American literature's first psychedelic travel narrative" (126), it is more accurate to say, with Terrence McKenna, that it is the founding text of a "pharmo-picaresque" tradition (163). My point is that the version of Burroughs' *yagé* encounters given in the published text is significantly framed and regulated by Lee's identity as a picaro and must also be recognized as highly selective: despite the decade-long delay in publication, Burroughs made no revisions to reflect the more considered and scientific approach adopted for his "Yage Article." On the contrary, Lee's cynical persona dictates that his attitude towards *yagé* seems a mere extension of that in *Queer,* where he is presented as an ignorant and mercenary opportunist, a hustler who tries to "come on like a scientist" to Dr. Cotter, while looking for a "buck in the deal" (Q 121, 116). He is engaged in what we would now recognize as a local act of pharmaceutical "bioprospecting" or "biopiracy," as defined by the environmentalist Vandana Shiva: the theft of ancient indigenous knowledge of the natural world for profane commercial profit[24] (76). If in *Queer* Lee had "no access to *Brujo* secrets," unlike the "white *Brujo*" Dr. Cotter (121), then little—or rather, not enough—seems to have changed in "Yage."

Each of Lee's first two *yagé* encounters are introduced in the soured tones of a skeptic: in Puerto Limón, he mocks the shaman as an "old drunken fraud" (*YL* 16); impatient to get his "Yage kicks" in Macoa, he quips, "You can't hurry a Brujo" (23). Lee's attitude implies a need to separate the shaman and his rituals from the substance itself, a need, that is, to naturalize the power of the drug in reassuring Western terms. The central issue for Lee is therefore the question of control—but of himself, not others, and of a critical distance that must be maintained to safeguard existing paradigms of knowledge and being. As the *chuma*, or intoxication, takes effect, Lee's initial responses all try to translate back into familiar terms of reference (23–24). But this effort must cede to the sheer power of the *pinta*, or visions, as the drug transports Lee to Easter Island and then dumps him on the ground, wracked with nausea and helpless misery. Numbed by experience of *la purga*, Lee tries to escape: "I was saying over and over, 'All I want is out of here.' An uncontrollable mechanical silliness took possession of me. Hebephrenic meaningless repetitions. Larval beings passed before my eyes" (24). This is a key moment for Lee: "All I want is out of here" means something other than "I have to leave right now." The identity that desires, desires exit from itself, from its location in time and the body. But what happens is that Lee's very repetition of the words brings about exhaustion of the verbal and brings on visions of life-forms in the early stages of metamorphosis.

What Lee's account leaves implicit is that the traditional colonial effort to assimilate native knowledge has collapsed under that knowledge's irresistible transforming power. You can't hurry a skeptic—Lee hails from Missouri, the Show Me State—but *yagé* converts him in the end. That it was left implicit—or rather, that something once fully explicit was *left out*—is absolutely clear from the fullness, the fulsomeness, of Burroughs' contemporaneous reports. Written from Pucallpa, the key letter is dated 18 June, but crucially, not a word of it appears in the letter that bears the same date (but a different place) in the published text.

> Hold the presses! Everything I wrote about Yage subject to revision in the light of subsequent experience. It is *not* like weed, nor anything else I have ever experienced. I am now prepared to believe the *Brujos* do have secrets [. . .] I feel rather like a male Dorothy Thompson who rushed down here to get the story on Yage in two weeks. (*L* 171)

Hold the presses: that's just the point—Burroughs *didn't*. He allowed the journalistic shallowness and skepticism of his initial reports to stand unrevised. The fact that parts of the sensational account of his Pucallpa visions would appear in *Naked Lunch* (*NL* 109) should prompt us to recognize two other things: First, the overlooked place of *yagé* in *Naked Lunch,* where the drug has stayed a kind of open secret, its significance eclipsed entirely by the relentless overdetermination of junk and addiction. Second, the eclipse in "Yage" *itself* of the *yagé* experience, which amounts to less than three pages (*YL* 16, 24–25). The effect of displacement becomes even clearer when we bear in mind that the Composite City vision, which announces that "Yage is space-time travel," was also included in *Naked Lunch* (106–10) but didn't appear in *The Yage Letters* until the 1975 edition (44–46). To grasp the upshot of this curious editing history, we have to note and contextualize the key features of Burroughs' Pucallpa vision, as given in his 18 June letter and in the original notes typed up in early July.

YAGE IS IT

First, *yagé* produced "the most complete derangement of the senses" (*L* 179) and so fulfilled explicitly the hallucinatory and metamorphic logic of Rimbaud's project for a dissolution of self that goes together with a deconstruction of language. Second, the connection to a tradition of radical, visionary poetics in turn produced a connection to a history of visual aesthetics, since for Burroughs the *pinta* were just that, *pictures:* the world comes to "writhing life like a Van Gogh painting" (180). This is the beginning of Burroughs' creative turn towards a visual and materially based aesthetics. "If I could only paint I could convey it all," he claimed (180), and later that July, he filled several pages of at least one notebook with a kind of automatic script of *yagé* glyphs.[25] Two years later, Burroughs would recognize more precisely the profound visual impact of his *yagé* experience in the work of Paul Klee, identifying one as an "exact copy" of his Pucallpa visions (289, 290).[26] Finally, Burroughs speaks of *yagé* producing an "overwhelming rape of the senses," a figure immediately literalized through his vision of achieving a total sexual and racial transformation: "I feel myself change into a Negress [. . .] Now I am a Negro man fucking a Negress" (*L* 179–80). This final metamorphosis, with its reversals of white/black, passive/active, male/female, is glossed in terms of attaining "the most complete negation possible" of "that preposterous condition known as self respect" (180, 181), by which Burroughs means rather more than Kerouac's Sal Paradise's "wishing I were a Negro" in *On the Road* (163). This is neither identification *with* nor *as* an "other" in hope of accessing what Jonathan Paul Eburne refers to as the "privileged experience of cultural subversion" (69). The metamorphosis experienced in Pucallpa breaks apart the colonial authority of white maleness, while the full upshot of such radical illumination is a larger breakdown still, a larger *breakthrough.* In absolute contrast to the fantasized power of *yagé* in *Queer,* in "Yage" the horizon opened by the drug for Lee is not a self-protective, narcissistic assimilation or consumption of the other but a dissolution of the self, a dispossession of the very basis to the will-to-possess. This is a vision of self-overcoming without the lacerating masochism of abject self-humiliation, an apparently *desirous* rather than disastrous disintegration of identity.

When Burroughs invoked Klee in 1955, it was in the context of

incredible journeys of exploration, expression in terms of an *extreme act,* some excess of feeling or behavior that will shatter the human pattern.

Klee expresses a similar idea: "The painter who is called will come near to the secret abyss where elemental law nourishes evolution." (*I* 128)

So too, Burroughs was "called" under the influence of *yagé*, his Pucallpa visions leading logically on to Lee's final destination, the Composite City: "new races as yet unconceived and unborn, combinations not yet realized passes through your body. Migrations, incredible journeys through deserts and jungles and mountains [...]" (*YL* 44). One of Burroughs' most extraordinary texts, this is a precise variation upon the *Villes* of Rimbaud's *Illuminations* and St. John Perse's *Anabasis* that borrows not just their themes but their visionary poetics, their elliptical mosaics of imagery and long, densely rhythmic catalogs. In Burroughs' phantasmagoric cityscape, metamorphosis is permanent through continuous juxtaposition, so that, like Rimbaud's, this landscape is an *anti-paysage* marked by the volatility of shifting perspectives and elements that cannot be mastered into coherence. Here, the key words are all *sous rature:* "unknown," "unconceived," "incredible," "unborn," "inhuman," "unthinkable," "unspeakable," but above all "unknown" (44–46). This is the antiknowledge of Rimbaud: "He reaches the unknown, and when, bewildered, he ends by losing the intelligence of his visions, he has seen them!" (307).

This *anti*knowledge may, as Burroughs' citation from Klee suggests, be just the visible form of an evolutionary *ante*knowledge: gestures towards a posthuman world that, from here, from the vantage of the human, cannot be known in advance and so can only be defined at the extremes, negatively. As Foucault put it, beyond "man" there can only be "something that absolutely does not exist, about which we know nothing," something "entirely different" (qtd. in Dollimore, "Sex" 40). What *yagé* produces is a visionary text of functional dysfunctions, unwilled biological and racial mutations whose political efficacy has been well put by Steven Shaviro: "every breakdown brings to the fore an immense reservoir of new, untapped differences and mutations: material in random variation upon which selection can operate" ("Two Lessons" 53). Shaviro is generalizing from Burroughs, but he might be describing the Composite City of "Yage." Here is the energy of continuous evolution, of "all human potentials" in a state of passage and becoming, a chaos of open-ended mutation as opposed to the fixed closure of being and "stasis and death in closed mountain valleys" (*YL* 44). The spatial and temporal limits are off: "Yage is space time travel."[27]

Conclusion? "Yage is it." "Yes Yage is the final kick and you are not the same after you have taken it. I mean literally" (*L* 180, 184). Or as Burroughs spelled out the implications of his Pucallpa visions in his "Yage Article":

I glimpsed a new state of being. I must give up the attempt to explain, to seek any answer in terms of cause and effect and prediction, leave behind the entire structure of pragmatic, result seeking, use seeking, question asking Western thought. I must change my whole method of conceiving fact.

In short, we have the answer to the question posed in 1964 by Donatella Manganotti, in what has remained the only extended commentary on the text: "Was Yage the *real* thing, the 'final fix' and as such too important to be told in so many words—like esoteric mysteries of the past?" (84–85).

And yet *yagé* is *not* it.

When William Stull constructed the quest structure of Burroughs' first decade, on the published evidence he was absolutely right to observe that in "Yage" the quester's "boon is not forthcoming" (23). Whether or not *yagé* was the real thing for Burroughs, it is clear that he refused to allow *yagé* to be "the final fix," the archetypal *grail* promised at the end of *Junkie*. "In Search of Yage" is not Burroughs' version of *A Yaqui Way of Knowledge* fifteen years ahead of Castaneda (and of his own interest in Castaneda), any more than *Naked Lunch* is. To conclude that *yagé* is the suppressed secret of "Yage" leaves us with two final questions: *why* Burroughs decided to withhold the secret, and *what else* he put in its place.

A WHOLE DIMENSION EXCISED

To answer the first question requires knowing *when* he made the decision, which in turn requires some awareness of the concealed manuscript history of "Yage." When Burroughs called out "Hold the presses!" in his letter of 18 June 1953, he was asking Ginsberg to disregard the "Yage MS" he refers to having sent him in his previous two letters (*L* 168, 170). The "revision in light of subsequent experience" (171)—his Pucallpa *yagé* experience, with its "rape of the senses," sexual and racial metamorphosis, radical negation of "self respect," and so on—all this was still in Burroughs' manuscript when he began in early 1955 to rework it.[28] The fate of this material is undoubtedly tied to that of Burroughs' key text about quests and secrecy, also begun in early 1955, "The Conspiracy." For here, Burroughs is even more explicit about *yagé*, which now represents the creative life force in a global historical conflict against the powers of death. This was itself a scenario that extended the "fundamental split" that Burroughs identified in "Yage" through the Colombian Civil War, "between the South American Potential and the Repressive Spanish life-fearing armadillos" (*YL* 34).

In "The Conspiracy," on one side, there is the "anti-dream drug" based on junk, a scientifically perfected means to produce a socioeconomic order of rational automatons; and on the other side, *yagé*, revealed as an archaic, utopian antidote that, drawing on the prized dream experience of nostalgia, "increases the symbolizing faculty" that "everyone has to some degree as a child" (*I* 109). Therefore, in removing "The Conspiracy" from *Naked Lunch* and the conclusion that *yagé* "is it" from "Yage," Burroughs himself eliminated the antidote to his dystopian vision of a world in which "it is possible to eliminate nostalgia," so that "a whole dimension [is] excised" (108, 109). Now, the *why* becomes clearer: once again, as he had when cutting from *Junkie* his invocation of Wordsworth's dream, Burroughs bluepenciled the call of Romanticism. He refused the lure of the "false secret" of a philosopher's stone or a holy grail, a final secret of hidden content, which is what *yagé* would have become, whether it were taken *allegorically* (as a figure in Burroughs' war against Control) or *literally* (as an actual drug that works). And so finally, we can answer the second question, what Burroughs put in place of *yagé*.

Instead of holding the presses and revising his conclusions about the drug, Burroughs turned its semiotic and metamorphic potency into a practice of *writing* and did so not once but twice.

The Composite City that concludes "Yage" is so called for a very good reason. Here, it is not only architecture, geography, and biological evolution that exist in a state of shifting intertextual plurality, as Robin Lydenberg has noted (*Word Cultures* 47), but the very text of the Composite City itself. This is a literally *composite text*. It is traversed by cuts and pastes, fragmentary ellipses, and juxtapositions of a whole series of variations upon phrasings already read in earlier parts of "Yage," so that, whether the process is consciously recognized or not, the experience of space-time travel is embodied and reproduced materially in the reading experience itself. "Hebephrenic meaningless repetitions" (*YL* 24) are here themselves repeated in "Hebephrenic shorthand" (46). Figures are rendered literal, fantasy reappears as fact, and metaphor is animated into metamorphosis, as image after image is rewritten in abbreviated or expanded variation, to create the effect of cinematic and chemical *flashbacks*. If the sensual derangement of the *yagé* experience could not be described in words, it is here rendered verbally, not in terms of image content but through structural rearrangement and formal recombination. Lee's accounts of visionary metamorphosis have themselves turned metamorphic. Sentences lose their verbs, words turn material and become, in effect, *yagé letters*.

The dense and disorientating intertextuality of the Composite City works backwards, on the text already read out of which it is constructed, but clearly enough, it also has the significance of a new departure in Burroughs' writing that predicts his cut-up practices ahead. No coincidence then that the first literary texts Burroughs would submit to his scissors in 1960 should be by Rimbaud and St. John Perse. We can now see, in the very structure of "Yage" within *The Yage Letters,* the second way in which Burroughs refused to allow Lee's figurative "trip" to conclude his literal one. For he makes acquisition of the drug initiate another adventurous quest for frontier knowledge and knowledge of frontiers by way of including letters and texts from the next decade that introduce his cut-up methodology. The original quest's end is displaced therefore by Burroughs' new *techné* of montage. This is one of the great interests of *The Yage Letters,* that it makes so readily available, if not positively invites, comparisons between Burroughs' writing across decades.

The performance of *yagé* as space-time travel in the Composite City confronts us, however, with the paradox, maybe the oxymoron, of *The Yage Letters* as a title. For if the experience of *yagé* reveals an epistemological and ontological dimension that can only be verbalized in any measure by such montage effects, what then of the letter as a form of narration, identity formation, and communication?

NO LETTERS

The essence of the epistolary is that writer and reader share neither the same space nor the same time, so that, whereas the telepathic horizon of *yagé* is the absence of language, the epistolary is forced to speak the language of absence. The letter can only dream of presence, of proximity, of bringing bodies together, especially when it plots the course of love. That is Lee's dream for Allerton in *Queer* but not for Al in "Yage." There is no fantasy of reunion here, and so, against all our expectations, no obvious continuity with *Queer.* What kind of plot animates the letter writing of "Yage" then and mediates what kind of presence?

Even if Lee doesn't seek out a shaman to exorcise *mal aires,* he is clearly driven by some force, some evil spirits from the past; but the motivation—for the journey and the letters alike—is withheld from us, as it seems to be from him. Perversely, we learn little about Lee despite the confidential medium of intimate correspondence. Lee eludes us, disappearing into the social and political scene he documents, as if making reports on the present *in order to* close off reflections on his past, sticking to exteriors to avoid interiors and depths. In this, he is far nearer to the narrator of *Junkie* than ought to be the case. The only significant exception is in the first letter, which incorporates as a postscript a routine that stands in for a preface and so occupies the same relation to the letters that follow as the preface to *Junkie* does to its narrative. Standing out from the rest of "Yage," it constitutes a parallel queer autobiography and queering of autobiography.

Given as a postscript to Lee's first letter, the Billy Bradshinkel routine encrypts the past that Lee otherwise keeps absent. Anomalous within "Yage," this routine is therefore fully continuous with Burroughs' previous writing: in its narration of sexual desire and emotional trauma, the routine follows on from the central scene of *Queer,* and in its familial references it connects to the short stories Burroughs first drafted at this time. In fact, Billy seems to be a kind of ultimate synthesis, an apocryphal composite of all the main figures in Burroughs' emotional and erotic biography from early adolescence onwards. The routine's point of departure is a rare moment of nostalgic recollection prompted by two encounters in Lee's present experience. First, there is a bar outside Panama City that reminds him of a prohibition-era roadhouse of his adolescence. Memory stirs emotions, and Lee turns lyricism into parody and then self-mockery: "How sloppy can you get?"[29] (*YL* 4). The sloppiness is both stylistic and emotional, so that the postscript's long routine seeks to exorcise the sentimentality of nostalgia by killing Billy Bradshinkel in a fatal rerun of "Driving Lesson." To kill Billy is to bury the past and its traumatic emotional freight: "Billy" is more than a cognomen Lee shares with Bradshinkel, it is a compound of the entire identity. It also confirms Lee as his mother's son: Bill Lee writes little Bill-Lee into existence in order to erase himself as an adolescent, someone caught up in the desire of the other and of the mother. What the routine suggests then is that Lee's geographic movements in the present should be read not just as a search for *yagé* but as a bid to escape from the ghosts of his past, a desire to escape desire.

The second prompting encounter is easy to overlook, but it is the crucial one. The prompt comprises just two words, ominously slipped in between references to desire and drugs when Lee stops off at the American Embassy: "Smell of excrement and sea water and young male lust. No letters. I stopped again to buy two ounces of paregoric" (*YL* 3). *No letters:* meaning, no letters waiting for Lee at the embassy. Extraordinarily, this briefest of references in the negative is the only reference Lee makes in his whole epistolary text concerning the receipt of letters. After Billy Bradshinkel breaks off the romance—"'But why Billy? Why?'"—Lee describes his failure to restore communication, first by telephone ("he always hung up when he heard my voice") and then: "I wrote him a long letter which he never answered" (6). We are borne back to *Queer*, to its broken telephonic connections standing in for severed epistolary relations and to the eternal return of the compulsion to repeat. *No letters.* No letters from whom? We aren't told or able to tell, but it isn't Al. The original manuscript holds the key.

The final page of the 8 July letter that concluded "Yage" in the first edition of 1963 derives from a ten-page typescript Burroughs mailed to Ginsberg on 3 August 1953 intended to complete "Yage."[30] Thirty years later, the other nine pages were used to form the epilogue to *Queer*, "Mexico City Return," which ends with the Skip Tracer's quest to repossess Allerton. The typescript begins with these vital lines, edited out for *Queer* for understandable reasons but with the effect of concealing an essential continuity: "Back in Lima. No letter from Allerton. I felt sick and discouraged and sat down for several minutes in the embassy. Why doesn't he write?" *No letter from Allerton.* The original manuscript confirms that the Skip Tracer's fantasmatic pursuit is sustained by an epistolary economy of distance and desire, and this is reconfirmed by Burroughs' covering letter to his enclosed manuscript: "I never heard from Marker after I left Mexico, though I wrote ten letters to his home address" (*L* 187). Within the manuscript itself, this economy is made fully explicit in another line cut for publication of *Queer*. Lee has asked Gale about Allerton's absence: "I put the magazine away slowly and walked outside and leaned against a post. '*He must have gotten my letters. Why didn't he answer. Why?*'" (my emphasis; cf. *Q* 130). And just as this manuscript provides vital evidence for our reading of *Queer*, so too it bears upon our reading of "Yage." For it is crucial to note that the Skip Tracer routine—and therefore Allerton—was still a part of "Yage" throughout the 1950s. As with *yagé*, so too with letters, what Burroughs took out is as significant as what he left in, and the text bears the traces of his scissions and decisions.

The restored manuscript confirms what the published text of "Yage" leaves implicit: that Lee is defined as a writer who does not get back what he sends out. Here lies the paradox: without these original references to Allerton, which thematize explicitly the epistolary anxiety of transmission and reception, Lee is left in the Billy Bradshinkel routine fictionalizing a traumatic failure of sexual and textual reciprocity in the distant past, in the course of giving us in the present only his own half of a correspondence with "Al." In the context of Lee's isolation and alienation abroad, this absence ought to be another occasion for crisis. In June 1952, the definitive form of Marker's rejection was his failure to reply: "No answer. I guess he means no" (*L* 131). But in "Yage," no answer equals no problem. If the question of receipt should occur to us, then even though there is no evidence that Al ever receives them, we are likely to assume that Lee's letters do reach their destination, not the dead letter office.

Why do we make such an assumption? Because of the nature of Al's presence. To begin with, Al or Allen is not Ginsberg. Contrary to the book's presentation, these are not letters from "William Burroughs to Allen Ginsberg." In "Yage," all traces of the historical Ginsberg have been carefully expurgated, while Burroughs' fictional identity is dispersed across letters that sign off in five different forms (Bill, William, Willy Lee, W. Lee, William Lee). Diane Cousineau observes that the letter form "reifies such principles as stable and unified identity (signature), certainty of destination and destiny (address), and the possibility of human exchange" (17), but none of these essential guarantees appear operative in "Yage." The Al of Lee's letters is not so much a figure of absence as a simply absent figure. Despite Lee's isolated exile and "the lonely scene of writing" distinct from the shared ground of speech (Dowling 10), it is not Al's absence that motivates the letters, only Lee's presence as a writer traveling abroad. As a receiver, Al should represent a point of fixed reference against which the nomadic Lee can write letters to chart his shifting coordinates in space, time, and emotional geography. But even this stability is abstracted: unlike Ginsberg, Al has no (spatial) address or (temporal) existence of his own. Lacking not just specificity but subjectivity, Al inside the narrative coincides too fully with the extra-diegetic reader of "Yage." He is less elsewhere than *nowhere*. Janet Altman notes that in epistolary texts the "confidant is rarely a purely passive listener" (51). "Yage" would be such a rarity. Would be but isn't, because despite sharing some of its physical features, "Yage" lacks the major functions of an epistolary text.

On any map of the epistolary as drawn by its scholarly cartographers, "Yage" appears only on the margins. It develops scarcely a single feature of epistolarity, exploits hardly any of the genre's rich resources. Although the structure of sender-receiver is inherent and a preoccupation for Burroughs, Lee's letters do not foreground mediation by making them a *mise en abyme* for the writer-reader relationship; nor do they concern themselves with the problematic of transmission and reception or emphasize either the distance that divides or its bridging, either isolation or relief, either the compensatory power or the poverty of language (Altman 88). As a narrative, "Yage" goes against the grain of the genre, or at least its most interesting potentials, by detaching the letter from its plot and by using all four of the methods listed by Altman for maximizing continuity and coherence: its plot is singular; time is effectively linear; there is only one writer to one addressee; and no emphasis or significance is given to the lacunae between letters. By definition, the form encourages discontinuity, conflicting perspectives, fragmentation, a mosaic structure. Where is the formal experiment or self-reflexivity or critical metalanguage in "Yage"?

If at its most basic, epistolarity is dependent on the "imaginary copresence of the other—on the relevance of the recipient," as Claudio Guillen has noted (7), then "Yage" does not possess it. The problem is not the absence of replies but the lack of intersubjectivity. Here, the other half is fractional: ostensibly one-to-one, Lee's letters are strictly one-way, are simply not involved in an economy of social exchange or relations of power. To recall Altman's definition, just as Lee's routines in *Queer* are marked by an entirely unsuspected epistolarity, so his letters in "Yage" are marked by its equally unexpected absence. Lacking the basic drive to address and affect the other, generically this writing "does not differ significantly from a journal, even if it assumes the outer form of the letter" (Altman 89). For the most part, Al is an entirely formal device, and Lee is a correspondent more in the journalistic sense of someone who files news reports from the front line.[31]

If the routines of *Queer* cannot be understood as simply written versions of originally oral material, in a parallel reversal of expectations, the letters of "Yage" cannot be understood as simply edited versions of original epistolary material. The situation is more complex, more problematic, but the starting point is this: while Burroughs journeyed through Central and South America, he did not conceive of this writing taking epistolary form. "Yage" retains the barest trace of this situation, gesturing to writing beyond itself when Lee refers to seeking out "additional Yage material" (*YL* 31). Burroughs' own letters spoke anxiously of the writing still to come. "I have written nothing yet," he noted in his real letter of 3 March 1953 (*L* 152; cf. *YL* 21). By the end of April, little had changed: "So far no success writing anything on Yage. My info is incomplete or some essential impetus is lacking."[32] He only announced having "started last night" on 4 May, after four months of traveling.[33] What he called the "Yage MS," completed just before his momentous Pucallpa visions, was finally mailed to Ginsberg on 5 June—"Write me what you think" (*L* 170)—and turns out to be two-dozen pages of first person narrative, travel reportage, and research, diaristic in some senses but not epistolary in form. What makes this urmanuscript so significant is that it corresponds, mostly near verbatim, to the text published as the first six letters of "Yage" (*YL* 3–29). The majority of "Yage" was something other than a reworking of actual letters no longer extant, and the closer those letters that do survive are scrutinized against the text of

"Yage," the clearer the case becomes: reversing the logical order of priority, most of this material was not derived from, but only later put into, epistolary form.

To summarize briefly: For only four out of the twelve letters in "Yage" are there originals that match in any way those in the published text, and all the letters in "Yage" derive from more than one original. In the case of the sixth letter, for example, dated 15 April, a few lines derive from the real letter of 12 April, a few from the "random notes" presented in that of 8 July, and several more from the letters of 22 April and 8 June. Equally significant are the local details, such as the addition for "Yage" of the phrase "my dear" to give an impression of epistolary address, even though this phrase is absent from the corresponding passage in the real 12 April letter (*YL* 22; cf. *L* 156). In short, Ginsberg's claim for Burroughs' early writing as "one half" of their written relationship turns out even here to be highly problematic.

Instead of referring to letter material, having sent the first draft manuscript in June, Burroughs speaks repeatedly of adding "notes as they are in the note-book" to what he called "the Yage section" (*L* 162, 173).[34] He clarifies these are "at random in no order" and that he retypes his miscellany of notes precisely "to get them in some sort of order (173, 178). Back in Mexico City after his travels, Burroughs mailed Ginsberg "more notes" and commented: "I have been working ever since I got here sorting out notes and re-writing" (187). Yet again, he fails to mention letter material as such. But perhaps we see here one ground for Burroughs' decision to generalize rather than expunge the epistolary form: he recognized the advantage of a form that set him free from regular beginnings, continuities, and conclusions. The epistolary format allowed him to reconstruct events "more or less chronologically" (*YL* 15), without imposing a narrative architecture, novelistic unities, the closure of formal control. Burroughs wasn't interested in exploiting epistolarity as a set of specific formal features, and references in his "real" letters that would have thematized the epistolary were not retained but were actually cut out.[35] Above all, the absence of the routine form in "Yage"—with the exception of "Billy Bradshinkel"; "Roosevelt after Inauguration" he termed a "skit"[36]—confirms the paradox that it is *Queer,* not "Yage," that bears the impress of writing as a compulsive act of communication, a drive to impose identity on an other, and therefore it is *Queer,* not "Yage," that initiates a textual politics based on the epistolarity of the routine. There is no desperate necessity for shared understanding in "Yage," no demand for an other half felt so urgently it must be resisted, either via routines or the letter itself.

As with *yagé,* so too with "Yage": neither is *it.* On the basis of its epistolary form, it seemed initially reasonable to claim the centrality of "Yage" within the trajectory of Burroughs' writing as irrefutable evidence for the letter principle, but this turns out not to be the case. Although the gap between letter and literature does narrow materially, in the end "Yage" gives us little more than the empty shell, the dry husk of the letter form, its formal tops and tails. The paradox of "Yage" comes down therefore to this: that because of Burroughs' vital investment of pathological and political energy in writing mediated by the fantasy letter-relation, there is more of an epistolary economy in *Queer* than there is in "Yage." So "Yage" remains anomalous after all, a curio, a strange text on its own terms and within Burroughs' development. Its true significance lies in fact on the horizon, as Burroughs traveled to New York City with a suitcase of *yagé* vine and assorted manuscripts to rendezvous with Ginsberg in fall 1953 en route to his next destination: Tangier.

5

The Real Novel

In my letters it is my perpetual concern to free you of me, but when for once I seem to have succeeded, I go raving mad.
—Franz Kafka, in a letter to Félice Bauer

I relish the idea that in the night, all around me in my sleep, sorcery is burrowing its invisible tunnels in every direction.
—Paul Bowles, *Without Stopping*

UN HOMME DE LETTRES

PAPER CITY

Tangiers, February 1st 1954: "Dear Allen, Cold here like the Penal Colony" (*LG* 16). Tangiers, February 9th: "This town seems to have several dimensions. I have experienced a series of Kafkian incidents" (*L* 196). Falling four days either side of Burroughs' fortieth birthday, an anniversary celebrated alone in a strange city three thousand miles from his correspondent, these letters frame that most traditional of autobiographical milestones with allusions to Kafka. The names of Kafka and Tangier go together, because Tangier was a "paper city" in multiple senses (Finlayson 83). The city's identity as an "International Zone" was always a legal fabrication, a "diplomatic fiction" drawn up by colonial powers in the 1920s; as Ian Finlayson notes in his history of Tangier, "the dreamscapes of consular colonialism, the illusory charade of foreign authority" would simply melt away at the touch of independence in October 1956 (11). The other paper that ruled Tangier in its heyday—until riots in 1952 collapsed confidence—was the promissory note, circulated and speculated on the free exchange market, when the city was host to several hundred banks and when fiscal deregulation verged on financial anarchy. An international fiction and a microcosmos of raw, free market capital, a hybrid of decaying and emergent identities, the spelling of whose very name shifts restlessly in Burroughs' letters—*Tangier, Tanger, Tangers, Tangiers*—this zone of unstable political, economic, and cultural juxtapositions was less a unique and anomalous outpost bound by its historical determinants than an augury of the future as cityscape collage. In Foucault's terminology, it was a "heterotopia," in Burroughs' terms, a "Composite City" or metamorphic "Interzone": "the prognostic pulse of the world, like a dream extending from past into the future, a frontier between dream and reality—the 'reality' of both called into question" (*L* 302).

On the other hand, Burroughs saw the town as a Kafkian trap, a penal colony, because its social license was, as he put it in his own portrait of the place, "International Zone" (written in 1955), a negative function of capital approaching a state of final reification: "People sit at café tables, silent and separate as stones. No other relation than physical closeness is possible. Economic laws, untouched by any human factor, evolve equations of ultimate stasis" (*I* 49). But if Burroughs recognized an alienating economic determinism, his vision is not that of an economic determinist. Tangier was "a sanctuary of noninterference" for him, a relative haven from forces that in turn defined the socioeconomic as secondary and symptomatic extensions: "Control, bureaucracy, regimentation, these are merely symptoms of a deeper sickness that no political or economic program can touch. What is the sickness itself?" (69). This was a question, posed in early 1955, whose answer he would come closer and closer to formulating during the Tangier years. In the meantime, as addict, homosexual, and privileged foreign national, Burroughs hoped to find in Tangier refuge and opportunity. But unlike Mexico City or the jungles of Central and South America, Tangier uniquely drew Burroughs as the paper city of *literary* invention and fantasy.[1]

In a footnote to Burroughs' letter of 1 February, Ginsberg simply says: "*The Penal Colony:* Kafka's story was on our minds" (*LG* 17). This is precise, but there is more to it. To begin with, Kafka greets Burroughs in Tangier because it is Kafka who brings him here, via Paul Bowles. The literary fascination is uppermost: "Why Tangier? I came solely because of a book by Bowles: *Let It Come Down*" (qtd. in Rondeau 189; my translation).

In fact, there was also Bowles's first novel, Moroccan-set but not Tangier-bound, *The Sheltering Sky*. Here, in the form of an epigraph, Burroughs encountered the conjunction of Bowles, Morocco, and Kafka and a possible intersection with his own trajectory: "From a certain point onward there is no longer any turning back. That is the point that must be reached."[2] These lines were a kind of key for Bowles, a wager he placed during the writing process of each novel, but the aphorism terrified his wife, Jane, who read it as "prophecy," his account of her destiny (Dillon 176). Burroughs would surely have understood.

The forty-year-old Bowles's debut novel had entered the best-seller lists of the *New York Times* at New Year 1950, shortly before Burroughs began his own first novel, and shortly before he started on his sequel, in February 1952 *Let It Come Down* appeared. The parallelism may seem distant between Bowles's sudden rise to literary notice, a *succès de scandale,* and Burroughs' first efforts in the same line, but the intersections for Burroughs would have been particular. Geographically and socially their paths had crisscrossed often without ever touching, and the precise nature of Bowles's success—as a married homosexual and an international socialite, as a peripatetic expatriate and the author of cold, cruel existential thrillers—might have been a fantasy mirror for Burroughs. Bowles may not have inspired Burroughs to write but perhaps to identify with a certain stylized *image* of the writer and to consider Tangier a rendezvous with his writing destiny: a site of fascination that opened onto both a terminal trap and the dream dimension. For Burroughs as a writer arrived in Tangier at a turning point: quite simply, make or break. Looking back, he would single out for praise "the typhoid dream from *The Sheltering Sky* and the hashish delirium at the dead-end of *Let It Come Down*" (qtd. in Pulsifer 14), instances of breakdown and breakthrough, the second under the power of the novel's true protagonist, Tangier herself: the city as *femme fatale.*

Then again, for Burroughs the social reality of Tangier in 1954 was less noir thriller than a dead end for an assortment of last chance exiles; misfits, as he himself put it, "trying to mitigate the dead gray of prosaic failure with a touch of borrowed color" (*I* 52). When a film company arrived just a few months after Burroughs, the local English paper, the *Tangier Gazette,* summed up the city's current fate: "Let us at least be thankful that the world still takes an interest in us—even if it always cast us as the villain" (Beckett 6). Surely, this is why Burroughs and Tangier were so well matched; because the fantasy image of the city lent itself to a special form of self-dramatization, an art of living generically that intensified Burroughs' growing investment in a paper-thick identity. When the *Gazette* reported the local news in March 1956, it would publicly seal, make official as it were, the conflation of prosaic and fantasy selves: "Author William Lee tells us that he is off to spend a couple of months in London" (Gifford 7). It would be another year before Kerouac, after his visit there, could safely speak of "he, Burroughs (not 'Lee' any more)" (qtd. in Harris, Introduction xxvii).

It is said that before the war Pinkertons used to train their fledgling detectives in the art of shadowing suspects by sending them to the medina of Tangier, so subtle was the play of sunlight and so unexpected the twists of its alleys (Schneider 33). This anecdote might be regulatory for the task of retracing the footsteps of *Naked Lunch*, a pursuit that must take into account the particular fascination exercised by the intersection of a writer and a place so potently defined by the devious seduction of their images. What is at stake here is visible in another Tangerine anecdote, when David Cronenberg describes having to give up plans to shoot his movie of the writing of *Naked Lunch* on location: "the assumption was made by all of us—a mass hypnosis—that we must go there," he recalls, before deciding that this was not only unnecessary but a mistake, because "we had been seduced by the biographical element" (qtd. in Rodley, *Cronenberg* 168). Although Cronenberg's film is an easy target, it isn't hard to see the consequences of bringing Tangier to Toronto and making Interzone a "state of mind." His film became the definitive instance of that blurring of fact and fiction, of product and its producer, that for forty years has mystified and mythologized the writing of *Naked Lunch*.

A final anecdote: throughout the 1980s, I found myself making one trip after another to research Burroughs' experience in Tangier, until I could no longer tell whether it was the writer or the place that kept drawing me back. On my last trip, in summer 1991, I attempted a vast, impossibly detailed map of the medina, getting up at dawn each day to photograph all the alleyways and plot their every twist and turn, down to the last blind passage. Methodically tracing these labyrinthine circuits so rich, as Bowles once observed, with "prototypal dream scenes" (*Without Stopping* 128), I experienced curious disturbances of memory, not only déjà vu but, as Burroughs himself put it, the experience of "always finding streets, squares, parks you never saw before" (*I* 58). It was only later on, after the poet and photographer Ira Cohen had turned my map making into an absurdist joke,[3] that I saw what I had been doing. In my unremitting fidelity to factual detail, trying to discover the real scene of Burroughs' Tangier, I had unconsciously reproduced the disturbing experience of reading the very text he wrote there. Trying to fix the location of *Naked Lunch*, to find Interzone in Tangier, I had created only another paper city and once again lost myself in its textual labyrinth.

Putting these anecdotes together, it becomes clear how a materialist approach risks creating a falsely objective scene, unless we take into account the material, but entirely subjective, dimension that is only proper to the unique fascination of *Naked Lunch*. For we can never hope to catch this text square on with an objective critical eye but only, if at all, awry, tangentially, by default, in circuitous and repetitive form. It therefore poses challenges of an entirely different order to those set by *Junkie, Queer* or "Yage." A text so visibly hostile to criticism, it has proved enduringly elusive despite being the center of so much analysis; but at least that attention means there is no need here to redress a state of critical neglect. My emphasis, therefore, will be far more on pursuing a material history of the genesis and reception of *Naked Lunch* than on the impossible task of making this text fully present. Then again, while the genetic histories I have established of Burroughs' previous novels do prepare the ground to some extent, that of *Naked Lunch* is also of an entirely different order. It could hardly be otherwise for a text so radically different, so perplexing and unique. Since the text of *Naked Lunch* has eluded every critical grasp, why should it be any easier to give an adequate account for its coming into being?

Does this mean conceding to Burroughs that, in this instance, "there is no accurate description of the creation of a book"? Not entirely. Rather, it is a question of needing to reckon with everything that comes before *Naked Lunch* that has mediated its reception with myths of its production and of seeing my pursuit of an accurate description of its genesis as itself, in the last analysis, whatever its material and useful results, only another displaced response to the fascination of its form.

IT WAS MY OTHER HAND

"*The Penal Colony:* Kafka's story was on our minds." Ginsberg's allusion is also highly specific, referring to Burroughs' own story of the same title, and it was on their minds because of the exchange between Lee and the boy who Lee tries to blackmail with gifts of severed flesh:

> "Well, I will cut off my foot and shrink it down by a process I learned from the Auca, and make you a watch fob."
> "What I want with your ugly old foot?" (*I* 45)

Replaying the scene from "The Finger," here the boy is modeled not on Jack Anderson but on Lewis Marker, while the rebuff quotes Allen Ginsberg and takes us back to fall 1953. This was when Burroughs stayed with Ginsberg and they worked together on the manuscripts of "In Search of Yage" and *Queer*. At first, Ginsberg described their meeting as a "great psychic marriage," but when it became a one-sided sexual affair, another fantasy of absolute desire, the result was an abrupt physical divorce: "In the end, despite my admiration and affection for my teacher, I had rejected his body. 'I don't want your ugly old cock'" (*LG* 5). Ginsberg gave this account in 1981 when writing the introduction to *Letters to Allen Ginsberg, 1953–1957,* a transatlantic correspondence initiated precisely by their separation that fall.

This context is crucial because it was the publication of these letters that at last forced Burroughs to revise his account of *Naked Lunch*'s genesis, an account most famously given in "Deposition: Testimony Concerning a Sickness," the introduction that has physically mediated all editions after the first. In *"Un Homme de Lettres. Un Poème Moderne,"* his preface to the volume of letters to Ginsberg, Burroughs writes with strained impersonality and surprise:

> Despite the writer's subsequent claims that junk is absolutely contraindicated for creative writing, and that *Naked Lunch* could not have been written unless he had gotten off junk, one is amazed to discover that a great deal of *Naked Lunch was actually written* in these letters to Allen Ginsberg, at a time when the writer was often heavily addicted [. . .] (*LG* 2)

Irrefutable epistolary evidence makes Burroughs revise his own genetic record, while the revised record has to admit the centrality *of* the epistolary. However, far from undoing the account given in his introduction to *Naked Lunch,* Burroughs here reveals a secret with one hand, only to conceal it with the other. This makes it a doubly significant text in the strange history of the letter and *Naked Lunch.*

Written in the third person, Burroughs' preface converts the volume of correspondence into an occasion for the "ghostly sensation of being called upon to comment on someone else's old literary letters" (*LG* 1). This curious move grants Burroughs the distance for self-mockery, but it also allows him to merge his own particular letters into those of other, more familiar literary scenes. First, there is the writer's private record of a struggle with addiction, the "saga of a moaning man of letters," which he invokes by juxtaposing fragments of his own letters alongside one attributed to F. Scott Fitzgerald. Second, there is the Romantic tradition of creative drug-use, invoked by references to Coleridge and De Quincey. Two traditional literary topoi therefore contextualize and guide reading of Burroughs' own individual circumstance. The first establishes the axis *letters-addiction;* the second, the axis *drugs-writing*. The implication of this distinction is not at first clear, but that is because the acknowledgment that is forced by the volume's evidence—"one is amazed to discover"—is framed by Burroughs in ways that obscure and completely redirect its significance.

Immediately before it, he speaks of Livingston Lowes's genetic enquiry into the literary sources of *The Ancient Mariner,* as if this were a necessary and natural archetype. As in Burroughs' introduction to *Queer,* the allusion serves rather to foreclose political meaning by abstracting and aestheticizing his own personal history. The effect is to distance his letters from the specificity of the period they cover, from the place they were written in, and from the person to whom they were addressed. Burroughs then appears to set up an unlikely equivalence between Coleridge's literary reading and his own letter writing as sources of "poetic imagery," only to shift attention away from the epistolary altogether: "These letters to Allen Ginsberg present a devious road to *Naked Lunch* from the raw material of junk experience, as set forth in *Junky* and in these letters" (*LG* 2). The circularity of sentence structure is itself a sign of deviousness, since the effect of it is to further tie both Burroughs' writing and his letters to drug addiction. This move invites the second framing, a bland generalization about the way "all experience is transmuted by the writer into what we call art" (3). The abstraction "art" maintains the implicit binary distinction: letter writing and the writer on one hand, writing and addiction on the other. That is, the left-handed writer of letters set against the right-handed author of what we call art. What would be extraordinary and unique to Burroughs, the third term, does not arise; namely, the integral relationship between letter writing and literary production.

Unsurprisingly then, when this volume was reviewed and assessed for what it reveals that is "new about a writer and his works," it would be judged only of "interest to Burroughs cultists and collectors" (Guzlowski 741). Since these letters are in fact momentous for the particular writer and for the epistolary as a category, the reviewer, like so many others for twenty years, had been hoodwinked.

Of course, when it comes to the mystification of *Naked Lunch*'s genesis, no text has proved so enduringly influential as Burroughs' "Deposition," an introduction whose effect has been every bit as disastrous for Burroughs criticism as the one he wrote for *Queer*. However, in marked contrast to the radical oversight of *Queer*'s genetic history, that of *Naked Lunch* has been subject to a mass of biographical and critical (not to mention cinematic) treatment. Far from being neglected, the time and place of this writing has become inseparable from the text's existence in the popular imagination and in critical accounts alike. But once again, the alternative responses of gullibility and skepticism have either let material confusions stand uncorrected or simply foreclosed further investigation.[4]

The production history offered in the introduction has guided the text's reception in numerous ways but two in particular. First, it has installed opiate addiction as the sole and self-evident *biographical* ground for the writing that took place in Tangier and as the equally self-evident basis to the *metaphorical* "Junk Virus" that gives the text its central interpretive principle. Second, it has promoted addiction as not just the subject of the text but as the key determinant of *textual production* itself. In Burroughs' famous account: "I apparently took detailed notes on sickness and delirium. I have no precise memory of writing the notes which have now been published under the title *Naked Lunch*" (*NL* ix). At this point, it is tempting to state quite baldly that Burroughs' account falsifies the history of the text and then to establish how. But it is just as important to observe exactly why and how Burroughs criticism has for so long missed what is missing from it. The clearest instance is provided by Carol Loranger, not because she exemplifies the poverty of Burroughs scholarship but on the contrary, because she has published by far the most detailed and well-researched account of the textual history of *Naked Lunch*.

After dealing with "Burroughs' fabled passivity during the production of the novel" and how the body of the text was drawn "according to the mythology, from letters, sketches and a detective pot-boiler written by Burroughs during the Tangier period" (5), Loranger concludes:

> My aim in referring to the above account as part of the mythology of *Naked Lunch* is not to contest its truth-value, but to specify its function. The story of the novel's production is so much a part of its initial reception and continuing apprehension that it forms part of the novel's aura. (7)

The truth of her second sentence could not be expressed more forcefully, but it remains fatally flawed by her preceding refusal to contest the truth-value of Burroughs' genetic mythology. This has become the alibi for an endemic disregard of factual accuracy that is a scandal within Burroughs criticism. Take the example of Timothy Murphy, a major critic of manifest *interpretative* ability, when he discusses the "mosaic structure" of *Naked Lunch*. Taking it as the sign of Burroughs' rejection of artistic control, Murphy observes that this structure was "created, according to Beat legend, when the routines were simply sent to the printer in the order that they were typed up by Kerouac and Ginsberg" ("Intersection" 87). Based on readily available material evidence, it is not hard to contest the "truth-value" of everything here: Burroughs had already established a mosaic structure in October 1955; he never referred to the text's separate sections as "routines"; Kerouac, Ginsberg, and Alan Ansen typed up a manuscript in early 1957 that was absolutely distinct from the final text; it was Burroughs, Brion Gysin, and Sinclair Beiles who prepared the material for Olympia Press in July 1959; and Burroughs subsequently relocated at least one major section of text. In Murphy's account, the term "Beat legend" obviates the need to know this history, a spectacular failing, since a false material base must in turn have material consequences for textual interpretation.

Murphy's failure is particularly instructive because it goes together with his insistence that in the "Atrophied Preface" that concludes *Naked Lunch,* as in the "Deposition" which begins it, Burroughs is *not* being ironic in his accounts of its method, *not* "parodying the explanatory preface much as deconstructive critics do" ("Intersection" 100). In fact, the question of credibility is subject to a systematic deconstruction in the "Deposition," which mimics and belongs to that Romantic tradition of false prefaces perfected by Coleridge. It therefore set the example for Burroughs' later introduction to *Queer* and his preface to *Letters to Allen Ginsberg,* both of which, by no coincidence, name Coleridge. The "Deposition" is less a genetic history of *Naked Lunch* than a prelude to it, being consistent in its rhetorical ambiguity with all that follows. It is, as Michael Leddy has ably demonstrated, a flagrant "attempt to deceive the audience (if we assume that there is an objective reality, or at least greater and lesser degrees of accuracy)" (34). This is exactly the point that Loranger makes so forcefully; that given Burroughs' "career-long, semi-ironic self-identification as a huckster, one can never be certain about what actually happened" (7). The upshot is that this very "uncertainty, too, is part of the aura of *Naked Lunch,*" a conclusion that mirrors her claim that it would be an "editorial sin" to stabilize its multiple and conflicting textual states: "*Naked Lunch's* enduring appeal arises in large part from its instability, its openness to multiple and alternative readings" (23). In other words, here we have in definitive form that paradoxical scenario in which a critic trying to narrate an objective material chronology is fated to miss an essential point: exposing its secret source misses the *effect* of fascination.

Doomed in principle, however, certainty and stability can remain fully valid in local practice. Let us recall the elements of Burroughs' version of events: that he "apparently took detailed notes" on addiction; that he had "no precise memory of writing the notes"; and that the title "was suggested by Jack Kerouac" (*NL* ix). As evidence for the suppression of the epistolary and arguing *ex silentio* as proof of its importance, I would say this is clear-cut. Since Burroughs himself introduces the circumstances of writing—addiction—the method of writing—notes—and his text's debt to a Beat relationship—Kerouac—it makes all the more dramatically significant the circumstances, method, and Beat relationship he disregards: the fact, in his own words, that "a great deal of *Naked Lunch was actually written* in these letters to Allen Ginsberg." In short, behind "Beat Legend" and beyond "the mythology of *Naked Lunch,*" there lies another story, one whose importance is inseparable from the history of its concealment: it is only by going back to the "Deposition" and to the preface to *Letters to Allen Ginsberg* that we can see how the epistolary went from being an absolute secret to an open secret, hidden now because apparently not hidden— *apparently not worth hiding*—at all.

Along the devious road to *Naked Lunch,* prompted by Ginsberg's claim, *Junkie* appears as Burroughs' pre-epistolary text. As a result, sections of *Junkie* return only after the most thoroughgoing rewriting, giving voice and body to all that is silent in the first narrative. In the opening pages, Lee therefore takes on the dimensions of Barthes's huge tongue, his direct address abusing to the full a narrator's authority to exploit and seduce the fruit/asshole/jerk, the listener who stands in for the reader. *Naked Lunch* begins, in other words, by retyping *Junkie* on the epistolary writing machine. The inverse of *Junkie*'s zero-degree narrational contract, the intense rhetorical force of these first pages also ridicules the claim of the "Deposition" for a text made from found notes. This offers a private and autonomous form of writing, disinterested and authentic, a form detached from intentionality and exchange, detached from the whole desire-driven economy of production and consumption, and so makes no sense at all for a reader of the opening pages of the text. Indeed, a fifth of the book goes by before the first section introduced as "Notes" appears (*NL* 55). Equally, since the central action of *Naked Lunch* is "the moment by moment relation of narrator and reader" (Hilfer 253), it is clear enough that this relation is central because it comes from, and can be understood in terms of, the letter-routine economy and so the textual politics that only emerged after the writing of *Junkie.*

In the case of *Queer,* although the material evidence for Burroughs' epistolary practice is largely secondhand or circumstantial, we can clearly recognize the force of epistolarity within the novel's (barely) naturalistic setting as the written address of Burroughs' routines disappears into the oral performance of Lee as a character. For *Naked Lunch,* Burroughs would select favored elements of these routines—Tetrazzini, the Duc de Ventre

(*Q* 61, 165)—and put them in the mouth of Dr. Benway. This is conventional cannibalization of unpublished material, but it is also a deliberate textual gutting, another kind of rewriting and undoing. Burroughs' selective use of *Queer*'s routines is a method of decontextualization, whose effect is to confirm the emergent autonomy of the routine, its capacity to be taken out of an intersubjective narrative context. This move therefore rids the routine of its unwanted autobiographical foundation, one that would have naturalized it as only a fantasy mode of personal expression.

With "Yage," the epistolary form is in full view, but it gives us little more than framing features and lacks significant epistolarity. This is for two clear reasons: first, unlike the routines of *Queer,* the letter writing of "Yage" is not invested with desire and power, does not reproduce in the writer-reader relation the previous text's relationship between speaker and listener; and second, much of its material was originally written not in the form of letters but as entries in the traveler's notebook. Once again, Burroughs cannibalized the unpublished "Yage" for *Naked Lunch,* but significantly, this material is introduced here as "Notes from Yage state" (*NL* 109). In practice, both texts expropriated material from letters and notes, but whereas "Yage" retains only the empty letter form, *Naked Lunch* retains only that of the note. Each decision has the effect of promoting one stage of production or formal organization at the expense of the other.

Here then is the apparent paradox of the letter and *Naked Lunch:* Burroughs' published correspondence enables us to revisit the fantastic terrain of his epistolary relationship with Ginsberg—most significantly between 1954 and 1956—and so begin to grasp its exacting psychological hold and dynamic productivity, while signs of the aesthetic and economy of power particular to the letter never appear *visibly* in the published text. This absolute absence has had ironic results, seen in Arnold Weinstein's comparative analysis "Freedom and Control in the Erotic Novel," which he bases on a "sharp intuitive sense that the vastly dissimilar *Liaisons dangereuses* of Laclos and Burroughs's *Naked Lunch* are not so dissimilar after all" (29); his intuition couldn't be sharper, but what is really instructive is the assumption that this similarity to an epistolary novel has nothing to do with *letters.* For Burroughs criticism as a whole, this failure to recognize the missing material link is less an irony than a massive structural limitation. Then again, could we usefully read *Naked Lunch* in light of any single genetic factor, any developmental master narrative? Wouldn't this just repeat the reading imposed by Cronenberg's movie, forging a unified allegory of writing out of a radically heterogeneous and decentered text? And that is the point: *Naked Lunch* visibly bears the marks of multiple and conflicting histories of production and foregrounds in the reading experience the problem of its construction. That is why we must deal with Burroughs' genetic myths, with *their* totalizing tendencies, as well as with received critical wisdom.

One of the "Habit Notes" in the "Hospital" section reads: "Last night I woke up with someone squeezing my hand. It was my other hand. . ." (*NL* 66). These lines, which come from Burroughs' letter of 27 February 1956, may stand for the conflicted divisions between the left-handed labor of the letter and its right-handed other. The question is: which hand wakes the sleeper? Which exerts control, which will gain, as they say, the upper hand? Maurice Blanchot, discussing the pathology of "tyrannical prehension," observes:

> The writer's mastery is not in the hand that writes, the "sick" hand that never lets the pencil go [. . .] Mastery always characterizes the other hand, the one that doesn't write and is capable of intervening at the right moment to seize the pencil and put it aside. (*Space* 25)

Naked Lunch is written out of such a struggle for mastery.

AND SOME PANSY SHIT

During the Tangier period, Burroughs rehearsed his routines in letters to Ginsberg and expropriated them for his fiction. This much no longer needs arguing: the published evidence is clear, and my own introduction to *The Letters of William S. Burroughs, 1945–1959* establishes the general case. The letters also clearly narrate the key phases of Burroughs' epistolary-driven relationship with Ginsberg: their meeting in New York during fall 1953, after six years of long-distance correspondence, and the split-up that initiated a new stage of letter-courtship; Burroughs' panic of spring 1954, caused by Ginsberg's failure to reply; Ginsberg's formal letter of rejection in fall 1954, provoked by Burroughs' threat to rejoin him in America; and the intensely creative, progressively less fraught period up to early 1956 and Burroughs' apomorphine cure. What still needs to be developed is the specificity of the letter phase as a site of textual production and the relationship between the letter routine and the text of *Naked Lunch* as a whole. Robin Lydenberg astutely recognized that the "most obvious" value of Burroughs' letters for his texts, namely their actual content, is not the most significant (*Word Cultures* 98). Or rather, Burroughs began with the value of content and, by acting as both reader and editor of his own letters, was then led to understand that their chief value for his work was to be found elsewhere: in the rhetorical strategy their economy invested in his routines and in the structural possibilities their cannibalization revealed. To explore what Linda Kauffman terms "the fluid boundaries between the letter as literature, literature as a letter" (*Discourses* 160), therefore brings us to Burroughs' textual politics and by no means requires engaging in a narrow psychoanalytic approach that would reduce the art to the life. Typically, Burroughs is there before us, when self-consciously "thinking about routine as art form": "And some pansy shit is going to start talking about *living* his art" (*L* 216).

If the particular meanings and values of the routine form are determined by its genetic history, then since aesthetic production is inseparable from the idea of consumption, this must include the actual conditions of reception. This was material written and read under precise personal and historical conditions;[5] rather than simply a facilitating procedure, Burroughs' letters made Ginsberg his literary *agent* in the strongest sense of the word. Not only a necessary archivist, the dedicated custodian of Burroughs' scattered manuscripts, he became, to borrow Vincent Kaufmann's terms, an "unavoidable relay" in the genesis of Burroughs' writing ("Valéry's Garbage" 78). Through the letter, Burroughs' sexual and textual economies were materially integrated, and this scene of production has to be recognized as a vital ground for *Naked Lunch*'s analysis of, and own relation to, the exercise of power.

One problem that needs to be addressed here comes from what Elizabeth MacArthur terms the "epistolary form's unstable proximity to life" (273). That is the question of documentary authenticity, the assumption that "letters are pure, undistorted reflections of life" (117), which are therefore available for historical and psychological use. As MacArthur argues, the narrative formed via correspondence is not transparent mimesis but essentially fictive, a performance that mediates two "epistolary constructions" (119). In the case of Burroughs and Ginsberg, an awareness of the personae created by letter writing emerges as an acute awareness of the verbal per se. When Burroughs writes in October 1955 that their difficulties "exist only in the imagination of both of us, and have no bearing on the realities of our relationship," he concludes: "I can not exactly make this clear in words because exactly what I am referring to is understanding on a non-verbal basis. That is why there has been so much misunderstanding in our exchange of letters" (*L* 286). Later the same month, Burroughs acknowledges another side to the letter relation: the compulsive temptation to impose authority. When he reworks the lyrics from *Porgy and Bess* to say that "it ain't necessarily so like a lot of things you're liable to read in my letters" (292), his substitution of "my letters" for "the bible" is a tacit recognition of the need to resist taking his own texts at their authoritative, authentic-seeming face value. The personal letter exchange intensified—and intensified Burroughs' awareness of—the power relations of representation inherent to writing.

Finally, if we can't talk about Burroughs *living* his art, we certainly have to acknowledge the ethical implications of reading his letters in the first place. Scholarship has no less an appetite than the popular media for erasing the line between private and public, and the mere fact of publication doesn't make the critic any less complicit in the invasion and exploitation of epistolary intimacies. However, at least I can say that the biographical Burroughs I invoke is of a specific kind: not the author's life as the source of writing but the writer's textual relationships as a particular point of material origin, a point at which it is the writing itself that now seems to come alive.

THE REAL NOVEL IS LETTERS TO YOU

IMAGINING ALL SORTS OF THINGS

We are dealing with two economies of production-consumption and their relation. The first is traditional, that of the letter as an engine of desire: writing what modesty forbids to be spoken, the letter expands its own force of motivation, a dynamic that goes back to Phaedra in Ovid's *Heroides*. Thus of Marianne, the nun who writes *Lettres portugaises,* Claudio Guillen observes: "Her passion grows as she writes and the words multiply as the passion increases" (20). The second economy is particular to the writer who must distinguish the letter from the literary: private from public, personal from professional, waste from work, left hand from right.

To begin with, exchange is not equivalence: "communicative relationships are generally asymmetrical" (Roger Fowler and Bob Hodge, qtd. in Reid 104). In the case of epistolary relations, this commonplace about the unequal economic distribution of authority takes on a material and inexorable momentum. It is this very visibility, endlessly re-presented, that drives the letter writer into perversion, into vicious circles. Self-awareness presses relations of power in both directions, fuels the fire: authority and desire oxidize into dependency and exploitation. With Burroughs and Ginsberg, we see the two basic generic categories of epistolary tradition—the educational and the erotic—transformed over time, as mentor becomes seducer, and then each becomes its opposite: anti-teacher, anti-lover.

Whereas in spring 1952, Marker leaves and refuses to write back to Burroughs, so preventing the relationship from being reconstituted as a paper courtship, a letter love, with Ginsberg two years later the situation is very different. To begin with, Ginsberg was available to Burroughs throughout his earlier crisis, a ready and sympathetic receiver. Drawn closer together by this proxy erotic intimacy when, in a characteristic act of transference, the epistolary relationship shifts to Ginsberg, Burroughs has no other outlet. He loses his only confidant in the process of turning him into his object of desire, while Burroughs' relocation from Mexico to North Africa intensified the exile's sense of isolation. In spring 1954, Burroughs panicked at Ginsberg's repeated failure to reply—he was traveling in Mexico, effectively incommunicado—and in this moment of crisis, it becomes evident that the only possible satisfaction for desire generated by writing is more writing. In other words, it is a matter of producing desire, not reproducing it, by the letter. Burroughs doesn't write to Ginsberg because he already desires him; he comes to desire Ginsberg because he writes to him, because for six long years he *has* written to him, knowing that his letters will be read.

This is the meaning of "Yage": not an amorous discourse in itself, it is the epistolary prelude to erotic investment, which took place in New York in September 1953, when Burroughs and Ginsberg met up for the first time since 1947 and edited the work together. When Ginsberg anticipates Burroughs' return to America in fall 1954, he knows he will once again "have to sit and listen to him and routines mercilessly applauding [. . .] Bill is a power of solitude—got to give him *all* attention" (qtd. in Miles, *Ginsberg* 174). Up to fall 1953, their six-year friendship by correspondence maintains a relationship that falls under the category mentor-student, with its own hierarchy of power and its latent sexuality. As Ginsberg admitted, it was precisely Burroughs' experience, his authority and seniority—"my admiration and affection for my teacher"—that had to be resisted. During 1954, the teacher-student axis gave way to the romance plot: calculating seducer and virtuous victim.

Was Ginsberg the virtuous victim? As John Muckle recognizes, Ginsberg suffered an "inability, or unwillingness, to set boundaries between self and other, and a consequent tendency to welcome imposition, abuse, exploitation" (33): "A constant theme in the early biography is of being invaded, taken over, robbed of identity, displaced by others" (32). Muckle refers to Herbert Huncke, abuser of Ginsberg's enormous generosity or feeder of his masochism, but the relationship to Burroughs is more interesting because of the secret similarity and reciprocity of their fantasies. Their letter relation follows and then runs in parallel to Ginsberg's other epistolary "master-slave" relationship, begun in 1947 with Neal Cassady: "Realization of the total masochism I feel toward Neal," he writes in August 1954, "and curiosity as to how far he can be pushed sadistically" (*Journals Mid-Fifties* 54). Ginsberg was therefore uniquely attuned to the penal economics of Burroughs' dependency. He was also uniquely placed to grasp the relation between desire, epistolarity, and creativity, since Ginsberg wrote his "break-through" poem, "The Green Automobile," and openly stated its equation of literature with letter during the very week in September 1953 that Burroughs had come to stay. Writing to Cassady about having sorted out Burroughs' crisis of spring 1954—"He just never got my letters & began imagining all sorts of things"—Ginsberg observes of this "psychotic" response to rejection: "He had it with Marker, with some reason. However this kind of need with which I cannot but sympathize [. . .] will be real problem" (*As Ever* 179). Sympathy, a defining characteristic, perversely enables Ginsberg to grasp the necessity of the asymmetry of power, even in the course of falling under its dominion. He appears to have grasped the two key economies of writing that would carry over from *Queer* to *Naked Lunch:* that Burroughs' letter-borne fantasies realized a dark Hegelian/Lacanian truth about intersubjective relationships, disclosing "the Real of the traumatic social antagonisms, power relations, and so on which brand the space of social exchange with a pathological twist" (Hurley n. pag.); and that Burroughs' psychotic creativity—"imagining all sorts of things"—was directly tied to the sending and receipt of letters.

In his own introduction to *Letters to Allen Ginsberg*, Ginsberg likens Burroughs' letters to "Shakespeare's sonnet sequence to his boyfriend Mr W. H." and half rejoices ("I'm almost glad") at the one-sidedness of the published record: "If nothing else of my own history survives, I'd be happily remembered as the sympathetic kid to whom W. S. Burroughs addressed his tender intelligence in these letters containing major sketches of *Naked Lunch*" (*LG* 8, 10). Ginsberg's act of self-sacrifice may be a retrospective fantasy, but it is entirely in keeping with the original circumstances. It is therefore a tacit affirmation of what is most paradoxical about Burroughs' epistolary practice: the self-sufficiency of its results.

It is reasonable to assume that his epistolary activity was in itself an element of collaborative production, and this is one of the few things critics have had to say about it. But to argue that Burroughs saw his "readers not simply as auditors, but as editors and even collaborators" (Lydenberg, *Word Cultures* 101) is to generalize and conflate several quite distinct histories and functions. It is also to miss both the psychology of the Burroughs-Ginsberg relation and its political extension in Burroughs' fiction. What is particular to their relation appears clearly in the context of the tradition studied by Wayne Koestenbaum in *Double Talk: The Erotics of Male Literary Collaboration*. Koestenbaum shows how the desire to collaborate proceeds typically from anxieties and splittings of the author and where his writing features "the desire and the pursuit of the whole—the wish to unite with a lost twin and to form a blended soul" (4). Clearly, the fantasy of union that Burroughs called "schlupping," the governing fantasy of the routine as a form, is the dark side to such utopian desire for correspondence: a fantasy of power to resist, not a partnership to pursue. Or as Ginsberg himself put it in November 1954: "My objection wasn't to queerness but to the wild strange frightening (antipathetic symbiotic) uncanny Bill."[6]

The letter is an enabling device for the routine because its addressee— Ginsberg—is already internal to the form: the relative autonomy of the letter coincides with the rhetorical economy of the routine. Replies are needed to maintain the flow of production, operating as a kind of feedback signal in which Ginsberg's reply tests the line, as it were, confirming Burroughs is still on air. If Ginsberg can imagine himself as Shakespeare's boyfriend, silencing himself as a writer before his master's voice, it is because, despite his regular critical support and positive form of editorial collaboration, this describes the core economy of their relationship. Burroughs' desperation for a "receiver"—the passive end of a speech act, or better still, of a radio broadcast—should force us to revise what Elizabeth MacArthur identifies as the "fundamental tendency of letters to engender exchanges" (63–64), by already insinuating the unilateral force of Burroughs' epistolary transmission.

In their remarkable analysis of Kafka that must serve here as a necessary touchstone, Deleuze and Guattari speak of the *"pacte diabolique"* he makes through his correspondence with Félice Bauer: "that she should write twice a day. That is the diabolical pact. The Faustian diabolical pact is derived from a distant source of strength, as opposed to the closeness of the marriage contract" ("Kafka" 594). The parallels that begin here are revealing, perhaps more so than the typical critical association of Burroughs and Kafka.[7] Kafka warns Félice that their epistolary communication was "almost an instrument of Black Magic (without seeming to be)" because of the tariff on "natural communication" it charges (*Letters to Félice* 23), which Deleuze and Guattari dub "the vampirelike revenge of the phantom" ("Kafka" 593). In the case of Burroughs, the sorcery is a fantasy of projection and one-way power: "That was what the whole *Naked Lunch* correspondence was about," Ginsberg recalls, "sending me all that magical material, getting more deeply involved with me by mail" (*Journals Mid-Fifties* 177).

In Burroughs' own diabolic pact, he also demands letters but primarily as proof of receipt. It is one-sided and one-way: reception—predictable, passive—rather than reciprocation—spontaneous, active—is the driving force. "In some respects situation quite horrible you know," Ginsberg confided to Cassady in May 1954, "a kind of evil which in other situations I would not dream of putting up with or being cause or object of; in this case not really dangerous since Bill ultimately sane somehow & anyway I do not believe in black magic" (*As Ever* 179). The final phrases suggest, however, that Ginsberg *did* believe, although it is clear that he would rather he didn't. After all, he had already witnessed how Burroughs "had it with Marker."

UN DRACULA PAR LETTRES

Burroughs' crisis of the dead letter in April 1954 was a crucial moment in the genesis of *Naked Lunch,* just as the crisis in April 1952 with Marker had been one for the writing of *Queer.* Here, we begin to see the convergence of letters and novel and to suspect an underlying strategic purpose. In his letter of 7 April, the first to be driven by the acute crisis of Ginsberg's failure to write back, the first to feel the horror of letters "returned unclaimed" (*L* 200), Burroughs begins: "Dear Allen, I have written and rewritten this for you. So please answer" (201). In his letter of 11 May, the first written after restoring contact, he ends with a postscript: "Note material in novel from letters" (212). By collapsing the distance between each form of writing, the stakes are doubled: to reject one is to reject the other. In the terrifying panic of his 7 April letter, Burroughs' need for Ginsberg is fully displaced onto the need for his writing to be received, a need policed by dangers as well as demands:

> I have to have receiver for routine. If there is no one there to receive it, routine turns back on me ~~like homeless curse~~ and tears me apart, grows more and more insane (literal growth like cancer) and impossible, and fragmentary like berserk pin-ball machine and I am screaming: "Stop it! Stop it!" (201)

As a structural key to Burroughs' writing, this extraordinary passage can be taken in two stages. First, there is the absolute integration of the receiver into the routine; which is to say, the routine's organization as an economy. This might make the love letter appear as a kind of ultimate talismanic ritual, a perverse version of the writer's perennial need to associate success with a particular set of working conditions; in which case, desire is only a literal *pre-text.*[8] This was the situation in January 1955: "Dear Allen, I need you so much your absence causes me, at times, acute pain. I don't mean sexually. I mean in connection with my writing" (*L* 255). The dangers of such an economy are immediately apparent: the agony of Ginsberg's absence and of Burroughs' emotional and erotic failure become the necessary condition of a writing tied to the epistolary principle. In his letter following that of 7 April 1954, Burroughs is again "in urgent need of routine receivers" (204), and he presses a visitor to Tangier into service as a substitute. But since the routine is *really* "meant for loved one," and since Ginsberg is not present for speech but absent for writing, then speech is for substitutes; writing is for the real audience. In this way, the epistolary performs a double seduction, since Burroughs doesn't only write letters in order to seduce Ginsberg but is himself seduced by the act of writing them, by the sound of his own voice in them. In a rare analysis of this dimension, Vincent Kaufmann argues that when they become workshops for creativity, letters "give the writer a chance to avoid dialogue": "Although letters seem to facilitate communication and proximity, they produce instead a distance in which writers find the chance to become writers" (*Post Scripts* 4). For Burroughs, the modes of epistolary seduction are therefore not just double but antagonistic, and his writing arises in the irreconcilable tension between them. If the routine is writing from the impasse—"the impasse of unrequited affection" (*L* 204)—then here is the answer to the question Kerouac put to Burroughs at the time of Ginsberg's apparent desertion: "If I love Allen why don't I return and live with him?" (213).

The letter has to be grasped as far more than a medium that enabled Burroughs to generate fictional material, a facilitating but essentially empty vehicle. Quoting from the 7 April letter, David Savran observes that Burroughs' letters to Ginsberg "contain so many pieces of what will become *Naked Lunch* that he finally confesses, 'Maybe the real novel is letters to you'" (*Taking It* 86). However, these "pieces" were not so much *contained* in letters as produced through them, because they are a product of the letter economy and its self-divided, fragmentary aesthetic. To recognize this enables us to see how far the epistolarity of the routine form determines the textual politics of *Naked Lunch*. In which case, we also need to recognize that it is not the case that Burroughs "finally confesses" the real novel is letters to Ginsberg: both because there is no "confession" here—in context, the line reads more like a threat or the imposition of an obligation—and because it was not "finally" but at a very early stage in the writing of *Naked Lunch* that Burroughs thought of it this way. *Finally,* he would come to think completely differently about it. Equally, we need to bear in mind that these letters to Ginsberg describing the importance of letters to Ginsberg are inevitably determined by their desired effect. Burroughs' acute sense of audience underwrites everything in them, including their truth-value.

If "the audience is an integral part of the routine" and if the routine can endanger both performer and audience (*I* 127), it is also because the epistolary medium, whose "principal message is the act of communication itself," dictates it (Guillen 9). The will-to-communicate is understood as a dictation: dictated to the routine sender who in turn dictates to the receiver. Reciprocity here is an illusion, since the dialectic of sender-receiver conforms to the model of economic exchange in which it is the system that reproduces itself. Burroughs finds himself, to recall the situation of Lee in *Queer*, condemned to transmit the discourse transmitted to him, forced to pass it on like a curse. This is one reason why the routine must have a receiver. Or perhaps the receiver is necessary because it takes an other *out there* to unlock the secret other *in here:* as an epistolary terminal point for Burroughs, his "only point of reference" (*L* 311), Ginsberg structures the letter exchange as a kind of analysis by correspondence, in which the routine is offered symptomatically, as an enigmatic signifier. This is precisely what Lacan in 1955 meant by his famous equation of the patient's disclosures with "purloined letters," where it is only his fee that saves the analyst from an interminable libidinal circuit of debt and restitution (*Ego* 204). The Burroughs-Ginsberg correspondence creates therefore an analytical space, another version of the encounter staged between Lee and Allerton in *Queer:* the absent lover or silent analyst possess a virtual reality, giving free reign to the imagination, allowing the delights and terrors of narcissistic fantasy to run riot. In which case, the unilateral need for a receiver makes another kind of sense: Ginsberg as analyst is obliged to be all ear; Burroughs as analysand is one huge tongue.

In a second approach to the 7 April letter, there is the revenge of the routine; a violence of words turning back on the writer that Burroughs blames on Ginsberg's failure to receive, where receipt can only be proved by the return of writing. The revenge of the routine is intensely literal—return to sender—and the four-fold terms of this revenge are highly particular. First, there is the "homeless curse," a phrase heavily struck through. Inevitably, the erasure signifies, recalling a previous erasure: "I do not contemplate any curse, that is absolute end of wrong line. ~~The picture of him slipping further and further away from me,~~" and so on (*L* 128). First Marker, now Ginsberg, and in each instance the curse, as a form of "black magic" to "coerce human love," is canceled out like a double negative. In July 1954, Burroughs writes that "salvation lies not in receiving love but in giving it" (221). Is this the generous logic of the gift in its ideal state—"The gift is the alternative to the dialectic of master and slave" (Godbout 220)—or should the writing gift be equated with "an assertion of mastery, of power, of pleasure, of solitude," in which there is not benevolence but terror (Barthes, *Lover's Discourse* 78–79)? How did Ginsberg respond to Burroughs' letter? "In some respects situation quite horrible you know, a kind of evil[. . . .]" Burroughs' letter is nearer the poisoned gift than the utopian gesture. Indeed, since Ginsberg claims that Burroughs blue-penciled or burned "the most extravagant passages, abject letters of complete schlupp-longing, and prophetic curse" (*LG* 8), the published evidence doesn't even give the worst of it.

The second term of revenge images the routine's blocked economy in embodied terms familiar from "The Finger" short story but in reverse order: whereas in the story Lee makes an obligating gift out of his ablated finger joint, literalizing his image of emotional fragmentation ("It's tearing me all apart"), here in this letter it is the routine, as a drama of writing that is not received and so cannot be given, that causes a figurative self-morselization of the writer. Third, the routine that is figured as dismembering the writer's body is itself described as both fragmentary and self-replicating, cancerous, viral. The body in pieces becomes the body *of* pieces, alternative models for scattered integrity and lost agency.

Finally, this menacing drama reaches a climax with its definitive image, that of the autonomous machine gone berserk: the control machine out of control, the machine turned against the mechanic, as in Kafka's "Penal Colony." The revenge of the routine therefore recalls the trap that Deleuze and Guattari see as the source of Kafka's panic: "that the typewriter which writes the letters might turn against the typist" ("Kafka" 596). Is this terror a specific potential of the epistolary for a certain kind of writer? Richard Hardack notes that the intertextuality of Melville's letter exchange with Hawthorne had a sinister—a left-handed—side: "Melville's body becomes a kind of player piano for texts" as "the writer is ground up by his own mill [. . .] The Melvillian writer is endemically situated as a victim of a Dionysian force he cannot control" (131–32). If correspondence hopes to overcome all physical distance, then fragmentation and dismemberment are really signs of a failed merger. Kafka tells Félice he wishes she were "entirely within" him or he was "entirely within" her, because either way, "there is one too many of us; the separation into two people is unbearable" (*Letters to Félice* 284).[9] This is Kafka's version of Burroughs' narcissistic fantasy of "schlupping," and of course it succeeded by keeping Félice—"Félice, whose curse I am" (347)—at a permanent distance. Kafka is therefore free to practice a form of parasitism that Deleuze and Guattari call his "epistolary vampirism" ("Kafka" 592). For them, Kafka's letters "are as many bats" that "must bring blood" (592, 593). Burroughs writes to Kerouac, shortly after his 7 April letter: "The withdrawal symptoms are worse than the Marker habit. One letter would fix me" (*L* 205). A shot of the epistolary would not satisfy Burroughs' need to receive, however, but his need to *send;* "see that he writes me a fix," he continues. "I am incapacitated. Can't write" (205). Had Burroughs forgotten the lesson of Marker? Namely, the difference between desire and need, that the other doesn't possess what he desires: "You can't fix me if you want to" (132). Not at all: "Tell Allen I plead guilty to vampirism and other crimes against life" (206). It is Burroughs who is, who recognizes himself to be, not so much *un homme de lettres* as, like Kafka, *"un Dracula par lettres"* (Deleuze and Guattari, *Kafka* 53; my emphasis).

HIS ENVELOPING PRESENCE

The dilemma of isolation and dependency gives rise to a solution of union and total control, a final solution in which the other is made fully predictable, not a subject but an object—as in that telling phrase: a "love object" (*L* 224)—not another sender but only a receiver, or better still, entirely internalized, eaten. Douglas Kahn writes perceptively when arguing that Burroughs needed someone to listen "who understood him completely, so he could reproduce this understanding in himself through autoingestion" ("Three Receivers" 85). However, when Kahn claims there was "nothing necessarily pathogenic in the love for Ginsberg or the lust for Allerton" (*Noise* 302), it is hard to agree with him (and not just because of his slide from real to fictional identity); Ginsberg's predisposition to receive does not thwart the drive towards colonization of the other, and this was not a process of true communication. Consider the terms of Ginsberg's rejection, which amounts to a reassertion less of his own needs than of his very subjectivity: "But he had pushed me to it, after long ambivalence, by offering, nay, threatening, to 'schlupp' with me, i.e., devour my soul parasitically, as Bradley the Buyer does to the District Supervisor in *Naked Lunch*" (*LG* 5). Is this what Burroughs meant by *"living* his art"?

Significantly, the routine Ginsberg specifies here is delivered by Lee in the text's opening section, a scene that exercises the fantasy seductions of narrating authority as an exemplary act for the reader to resist. But the force of the scene is directed not only at the power economy of interpersonal relations but at the power of an inner psychic economy: "Hustlers of the world, there is one Mark you cannot beat: The Mark Inside" (*NL* 10–11). Schizophrenically, the Buyer thinks he has "a Man Within," which makes him "the only complete man in the industry" (15). But this fantasy of absolute self-sufficiency, as a grotesque resolution of subject-object dualism, is what will lead to the equal and opposite fantasy—"Schlup . . . schlup schlup" (17)—of vampiristically consuming the Man Without, as he goes on to assimilate first the District Supervisor and then the Narcotics Commissioner. The Buyer's fantasy of total autonomy, of rejecting the whole universe because it is already inside, then breaks down catastrophically as "a yen comes on him like a great black wind through the bones" (15–16). This is significant phrasing because originally it occupied a vital place in Burroughs' letter of 13 October 1956, which is in turn a significant letter, marking the turning point in Burroughs' epistolary relationship with Ginsberg.

"I don't see our roles reversed exactly," he begins, "but expanded and altered on both sides" (*L* 329). Not reversed: a vital clarification, because it admits that this would only replicate the vampiric power-relations of their previous correspondence. These relations are demolished here in terms of religious authority through a routine given in *Naked Lunch* as "The Prophet's Hour." The letter's key passage follows immediately:

> And I want you fellows to control your most basest instinct which is the yen to control, coerce, violate, invade, annihilate, by any means whatsoever, anybody else's physical or psychical person [. . .] And remember, *when the control yen rips through your bones like a great black wind, you have connected for Pure Evil* . . . (*L* 333–34; my emphasis)

Burroughs could not be clearer: what he denounces describes the workings of the routines Lee addresses to Allerton in *Queer* and of his own past epistolary relationship with Ginsberg, each a fantasy instance of evil sending.

In the introduction to *Naked Lunch,* Burroughs' claim that the "face of 'evil' is always the face of total need" is firmly tied to the "total sickness, total possession" of narcotic addiction (*NL* xi). But the account offered in this letter confirms our need to shift the junk paradigm, to see addiction as providing certain terms rather than the defining ground of control. This is the other great mystifying effect of the "Deposition": *to reduce everything to junk.* The Bradley the Buyer routine sets the example by simply translating Burroughs' epistolary fantasy of homosexual desire into a tale of junk possession. And as junk overwrote the queerness of *Naked Lunch,* so it displaced the productive relation between sexuality and textuality so evident in its epistolary-driven routines.

Junk may be central to *Naked Lunch,* but we have to kick the junk paradigm if we are to reinstate the material, not metaphoric, origins and economy of the "yen to control." Only then can we recognize *Naked Lunch's* technological and economic extensions of the epistolary, its aesthetic consequences, and its textual politics. Most obviously, the power exercised through the epistolary medium by the sender against the receiver, and both conjured and exorcised through the letter-routine, is instantly recognizable as Burroughs' model for modern technologies of communication as methods of control. This recognition will bear repeating because it is so fundamental: the postmodern electronic culture of McLuhan, Baudrillard, Debord, Deleuze and Guattari, Jameson, Kroker, et al., this variously constructed technoculture of the image and its dehumanizing effects is, for Burroughs, a realm of intensification but not of origin. As a motor for *Naked Lunch,* and in context of the postwar communications revolution, the epistolary principle is an old technics, of course, and no doubt this is a major reason for critical disregard of the epistolary in Burroughs: simply, the anachronism of the letter, the difficulty of even seeing it *as* a technology.

In *Naked Lunch,* Benway is a "black magician" and the inheritor of Lee's routines from *Queer,* because the goal of his chemical, psychological, and technical research is also the production of "automatic obedience" (*NL* 123, 26). This is also the aim of the Senders, whose science fiction techno-fantasies of "biocontrol" (162) Burroughs only had to take verbatim from reports of the Norden-Ketay Corporation's electrical engineering researcher, the real-life namesake of Benway's colleague, a certain Dr. Curtiss Schafer;[10] "The National Electronic Conference in Chicago" is in turn only the scene for a technical updating and generalization of the diabolic principle that drives the epistolary machine. Like an isolated and unilateral letter writer, the sender "can never receive," "has to send all the time," and "can't ever recharge himself by contact" (163), and such "one-way telepathic broadcast" is denounced by Burroughs with unusual directness as "an unqualified evil": "We oppose, as we oppose atomic war, the use of such knowledge to control, coerce, debase, exploit or annihilate the individuality of another living creature" (167). Borrowing verbatim from his 13 October 1956 letter, Burroughs' denunciation establishes that it is a quite literal and material *sending* that underwrites this evil.

Now, it becomes clear how Burroughs formulated his answer to the "deeper sickness" of Control that, in early 1955, he saw as beyond the reach of political or economic programs. In *Naked Lunch,* these are "symptoms of The Human Virus" (*NL* 168). And what is the "Master Virus: Deteriorated Image" of the human species? The Sender. Of course, the Sender is therefore "not a human individual"—let alone a letter writer—but Communication itself, which Burroughs always presents in the abstract, as he does Control. This seems to make each term monumental and both naively immaterial and ahistorical; but it might equally be thought of as a way to render the elusiveness of an always absent cause. As the viral or virtual Real of cybernetic power, the Sender is not itself fully alive or fully material or even visible but needs human individuals to materialize Communication and Control historically and symptomatically. Hence of the "U.S. drag," Burroughs insists: "You can't see it, you don't know where it comes from" (12). In the science fiction scenario of his cut-up trilogy, where the Sender is now a Nova Criminal, he would spell out the same analysis in updated form: "You see these criminal controllers occupy human bodies—ghosts? phantoms? Not at all—very definite organisms indeed—True you can't see them—Can you see a virus?" (*Ticket* 58).

In Burroughs criticism, a figurative language of power has almost always tended to displace the literal power of language; a rare exception is Cary Nelson, with his insistence on giving absolute priority to "the inescapable facts of the reading experience" (121). But the rule of displacement is understandable, since if we say that the site of action is literal not thematic, a matter of visceral experience not verbalized ideas, then the more that is said, the less material it seems to become. One more reason is that the ground of Burroughs' writing, the material basis to its material effects, has been displaced. In the case of *Naked Lunch,* the complete absence of the epistolary base exists in direct proportion to the ubiquity of junk addiction in both the text and its framing commentaries.[11] Whatever the motives for its abolition as a genetic factor, the letter's absolute suppression from *Naked Lunch* has, however, had a paradoxical formal effect: precisely to forestall translation of the literal—Artaud's "the very cry of life"—into a rhetorical figure; that is to say, to foreclose the text's potential recuperation as a narcissistic narrative, like John Barth's *Letters.* In this sense, Burroughs' generalization of addiction—as private autobiographical and world medical crisis—has had the effect of maintaining a psychology and politics intimately bound up with his epistolary economy, while avoiding the textualizing, aestheticizing effects of acute literary self-consciousness.

The letter's suppression need not be taken as a conspiracy of silence then, the deliberate burying of an undesired etiology. But it is still significant that when Robin Lydenberg briefly discusses Burroughs' "early letters" and relates them to the typical subject of his routines ("the need for human contact and the fear of isolation"), she should claim that he "often expresses these feelings in epistolary images" (*Word Cultures* 98). For the examples she gives from *The Soft Machine*—"dead postcard," "sending letter to a coffin"—actually prove the exact opposite of her case: she has just cited the few examples of epistolary images there are to find. Ironically, by trying to give some critical space to the letter—the first critic to do so—Lydenberg is trapped into overplaying her hand, because all the court cards are missing. This brings us back to the place of the letter in the proper chronology of *Naked Lunch,* to the decisions for and against it that shaped the history of Burroughs' manuscript. If in June 1954, the "real novel" was letters to Ginsberg, in the final text of *Naked Lunch,* the epistolary leaves only the faintest and most uncertain of traces. The one potential image is, however, significantly phrased and placed as the conclusion to the schlupping routine of Bradley the Buyer: "Like a vampire bat he gives off a narcotic effluvium, a dank green mist that anesthetizes his victims and renders them helpless in his enveloping presence" (*NL* 18).

DIRT AND DISORDER

POSTHUMOUS BIOGRAPHICAL MATERIAL

If the first economy of production-consumption is that of the letter as an engine of desire, the second concerns the relationship between letter and literature, left hand and right, waste and work. This relation may have many potential modes, some harmonious, others antagonistic, some visible in the final form, others vital at only a specific genetic stage. Kafka's correspondence with Félice, for example, marks a particularly precise and dramatic turning point in his creativity.[12] So too does Kerouac's, for that matter, although his correspondence with Cassady shows a more direct relation to the form of *On the Road.* Equally, it should go without saying that the material history of Kerouac's novel, written on one long roll in a three-week burst of energy, could not be more different from the protracted, piecemeal epistolary genesis of *Naked Lunch.* Unlike the letter and epistolary fiction taken separately, this kind of genetic relation between writing hands has almost no critical history: Vincent Kaufmann's *Post Scripts,* focused on early European modernists, is a brilliant exception. But the relation between letter and literature must itself be historically as well as biographically determined. In the case of Burroughs, the confusion of left hand and right, their virtual identification at a key stage in the evolution of *Naked Lunch,* is an economic dilemma. This is because it announces a merger of economies of production and consumption, and therefore of desire and aesthetics, in unresolved conflict. This merger falls under three related headings: the journal, the waste product, and the whole. Each opens out onto the key formal problematics that faced Burroughs en route to *Naked Lunch.*

The journal: we should begin by dealing with the larger critical claim for *Naked Lunch* as "a diary that records experience as it happens, and the act of recording is part of the experience" (Skerl 44). Such an interpretation extends to the limit Burroughs' own genetic myth given in the "Deposition" ("I apparently took detailed notes [...]"); it performs both a sweeping formal totalization of the text and a refusal of either the value of shaping artistic labor or of writing as a transitive act. The very inadequacy of this account is revealing. At a certain point in early 1955, this is exactly how Burroughs conceives of his work in progress: "Tanger novel will be Lee's impressions of Tanger," because "*I include the author in the novel*" (*L* 251). Such a move might suggest the choice of a traditional modernist aesthetic, the self-reflexive journal novel, as perfected by Gide in *The Counterfeiters,* for example. However, this is not the case. Burroughs considers a recursive literary structure because of his urgent need to find a solution to the disabling merger of writing hands, as the full context makes clear. To transcribe "Lee's impressions" is a way of "solving the contradictions raised by dissipation of energy in fragmentary, unconnected projects." The specific moment of writing these lines in this letter itself becomes an instance of what he means and a sign of why its naturalizing ambition will not work:

> I feel guilty even writing this letter when I should be up to my balls in the work. But "nothing is lost" . . . (A horrible vision of suffocating under the accumulated shit and piss and nail clippings and eyelashes and snot excreted by my soul and body, backing up like atomic waste: "Go *get* lost for Chrissakes.") I already made a novel outa letters. I can always tuck one in somewheres, bung up a hole with it, you know. (251)

What is apparent is that Burroughs' "work"—as authored and authorized labor, as a noncontradictory product fit for consumption—is forced to depend on its other, on the fragment, on the letter, on waste products. Nothing is lost: his own private voice, his own personal space of writing, the expressive and intersubjective liaison of the letter, all is fully implicated in the same total economy. This is not literary self-consciousness in any conventional sense, a turning in on oneself from a reflective distance; it is physical self-exploitation, self-parasitism, self-cannibalism. After shit, piss, nail clippings, eyelashes, and snot, *blood* is the significant omission in his list of bodily substances: it is the work that is vampiric.

Or rather, the work occupies a middle and mediating position in a food chain. Below is Ginsberg, since Burroughs feeds off writing that is not private to himself but comes into being primarily through their epistolary relationship. Hence, the guilt of writing his letter when he should be up to his balls in work is doubly ironic: "Tell Allen I plead guilty to vampirism" (*L* 206). We are back to Kafka's letters as bats that "must bring blood."[13] And vampirism above? The only other instance of the term in Burroughs' correspondence occurs in April 1952 and coincides with his self-identification as a professional writer, when he refers to "those vampires going round sucking off the talents of we authors" (120), meaning his publishers. Burroughs finds himself caught in a hierarchy of vampires.

Lee, as we know, was a persona effectively born in the epistolary medium. By placing the letter under the signature of Lee—from "Willy Lee—That Junky writin' boy" in April 1952, to "Pop Lee Your Friendly Prophet" in October 1956 (*L* 121, 335)—Burroughs elides the gap between the signed letter and the authored work and so closes off any space to breathe. There is only the constipation of accumulation and of recycling what should be put outside as waste, taken away. Burroughs therefore lacks the option described as a necessity by Blanchot: recourse to the journal. For Blanchot, this provides a vital means for the writer to remember "who he is when he isn't writing": "The journal represents the series of reference points which a writer establishes in order to keep track of himself when he begins to suspect the dangerous metamorphosis to which he is exposed" (*Space* 29). This is exactly Burroughs' fate: to have lost a way back. In Blanchot's terms, since in the journal a writer "retains his name" and preserves a mundane chronology, without one he passes "from the first to the third person" and enters that realm of "the solitude in which fascination threatens" (33). The redemptive option is lost for Burroughs because he is always using himself, feeding off himself, making everything pay. Hence, the production of "Lee's Journals"—rather than Burroughs' own—and also the inclusion in them of a suitably reworked version of his January 1955 letter's proposed solution of including the author: "This could go on in an endless serial arrangement" (*I* 82). When he transcribed a draft letter written the same day, the original is worked over until overworked, until it seems self-parody: "Oh, God! Sounds like posthumous biographical material—Lee's letters to his beloved agent and friend" (89).[14]

THIS LETTER

Very little of such self-reflexive material was retained for *Naked Lunch*, but during 1955 the epistolary-diaristic format was essential to Burroughs' work in progress. That October, he identified "Chapter II of Interzone novel," running to some forty pages, as "Selections from Lee's Letters and

Journals": "With this gimmick I can use all letters including love letters, fragmentary material, anything" (*L* 288). This self-cannibalizing chapter was the logical fruition of the practice Burroughs described in June 1954 when he told Ginsberg that he always kept "a letter to you on the stove and put in miscellaneous ideas, a sort of running diary" (216). In Burroughs' practice, the letter already points towards the journal form, and the reason for the journal's potent attraction for him was undoubtedly its lack of rule-bound definition; that is, the license it gave to use anything as material and to be no one thing as a result. In *The Diary Novel,* Lorna Martens notes that "almost any piece of writing that is too formless and chaotic to deserve another name can be termed a 'journal'": "The diary is a loose form. It is not cohesive; it consists of pieces" (186–87). "Pieces" was exactly what Burroughs had at his disposal or had to dispose of in some way. As an open form receptive to contingency, the letter journal therefore promised Burroughs a technical solution to intransigent problems of organization, internal coherence, and structural continuity. However, within the form there remained crucial aesthetic and autobiographical decisions to make. "If an author chooses to suppress the kinds of content that collaborate with the sequential implications of narrative, such as individual biography, in favor of kinds that do not," Martens continues, "there is no reason why the diary cannot be converted into a collage of fragments or a random-order construction that can be opened and read anywhere" (187). She might be describing the final form of *Naked Lunch.* The paradox then is that while Burroughs' text evolved radically new and highly influential potentials for montage, it did so by taking its organization initially from the much older tradition of the letter journal.

It also becomes clear why Burroughs' simple "gimmick" forced him to consider aesthetic and autobiographical issues absolutely central to the development of *Naked Lunch.* By October 1955, the process of "selecting, editing and transcribing letters and notes from the past year" resulted in the chapter of "Lee's Letters and Journals" that formed "a sort of mosaic with the cryptic significance of juxtaposition, like objects abandoned in a hotel drawer"[15] (*I* 128). Because this phrasing reappears in *Naked Lunch* (116), critics have often taken it as a "succinct description" of "the compositional method" of the text (Murphy, *Wising Up* 85), but this is to oversimplify both *Naked Lunch* and its material history. First, the final form of the text itself shows in its heterogeneity that Burroughs' methods of composition were multiple and in productive conflict: the method he describes in late 1955 is not identical to that of *Naked Lunch* in 1959.[16] Second, he contemplated this form in October 1955 only to reject it immediately: "The

mosaic method is more suitable to painting than writing" (*I* 126). His epistolary-based mosaic structure offered a potent but, at this time, essentially
unworkable model. Finally, because the sections published in the *Interzone*
collection as "Lee's *Journals*" and "Ginsberg *Notes*" tell only half the story;
they leave out the *letter* and so gloss over entirely the extent to which this
urmanuscript of *Naked Lunch* was epistolary in surprisingly explicit ways.

In the *Interzone* collection, the genetic debt of Burroughs' mid-1950s
material to the letter is entirely insignificant and its formal debt completely
invisible. However, it takes only a brief comparison of how this material is
presented here to how it is presented in its earlier published form, in *Early
Routines,* to begin to see the extent of what was lost in reediting. Signs of
the epistolary were edited out of the *Interzone* material in two small but
significant ways. Sometimes, it is only a matter of deleting a single word:
"I feel guilty writing this when I should be up to my balls in work" (*I* 82).
The reduction to "this" of the original phrase "this *letter*" (*Early* 41) cuts
this material off from its epistolary source (Burroughs' letter of 6 January
1955), just as its presentation under the general heading "Lee's Journals"
(*I* 63), rather than "Extracts from Lee's Journals and Letters" (*Early* 25),
removes the material from its original formal organization.[17] In fact, comparison with the original manuscripts reveals more: that the *Early Routines*
version had already edited out numerous epistolary frames and references;
and that the same process of concealment by revision applies to the "Ginsberg Notes" section of *Interzone* (not published in *Early Routines*). Here
too, the appearance changes entirely by again turning the phrase "this letter" into plain "this" (*I* 125) and indeed by omitting the heading of address,
date, and place that identifies everything here as not a journal of notes but
a letter: "Letter to A," signed, "Love, W. Lee."[18] The effect of this two-stage
editing process carried out during the early and mid-1980s is to further
hide from view the already obscure history of the letter and not only as a
material source for much of Burroughs' writing but as a major formal device for its presentation. That Burroughs himself went on to edit out this
material is an entirely separate matter from the editing of the *historical
record* of this revision. On the other hand, such changes were largely a by-
product of the need to impose some editorial coherence on Burroughs'
messy material. Also, unlike the text that follows it, Grauerholz's introduction to *Interzone* hides nothing. Far from neglecting the letter's historical
role, it is very informative: it is criticism that has neglected Grauerholz's
introduction. And so, if the disappearance of the epistolary is too consistent and pervasive to be no more than a matter of mere contingency, it is
also something less than a calculated conspiracy.

Finally, there are also significant surprises in the content of material that Burroughs considered using within "Lee's Journals and Letters," such as this barely reworked version of his letter from 16 July 1954: "Dear A, With your letter receive a note from that idiotic agent who is supposed to be handling *Junkie* in England: 'We have now received letter [...] making clear that you have signed contract with Star Books.'" Such material is inconceivable in *Naked Lunch* as we now know it. Although he would return to the *structure* suggested by the juxtaposition of cannibalized letter material, in late 1955 Burroughs had already made his first major decision against the recognizable authorial *voice* of the letter.

NO USE HAS BEEN FOUND FOR IT

When Barthes deliberates on the journal form, he deals with its necessary self-consciousness, the impossibility of authenticity, but focuses on the problematic relation of "worth" and "work": "on the one hand, I experience it, through its facility and desuetude, as being nothing more than the Text's limbo, its unconstituted, unevolved, and immature form; but on the other hand, it is all the same a true scrap of that Text, for it includes its essential torment" (*Barthes Reader* 495). Barthes's two hands want to join, to overcome the separation of private from public and so—his silent subtext—recover the worth of writing from that of the published, that is, sold, work. It is therefore no surprise that Burroughs' subject matter should return images of the worthless put to work. In the novel opening he describes in December 1954—which appears in the "Interzone" section of *Naked Lunch*—Burroughs planned to "incorporate" all his "scattered" material. It starts with "a deal to import and sell 'a load of K. Y. made of genuine whale drek'": "Whale drek is what remains after they get finished cooking down a whale. A rotten, stinking, fishy mess you can smell for miles. No use has been found for it" (*L* 243).

The conjunctions here are clear enough: to incorporate fragments, making a textual body out of miscellaneous parts; to make the rotten mess ripe for marketing. Drek is therefore junk. "What is junk?" asks Miles Orvell.

> Junk is the antiworld of the technological civilization, the stuff that is useless, discarded, utterly lacking in appeal, the unadvertized object. We are aware of junk as a symptom of disorder, of things gone wrong, of waste, a negative in the balance sheet. (287)

Burroughs projects a scenario in which a use *is* found so that money can be made from drek, detritus, shit. Nevertheless, Burroughs was faced with a self-evident but pressing problem: to "attempt a complete work" out of material he knows is both fragmentary and in his "most extreme line" and so can only be "unpublishable" as usual (*L* 243).

When he moves on from the economics of waste in his December letter to Ginsberg, Burroughs offers a definition of the routine in the very image of the epistolary:

> Routines are completely spontaneous and proceed from whatever fragmentary knowledge you have. In fact a routine is by nature fragmentary, inaccurate. There is no such thing as an exhaustive routine, nor does the scholarly-type mind run to routines. (*L* 244)

By bringing together spontaneity of production, incompleteness of results, and an antiacademic disposition, he premises the routine on the letter's traditional grounds of contestation with the literary: the productivist ideology of capital criticism that invests value in time spent, hard labor, and unified, productive results. What Burroughs offers is the unassimilable, the refusal, or refuse. "'Junk,' 'muck,' 'excrement,' 'waste,'" writes Christopher Nash, are "the detritus of culture's frenetic efforts to make sense (and where value is missing, *all* effort lies 'waste')" (219). The letter, in short, drives both the content and form of the routine in the same direction of excess, towards a horizon of impossible limits: "There were even some letters I *destroyed* as too extreme," Burroughs delights in telling Ginsberg (*L* 211).

The excess of the letter routine and its inherent inaccuracy and incompleteness is a sign therefore of the entrance it gives to the impossible, unsymbolized Real of desire, as is suggested in Burroughs' fully Lacanian account from November 1955: "The meaning of Interzone, its space-time location is at a point where three-dimensional fact merges into dream, and dreams erupt into the real world . . . ~~The very exaggeration of routines is intended to create this feeling~~" (*L* 300). Shattering divisions between "reality" and "fantasy," the routine cannot be situated within either term and so becomes *uncanny,* in the sense that, as Mladen Dolar observes, in the presence of the uncanny the "status both of the subject and of 'objective reality' is thus put in question" ("'I Shall'" 6). The hallucinatory effect fulfills the logic of rendering an encounter with the irreducible "Thing" and so completes the vital transformation that took place in Burroughs' writing from *Junkie,* defined as an "accurate account," to *Queer,* defined as an *in*accurate "*attempt*" to render the *un*accountable (*L* 83, 126). Now, we can see how the meaningless materiality of "whale drek" identifies a basic truth of both the routine form and the Interzone. It defines a limit to interpretation as well as to commercial use and so undermines language's claim to know and render all of reality, its claims to transparency and reference.

As "reject material" (*NL* 179), "whale drek" insists on the useless but disturbing opacity of the sign, on what stubbornly *remains,* and of course the whale itself summons *Moby-Dick,* the "inscrutable thing" that exercises fascination, exceeds meaning, and so embodies what Lacan called "enjoyment."[19] The eruption of the traumatic Real that horrifies and fascinates is, in *Naked Lunch,* precisely a matter of laying waste to sense and of dirty enjoyment, and the problem of the text for the reader is the problem of waste disposal, of what we are to *do* with it. Making money out of "whale drek" is no more absurd than making a novel out of *Naked Lunch,* and this was exactly Burroughs' problem at the time of writing.

The letter journal form therefore offered a technical solution to Burroughs' problems of structuring fragmentary, "useless" projects but still functioned to naturalize his material, to reproduce an essentially modernist requirement for order and stability, for system and structure. It is these requirements, reflecting needs to secure an ordered self and an ordered world, that demand obstacles to order to be defined as forms of the Other. Such obstructions, as William Connolly argues, "become dirt, matter out of place, irrationality, abnormality, waste, sickness, perversity, incapacity, disorder, madness," obstacles therefore in need of "rationalization, normalization, moralization" (*Political Theory* 13). Connolly, writing in the context of political theory, clearly draws on Mary Douglass's anthropological case for dirt as an offense against order and for disease as a structural crisis: "dirt is essentially disorder" (2). There is no need to insist on an absolute homology of textual and political bodies to see that what is true at a social level also applies at the artistic level; namely, that it is the normalizing pressure for unity and order that manufactures fragmentation and abnormality, so that Burroughs' insistent search for principles of coherence and control can only enlarge the field of the disorderly.

Over and over again during the Tangier years, Burroughs was desperately seeking a schema, a plot, a narrative line, seizing upon first one and then another way to structure his material. From April 1954—"Attempt to organize material is more painful than anything I ever experienced"—to October 1955—"Horrible mess of long-hand notes to straighten out, plus all those letters to go through"(*L* 201). "It is terribly painful" (287)—Burroughs describes his formal problem as a *physical* agony, on a par with the pains of addiction. When these two chronic conditions coincided during the editing of "Lee's Letters and Journals," the result was a disturbance of tense and person and of time and place, arrived at through the physical process of textual manipulation: "What levels and time shifts involved in transcribing these notes [and letters]: reconstruction of the past, the immediate present—which conditions selection of the material—the emergent future, all hitting me at once, sitting here junk-sick" (*I* 84). Without quite realizing it, Burroughs had just hit upon his trademark technique of spatial juxtaposition, where chronology and identity can slip and segue in any direction. In the meantime, the problem of organization and order remained a resolutely *material* problem for him: "My room and papers are in a mess that seems hopeless," he tells Ginsberg in August 1954. "I try to sort and classify, but the wind-up is moving papers from one place to another" (*LG* 62). Burroughs' novel was "bogged down" precisely because he assumed it needed cleaning and tidying up. Hence, the irony of his despair, that December, when he sat down to write his "best-seller Book of the Month job" and, as he told Kerouac, failed miserably: "I can just see that serialized in *Cosmopolitan* or *Good Housekeeping*" (*L* 242).

The day before, writing to Ginsberg, he spelled out in more detail the consequences of holding onto a typically modernist faith in what William Connolly calls "the code of integration and coherence" (*Identity/Difference* 60):

> I am discouraged about my writing. It seems impossible for me to write anything saleable, or, in fact, anything that achieves artistic unity or wholeness. What I have written reads like the notes for a novel, not the novel itself. The act of creation needed to unify material into a finished work, seems beyond my power. All I can write is pieces of a novel, and the pieces don't fit together. (*LG* 76)

Burroughs' pieces do not fit together into a whole novel precisely because they are not fit pieces for a novel, the ethical content of his routines proving as awkward as their aesthetic organization. But with his right hand, Burroughs still clearly remained committed to unity and coherence, to solving contradictions, and so to meeting norms of what Pierre Machery terms "ghostly perfection" (qtd. in Levinson 201). And as Marjorie Levinson has argued in the case of the Romantic "fragment poem," such norms are not "obvious, timeless, and universal" (8, 13). In other words, the self-thwarting of Burroughs' formal intentions designates a site of ideological impasse. Most importantly, the epistolary-aesthetic axis did not exist in isolation from the aesthetic-economic axis, as Burroughs was all too aware: the line between writing "anything saleable" and "anything that achieves artistic unity or wholeness" was as short as it was unbroken.

And so in late 1954 and early 1955, Burroughs finds himself returning to a familiar crossroads. In one direction, there lies work approaching the commercially anonymous (approaching it, that is, for Burroughs). In fall

1954, he will write up his story "Driving Lesson" so that it comes "near to being perfect and finished" and is therefore salable but uncharacteristically "conventional" (*LG* 63, 51), or he will work on a journalistic report like his "Letter from Tangier" aimed at the *New Yorker:* "so flatly an *article* like anybody could have written" (*L* 258). This latter was out-and-out "hack work" (255), a resonant term with a history for Burroughs, going back to April 1952 and his first draft of "The Finger" (120); *hack* denotes a writer who would always complete his work, a mere professional drudge who works to order. It comes as no surprise to find Burroughs repeating his comments in 1955 for another story: "Incomplete, of course. What you think I am, a hack?" (*I* 77).

This refusal of commercial finish and narrative closure is essentially a refusal of the philosophical category of the whole: in this view, the part isn't monstrous, except in terms of a totalizing rage for order. However, for Burroughs to see the fragment as not his problem but the solution, to find self-realization in self-thwarting, this was only available to him in retrospect. He moves in halting stages towards a certain way of contesting the forces of systematization, one that will give the fragment what Balachandra Rajan in *The Form of the Unfinished* calls "its right to significance without incorporation" (309). This is because, to borrow Rajan's terms, what the protracted labor pains of *Naked Lunch* signal is an extreme form of "the ongoing encounter between a creating self and the developing otherness of a work which increasingly claims its autonomy from that self" (308). It is in this sense that in *Naked Lunch* the writing comes alive.

It is therefore not necessarily masochism that causes Burroughs to describe his work in October 1955 in these terms: "This writing is more painful than anything I ever did. Parentheses pounce on me and tear me apart. I have no control over what I write, which is as it should be" (*L* 289). Burroughs demonstrates here any number of modernist writers' "painful sense of the irreducible gap between their need for order and the disorderliness of reality" (McHale, *Constructing Postmodernism* 22), up until his telling, final phrase; this is "as it should be." To recall Blanchot's case of "tyrannical prehension," here Burroughs recognizes that, as Steven Shaviro puts it, the "imposition of order is itself the most compulsive, the most unfree and inauthentic, of actions" (*Passion* 127). But of course, in the mid-1950s, to surrender control, to abandon narrative and to short-circuit self-censorship, all this meant renouncing any chance of commercially viable writing. It meant giving up any chance of an *audience,* an audience other than Ginsberg.

In the other direction, there lies work that contests salability and wholeness, that forces an inexorable aesthetic-economic binary, scoring an ironic victory for the "other" writing hand, as when in December 1954 Burroughs "sat down seriously to write a best seller, and the result is another routine" (*LG* 76). The term "routine" has become shorthand for the unsalable, the unusable. One month later, writing on a typewriter verging on breakdown and suffering from a "feeling of complete desolation," Burroughs defined his work-in-progress in the course of once again describing his house, where he now lived "in slowly accumulating dirt and disorder" (*L* 258). He was just two weeks away from his first anniversary in Tangier and the writing of his definitive routine of dirt and disorder: "The Talking Asshole." If, as Blanchot observes, it is "difficult to grasp this speech of fragment without altering it" (*Infinite Conversation* 152), then this routine is ideally placed to test that "difficulty of grasping" posed so materially and so relentlessly by *Naked Lunch* as a whole.

6

Naked Lunch: Master-Pieces

I feel the work is sufficiently complex I couldn't begin to see—I found it
absolutely fascinating because it draws me to read it further and further.
> —Norman Mailer, qtd. in "Excerpts from the Boston Trial of *Naked Lunch*"

Such a paradoxical space [...] is best exemplified by a well-known Hegelian
dictum according to which the secrets of the ancient Egyptians were also
secrets for the Egyptians themselves: the solution of the riddle is to redouble it.
> —Slavoj Žižek, *The Sublime Object of Ideology*

EVERYONE MAKES A LITTLE DUMBNESS

A HISTORY OF VOICE AND BODY

A popular and critical consensus says that *Naked Lunch* is Burroughs'
masterpiece and that the masterpiece within it is "The Talking
Asshole." Why focus again on this "most famous and most analyzed
routine" (Murphy, *Wising Up* 91–92)? To begin with, because it is
the exemplary instance of all the interminable critical problems that make
Naked Lunch so fascinating, including the problem of the exemplary itself.
Almost always the routine is read as central, representative, a template; but
central to, representative of, and a template for precisely *what* changes from
one approach to another. That "The Talking Asshole" can be the best sum-
mation of the "world of Interzone" (Tanner 117), the "most important epi-

sode" illustrating the effects of addiction (Skerl 39), a "parable of writing" (Grunberg 103), a "parable about giving too much power to transgressive desire" (Beard 838), the "quintessential example of Burroughs' 'routine' style," and a "blueprint for understanding the radical nature of Burroughs' fiction and theory" (Lydenberg, *Word Cultures* 26, 28)—that it possesses such a promiscuous ability to satisfy all comers suggests that criticism doesn't freely focus on this material but is sucked in according to a certain logic of criticism itself when faced with *Naked Lunch*.

In other words, "The Talking Asshole" stands for the intractable difficulty of *Naked Lunch* insofar as it is a part readily taken for the whole. This fate is doubly ironic, however. For the relation of part to whole is a problem at the very heart of the routine, and critics usually treat the anecdote of the man who taught his asshole to talk as a whole in itself, when it is actually one part of a larger routine made, like *Naked Lunch* overall, out of many conflicting modes of writing. It is less a singular Burroughsian masterpiece than multiple pieces only mastered into singularity by critical will. This is the problem faced by Burroughs criticism. For at its roots— from the Greek "to separate or choose"—*criticism* depends on generalizing from the particular, on motivating the text as a whole even while reading its parts out of context and ventriloquizing its words. Four decades of reading *Naked Lunch* may have dulled its ethical offensiveness, its "dirt," but its aesthetic offenses, its "disorder," remain as recalcitrant as ever: to be fit for critical purposes, "The Talking Asshole," like the book, has to be cut to fit.

Overlooking this complexity, "The Talking Asshole" has been added to a specific category of textual elements. This is the class of those parts that present the reader, weary from the teeming heterogeneity of *Naked Lunch*, with what appear to be master keys to the text. These are its most seductive but also its most suspect parts, because they promise to save us from the reading experience itself, from its disorienting material contradictions and aggressive rhetorical self-subversions. "The Talking Asshole" joins therefore not only the "Deposition" but a range of eminently quotable passages, such as "The Word is divided into units which be all in one piece" (*NL* 229), that seemingly offer "a perfect description of the book" (Seltzer 343). Robin Lydenberg has shown what is wrong with this approach methodologically; how "the notion that unity and structure 'justify' a text" rests on the very critical foundations Burroughs attacks (*Word Cultures* 21). But just as revealingly, it is wrong *materially*. For instance, in the above case, this line originally opened the sixty-one-page manuscript section titled "The Word" that in turn originally began Burroughs' Interzone manuscript dating from 1957, so that critics have applied to *Naked Lunch* as a whole a claim that referred properly to only one of its parts, and a part that was almost entirely left out.

What is at stake here becomes even clearer in the case of Timothy Murphy's use of the same line. He reads this as a *continuation* of the equally quotable "mosaic of juxtaposition" passage, one that in 1955 described another rejected manuscript, the "selection chapter" of "Lee's Letters and Journals," and Murphy uses both to support his broader claim that "Burroughs himself offers a straightforward, practical pedagogy of his writing within *Naked Lunch*" ("Intersection" 84). The text may invite such a case, but both materially and rhetorically, *Naked Lunch* refuses to sustain it, and not just because it leaves out all those parts that don't fit. There is something else in Murphy's approach that is visible in the five tables he constructs, listing themes, characters, and refrains as they recur page by page. Why is it that these lists immediately struck me as *essentially useless?* Because they reminded me of my own lists, which over the years grew ever longer and more complex and more useless, until I realized what their real function was: not simply to map the text but to *master* it. This is the first lesson to learn from fascination: that no matter how long a list you draw up to account for it, the list must remain always incomplete, not because of something missing that could be included but because for an object to exercise fascination our relation to it must include some symbolic lack or surplus that remains unaccountable. Once everything *can* be listed, then what it describes is no longer fascinating. Norman Mailer said that *Naked Lunch* is "absolutely fascinating because it draws me to read it further and further,"[1] but the opposite is also true: I am drawn to reading it further and further because it is so absolutely fascinating, because I can never quite grasp even the truth that I can never quite grasp it.

Rather than taking anything away from its precise political and literary-historical importance, it surely adds to it to say that this is one of *Naked Lunch*'s major cultural functions: to torment us by presenting an experience we cannot master. Paradoxically, this is both the lure of the text and its admonitory lesson, and here we recognize Burroughs' acute awareness of the relation of desire to authority. In this sense, *Naked Lunch* fulfills the economy of fascination mapped out in advance by Kerouac in *The Town and the City,* which dramatized for Burroughs at the very start of his writing career the seductive authority of the teacher supposed to know the secret. "The lesson of the master," Adam Phillips has observed, referring to Jacques Lacan but effectively glossing both Kerouac's scene and Burroughs' text, "is the one we should stop listening out for" (112). Perhaps inevitably, responses to *Naked Lunch* have either surrendered to or imposed upon it this very authority.

If criticism gives insufficient attention to "The Talking Asshole" as a material but self-divided whole and as a part within *Naked Lunch,* it goes without saying that none at all has been given to the routine within its original, epistolary text—Burroughs' letter of 7 February 1955—let alone to the relation between the two. Robin Lydenberg, whose analysis is the most critically sophisticated, approaches "The Talking Asshole" as a "history of voice and body" (*Word Cultures* 22). I propose to take her case literally, by attending closely to the material textual body of its voice; or rather, to its many voices and its *two* historical bodies. The movement here, therefore, is not from published text to letter context: the letter text is to be taken as itself a whole, one that Burroughs himself partialized, took out of context, and ventriloquized long before his critics.

Between 1954 and 1956, Burroughs first wrote numerous routines in letters to Ginsberg: "Leif the Unlucky" (*L* 218–19; *NL* 181–82), "The Prophet's Hour" (*L* 332–34; *NL* 112–16), "The Oblique Addict" (*L* 309–10; *NL* 67–68), and so on. A comparative analysis would show the degree to which each was written within an epistolary economy rather than simply contained in a letter, and therefore how their recontextualization within *Naked Lunch* preserved or lost what was produced specifically by their initial intersubjective origin and framing. But if we must resist the reductive temptation to seek models of the text taken from within it, so too we can't generalize about the debt that the textual politics of *Naked Lunch* owes to the letter routine. What then does my analysis of "The Talking Asshole" hope to achieve? A specific, rather than representative, case history, to let us grasp the complex relation between the published routine and the formal, cultural, and political economies of its epistolary original. The difference of the "original" from the published text does not stabilize its meanings or simply multiply them but on the contrary shows that there can be no satisfactory resolution of a text whose meanings are not ambiguous but antagonistic. This is surely a major source of its innovative power and of its fascination as a subjective experience: that *Naked Lunch* is made of and effects a *contrariety.*

SHAKEN AROUND AND POURED OUT

Here, I will not quote extracts: it is essential that "The Talking Asshole" be read in its entirety as it appears in *Naked Lunch* (131–35).

Located in the middle of the "Ordinary Men and Women" section, "The Talking Asshole" is quite clearly constructed in five parts: part 1, the framing dialogue between Benway and Schafer; part 2, the main anecdote of the carny man who taught his asshole to talk; part 3, a paragraph of cultural comment; part 4, a political allegory about bureaucracy; and part 5, a short anecdote about an Arab boy who played the flute with his ass. These parts are all linked, but each is nevertheless formally or thematically quite distinct, which is why the material can only be mastered into coherence by being partialized—cut down for analysis—and naturalized—responsibility for it passed onto a familiar source.

The key self-contradiction of "The Talking Asshole" is the most elementary: that Benway's speech is not spoken by Benway. At first, there seems no problem relating Benway in dialogue with Schafer to his anecdote of the ass. Wayne Pounds sees none, even though he makes one apparent:

> The context here, mad Dr. Benway discussing medical efficiency, draws attention to what Burroughs' own performance makes obvious (or would have made obvious, had the reader heard it): this is full-blown parody, a parody of the discourse of scientistic, behaviorist human engineering. (219)

Pounds invokes Burroughs to resolve into "parody" the contradiction between framing context—Benway and Schafer as unbridled mechanics of bodily reconstruction—and the anecdote that follows, now crudely translated into a parable warning against behaviorist experimentation. For both scientists share the same fantasy of doctoring the body into "one all-purpose" structure, an organism so unified and controlled that it cannot "get out of order" (*NL* 131). By turning into a giant centipede, Schafer's "Master Work" betrayed Schafer, turned his modernist dream of totalizing perfectibility into a nightmare (103). As a narration whose result is another disorderly metamorphosis, the anecdote of the ass betrays its own narrator, betrays Benway. In dialogue with Schafer, Benway proves himself a master of different discourses and languages, citing German maxims, Shakespeare quotations, antiquated Anglicisms, technical terms, and so on. In the monologue, it is the multiple discourses that master him, autonomous words that talk through his mouth and in his name but against his and Schafer's beliefs. To call this *parody* makes sense from the point of view of Burroughs but no sense at all from Benway's or Schafer's.

If part 1 soon collapses as a framing dialogue, the transition from the main anecdote of part 2 to the cultural criticism of part 3 is still less secure: "That's the sex that passes the censor," it begins (*NL* 133). Given how clearly the anecdote had been set up in terms of scientific rationalism, we might have expected a line beginning, "That's the *science* that . . ." How are we supposed to understand this sudden shift of reference to sex and to "popular songs and Grade B movies" (133)? Is this meant to be the real point of the routine? And in any case, in the context of *Naked Lunch*'s actual publication history and obscenity trials, isn't the point entirely backwards? Surely, this is the sex that in the 1950s *couldn't* pass the American censor. Within the routine in the text, however, the abrupt shift from bodily reconstruction to cultural production is not surprising, insofar as it is just one more contradiction that we can only overlook or fail to understand. Indeed, the same shift takes place in reverse in part 3, which begins with cultural criticism only for the image of "American rottenness" to spawn tropes that take on an entirely literal and physical sense, so that we end up back with "human parts shaken around and poured out any way they fell" (134). This is an apt figure for so disorderly a *textual* body, where one part is continually being taken over and transformed by another.

And so the political science allegory of part 4 shifts the ground once again, now onto the figurative body politic, and again with a force that suggests that this is not an alternative but the real "point" of the routine. This allegorical political critique is in turn displaced once more by the physical body, by culture, and by the erotic in part 5, the story of the flute-playing Arab boy. The jump between parts 4 and 5 is the last and most startling of all. Alvin Seltzer's solution is a final will to integration: for him, this material rescues the first anecdote of the talking ass, no longer "an apparently pointless tale" but "an allegorical equivalent to bureaucracies that feed off their host" (345). Quite properly, Lydenberg has argued against this as a "reductive mode" of explanation, and she proceeds with her case for the physicality of the asshole, for the literal body, against any allegorical reading of the anecdote (*Word Cultures* 21). But what makes the inter-critical dispute interesting here is that, by opposed routes, each arrives at the same destination. By allegorizing the whole, Seltzer demands disciplining the parts into an order they actively subvert within and across one other. By literalizing a single part, Lydenberg must suppress the whole to which it belongs in so problematic a relation. Each unifies and makes sense of a text that cannot be resolved because it is composed of a struggle between competing agencies and orders of meaning.

Since Benway cannot be mistaken for a realistic character "possessed" by his speech or as a stand-in for the author, in the way that Lee may be by the Slave Trader, how is the reader to understand the routine? One approach is to see all the contra-dictions as strategic. The routine then becomes Benway's punishment that fits the crime: the master of control is subjected to the ventriloquizing of a routine about ventriloquism; the master bureaucrat is made to speak out against bureaucracy; the architect of bodily regulation is forced to narrate a story about bodily disorder; the manipulator of sexual identity for purposes of state control is given an anecdote about sexual identity running out of control; and so on. Such a strategy would be reciprocal: as Benway is forced to speak against his own position, in the same breath Burroughs forces *his* own—most didactically, the cooperative as "the road to follow" (*NL* 134)—into a mouth that must render it suspect. This would be a strategic art of self-subversion in which authority is not challenged directly but turned against itself. This is one way of making it hard for us to listen out for the lesson of the master.

However, there are at least two objections to this approach. First, it ignores all that is *particular* to the main anecdote: Benway's narration of the routine may suggest a complex relation between science, power, bureaucracy, the body, and sexuality, but it leaves a key question unanswered, if not unanswerable: why should the center ground be given to American popular culture? Second, a strategic approach would get rid of all the self-divisions and contradictions, all the proliferating possibilities of contrary meanings and effects by calling on the author, on Burroughs' *purpose.* Authorial intentionality is too single-minded, too reassuring a security blanket for either "The Talking Asshole" or *Naked Lunch* as a whole. Norman Mailer was merely stating the obvious when he registered "a feeling of great torture in the composition" of the book,[2] a feeling necessarily reproduced in the process of reading; in the end, it is this trauma that needs to be preserved from the aim of critically mastering it.

In the relation of ventriloquist to dummy, the duet of a communicative exchange becomes a solo, in which both speaker and listener simply disappear inside the autonomous workings of the text. Since there is no intersubjective dimension between characters—Schafer's disappearance stands in for the fate of any internal audience in *Naked Lunch*—the force of language is thrown fully onto the reader, with similar and similarly disturbing effects. Words that are alien to the speaker become alienating for the reader, and all utterance takes on "the uncanny air of citation" (Nathanson 307). Anyone who has reread *Naked Lunch* with pencil in hand will understand: the pages flicker back and forth, the pencil scratches cross-references along the margin as phrases replicate across the text, traveling from one context and speaker to another, creating a labyrinthine network of verbal repetitions and variations that can be collected and collated and arranged into lists but that, finally, yield eerie surface effects of uncanny *recognition,* of disturbed memory, not deeper levels of meaning. For every part of *Naked Lunch* that refers to some reality beyond the text and invites pointed interpretation, there are always others that we can't explain away. Its redundant doublings and frequent hermetic passages speak an opaque language, a meaningless materiality that cannot be absorbed into the reassuring realms of representation or expression.

Many critics have followed Mary McCarthy's example and naturalized the text's ventriloquial voices by passing them back to Burroughs' alter ego, on the basis that the "action of *The Naked Lunch* takes place in the consciousness of One Man, William Lee, who is taking a drug cure" (35). However, it is only too convenient to ground the text in Lee/Burroughs' consciousness, scattered by the effects of withdrawal, even though it does not quite add up like this. To recall Cronenberg's achievement, such a reading views *Naked Lunch* as the product of a traumatized memory, which serves to disavow what it inflicts on the reader: namely, the effect of *producing* trauma and memory. There is also a more material reason. Especially during the first three years of its history, Burroughs was still committed to solving contradictions, not enlarging them; if it "read like the notes for a novel, not the novel itself," this was a chronic failure (*LG* 76). By late 1957, he knew it was "not a novel" (*L* 367) nor meant to be one, and this would stay his verdict, but the earlier history remains in the text. *Naked Lunch* supports entirely contrary readings because of the fertile but finally unresolved conflict between opposed writing hands. This is why a material genetic history is so valuable: it shows over time the pull of antagonistic forces—aesthetic but also economic, cultural, and political—at their point of emergence, and this is significant above all in the case of the letter routine.

TYING THE GARBAGE UP

DO YOU DIG WHAT HAPPENS?

To begin with its most limited value, what does the letter text original of "The Talking Asshole" tell us about the published version? First, it establishes the overall structural integrity of the routine in *Naked Lunch,* and second, it shows three small but crucial areas of revision. Most significantly, the framing Benway-Schafer dialogue does not appear in Burroughs' letter of 7 February 1955 and was certainly added at a much later stage. This frame in turn replaced an original first paragraph and a second paragraph that Burroughs cut down heavily. This is the original opening of the letter routine:

> "The incredibly obscene, thinly disguised references and situations that slip by in Grade B Movies; the double entendres, perversion, sadism of popular songs; poltergeist knockings and mutterings of

America's putrefying unconscious, boils that swell until they burst with a fart noise as if the body had put out an auxiliary ass hole with a stupid, belligerent Bronx cheer.

"Did I ever tell you about the man who taught his ass hole to talk?" (*L* 259)

Clearly enough, this paragraph accounts for one of the main contradictions in the *Naked Lunch* version: the anecdote of the ass was not introduced as an instance of the physical body's scientific and rational reconstruction from above but originally developed by taking literally a figure tied to the popular-cultural body and its barely sublimated libidinal energies below. When this cultural material is repeated in part 3 of the routine, immediately after the main anecdote, the original constructs a symmetrical frame that in *Naked Lunch* is simply lost: what the text version's unaccountable shift shows is the hand of editing against the original's grain. Likewise, it now becomes clear where the "sex that passes the censor" comes from, although as another small change at the start of part 3 indicates, this comment did *not* apply to the anecdote of the ass: instead of "That's the sex that passes," in the letter routine Burroughs wrote, "So what I *started* to talk about was the sex that passes" (*L* 260; my emphasis). In other words, in the letter original, the anecdote digressed from the point, transgressed its own exemplary aim, while the published version doesn't so much change this meaning as creates a contradiction that is quite meaningless.

In contrast, the framing of the routine within its original letter text establishes a highly determined reading. This is no casual framing. It is symmetrical and precisely phrased, showing, like the routine itself, a keen awareness of the regulatory functions of any frame: on the one hand, that "perceptions of coherence depend upon acts of *framing*," and on the other, that "any framing has the intent of fixing an exchange rate" (Reid 9, 13). Burroughs' remarks here ask to be admitted into the text, into textuality, into relation with the routine text that they contain—or rather, do *not* contain, since the original handwritten letter runs on as a continuum and draws no line to separate epistolary preamble from fictional routine. This is a frame precisely concerned with the production of meaning and value:

Dear Allen,

Here is my latest attempt to write something saleable. All day I had been finding pretexts to avoid work, reading magazines, making fudge, cleaning my shot-gun, washing the dishes, going to bed with Kiki, tying the garbage up in neat parcels and putting it out for the collector (if you put it out in a waste basket or any container, they will steal the container every time. I was going to chain a bucket to my doorstep but it's like too much trouble. So I put it out in packages), buying food for dinner, picking up a junk script. So finally I say: "Now you must work," and smoke some tea and sit down and out it comes all in one piece like a glob of spit [...]

This is my saleable product. Do you dig what happens? It's almost like automatic writing produced by a hostile, independent entity who is saying in effect, "I will write what I please." At the same time when I try to pressure myself into organizing production, to impose some form on material, or even to follow a line (like continuation of novel), the effort catapults me into a sort of madness, where only the most extreme material is available to me. What a disaster to lose my typewriter, and no possibility of buying one this month. My financial position slides inexorably. (*L* 259, 262)

As long ago as 1979, Serge Grunberg called "The Talking Asshole" a "parable of writing" (103), but Burroughs' original letter does not simply confirm this as one possible reading among others. This is because, whereas Grunberg refers to writing in the abstract, just as Lydenberg refers to the routine's "exposure of the dynamics of linguistic power" in the abstract (*Word Cultures* 26), the letter frame establishes the historically specific ground of the routine in Burroughs' particular material conditions of writing. With this frame, the routine returns to its epistolary context as a condensation of Burroughs' economies and economics of writing: returns to a dialectic of work and waste, production and rejection, the machine and the mechanic, dirt and disorder. For convenience, two double axes can be isolated, each speaking to basic divisions of the writer: first, the relations between economy and culture and between psyche and productivity; second, the relations between spontaneity and control and between form and theme.

THIS IS MY SALEABLE PRODUCT

Burroughs begins by acknowledging the economic destiny driving the cultural production of his routine: as the "latest attempt to write something saleable," it completes a yearlong history of writing where success is defined entirely—and not entirely ironically—in terms of popular culture, mass circulation, and mainstream commercial readership. And so, in his comments following "The Talking Asshole," there is a brutal insistence on productivity, on "saleable product," "writing produced," and "organizing production." Having already seen *Junkie* packaged as a pulp "Double Book,"

Burroughs' apparent ambition is to emulate the Grade B movie, to give the fruits their B productions.

As such, Burroughs dreams of entering the standardized mold that defines his own work by negation and rejection, the saturated "book market" (*I* 72). In the postwar era, Marx's insight into production—that it creates a human subject for the commodity object—took on new meaning for American writers precisely because the distribution of culture on an unprecedented mass scale was so fully integrated into consumerized conformity. This in turn served cold war politics by positing the joyous but passive loyalty of what Stewart Ewen terms "economic nationalism" (211); hence, Burroughs' fantasy of writing for *Good Housekeeping,* Book-of-the-Month Club, and *New Yorker* (*L* 231, 241, 258). To cold war liberals, such a vision of conformist commodification is the nightmare world of "mass culture," Dwight Macdonald's hugely influential updating of Clement Greenberg's "kitsch," the culture that "predigests art" for ease of consumption (qtd. in Lears 47). Writing in 1953, Macdonald warned of a culture that threatened to "engulf everything in its spreading ooze," a vision of suffocating horror straight out of contemporary science fiction movies, but one that was, as Jackson Lears notes, an apocalypse "being promoted by the Book-of-the-Month Club" (47). Using the same rhetoric and range of reference, in "The Talking Asshole" the cancer of "Undifferentiated Tissue" that engulfs the ventriloquist dramatizes (among other things) Burroughs' version of Macdonald's vision. To describe this cellular takeover, Burroughs twice uses what he knew was a key word here, a pathological term for entropy loaded with a heavy history of political, sexual, and artistic associations: *degenerate.*[3] Burroughs' ambition to write a best-seller Book-of-the-Month Club job returns in the anecdote of the talking asshole as a biological and moral catastrophe, the realization of "America's putrefying unconscious." Of course, in Burroughs' scenario, the ventriloquist is not the duped consumer of commercial mass culture but one of its producers. If, in the neo-Marxist vision of mass-culture critics, postwar American capitalism set about "ventriloquizing an inert and prefabricated mass of consumers" (A. Ross 35), then Burroughs suggests in "The Talking Asshole" what the colonization by culture might look like from the other side. What the letter routine does is to bring together the unconscious economies of individual and mass cultural production, and Burroughs' references to popular culture are deployed with precision to this end.

One of Robin Lydenberg's most valuable contributions to reading the anecdote of the talking asshole was her analysis of Le Petomane, the late-nineteenth-century French music-hall anal ventriloquist. For the rise of the music hall in France and England, like the rise of vaudeville in America, incorporated ventriloquist performances within the "rapid turnover of acts on a variety bill" (Connor, *Dumbstruck* 397), which in turn suggests the entirely fitting location of the carnival performer within *Naked Lunch* as a whole, both culturally and structurally. In the 1920s, Viktor Shklovsky commented on the interpolated numbers of vaudeville that they belonged to one of the "most vital genres in contemporary art": "the collection of articles and the variety show, which depends for its interest on the individual components, not on the connective tissue" (81). Since Shklovsky made these comments in his unique letter novel, *Zoo: or, Letters Not about Love*, this is also a reminder that the epistolary model of juxtaposition can, without much effort, approximate and accommodate on the page the literal variety of vaudeville, which, of course, is where the very term "routine" originates. However, the material source for Burroughs' routine was a more contemporary cinematic treatment of the stage ventriloquist act, namely the section directed by Cavalcanti of the portmanteau, noirish British classic *Dead of Night* (1945). Characteristically, Burroughs doesn't identify the film by name, but in fact "The Talking Asshole" does name its location within a broader sweep of American cultural history through the very title of the carny man's act: "The Better 'Ole."

"The Better 'Ole" takes us back to 1926, the last year of the silent film and the birth of the talkies in Hollywood, when Warner Brothers premiered a largely neglected variety burlesque of that title. The film's particular significance is double. First, as the film historian Harry Geduld notes, it confirmed the understanding that from this point on, the "whole range of vaudeville could now be presented on the screen"[4] (150). Second, the film confirmed Vitaphone, Warner's synchronized sound system, as a landmark in the technology of cinema. *The Better 'Ole* pioneered the talking picture and so marked the development by Hollywood of a technology of word and image that would convert cinema itself into a mass technology of ventriloquism, not just a convenient screen on which to represent it. The demonic dummy therefore stands for the autonomous power of the medium as such since, as Steven Connor observes, "a 'talking picture' is both a picture to which talking has been added, and a picture that has started to talk for itself" (*Dumbstruck* 411). Once Hollywood taught it to talk, like the carny man's ass, it would never shut up.

If "The Talking Asshole" encodes a stage of significant development for Burroughs' future interest in film, we have also to see the significance of his overt allusion, repeated twice in the letter routine, to B movies. Where ventriloquism explores the theme of the double, Burroughs' citation of B-movie culture is invoking a history of film production driven hardest by the profit motive, like his own determination to write a saleable product. B movies held an emphatically inferior position in the hierarchy of exhibition, and this is where their cultural function doubles that of Burroughs' routine. B films, runs the standard glossary, "were used to fill the bottom half of a double bill when double features were standard" (D. Cook 960). Burroughs makes the anal and schizophrenic potential of B production absolutely literal in the carny man's performance as the revenge of the bottom half. His desire to expose the "double entendres, perversion, sadism" of popular culture pits him, therefore, against those who saw in such postwar forms as film noir a way to contain and channel otherwise repressed desires and disavowed fantasies. Where C. L. R. James argued that in such films the American people therapeutically "released the bitterness, hate, fear and sadism which simmer just below the surface" (qtd. in Corber, *Homosexuality* 28), Burroughs' approach is to invert the therapy.

If "The Talking Asshole" alludes to the decline of live vaudeville, the rise of the talkies, and the heyday of the cinematic bottom half, it relates this history of cultural production to psychological ventriloquism via the effects of censorship. The libidinal energies that pass the public censor, hungering desires so alienated that they can be commodified as images and fed back for consumption, emerge in fantasies of communication coded to bypass schizophrenic self-division. This is most explicit elsewhere in *Naked Lunch,* as in the lines immediately following the nightmare image of self-division where one hand squeezes the other: "Obsessed with codes. . . . Man contracts a series of diseases which spell out a code message. . ." (*NL* 66). In the letter original of this passage, dated February 1956, the relation between bodily and cultural symptom was even clearer: "Or he gets message from subsidiary personality by farting in Morse code. (Needless to say such obvious devices as automatic writing would never get by the Censor)" (*L* 311). Given Burroughs' direct reference to automatic writing immediately after the letter routine of "The Talking Asshole," it becomes clear that the routine integrates two economies of censorship: the Freudian kind as well as that of the Hays Production Code.

NOW YOU MUST WORK

Burroughs' awareness of the conditions determining his own productivity was a base for his insights into cultural production, censorship, and economy more generally. In which case, we should return to examine the opening frame of his 7 February 1955 letter. Here, Burroughs' account of a writer's habitual diversions and distractions—albeit rather less habitual than most—is more than a description of mundane circumstance: "All day I had been finding pretexts to avoid work," the second sentence begins. As "pretexts to avoid work," the particulars of his daily routine don't simply precede or defer the text to come but define it as undisguised *work,* as the alienation of labor that life would much rather evade. He troubles most of all over the problem of waste disposal, which in the larger context of his letters and letter routines becomes a literal play on tropes with a history of particular use. The network of association becomes clear in another smaller revision in the letter's first paragraph, where Burroughs wrote of "tying the garbage up in neat parcels and putting it out for the ~~inspector~~ collector."[5] With a slip of the pen, the local Tangier garbage collector is mistakenly identified as a censor, in the form of an inspector of food hygiene.

This is a role that Burroughs himself plays in the letter routine's second paragraph, when he describes rejecting material that is itself about "second-run reject liver that doesn't pass the inspector" (*L* 259). The routine itself begins by addressing "the sex that passes the censor," which is also the sex that in cold war America dare not speak its name, only to subvert its desired Hays Code certification because restraint invites transgression, censorship intensifies the will to pornography, and demonization inflames homosexual desire. The excessive display of private parts that drives Burroughs' epistolary routines—and no part is so private as the asshole—triumphs over the production codes of public property. The lines blur between collector, inspector, and censor to form a composite authority who examines waste products to see if they are fit for consumption.

The letter frame sets up a drama in which Burroughs plays double and divided economic roles: "So finally I say: 'Now you must work.'" Here "you" is work shy, the one who would prefer not to labor, and "I" is the one who insists on equating writer with worker, literature with labor. "I" is the capitalist-as-writer: one who observes the dictates of capital that all production is for the market, so that writing is defined in terms of its salability. This is, to repeat, the *latest attempt;* but despite the dictatorial command to work, also the latest failure. These are related inversely: not despite but *because.* If the routine is crudely introduced as the artistic means to financial ends, then the result is recognized as evidence of another form of resistance—resistance to compulsory alienation and commodification: "you *must* work" gets the reply, immediately after the letter routine, "I will write what I please." Writing socially for profit with the right hand turns into its opposite, writing selfishly for pleasure with the left. This is the interesting thing about Burroughs' relationship to the marketplace: that he does not present himself as consciously antagonistic at all. He doesn't identify himself as a writer setting out to contest the relation between art and economy but as one whose work arises against his own will, in reaction to his very attempts to abide the terms of that contract. The repressed returns in the form of a dirty dictation because, not despite of, capital's dictates and despite, not because of, the writer's ambition.

Both "The Talking Asshole" routine as a whole and the ventriloquist's fate within it therefore become the revenge enacted on capital's demand that the writer go to market: they are *symptoms* in the sense of apparently pathological forms that actually manifest the hidden logic of the system. "The Talking Asshole" simply takes literally the monstrous, self-cannibalizing economic imperative at the base of capitalism, right down to the bottom dollar. The symptomatic pathology of the routine and of *Naked Lunch* in general is caught in precise terms by Marshall Berman, whose unmarked pun shows that he knows where the real monstrosity originates:

> The drug-crazed nihilism of William Burroughs, a favorite bête noire in anti-modernist polemics, is a pale reproduction of his ancestral trust, whose profits financed his avant-garde career: the Burroughs Adding Machine Company, now Burroughs International, sober nihilists of the bottom line. (123)

In the routine, the man begins by teaching his ass to talk, instructing it with an unnatural knowledge and function. Its worthless productivity is denatured by being transformed into productive worth, the work of value: shit is repressed and made into use-value by being replaced by words. The crucial economic context here, which has gone entirely unnoticed in all the criticism on this routine, is that this man "worked for a carnival, you dig" (*NL* 132). His words are therefore meant to be turned into wages, into money that will feed him. Everything is implicated in economy. As the man works for the carnival, so he puts his own asshole to work: as above so below. And from above to below: his own ass becomes an asset. The moral of the story would be, as Deleuze and Guattari put it, that "it is not the anal which is meant for sublimation, but rather it is sublimation itself which is anal" (qtd. in Hocquenghem 237).

If Burroughs begins by willing his writing to go to market, by unnatural self-division, by speaking to himself as an other, then it should be clear that these identities are less multiple than amenable to multiplication: in keeping with the routine, "I" and "you" are in productive rather than descriptive relation. Therefore, even when a binary relation seems stable and the stakes clear, another comes along to disturb it: there is no simple opposition here between a voice of repression and a liberating voice of pleasure but a whole series of oppositions.

I PISSED MYSELF LAUGHING

The body as a trash can of accumulated psychic refuse will lead to the catharsis so autobiographically explicit in "Word": "I will not be silent nor hold longer back the enema of my word hoard, been dissolving all the shit up there man and boy forty-three years" (*I* 144). The backing up of waste signals constipation as a literal fact of opiate addiction, of course, but the triumph of the asshole, the release of what has become "anal and violent, regressive, because it has been made Other" (Vernon 94), is not interesting in relation to Burroughs' addiction nor for his individual neurosis. Nor even, as Norman O. Brown claimed for that other great scatologist, Dean Swift, for his "insight into the universal neurosis of mankind" (168). The point is the historically particular relationship between psychic and cultural economies of production.

This production is not for consumption; *Naked Lunch* is less a manuscript than, as Gaétan Brulotte puts it, an *"anuscript"* (39). Hence, the emetic function of "Word" serves up the "Transcendental Cuisine" consumed by the intimidated customers of *Chez Robert,* who eat blindly on when the food degenerates into "literal garbage" (*NL* 149). The diners are like readers who have missed the point of the text's title or spectators aesthetically contemplating such antiaesthetic objects as Marcel Duchamp's urinal, *Fountain* (1917); Arman's rubbish assemblages, *Poubelles* (1959); or Piero Manzoni's tins of shit, *Merda d'artista* (1961). The responses to *Naked Lunch* of the notorious "UGH . . ." reviewer—"Glug glug. It tastes disgusting" (Willett 42)—and of Dame Edith Sitwell—"I do not wish to spend the rest of my life with my nose nailed to other people's lavatories" (qtd. in Skerl and Lydenberg 49)—were entirely proper, in the sense that they reacted physically to what we, busy contriving our analysis, now tend to swallow without blinking. What they lacked was the sense of humor to catch the indicting ironies of Burroughs' visceral imagination, so nicely appreciated in physical terms by one of the audience for Le Petomane: "When I saw this Frenchman farting away professionally and people paying to hear him, I pissed myself laughing" (qtd. in Lydenberg, *Word Cultures* 25).

It is when the private becomes public—like Le Petomane—and when publication becomes the self-invasion of privacy that *Naked Lunch* must advertise itself as a nonproduct. Writing during the postwar production boom, at a time when David Potter insisted that for Americans, his "people of plenty," "the imperative must fall upon consumption" (173), Burroughs fulfills the negating function of modernist art in a commodity society described by Fredric Jameson: "the vocation *not* to be a commodity, to devise an aesthetic language incapable of offering commodity satisfaction, and resistant to instrumentalization" (16). This is another way of saying, with Anthony Hilfer, that "the novel's paradoxically enabling gesture is to create readers capable of rejecting its most seductive overtures" (265). To some degree at least, these logics derive their impetus from Burroughs' economic devaluation of writing implicated in the sphere of epistolary desire. When he tells Ginsberg of writing up "The Finger" in December 1954, he passes its value entirely over to him as a mere spontaneous production, not the fruits of labor: "I don't think much of it, but got writing on it and couldn't stop" (*LG* 83). He describes sending "The Finger" "in another envelope" (as he had probably once sent its first draft to Marker), even while asking Ginsberg to "throw it away" (81). "Faeces as gift" (Brown 173) becomes the gift as feces. As Barthes says: "The gift is not necessarily excrement, but it has, nonetheless, a vocation as waste" (*Lover's Discourse* 76). What *was* Ginsberg supposed to *do* with "The Finger" or, two months later, "The Talking Asshole"?

Through the economy of his epistolary exchange, Burroughs could dispossess himself of his material by presenting it as ejections that invite rejection. This becomes, if it was not always, pointedly strategic. The situation described by Ginsberg in November 1954—"Bill was driving me to distraction (purposely?) by letter [. . .] I got sometimes 3 a day, it was like a letter spectre zipping around me"[6]—feeds into Burroughs' textual politics: coercion to the limit short circuits desire and enforces resistance. The response foreseen by Ginsberg in a previous letter—"Bill will enforce his idea so much he will *make* me reject it"[7]—is actively produced by *Naked Lunch.*

Barthes's ideal "writerly" text offers, in Terence Hawkes's ecstatic gloss, "the joys of co-operation, co-authorship (and even, at its intensest moments, of copulation)" (114), in which case Burroughs' text is certainly not writerly. Acceptance or rejection are the defining alternatives, and *Naked Lunch,* as itself symptomatic of the diseases it would cure, is not acceptable. And so while the cooperative may be the road to follow according to the polemic of "The Talking Asshole," Burroughs' fantasy jacket blurb for his planned novel, described to Ginsberg the previous month, spells out the intersubjective truth by figuring the relation of book to reader in grotesquely unilateral terms, as rape and torture: "It leaps in bed with you, and performs unmentionable acts. Then it thrusts a long cold needle deep into your spine and gives you an injection of ice water" (*L* 255). If one visceral response proper to *Naked Lunch* is to piss yourself laughing, then this suggests another. And this is the novel, Burroughs adds—as if *en passant,* as if failing completely to see the ghastly linkage—to be made from all the material, including "The Finger" and "The Talking Asshole," that is "scattered through a hundred letters to you."

AMERICANS HAVE A SPECIAL HORROR OF GIVING UP CONTROL

The carny man's ventriloquist act starts as a "scream," but when the asshole talks back, he begins "screaming at it to shut up" (*NL* 132). This is the very madness of the writing machine running out of control, the madness of Burroughs in April 1954 "screaming: 'Stop it! Stop it!'" In the context of Burroughs' previous writing, the routine draws on a history of "taking it like dictation" going back to 1952, as well as dramatizing to the limit a routine that appears "almost like automatic writing." Just five months before "The Talking Asshole," Burroughs would tell Ginsberg he was waiting on "the state like automatic writing I am in when I do my best work" (*LG* 64), and similar claims punctuate his writing during 1956–57. Why does he think it his best work? Because to be genuinely creative, the writer must escape self-control, while what he creates is therefore a defeat *for* control.

Immediately after presenting "The Talking Asshole" in his letter of 7 February 1955, Burroughs refers to having also just started to write a "Chandler-style, straight, action story," later completed as "Hauser and O'Brien," and notes that he isn't sure yet where it is headed: "Don't ask me what is going to happen I just don't know. May turn allegorical or even sur-realist. *A ver*"[8] (*L* 262). Speculating about one text, Burroughs used key terms for describing the other, emphasizing how his central opposition between spontaneity and control as themes coincides with one between modes of writing, between automatism (surrealist creativity *par excellence*) and allegory.

In the structure of "The Talking Asshole," the transition from physical to political body, from anecdote to allegorization, appears to manifest the reassertion of the controlling right hand over the spontaneous left. In this sense, allegory is a disciplinary and hygienic control machine, systematizing the healthy production of meaning: the rule of law and order, not dirt and disorder. The allegorical reading out of the main anecdote thereby reasserts the original command—"Now you must work"—by putting the anecdote to work. As the most "orderly" mode of literature, allegory declares the author's will to control over a text; in the Nietzschean terms of Brian McHale's analysis, it asserts "Apollonian order and repression" over "Dionysian anarchy and the pleasure-principle" (*Postmodernist Fiction*

143). Therefore, when the allegory of the body politic in turn gives way to the second anecdote of the flute-playing Arab boy, the work of allegorical rationalization is undone.

However, the simple antithesis does not hold: the bureaucratic-allegorical passages offer their own metacritique of allegory, a mode considered "lifeless and mechanical" in the 1950s (Leyburn 1). Substitute *allegory* for *bureaucracy,* and it is allegory that "is as wrong as a cancer, a turning away from the human evolutionary direction of infinite potentials and differentiation and independent spontaneous action, to the complete parasitism of a virus" (*NL* 134). Substitute *allegory* for *virus,* and it is allegory that is "the renunciation of life itself, a *falling* towards inorganic, inflexible machine, towards dead matter" (134). If the weakness of bureaucracies is, as Jean-François Lyotard observes, that "they stifle the systems or subsystems they control and asphyxiate themselves in the process (negative feedback)" (55–56), then Burroughs' allegory of bureaucracy fulfills this fate, because the allegorical will, the rhetorical control machine, itself runs out of control. In this reading, the polemic against bureaucracy is an extension of Burroughs' own creative situation, so that cultural production and the body politic meet through the common fate that befalls the attempt to impose control.

This conclusion brings us to the often-cited claim given in the "Atrophied Preface," where the authorial voice says he does "not presume to impose 'story' 'plot' 'continuity'" (*NL* 221). Taken out of context, this seems like a modest variant on a now familiar theme, on a par, for example, with John Hawkes's premise that the "true enemies of the novel were plot, character, setting, and theme" (qtd. in Klein 204), or with the claims of the so-called Blank Generation writer Mark Leyner: "I took off from the assumption that plot, character and setting were conventions to be manipulated and played with. Or abandoned. Or humiliated. Anarchy was my starting point" (qtd. in Young and Caveney 15–16). But what has been taken as Burroughs' clearly defined aesthetic position cannot properly hide a history of self-division and its debt to the mother of his invention—necessity. After the letter routine of "The Talking Asshole," Burroughs observes:

> At the same time when I try to pressure myself into organizing production, to impose some form on material, or even follow a line (like continuation of novel), the effort catapults me into a sort of madness where only the most extreme material is available to me. (*L* 262)

"I try to pressure myself" returns Burroughs to precisely where he started, to "Now you must work." Summing up a history of creative conflict, these

lines establish Burroughs' vital distance from work single-mindedly governed by a fixed ideological premise. The imaginative energy and fertility
of *Naked Lunch* is inseparable from Burroughs' struggle to master his own
drive to mastery; without this generative element of self-division, we fall
back into the binary alternatives of "amnesiac" automatism or "conscious"
control (Seltzer 23) and of allegorical unity or spontaneous chaos.

In Angus Fletcher's terms, allegory produces a "constricted work of art,
which in turn imposes its own constriction upon the reader" (323), while
the agency of allegory is one of "psychic possession," its ultimate figure that
of the mechanical man, the robot (289). Fletcher is speaking in terms of
full-length narrative, and it was precisely routines like "The Talking Asshole" that made *narrative* development Burroughs' central dilemma, above
all for the figure of William Lee. This is clearest from an earlier, incomplete story, "Lee and the Boys," an atypically self-conscious depiction of Lee
as a writer. After the line "Lee put down the pencil" (*I* 36), in an aside on
the manuscript Burroughs reflected: "I felt something was wrong with these
first few pages, a sort of constraint. Well I won't have Lee presented in
fraudulent terms, a dummy for a hidden ventriloquist."[9] Burroughs' problem was Lee's very proximity to life in general and in particular to his own
conception of life as he defined it, as a war between spontaneity and control. Inevitably, Burroughs would have to abandon not just presenting Lee
at work—"Lee often spent hours on a letter" (35)—but using him as a vehicle within a thematically plotted narrative, because each would impose
intolerable allegorical constraint, reducing his alter ego's agency to precisely
that of a mechanical man or a ventriloquist's dummy.

Now, we can see better the significance of the surprisingly precise relation between "The Talking Asshole" routine and the narrative that became
"Hauser and O'Brien," a relation that Cronenberg's movie renders by default. For here, the anecdote of the anal ventriloquist is given simply as the
master's trademark: the film in effect asks to be authenticated by its presence. The cinematic fate of "Hauser and O'Brien," on the other hand, is the
very opposite: to be generalized into a dominant narrative, framing and
sustaining William Lee's identity by the Chandler style and its own familiar trademarks. Of course, as Burroughs himself observes in the introduction to *Everything Is Permitted: The Making of Naked Lunch*, his text was
"composed of many small, fragmentary, kaleidoscopic scenes," so that
Cronenberg's distinctive achievement was to have "crafted a masterful
thriller from the disparate elements of the novel" (Burroughs, Introduction 13, 14). This is a diplomatic but backhanded compliment. In terms
of generic stability and narrative unity, the filmmaker achieved just what

the writer temperamentally and ideologically could not, or did not want to, achieve: mastery. This is what makes the production history of Burroughs' *Naked Lunch* so revealing. It exposes the habitual readiness of critics to tie up loose ends and resolve contradictions by reading parts into wholes as the one thing that was *not permitted*. By giving "a more traditional narrative structure, a psychological and emotional development, and tell[ing] the story through a main character," Cronenberg gives back to Burroughs exactly what Burroughs himself gave up (Cronenberg qtd. in Silverberg 61).

"Hauser and O'Brien" is therefore especially important, because it seems to frame the body of *Naked Lunch* not just *with* first person narrative but *as* first person narrative, to bring about apparent psychological unity and formal closure. It has tempted innumerable readers and far too many critics to understand Lee's journey through Interzone as a drug-induced dream state. What's wrong with this reading is clear: if from Washington Square subway station to the Hotel Lamprey off Broadway, Lee never actually leaves New York City, then Interzone becomes no more than a nightmare version of the Land of Oz, an unreal and strictly allegorical space. In fact, the structural logic of *Naked Lunch* is closer to films such as Adrian Lyne's excellent *Jacob's Ladder* (1990), where the status of dream and reality are revealed to be horrifyingly inverted, or the Warchowski brothers' highly Burroughsian *The Matrix* (1999), where the apparently real world turns out to be a computer-generated fiction, a conspiracy run by aliens to hide the ghastly truth (taken from Baudrillard) of the "desert of the real." In other words, far from reading the space of Interzone allegorically, we have to recognize the apparently realist narrative frame as the true fantasy, concealing the true horror of the real. Of course, one of the reasons why *Naked Lunch* is infinitely more potent than *The Matrix* is that Burroughs' protagonist is no mere dupe of power; on the contrary, he remains horribly complicit with the conspiracy imposing a false reality. As the opening frame demonstrates, Lee is himself an artist of the staged spectacle, exercising a cynical power of fascination by giving the asshole audience his Hollywood "B production" (*NL* 2). In "Hauser and O'Brien," Lee finds himself trapped within precisely such a B-movie world, so that when he shoots the detectives as agents of the Law, the Reality Police as it were, he discovers his *own* identity and agency has disappeared. Calling the narcotics bureau and asking for Hauser, Lee is now faced with the horror of an unanswerable question: "Nobody of that name in this department. . . . Who are *you*?" (216).

Since the Lee of "Hauser and O'Brien" is explicitly identified with the figure of the *writer*—the detectives' mission is to confiscate "all books, letters, manuscripts" (*NL* 209)—closure here would entail a self-conscious allegory of the creative process, while, as the middle term between book and manuscript, the letter registers its special significance to Burroughs' productivity. At this point, we need to recall "The Conspiracy," which formed the original ending to "Hauser and O'Brien," only to be replaced at a very late stage of editing by the two final pages (216–17). Taking the allegorical turn Burroughs envisaged, "The Conspiracy" thematized the essential conflict between spontaneity and control—the dream and anti-dream drugs, East and West, forces of life and repression—within a master narrative well able to organize the disparate elements of his work-in-progress. But it is more than a question of narrative coherence. When Lee hides out in Mary's flat off Columbia University,[10] he gives her the alibi that he needs solitude to "write his thesis" (*I* 108). A university campus is the ideal hideout for someone *with* a thesis, that is, a coherent project. If "The Conspiracy" was a narrative about a theory, it points to Burroughs' recurrent search for both a narrative and a theory to make his material accountable. In late 1957, he thought he had finally found one that worked, both scientifically and as an explanatory principle, which he called his "General Theory of Addiction": "Incidentally, this theory resulted from necessities of the novel" (*L* 367). Far from being incidental, it is very significant that the novel necessitated and produced the theory; this describes Burroughs' typical working procedure, in which it is the material itself that gives rise to a theory to account for and develop it, at which point it starts to become counterproductive. In other words, "The Conspiracy" provided the kind of schema Burroughs kept looking for, and yet it's for this very reason that in the end he aborted it.

That he was well aware of the problem is clear from "Hauser and O'Brien." First, when he began to sketch its "Kafkian conspiracies" of control versus spontaneity, he insisted that "it is difficult to know what side anyone is working on, especially yourself" (*L* 269); not just including but *especially* yourself. Second, there is what only seems a passing detail in the text itself, when Lee notes: "I am righthanded but I shoot with my left hand" (*NL* 212). This, as Michael Taussig observes, is "the hand that strikes the decisive blows in history with the strength of improvisation" (*Shamanism* 467). The left hand defeated the right when Burroughs recognized that an allegory of this conflict, in which the writer was placed clearly center stage and where the parts were unified within a whole, itself represented a triumph for control. If "Americans have a special horror of giving up control," as Lee remarks in "Hauser and O'Brien" (*NL* 215), then we can see how "The Talking Asshole" dramatized the horror of imposing it.

EQUAL RIGHTS

Finally, we return to Burroughs in April 1954 "screaming: 'Stop it! Stop it'" because, without Ginsberg to receive, the routines he has conjured "turn back" on him. The asshole might have shut up if the carny man had been prepared to listen as well as speak, to receive as well as to send, to enter into genuine two-way dialogue. But as Burroughs put it, anyone who "must always send, but never receive" becomes "an automaton, a ventriloquist dummy, withers in orgoneless limbo" (*LG* 148). For the carny man wants to do all the talking and collect all the profit: by throwing his voice to his ass, the ventriloquist expects to retain the monopoly of monologue. This is an *ethical* failure: to use Levinas's terms, the carny man fails to leave himself open to the "call of the other." He can accept the autonomy of the ass only by integrating it into his performance, and when it grows teeth and starts eating, he responds with yet more economic and artistic exploitation: he simply "built an act around it" (*NL* 132).

This is the turning point: the ass refuses to remain an "act" on a stage but takes to the street, demanding "equal rights" (*NL* 312). With this call, the asshole insists on a politicized reading, most patently in terms of oppressed homosexual identity. But the act is not sexual in isolation from artistic performance. At this point, the Arab boy of the final anecdote takes on new meaning, because to put the flute-playing boy in relation to the carny man enables us to see something otherwise easily overlooked: if the boy's individuality merits his status as "a great artist," then it reminds us that the carny man is an artist also. A whole series of oppositions now opens up, based on Burroughs' contrasting conceptions of anality and artistry: Arab (East) versus American (West); boy versus man; innocent versus unnatural; erotic versus economic; private versus public; mutual versus unilateral; personal versus professional; musical versus verbal.

Burroughs' valorization of the flute player is emphatic, and within *Naked Lunch*, almost unique. Each line of the anecdote features a superlative, some several: "Every lover had his special theme song which was perfect for him and rose to his climax" (*NL* 135). The child-artist doesn't exploit his own anal, erotic, and artistic talents for anonymous popular entertainment but gives playful, uninhibited pleasure for love, not for money. Using his ass to make music, the boy's greatness as an artist is defined by his ability to improvise "new combines and special climaxes, some of them notes in the unknown, tie-ups of seeming discords" (135). The emphasis on exploratory creativity is made therefore by reversing the logic of "tying the garbage up in neat parcels," which is also the logic of controlled aesthetic form as seen from the point of view of *Naked Lunch*. As an artist, the Arab boy achieves the wordless and erotic bringing together of bodies, where the carny man realizes the fate of bodily division by the word, so that the second anecdote returns to the body, to the anus, and to the artist but transforms the disgust and disaster of the first into a rare moment of idealized bliss.[11]

How, finally, might we read the anecdote of the Arab boy within the epistolary economy of the original letter context? It seems to stand as the very antithesis of that economy and therefore to show the anecdote of the talking ass as its anxious realization, its grotesque parody. For the carny man's act is built upon a false relationship that is imbricated in economic and artistic exploitation and control. Having "taught his asshole to talk," the carny man expects to maintain the mastery, the hierarchy of teacher over pupil. His master's voice depends, however, on the other's dependency. Two weeks after writing "The Talking Asshole," Burroughs writes to Ginsberg reassuring him that what he wants and looks for is not the "dependence set-up" he falls into by default but a true "relation of equals" (*L* 269). Having tried to sublimate his acute need for Ginsberg, displacing erotic desire onto the safer field of his writing, Burroughs only confirms the asymmetry of their relationship: the ideal horizon shifts from a meeting of mutually desiring bodies to the production of Burroughs' marketable textual body. The Burroughs-Ginsberg relationship aspires to collaboration as a creative ideal—for Wayne Koestenbaum, the symbolic anus is "the place where men conceive when they write together" (7)—but their relation remains a crisis of dependency, exploitation, and fantasized possession, as figured in recurrent images of vampirism, parasitism, automatic obedience, the *latah,* and the whole Burroughs bestiary of repulsive desire. Referring to Kafka's story "The Metamorphosis" and extrapolating from its hidden debt to his epistolary relation with Félice, Vincent Kaufmann claims that the "cockroach symbolizes the demise of the letter writer; it is a fragment of monstrous reality, a warning of what would happen if the epistolary distance were to disappear" (*Post Scripts* 23). Might we not say exactly the same of *Naked Lunch* in general and of "The Talking Asshole" in particular?

The conclusion has to be that "The Talking Asshole" is at once a parable and an instance of Burroughs' economic situation as a writer, both within a broader cultural history and within his epistolary-based routine practice. To the extent that any text internalizes its conditions of production, it makes itself an allegory of them; and in the case of the epistolary mode, this would also entail encoding the conditions of reception. Burroughs' account actively invites us (via inviting Ginsberg) to read the routine in terms of its compositional circumstance and the carny man in relation to the writer. This is a complex relation, since the relationship between the man and his ass corresponds *both* to that between the writer as sender and the reader as receiver *and* to the relationship between the writer and his own work. This is, in turn, the double economy of the epistolary, insofar as every letter is also self-addressed: "the dual relation between addresser and addressee must," as Diane Cousineau argues, "be founded on the doubling and division that inform the letter writer's sense of self" (30). Such a reading becomes visible by recognizing the specific conditions of Burroughs' writing and his routine's specific audience, both of which were lost by the routine's relocation from the letter to *Naked Lunch*. Indeed, since this is true for all the other epistolary-based routines, it makes clear one of the key features of the routine in its published form; that it is not self-reflexive, that the scene of writing is never materially present and remains far from obvious at the level of parable or allegory. To put this the other way round: imagine if Burroughs had retained his original second chapter, "Lee's Letters and Journals," and that he had included within it "The Talking Asshole," as in fact he did include "The Finger." Would we not have been invited to read it very much as I have above?

It is not conclusive, but there is in fact material evidence to show that Burroughs *did* think of keeping "The Talking Asshole" within its original letter frame for use in *Naked Lunch*. There exists a typescript, headed "William Lee," that reproduces most of the letter routine, including its crucial epistolary frames. After the date, it starts with a significant line of address: "Dear A ——: Here is my latest attempt [. . .]."[12] "A ——" is an identity halfway between the "Allen" of Burroughs' real correspondence and the "A" that appears in "Lee's Letters and Journals" in late October 1955, and so it seems most likely that Burroughs considered including this epistolary version of "The Talking Asshole" at some point within nine months after first writing it. Needless to say, the fact remains that this was not to be its final destiny, because by the end of 1957 at the latest, Burroughs had decided categorically against making visible his writing's source and destination in the letter.

In its final form, *Naked Lunch* did not simply cancel all its debts to an epistolary economy, however. Just how far the letter determined its textual politics may always remain an open question, but no account can properly choose to ignore it. The mystery is how a chain of events long since then has conspired, one way or another, to obscure the significance of *Naked Lunch*'s genetic and generic origins. From one point of view, this secreting of the letter's history seems no more than the net result of a series of local and unrelated contingencies; from another, it has every appearance of a sustained and deliberate conspiracy. This very equivocation is, needless to say, entirely consistent with the epistemological trouble made by *Naked Lunch* and its author. That is why it is impossible for me to decide what to make of Burroughs' own attitude towards the editing of his letters I undertook for publication in 1993: since he interfered in the 1982 edition, could it be that his cooperation now was some consummate double bluff, his warm support one more piece of legerdemain? The idea is at one and the same time completely ridiculous and fully in keeping with all we are invited to suspect about the man.

AS EVER

LETTERS HAVE NO PLACE

Four years separate the writing of "The Talking Asshole" from publication of *The Naked Lunch* in 1959. During this time, Burroughs wrote more fragmentary routines and more aborted narratives, until in 1957 he had what he could call a manuscript as such. This in turn underwent several major stages of material revision, expansion, and editing up until virtually the point of printing in July 1959. However, none of these stages was more important than the first, which brought Burroughs to finally decide against the letter, and it is this particular moment that properly concludes, rather than tries to complete, this material history of *Naked Lunch*.

In early 1957, Ginsberg, Kerouac, and Alan Ansen rendezvoused in Tangier to help Burroughs type up and organize his chaos of manuscripts. The meeting seems to have been first suggested by Ansen in August 1956, but Ginsberg had a unique advantage: he had kept everything Burroughs had mailed him, month by month, week by week, and archived all the fragments in order of receipt. "So how do you cohere them all," Ginsberg wondered, "string them together, and what would be the cohering principle?" (qtd. in Finlayson 216). His answer was simple:

> My idea was to present it chronologically, so that the theme or plot would be the actual development, in time, of the ideas as they changed through 3–4 years, visible to the reader, one superimposed on another, developing and integrating with each other, as they did in the letters, accounting B.'s changes of psyche, and extension of fantasy. (*LG* 9)

During the visit itself, this is how Ginsberg described the situation to Lucien Carr: "It's quite a piece of writing—all Bill's energy & prose, plus our organisation & cleanup & structure, so it's continuous and readable, decipherable" (qtd. in Miles, *William Burroughs* 72). Given the history of Burroughs' writing up to that point, summed up in images of dirt and disorder, of the fragment, of waste, drek, and excrement, Ginsberg's vocabulary of coherence and continuity could hardly be more resonant or revealing.

But there is a paradox here. The letter has been the work of what for convenience I have called Burroughs' left hand. But by proposing a structure that kept to the letter of the manuscript's chronology, Ginsberg was effectively imposing the work of the right, the hand of order. His plan would have naturalized Burroughs' material, making its unbound energies and its radical diversity strictly accountable in terms of the author's autobiographical identity as the point of origin and responsibility. In effect, what Ginsberg proposed was to preserve a complete record of the material history of *Naked Lunch*'s composition, making visible to the reader exactly the process and chronology that I have been attempting to recover. Ginsberg would have made this critical task almost redundant, since no reader of this *Naked Lunch* could have failed to see the direct and material relation between Burroughs' actual labor of writing and his work's textual politics.

Returning to Tangier after a summer trip through Europe, in September 1957 Burroughs delivered his verdict on Ginsberg's "cleanup & structure" manuscript:

> As regards MS., I think any attempt at chronological arrangement extremely ill-advised. To my way of thinking *Queer* and letters have no place in present work. It is not at all important how anybody gets from one place to another. [. . .] The MS. in present form does not hold together as a novel for the simple reason that it is not a novel. It is a number of connected—by theme—but separate short pieces. [. . .] But I do not see organization as a *problem*. The gap between present work, that is last year or so, and work before that is such that I can not consider the previous material as really pertinent, and trying to fit it in according to any schema could only result in vitiating the work. (*L* 367)

Burroughs' grounds for rejection are interrelated. He rejects chronology because he isn't interested in creating what his material never had in the first place: the traditional continuities of fictional time, space, and identity. He rejects *Queer* and letters—he might have meant Yage letters, but it's less likely—and classes them together, for the same reason, and because each would ground all his routines in a fixed and familiar biographical source. He rejects the need for novelistic unities because he has begun to turn structural problems into a creative solution. The ground of his writing had shifted. If Burroughs' epistolary economy was the main engine of textual production during the mid-1950s, by this point it was no longer necessary, because the intensity of dependence had finally gone out of his relation to Ginsberg. But it did not simply cease to matter. Rather, it now applied negatively, in the sense that Burroughs reacted against the chronology, continuity, agency, and authority imposed by the organizing structure, the master narrative, derived from the letter. At almost exactly this time, in Chicago, John Cage was delivering his lecture "Experimental Music," insisting that "nothing was lost when everything was given away," because the creative control that he seemed to lose was only a limit anyway (8). Burroughs' rejection of Ginsberg's advice set him on a similar path of experiment.

However, what Burroughs doesn't say in his rejection is just as interesting: that the presence of *Queer* and his letters would have risked locating his routines within an intersubjective economy, grounding them not only according to a point of stable creative origin but also a specific destination. Even if Ginsberg's solution avoided visible epistolary form, it would have generalized an economy of epistolarity. This communicative circuit of desire and power, in which writing depends on another as a relay in its genesis, now didn't fit Burroughs' idea of *Naked Lunch* at all. In the passage from *Junkie* to *Queer*, he had gone from a writing that blocked inner and intersubjective economies—witness Lee's absolute contempt for psychiatrists—to one that put a wild analytic encounter center stage. While *Naked Lunch* would channel that letter-driven psychic energy into its aesthetic and political extensions, the overwhelming affective force of the text would be redirected fully onto the reader to create a terminal feedback loop. Burroughs' response to Ginsberg in late 1957 therefore established that the real novel was no longer "letters to you." Or rather, if his letters to Ginsberg did form a "real novel," then Burroughs now reversed the two basic generic categories of epistolary tradition, the educational and the erotic: anti-teacher, anti-lover. *Naked Lunch* as an anti-novel and as *not a letter* to Ginsberg.

PAY NO ATTENTION TO ABOVE

This conclusion finds a precise echo in a series of letters written to Ginsberg between the time shortly after the appearance of *The Naked Lunch* and his next publication, *Minutes to Go*, the launching manual and manifesto of his cut-up method. In early October 1959, Burroughs wrote to clarify his attitude towards the past and to map out his future direction. He did this first by leaving no room for doubt about his relation to his previous, still unpublished work: "Yage letters by all means, but I really *do not* want *Queer* published at this time" (*L* 430). Clearly enough, one motive here is to suppress a novel that laid far too bare the trauma of his homosexual identity. But there is another significance: he doesn't object to the appearance of epistolary form itself but to a novel with a hidden genetic debt to the epistolary, one where textual and sexual economies were inextricably and traumatically linked, and as such, one that returned to the original ground of *Naked Lunch* and an even less desired history of desire.

This is a vital part of the background to his letter of 29 October 1959 in which Burroughs broke the news to Ginsberg of his "new method of writing" (*L* 434). While the dramatic developments that took place at the end of Burroughs' first decade as a writer belong to another history, this particular letter marks a significant point of closure for the history of his first decade. Here, Burroughs framed his announcement that he had a new method of writing with two striking comments. He begins the letter by referring to a "biographical exegesis" he has sent Ginsberg for publicity purposes, which he says is "by 'myself'" (434). This exegesis summarizes a two-paragraph biographical note enclosed in a letter two days earlier, where he had advocated his new method for erasing traumas: the first paragraph of this note started, "I have no past life," and its second, "In any case he wrote a book and that finished him" (433). Burroughs ends the 29 October letter: "In this game the point is to lose what you have, and not wind up with someone else's rusty load of continuity. Pay no attention to above. I know you won't anyway, and it isn't written for 'you' exactly" (434). In 1954: the real novel is letters to you. In 1959: it's not written by Burroughs and not meant for Ginsberg to read. Literally as well as symbolically, the history—and the trauma—of *Naked Lunch* seems to fall almost precisely in between.

The final letter, dated 21 June 1960, was included in *The Yage Letters*. This is Burroughs' "reply" to Ginsberg's own *yagé* report, where he recommended the newly published *Minutes to Go* and the cut-up method as a response to Ginsberg's panic: "You want 'Help'. Here it is" (*YL* 59). But in offering help, Burroughs' letter also acts as a visible negation of the very relationship constructed in 1953 by the epistolary principle in "Yage." Through deciphering its date ("Pre-Sent Time"), doubling the signature ("William Burroughs For Hassan Sabbah"), and interrogating both the possibility of communication ("You did not or could not listen") and the truth of his own speech ("My Voice. Whose voice?"), Burroughs explicitly deconstructs the epistolary model of sender-message-receiver, its principles of identity, subjective expression, and interpersonal exchange. This letter functions as an *anti-letter,* so that in his return as a mentor figure, Burroughs now tells Ginsberg to take his authority ("You are following in my steps. I know thee way") and literally cut it up. This is the key: that Burroughs turns the writing of the master, with its appearance of possessing secret knowledge and its power of fascination, *against itself,* to produce an exemplary renunciation of authorship and authority. Advocating the cut-up method by urging its physical use on his own letter, the very letter in which he advocates the cut-up method, Burroughs offers Ginsberg a material way to unlearn the master's lessons.[13]

Burroughs' insistence on offering the cut-up *method,* not selling a product for mass consumption but providing a tool for active, individual use, is a crucial feature of this first exploratory stage of practice and promotion. It signals the two central and distinguishing facts from which Burroughs' cut-up project started: that it was *experimental,* and that it was based on therapeutic as well as artistic *material practices.* "Don't theorize," as he insisted to Ginsberg. "Try it" (*YL* 59). A good deal has been written about Burroughs' cut-up texts of the 1960s since Robin Lydenberg's groundbreaking study of 1987 but almost nothing about *Minutes to Go* or the actual, physical activity of the range of methods it inaugurated. This is an absolutely crucial oversight, because it signals how the texts Burroughs produced after *Naked Lunch* have, like those he wrote before it, always been read outside their material history.

It is tempting to conclude by going on to sketch the various continuities and ruptures between Burroughs' two decades either side of *Naked Lunch,* making connections between their themes, their forms, and their situation in cultural history and drawing conclusions about their textual politics and so on, but what stands out most of all is simply the persistence of exactly the same basic problem, the problem of an accurate and sufficiently material history. For when it comes to Burroughs, no critical engagements with theme or theory and no textual analysis can escape the consequences of lacking an established material base. And if anything, this is an even *more* urgent problem in Burroughs' second decade, where critics have typically read his cut-up project outside its history by starting from theory and neglecting his investment in the physical procedures that produced his texts.[14] Worse still, critics have failed completely to reckon with the perverse literary history of his cut-up trilogy—*The Soft Machine* (1961; 1966; 1968), *The Ticket That Exploded* (1962; 1967), and *Nova Express* (1964)—which became so garbled by new editions that the first title has become the last text and the last title the earliest text. This peculiar trilogy has managed to reverse beginnings and ends, to lose its center, and for lack of due attention to *which* edition they are reading, to confuse the critics, so that none have been able to identify Burroughs' development over time or interpret one text in relation to another. To get a measure of the problem, imagine reading *Naked Lunch* then *Yage* then *Queer* then *Junkie* . . .

If we see through all the genetic myths, inadequate metaphors, misleading paradigms, all the glossy images and easy assumptions, and if we give due weight to the material activity and chronology of Burroughs' writing in its difficult, messy, often disguised, and typically painful history, then we must ask, where does that leave Burroughs' secrets and his power of fascination? In the last analysis, where they always were. For all the meanings I have made and all the material secrets I have unveiled, there remains a true secret of Burroughs that must go untold precisely because it can only have been a secret *for* Burroughs himself. This is why in Ginsberg's definitive portrait of Burroughs as a "Brother Sphinx," the most striking feature is the absence of the knowing, enigmatic smile. What completes the picture is the presence of our *own* gaze, which searches the inscrutable image to figure out its secret mystery, to penetrate and decrypt its hieroglyphic puzzle. Distorted by desire, our gaze not only projects and reincarnates Burroughs' fantasy identity on his behalf but serves to represent how Burroughs appears to *himself.* The picture is *posed* therefore like a question, and since it presents us with a riddle to which Burroughs has no solution, it constitutes a truly "enigmatic signifier." The appeal of the picture indicates that the true source of fascination lies not in Burroughs' possession of a fabulous secret we lack but in his embodiment of some internal mystery from which we are all hopelessly barred. There is no key, no secret someone else has that he can give you. How the fuck should I know? No glot . . . C'lom Fliday. I did not or could not listen, which is why I have not tried to hide the fact that, behind the mask of the rigorously objective scholarly investigator, I have been a dupe, or as Walter Benjamin would put it, a kind of lover.

This book should end therefore with the words Burroughs used to sign off his letters to Ginsberg during the 1950s, last words that suggested either a dream of immortality or the despair of a life sentence, either a promise or a threat, words that Ginsberg took up for his own letters, in imitation, in love, in all the deep ambivalence of the lure of fascination: *As Ever.*[15]

Notes
Works Cited
Index

Notes

1. THE SECRET OF FASCINATION

1. Note that I preserve the article in the title *The Naked Lunch* when referring to its original publication but otherwise use *Naked Lunch* to indicate the text reprinted since 1962. The complex differences between editions lies beyond the scope of this book; for the best available account, see Loranger. Except where noted otherwise, all citations are from the following editions: *Junky* (New York: Penguin, 1977); *Naked Lunch* (New York: Grove, 1992); *The Yage Letters* (San Francisco: City Lights, 1990).

2. For the most explicitly Lacanian approaches to Burroughs, see Dennis Foster, *Sublime Enjoyment;* Hummel; and Tietchen.

3. See Gresset, especially 157–82.

4. Although I have not been able to find the edition Burroughs would have read, the 1961 reprint remains an "impressive red volume with magnetic rays all over the cover" (*WV* 23) and includes not just all the commands he cites but the negative effects of yawning, smoking cigarettes, and eating cucumbers. See Shaftesbury, 126–27, 207.

5. In a journal entry for January 1954, Ginsberg imagines "a movie to be made, a la Mabuse, BILL IN EUROPE" (*Journals: Early* 35). Kerouac compares Bull Hubbard to Doctor Mabuse in *Desolation Angels* (314).

6. For help in identifying the sphinx in question, I am grateful to Claudia Farias from the Department of Egyptian Art, Metropolitan Museum of Art.

7. Burroughs, letter to Brion Gysin, 11 May 1971, Robert H. Jackson Collection, Arizona State University (hereafter cited as RHJ).

8. Of course, there is also Burroughs' own smile, which has proved peculiarly attractive. For example, see Hibbard (ix) and Caveney (19).

9. Indeed, the smile is taken not just from Kerouac: if the evocation of Gatsby's smile suggests the potency of a trope that in fact runs through American literature, we also need to recognize the particular source of Winston Moor's ghastly smile in another Fitzgerald text. Burroughs' source here, borrowed in detail and verbatim, is "A Short Trip Home," a haunting story of evil possession that would return in *Naked Lunch* and appear explicitly in later texts, from *Exterminator!* (15) to *The Western Lands* (132). Here, the unspeakably menacing Joe Varland not only wears a "sinister smile" and a "snarl" but passes these on to the victim he seduces; "there was," the narrator knows, "a contagion of evil in the air" (Fitzgerald 109, 124, 120). In other words, if Kerouac's scenario is not just a useful parable but a primary instance of how representations of Burroughs influenced his own writing, then to this we must add its role within Burroughs' emerging aesthetics of wholesale intertextual appropriation.

10. Tanner was an early and astute critic; I take issue only with the fact that the addiction paradigm has escaped critical reappraisal for thirty years.

11. My point is the uncritical perpetuation of paradigms; for example, *Junkie* remains "a blueprint" for Caveney (77).

12. The phrase appears twice in *Queer* (18, 96), but Ginsberg most likely misread the first instance, juxtaposed with the word "wrenched," to convert "lust" into "lunch."

13. Watson, for example, refers to *"Junky: Confessions of an Unredeemed Drug Addict"* (325), misaligning the title of one edition with the subtitle of the other. More generally, critics rarely use the titles with historical accuracy, while none have compared editions. There is no easy way to avoid confusion, but here I will refer to *Junkie* for the purpose of accuracy, while, because the 1953 edition is now extremely rare, all parenthetical citations to *"J"* will be from the text of *Junky,* for the sake of accessibility. Exceptions are clearly indicated by substituting *Junkie* for the abbreviation for material not present in *Junky* and by substituting *Junky* for the abbreviation for material not present in *Junkie.*

14. See Russell.

15. Except where noted otherwise, all citations are from the final versions of each of these texts: the third edition of *The Soft Machine* (1968) and the second edition of *The Ticket That Exploded* (1967). I cite the Grove (1964) edition of *Nova Express.*

2. *JUNKIE:* THE PROCEDURE HERE IS MORE OR LESS IMPERSONAL

1. While several critics draw attention to the packaging of the Ace edition, none have described the differences in text or in the organization of material between the two versions. *Junky* gained some 3,850 words of new material and lost 39 (13 as the result of an editing error), while the division and sequence of material was reorganized (the glossary initially preceded the text, and there were originally fifteen chapters), the preface was retitled "Prologue," the original editor's inserted disclaimers were cut out, and Burroughs' cryptic dedication ("To A. L. M.") was dropped. For a full account of the novel's editing history, see my introduction to *Junky: The Definitive Text of "Junk."*

2. The mirroring effect is missed by Murphy because he insists on identifying the reader here as "she" (*Wising Up* 89). This suggests the larger danger for Burroughs criticism of a politically correct rendering of the reader.

3. The immediate context for this writing is evident from a letter that Ginsberg, negotiating with Burroughs' publishers, wrote in June: "They want something covering Mexico in detail, queerness underplayed, and a theory of Yagi [*sic*], and a departure, or preparation for departure, for S[outh] A[merica]. [. . .] End of *Junk* will just hint at extension in *Queer,* so will be no conflicts" (letter to Burroughs and Kerouac, 12 June 1952, Ginsberg Collection, Columbia University; hereafter cited as GCC).

4. See also Tytell, *Naked Angels* 46; Gunn 221; Watson 160.

5. Naturally, this passage attracted one of Ace's inserted editor's notes, situated just before the phrase "Here are the facts" (*J* 18): "Authorities maintain that the marijuana smoker usually forms a psychological habit pattern; under present laws, the use of marijuana is in itself a crime" (*Junkie* 33).

6. See *L* 80 (28 January 1951). In fact, this passage was omitted from the Ace original, much to Burroughs' annoyance.

7. From the postscript to Burroughs' letter of 5 April 1952, GCC, edited out of the published version.

8. According to Lenson:

Clinical literature follows the empirical method common to all the natural sciences, seeking objectivity through controlled experimentation and analysis of the results. Because it is always looking for "facts," it can deal with subjective factors like feeling only circuitously [. . .] To enhance its objectivism, it depersonalizes the author [. . .] behind a deadpan narrative whose tone implies that the data has been gathered and interpreted *correctly*. (xi)

9. The two significant cuts comprised most of the Rio Grande Valley material— restored when *Junkie* was reedited for *Junky* in 1977 (105–10)—and a seven-page section that followed in which Burroughs related addiction to the theories of Wilhelm Reich.

10. Ms., c. 1952, Ginsberg Deposit, correspondence 1950s, box 2011, "Junkie" (Drafts). Note that the Ginsberg Deposit at Columbia was later moved to Stanford University.

11. In the poet's own words:

This poem rests entirely upon two recollections of childhood; one that of splendour in the objects of sense which is passed away; and the other an indisposition to bend to the law of death, as applying to our own particular case. A reader who has not a vivid recollection of these feelings having existed in his mind in childhood cannot understand that poem. (Wordsworth, letter to Mrs. Clarkson, December 1814, qtd. in Rader 170)

12. It is surely no coincidence therefore that what is missing here appears explicitly early on in *You Can't Win,* where Jack Black dwells precisely on his own recognition of the causal relation between reading and doing. Bored with his life as an orphan at the Sisters Convent School, Black reaches the turning point in his life shortly before his fourteenth birthday, when he describes becoming fascinated by newspaper reports of criminal adventurers: "Looking back now," he concludes, "I can plainly see the influence the James boys and similar characters had in turning my thoughts to adventure and later to crime" (12). Here is Burroughs' looking back, in his own foreword to a reissued edition of Black's book: "I first read *You Can't Win* in 1926, in an edition bound in red cardboard. Stultified and confined by middle-class St. Louis mores, I was fascinated by this glimpse of an underworld" (Black v). In fact, Burroughs read the book in 1927 when, like Black at the turning point in his life, he was still thirteen, and this was no doubt one more confirmation of a deep sympathetic bond and one more reason for the circuit in which fascination is communicated.

13. If we took up the psychoanalytical invitation posed by the preface and looked to Burroughs' biography for support, we would begin by wondering not only about the ambiguous presence of the boy's maid but about the striking absence of his mother. For an analysis focused instead on the father's ambiguous presence in *Junkie,* see Hummel.

14. The seven-page manuscript, which was almost certainly a part of the original "Junk" manuscript completed in December 1950, is held in the Ginsberg Collection, Stanford University (hereafter cited as GCS).

15. Korzybski writes: "For no 'facts' are ever free from 'doctrines': so whoever fancies he can free himself from 'doctrines' as expressed in the structure of the language he uses, simply cherishes a delusion, usually with strong affective components" (87).

16. Miles refers to the transposition of material from *Queer* to *Junkie* but not entirely accurately and without developing its significance; see *William Burroughs* 51. My analysis of the two novels' genetic history here depends on cross-referring manuscripts held in the Ginsberg Collection at Stanford University and in the Burroughs Collection at Ohio State University. Particular thanks are due to James Grauerholz for helping to make them available.

3. *QUEER:* WELCOME TO YOUR DESTINY

1. See, e.g., Miles, *William Burroughs* 48; Newhouse 85; and Ward, "William Burroughs" 345.

2. In fact, *Queer*'s mysterious thirty-year absence was perhaps not the main reason for the "legendary" status and "aura" of the book; for most readers, this was surely manufactured by the publisher's own hype, which they then had to deliver on.

3. Burroughs, letter to Ginsberg, 6 July 1952, GCC.

4. Of course, if we were to restore to *Queer* the material cut for *Junkie,* then Murphy's analysis would be correct; but he deals with the text *as published,* as should any interpretation in the first instance. To reconstruct the manuscript is to produce an alternative text, one whose meaning derives from the fact that Burroughs decided against it, rather than to contrive a replacement for the published text.

5. In fact, the idea that *Junkie* and *Queer* owe their distinct formal properties to the *writer's* addiction and subsequent withdrawal is flatly contradicted by evidence available in the published correspondence. He picked up "another habit" in early April 1952 (*L* 109), remained addicted until mid-June, and only began "really kicking" it in early July (134), by which time he had effectively completed the writing of *Queer.*

6. Savran *(Taking It),* for example, leaves behind the shooting incident in order to focus on sexuality in *Queer,* without considering how the one both hides and yet points to the other.

7. My discussion of Cory (pseudonym for Edward Sagarin) draws on D'Emilio.

8. Recall not just Burroughs' maxim in *Naked Lunch*—"A *functioning* police state needs no police"—but its typically overlooked context: "Homosexuality is a *political* crime in a matriarchy. No society tolerates overt rejection of its basic tenets" (36).

9. Clearly, I have not attempted to deal in detail here with the complex sexual politics marked by the historical progression from *homosexual* to *gay* to *queer.*

10. Using the work of Jean Laplanche and J. B. Pontalis, Silverman defines the *fantasmatic* as "the unconscious prototype for all dreams and fantasies, and as the structuring scenario behind symptoms, transferences and other instances of repetitive behavior" (3).

11. From *The Soft Machine* (1961): "a town in Ecuador can't remember the name, remember the towns all around but not that one where time slipped on the beach with my phantom and his precise disgust for my person—sex twice a week with 'intrusions' and 'plants'" (172–73). With the key lines cut, the same passage appears in the second edition (1966) on 174 and in the third edition (1968) on 163. The town he couldn't remember was Salinas; see *Q* 104.

12. To the degree that *Junkie* does become increasingly episodic in its final third, this needs to be understood in terms of material originally written for *Queer* and transposed from third to first person.

13. I am paraphrasing Abraham and Torok, who conclude: "The metapsychological

concept of Reality refers to the place, in the psychic apparatus, where the secret is buried" (157).

14. In Freud's classic formulation, parapraxes such as slips of the tongue or pen take "revenge" on the speaker for trying to suppress some disturbing truth that is then "put into words against the speaker's will" (*Introductory Lectures* 58, 65). Lee's routines stage such accidents flamboyantly, exposing the unconscious meaning precisely by canceling it out through transparently false "corrections"—"that is, of course," "I mean, of course," and so on; see, e.g., Q 39, 42, 66, 67.

15. According to Morgan, the job in CIC of the real-life model for Allerton, Lewis Marker, did indeed entail working on cryptographic machinery (185). In the revised *Ticket That Exploded* (1967), Allerton is again associated with intelligence agencies and endowed with a "CIA voice" (2). When Allerton returns in *The Western Lands,* he is described as "the perfect agent" and associated not only with the CIA and Mossad (23) but with "Margaras Unlimited," a "secret service without a country" (24), while Burroughs translates *Margaras* as "the Investigator, the Skip Tracer" (179).

16. *Queer* therefore provides the very prototype of ambivalent desire that Neal Oxenhandler takes to characterize the whole Burroughs oeuvre: "Constantly, he tries to keep us from learning the truth which he simultaneously *wants* us to know" (134). For a precise analysis of the dynamics of confession and secrecy, see Anspaugh. She reads the scene where Lee torments a cat in *Junky* (123; not published in *Junkie*) as a cryptic confession to the murder of Burroughs' wife by way of intertextual allusions to Poe's story "The Black Cat." Her convincing analysis, which resembles Abraham and Torok's practice of cryptonomy, can be enhanced by knowledge of the manuscript history, chiefly because this passage, a late addition, in effect belonged to the writing of *Queer.*

17. The borrowings are general and also precise: for example, both Joe Varland and the Skip Tracer have ominously "muffled" voices (Fitzgerald 124; Q 134).

18. Far from coincidentally, *Moby-Dick,* which Burroughs had in mind as he wrote *Queer,* became a key cold war text and Ahab a symbolic figure of totalitarian power. For a rare, if limited, analysis of the imperial theme in Burroughs, see Martinez.

19. On Hegel, see Pinkard 124–25.

20. In Hal Foster's gloss, fascist "armouring" is developed "against the other of the fascist subject, whether seen as a weak, chaotic interior (his unconscious and sexuality, drives and desires) or a weak, anarchic exterior (Jews, Communists, homosexuals, proletarian women, the masses)" ("Armour Fou" 95).

21. It is noticeable that Murphy, in his extensive analysis of the anti-Semitic in *Naked Lunch* (*Wising Up* 92–95), fails to trace its logic back to *Queer.*

22. Although there are as many Jews in *Junkie* as in *Queer,* the differences between their presence in the two novels is another measure of the essential gulf that divides them. Sol, Abe, Benny, and Moishe are just four more colorful characters in a rogue's gallery of addicts Lee meets in Lexington (*J* 64–66). They invoke neither a history of anti-Semitism nor a psychopathology of difference.

23. To recognize the historical contradiction it structures, Lee's crisis must be interpreted in the terms in which it is actually represented. Most obviously, this crisis should not be misread as essentially to do with *drugs*. When Newhouse, in an otherwise perceptive analysis, observes that "Allerton is a drug user, often besieged by junk sickness" and that "Burroughs' will to power is a consequence of junkie withdrawal"

(84, 85), his startling confusions—he obviously means *Lee* in one instance, and properly speaking, in *both*—show how much is risked when reading through the filter of Burroughs' introduction to *Queer*.

24. Sinfield argues that queers are "the perfect subversive implants, the quintessential enemy within" precisely because they "emanate from within the dominant" (281).

25. On the relation between Burroughs and public relations, see McNicholas. In fact, Ivy Lee eventually rejected the commission to represent Hitler.

26. "Old style Imperialism is done," Burroughs had noted in 1951, referring to the stalemate of the Korean War. "It doesn't pay" (*L* 78).

27. See Marks 203, which directly cites Burroughs' research into *yagé*.

28. Burroughs, letter to Ginsberg, 9 April 1952, GCC.

29. Ms., correspondence 1, box 2, folder 42, "Queer" drafts, GCS. I am grateful to James Drever for initially providing a copy of part of this material. Stanford holds two versions: one, the first pages of Burroughs' original typescript of *Queer*, the other, a corrected retype, both from summer 1952.

30. Jardine lists Burroughs as one of those male American writers who "obsessively fears disintegration into the incestuous nondifference of the maternal space" (233).

31. In a passage cut from his original manuscript in the course of revision during 1952, Burroughs let slip the relation between maternal union and sexual "shlupping," describing in an act of sex "the ma oeba [*sic*] reflex to surround and incorporate" (ms. page of "Queer," GCS).

32. Von Neumann and Morgenstern write: "if the theory of chess were really fully known there would be nothing left to play" (125). The continuity from *Queer* to the Nova Trilogy is confirmed by Burroughs' allusion to von Neumann, whom he would next name a decade later in relation to his cut-up techniques (*Third Mind* 32).

33. On the relation between Julia Kristeva's "powers of horror" and cybernetics, see Polan 161.

34. Ms. page of "Queer," GCS. The cut was made in 1952. Cf. *Queer* 4.

35. This scenario might be thought of as a kind of inverted updating of that staged by the famous Automated Chess Player, a machine first built in 1769 by Wolfgang von Kempelen and popularized in America through Poe's story "The Chess Player." This contraption, a large box featuring a puppet costumed as a Turk seated at a chess board, looked like a machine pretending to be human while, as everyone suspected but could never prove, there really was a little man hidden inside working the mechanism. As Sussman observes, what made it so fascinating was the way in which this "automaton raised the question: Where does human agency end and mechanical agency begin?" (89). When we examine such an apparatus to find the secret trick of how it works, we might end up scrutinizing our own functioning and wonder, what's the difference?

36. In the case of chess-playing computers, the thinking machine did achieve the "unthinkable" in 1997 when Deep Blue beat the world champion, Gary Kasparov—and so proved that the real winner of the symbolic cold war superpower game *par excellence* was the machine in the middle.

37. This is precisely the sociobiological vision of genetic determinism embraced by Dawkins: "We are all [. . .] robots, all von Neumann machines" (*Climbing* 259).

38. Such a vision recurs throughout Burroughs, from *The Soft Machine* (1961), where the "talking sickness" begins (153), via the "organism that *forces you to talk*" in the revised (1967) *Ticket That Exploded* (49), to the return of the epidemiological

catastrophe of the "Talk Sickness, also known as the Dummies, or the Yacks" in *The Place of Dead Roads* (257).

39. Burroughs, letter to Pierre Dommergues, 30 October 1973, RHJ.

40. In fact, Burroughs alternately spelled the name *Gene* and *Jean* during his writing of the 1950s. The name recurs throughout Burroughs' early biography, always tragically: from his childhood friend Eugene Angert, who went mad, to Eugene "Tiger" Terry, who was killed by a lion in Mexico and who featured in a lost short story. Perhaps there is a kind of determinism in the very recurrence of a name with such fateful associations.

41. Burroughs, untitled ten-page ms., enclosed with letter to Ginsberg, 30 July 1953, GCC.

42. For an excellent reading of Lacan's famous formula, see Žižek, *Enjoy* 10–28.

4. QUEER LETTERS AND *YAGE LETTERS*

1. If the implication is that Burroughs' actual speech was often monologic, there is ample firsthand evidence to sustain it. On 10 May 1952, for example, Kerouac wrote Ginsberg: "I schmeck twice a week with the old master . . . He talks to me all the time, I listen" (*Selected Letters, 1940–1956* 354).

2. See Harris, "Out."

3. When Burroughs started to write *Queer*, he insisted that the protagonists of his new novel were "to be regarded as derived from rather than copied from the originals" (*L* 105). It didn't occur to him to open up such a gap for his protagonist in *Junkie*, which suggests that he half anticipated a danger to which his writing increasingly exposed him.

4. My calculation here takes into account the fact that Burroughs would later cut much of this material to add onto his "Junk" manuscript.

5. Burroughs, letter to Ginsberg, 15 June 1952, GCC.

6. Burroughs, letter to Ginsberg, 1 July 1952, GCC.

7. Reckoning with that relationship, or rather with the epistolary relation it became, restores a crucial dimension missing from Savran's important analysis, in *Taking It*, of Lee's "pathological mourning" and from Caserio's brief but insightful analysis of his "masochistic contract." To Savran's analysis, we should add that Marker is a more immediate "lost object" than Joan; and to Caserio's, that the Burroughs-Marker relation was a fully *material* masochistic contract directly tied to the writing of the novel.

8. For this quotation, I have used Altman's translation as cited for her book's epigraph, rather than that in Kafka, *Letters to Milena* (229).

9. Here, I am adapting Žižek's own adaptation of Lacan's insistence that "there *is* no sexual relation." See Žižek, "Thing" 213.

10. As William Decker observes, it is because letters, like letter writers, exist "as bodies in time and space" that the "longing for transcendental or telepathic contact" is a recurrent theme in epistolary discourse (37). Lee idealizes telepathy as a fantasy of pure, unmediated access, outside the dialectical structure of sender-receiver. Of course, Burroughs didn't arrive at his interest in telepathy via the letter, but Lee's ability to "tune in on Allerton's viewpoint," which "caused him pain" (*Q* 61), fulfills the etymology of telepathic contact—"to suffer from afar" (Murphy, *Wising Up* 65)—in a way that suggests how emotional intensities are received as well as broadcast at long distance by the letter writer.

11. There is therefore nothing arbitrary or coincidental about the movie that Lee takes Allerton to see on their first date, *Orphée*, since Cocteau—also author of *The*

Human Voice, a play about the telephone's power of erotic control—is rightly credited by Lee with "his ability to bring the myth alive in modern terms" (*Q* 37). Here, technologies of sound and image, communication and transport, are nested one inside the other, the medium of film representing the poet's muse as a dictating radio inside a car. Since the disembodied voice of the radio can be "experienced as a spiritual or paranoid receiver, as well as an artistic muse" (Weiss, *Phantasmic* 80), the allusion to Cocteau serves to connect Lee's fraught creativity and equally fraught homosexual desire within the larger network of cold war fantasies of telepathic broadcast and control. Equally, while Burroughs' allusion seems to project his own dead wife in the place of Eurydice, it makes just as much sense to see the myth in terms of *Queer*'s origin in the loss of his present lover. After all, like Orpheus's song, the novel only comes into being at the moment that the real object of its address disappears. Taking its cue from Burroughs' introduction to *Queer,* Cronenberg's movie of *Naked Lunch* has put Joan's death at the center of a similarly Orphic myth, but it would have made more immediate genetic and sexual sense, if a less momentous drama, had he made the central figure a writer of terminally hopeless love letters.

12. Ginsberg, journal entry for 30 May 1952, series 2, notebooks and journals, box 4, folder 1, GCS. Clearly aware of its significance, Ginsberg used his journal to transcribe his letter to Burroughs.

13. Burroughs, letter to Ginsberg, 22 April 1952, GCC.

14. Complicating matters, none of the published versions of these texts dates from a manuscript contemporary to their initial writing.

15. These lines, referring to a version of "The Finger" written in 1954, are marginal autograph comments on the manuscript (RHJ), later published as "Lee and the Boys" (*I* 36).

16. This material derives from Burroughs, letter to Ginsberg, 20 October 1955, RHJ.

17. Confusions are inevitable: I refer to "Yage" to abbreviate "In Search of Yage" not as a text composed in 1953 but simply as the section published under that title. However, "Yage" within *The Yage Letters* has itself changed significantly through the book's several editions: the first (1963) ends with the letter dated 8 July; the second (1975) ends with that dated 10 July; the latest edition (1990) now includes "Roosevelt after Inauguration," suppressed from earlier editions.

18. Altman's study confirmed a resurgence of interest, but her project was to demonstrate the relevance for contemporary *critical theory* of a medium so self-conscious about the relation of writer to reader. By the early 1990s, the epistolary had found a new home in poststructuralist, feminist, and postcolonial territory, and the critical revival coincided felicitously with a new wave of letter fiction. However, as I have already suggested, this was a renaissance based on theory rather than on material practice, a situation implicit in Beebee's conclusion: "Letter fiction provides an *allegorical* treatment of problems commonly associated with postmodernism" (205; my emphasis).

19. Payne's chapter on Burroughs situates him alongside Kathy Acker, Jorge Luis Borges, and Luisa Valenzuela and follows an analysis of epistolary work by John Barth, Ricardo Piglia, and Manuel Puig.

20. See also *L* 224, 239, 273, 279, 312.

21. See the epigraph credited to Somerset Maugham in O'Hara.

22. The Burroughs Collection, Columbia University (hereafter cited as BCC), holds

two complete versions (twenty and twenty-five pages long) of the "Yage Article" manuscript, which was written during 1955, went through several stages of revision, and was completed by early 1956.

23. The first letter is dated 28 December 1954, the second misdated 5 January 1957 (actually 1956).

24. "One theory," Burroughs noted, "had me down as a representative of Squibb [Pharmaceuticals]. They were about to have a Yage boom" (*L* 173).

25. Ms. of the "Peru Notebook," Burroughs Collection, Ohio State University. The immediate impact of Burroughs' *yagé* writing recalls the mescaline glyphs of Henri Michaux and the calligraphic forms of Brion Gysin.

26. It is possible that the book of Klee's work Burroughs had in 1955 was the recently published edition introduced by Henri Michaux, which would have made concrete a series of further resonant connections: between writers who, dissatisfied with writing, turned towards more plastic experiments in verbal and visual form; between "Yage" and Michaux's travel diary *Ecuador* (1929); and between Burroughs' taking *yagé* in 1953 and Michaux's taking mescaline in 1954, experiences they would trade face-to-face when they met in Paris during the summer of 1958. Although Michaux hated mescaline and Burroughs never took *yagé* again, indeed warned against hallucinogens at the height of psychedelic popularity—"*learn to make it without any chemical corn*" (*Nova Express* 11)—nevertheless, in time his Pucallpa visions would be, as mescaline was for Michaux, a vital resource for adventures in experimental creativity.

27. This horizon is Burroughs' equivalent to Michael Taussig's *yagé*-driven "nightlong Dada-like pandemonium of the senses" (*Shamanism* 412). With inspired brilliance, Taussig brings Bertolt Brecht and Walter Benjamin to the jungle, relating "the theater of *yagé* nights in the Putumayo foothills" to both Benjamin's fascination with montage and the alienation effects of Epic Theatre (443). For Taussig, the ontological flicker induced by the "nonhomogeneous, fragmentedness of montage" is so violent under *yagé* that it "breaks up any attempt at narrative ordering" (441): it undoes the "totalizing compass of the Romantic concept of the symbol" in favor of "an image of truth as experiment" (443, 445).

28. Evidence for this is given in a list of corrections to "Yage" attached to Burroughs' letter to Ginsberg of 9 January 1955, BCC, not included in the published version; cf. *L* 254.

29. Burroughs' comments in the original "Yage MS" are revealing: he offers the passage as an "atrocity" committed when "drunk and sentimental" but written "in all seriousness too." The first lines are described as a "lapse into typical young U.S. novelist style," those following as "satirical comment on same." There are numerous congruences between "Billy Bradshinkel" and "Driving Lesson," from the drama of the wrecked car to identical depictions of Lee's mother.

30. Untitled ms., GCC. Burroughs almost certainly sent this with his letter of 3 August 1953. The Ginsberg Collection at Stanford University holds fragments of a retyped version clearly repaginated to fit into a larger manuscript of "Yage."

31. Manganotti astutely refers to "letters which should be intimate and personal and are in fact objective and aloof as reportage" (83).

32. Burroughs, letter to Ginsberg, 30 April 1953, GCC.

33. Burroughs, letter to Ginsberg, 4 May 1953, GCC.

34. This is almost certainly a reference to the "Peru Notebook" acquired by Ohio State University in 1999.

35. The most explicit and dramatic cut was Burroughs' citation of Pope's "Epistle to Dr. Arbuthnot" in his very first letter from Panama; see *L* 149.

36. See *L* 164 and footnote.

5. THE REAL NOVEL

1. Of course, there was a *tradition;* see Gunn.

2. Epigraph to bk. 3 of Bowles, *Sheltering Sky.* Burroughs later returned to these lines; see *WL* 12.

3. See Ira Cohen, "Minbad, Sinbad," in Pulsifer 27–36.

4. In case it seems that I exaggerate the claim to gullibility here, consider how a recent and otherwise astute reader such as Newhouse can state that Burroughs "recorded his fantasies on notes he scattered about the place" (112).

5. For the terms of this approach, see Levinson.

6. Ginsberg, letter to Kerouac, 9 November 1954, Ginsberg Collection, Humanities Research Center, University of Texas (hereafter cited as GCHRC).

7. On Burroughs and Kafka, see Meyer.

8. In October 1955, this was Burroughs' own conclusion, displaced onto Lee: "His love for anyone is always a pretext, a means to achieve something" (*I* 127). The material published in *Interzone* (124–30) derives from Burroughs' unpublished letter of 20 October 1955.

9. "The next step," Kafka had written earlier, "would be actual permeation" (*Letters to Félice* 169).

10. "The National Electronics Conference meeting in Chicago in 1956 heard electrical engineer Curtiss R. Schafer, of the Norden-Ketay Corporation, explore the startling possibilities of biocontrol" (Packard 196).

11. In his 1991 "Afterthoughts on a Deposition," Burroughs would offer yet another belated retraction—"When I say I have no memory of writing *Naked Lunch,* this is of course an exaggeration"—although not in order to give a more accurate account of the text's genesis but only to affirm and update a reading of the text in terms of the medical and legal "junk problem" (*NL* xxi). In the course of three decades, narcotic addiction had almost become *"public health problem number one of the world"* (xvi), but the seriousness of this global reality cannot explain what's missing from Burroughs' retraction.

12. Within two days of starting their epistolary relationship in September 1912, Kafka had written "The Judgement," a story actually dedicated to Félice and organized around a drama of letter writing. Within two months, he had also written the first chapter of *Amerika* and "The Metamorphosis."

13. Again, we might speculate that the fantasy scenario Burroughs shares with Kafka is not so much eccentric to the epistolary as its repressed dark secret, the demonic within the divine. In dilute form, Hardack found it at work in Melville, who "almost literally receives a blood transfusion, a fluid physical merger with Hawthorne, through their correspondence" (140).

14. This passage in *Interzone* derives from Burroughs, letter to Ginsberg, 6 January 1955, GCC.

15. Burroughs' precise phrasing recalls Rilke's comment, cited by Martens, that his *The Notebooks of Malte Laurids Brigge*—parts of which began as letters by Rilke—should be read "as if one had found disordered papers in a drawer" (186).

16. Indeed, the "gimmick" offered a "sort of framework" in which Burroughs could "alternate chapters of Letter and Journal Selections, with straight narrative chapters" (*L* 288), so that it was always a partial description in any case.

17. There are other instances, such as when "these notes" (*I* 84) replace "these notes *and letters*" (*Early* 43).

18. In the manuscript original, several major parts of "Lee's Journals" later published in *Interzone* are introduced as "Letter to A." Thirty-two-page manuscript sequence titled "Extracts from Lee's Journals and Letters," dated "received Nov 7 1955" by Ginsberg, RHJ. There is just a trace of these deletions left in *Early Routines* where the opening frame was cut but not the closing one, to leave "Love, W. Lee" stranded and apparently anomalous (52).

19. See Žižek, *Enjoy* 134. To analyze the whale in *Moby-Dick,* I have borrowed the terms Žižek uses to gloss the shark in *Jaws.*

6. *NAKED LUNCH:* MASTER-PIECES

1. Norman Mailer, qtd. in "Excerpts from the Boston Trial of *Naked Lunch,*" in *Naked Lunch* (New York: Grove Press, 1966), xv.

2. Mailer, qtd. in "Excerpts," xii.

3. Once applied by the Nazis to vilify avant-garde art and to justify their eugenic policies, by the 1950s the term would feature in the House Select Committee report on the mass-market paperback trade, condemned for peddling "immorality, filth, perversion, and degeneracy" (Gathings Committee report, qtd. in Haut 5).

4. Burroughs would have savored the local ironies too, since the film's lead, Sydney Chaplin, the brother of Charlie, played the part of "Old Bill" opposite a woman named Joan and ended up—this was light burlesque—as the front end of a pantomime horse.

5. From the original manuscript of Burroughs' letter, in the privately held Givaudan Collection. Erasures in letters were only given selectively in the published versions. I have restored the original manuscript's correction "inspector" to "collector" as a meaningful parapraxis.

6. Ginsberg, letter to Kerouac, 9 November 1954, GCHRC.

7. Ginsberg, letter to Kerouac, September 1954, GCHRC.

8. There are numerous close connections between these two texts, and unlikely as it first appears, we could read "The Talking Asshole" as a kind of extension or commentary on the embryonic "Hauser and O'Brien."

9. Ms. of "Early Routines," RHJ.

10. "Mary! That was the name, the answer," Lee declares (*I* 107). Recalling that in *Queer* another Mary had posed the question of Lee's identity ("Who is he?"), here he spells out the significance for psychobiographical criticism of the name's recurrence within the Burroughs oeuvre.

11. This is one reason why the anecdote of the Arab boy is so important. It functions as a positive counter to the negative homosexual identity described by Richard Dellamora as "apocalyptic" in *Queer* for want of social possibility (137) and as a vital corrective to Kendra Langeteig's reading of "The Talking Asshole" as evidence of homophobic "revulsion for the sexual body" per se (165). But if the Arab boy offers an ideal version of intercourse, it remains an exceptional instant that only proves the Burroughsian rule of sexual and social communication configured in his texts as a single and singularly virulent disease: the "Human Virus" (*NL* 168). Indeed, the an-

ecdote can also fall within this reading, if we see it as Loewinsohn does, as "a defense of colonialism" (582). This is a valid alternative, consistent with the routine's ability to undo every apparent binary. Even so, it is also possible to argue back that the Arab boy is not proof of sexual imperialism, if we were to take up Leo Bersani's case that "it is perhaps primarily *the degeneration of the sexual into a relationship that condemns sexuality to becoming a struggle for power.* As soon as persons are posited, the war begins" ("Is the Rectum" 258).

12. Ms., box 12, "Naked Lunch Note Books" blue file, RHJ.

13. To be precise, Burroughs says: "Take the enclosed *copy* of this letter" (*YL* 59; my emphasis). If the significance is not clear, Brion Gysin would soon make it clearer in "Cut-Ups: A Project for Disastrous Success." After giving an identical piece of advice, Gysin added, "after all, we are in Proliferation too" (*Third Mind* 51), so giving away an economic and artistic self-interest that would be bound to show itself over time.

14. See Harris, "It's No Calligraphy."

15. Uncredited front matter note to Ginsberg and Cassady's *As Ever:* "Allen Ginsberg's use of the closing 'As Ever' began in the early 1950s in imitation of William S. Burroughs."

Works Cited

Abbas, Ackbar. "On Fascination: Walter Benjamin's Images." *New German Critique* 48 (1989): 43–62.

Abraham, Nicolas, and Maria Torok. *The Shell and the Kernel: Renewals of Psychoanalysis.* Ed. and trans. Nicholas T. Rand. 1987. Chicago: U of Chicago P, 1994.

Adorno, Theodore. *Prisms.* Trans. Samuel and Shierry Weber. 1967. Cambridge: MIT P, 1981.

Allen, Donald, and Warren Tallman, eds. *The Poetics of the New American Poetry.* New York: Grove, 1973.

Altman, Janet Gurkin. *Epistolarity: Approaches to a Form.* Columbus: Ohio State UP, 1982.

Ansen, Alan. "Anyone Who Can Pick Up a Frying Pan Owns Death." *Big Table* 2 (Summer 1959): 32–41. Rpt. in Skerl and Lydenberg 25–29.

Anspaugh, Kelly. "The Black Cat Inside: Burroughs as Unredeemed Confessant." *Genre* 34 (Spring-Summer 2001): 125–48.

Ayers, David. "The Long Last Goodbye: Control and Resistance in the Work of William Burroughs." *Journal of American Studies* 27 (1993): 223–36.

Baker, Carlos. Introduction. *Hemingway: Selected Letters, 1917–1961.* Ed. Baker. 1981. London: Panther, 1985. ix–xxi.

Barthes, Roland. *A Barthes Reader.* Ed. Susan Sontag. Trans. Richard Howard. 1982. London: Fontana, 1983.

———. *A Lover's Discourse: Fragments.* 1977. Trans. Richard Howard. Harmondsworth: Penguin, 1990.

Baudrillard, Jean. *Simulacra and Simulation.* Trans. Sheila Faria Glaser. 1981. Ann Arbor: U of Michigan P, 1994.

Beard, William. "Insect Poetics: Cronenberg's *Naked Lunch.*" *Canadian Review of Comparative Literature* (Sept. 1996): 823–52.

Beckett, Richard. "Take a Ticket to Tangier." *Tangier Gazette* 22 Jan. 1954: 6.

Beebee, Thomas O. *Epistolary Fiction in Europe, 1500–1850.* Cambridge: Cambridge UP, 1999.

Bellarsi, Franca. "William S. Burroughs's Art: The Search for a Language That Counters Power." *Voices of Power: Co-operation and Conflict in English Language and Literatures.* Ed. Marc Maufort and Jean Pierre van Noppen. Liege: Belgian Assoc. of Anglicists in Higher Educ., 1997. 45–56.

Benjamin, Jessica, and Anson Rabinbach. Foreword. Theweleit 2: ix–xxv.

Benjamin, Walter. *The Origins of German Tragic Drama.* Trans. John Osborne. 1963. London: NLB, 1977.

———. *Reflections.* Trans. Edmund Jephcott. New York: Harcourt, 1978.

Berman, Marshall. *All That Is Solid Melts into Air: The Experience of Modernity.* London: Verso, 1983.

Berman, Ronald. *America in the Sixties: An Intellectual History.* New York: Free, 1968.

Bernstein, Jesse. "Criminal Mind." Lotringer 707–10.

Bersani, Leo. *The Freudian Body: Psychoanalysis and Art.* New York: Columbia UP, 1986.

———. "Is the Rectum a Grave?" Goldberg 249–64.

Bersani, Leo, and Ulysse Dutoit. *Caravaggio's Secrets.* Cambridge: MIT P, 1998.

Bischoff, Simon. "The Serpent's Eye: Paul Bowles as Photographer." Trans. Ishbel Flett. *Paul Bowles, Photographs.* Ed. Bischoff. Zurich: Scalo, 1994. 7–60.

Black, Jack. *You Can't Win.* Fwd. Robert Merrick. London: Macmillan, 1927.

Blanchot, Maurice. *The Infinite Conversation.* Trans. Susan Hanson. 1969. Minneapolis: U of Minnesota P, 1993.

———. *The Space of Literature.* Trans. Ann Smock. 1955. Lincoln: U of Nebraska P, 1982.

Bowles, Paul. "Burroughs in Tangier." *Big Table* 1.2 (1959): 42–43. Rpt. in Burroughs, *The Burroughs File* 15–16.

———. *The Sheltering Sky.* New York: New Directions, 1949.

———. *Without Stopping.* 1972. New York: Ecco, 1984.

Bredbeck, Gregory W. "The New Queer Narrative: Intervention and Critique." *Textual Practice* 9.3 (1995): 477–502.

Brown, Norman O. *Life Against Death.* 1959. London: Sphere, 1968.

Brulotte, Gaétan. "Le Déchet." *Le Colloque de Tanger.* Ed. Gérard-Georges Lemaire. Paris: Bourgois, 1976. 29–44.

Burroughs, William S. *The Adding Machine.* London: Calder, 1985.

———. *The Burroughs File.* San Francisco: City Lights, 1984.

———. *Cities of the Red Night.* New York: Holt, 1981.

———. *Early Routines.* Santa Barbara: Cadmus, 1981.

———. *Exterminator!* New York: Viking, 1973. Harmondsworth: Penguin, 1979.

———. Foreword. *You Can't Win.* By Jack Black. New York: Amok, 1988. v–viii.

———. *Ghost of Chance.* 1991. London: Serpent's Tail, 1995.

———. *Interzone.* Ed. James Grauerholz. New York: Viking, 1989.

———. Introduction. Silverberg 13–14.

———. *Junkie: Confessions of an Unredeemed Drug Addict.* New York: Ace Books, 1953.

———. *Junky.* Introd. Allen Ginsberg. New York: Penguin, 1977.

———. *Junky: The Definitive Text of "Junk."* Ed. Oliver Harris. New York: Penguin, 2003.

———. *The Letters of William S. Burroughs, 1945–1959.* Ed. Oliver Harris. New York: Viking, 1993.

———. *Letters to Allen Ginsberg, 1953–1957.* Ed. Ron Padgett and Anne Waldman. Introd. Allen Ginsberg. New York: Full Court, 1982.

———. *My Education: A Book of Dreams.* New York: Viking, 1995.

———. "My Purpose Is to Write for the Space Age." *New York Times Book Review* (19 Feb. 1984): 9–10. Rpt. in Skerl and Lydenberg 265–68.

———. *Naked Lunch.* New York: Grove, 1992.

———. *The Naked Lunch.* Paris: Olympia, 1959.

———. *Nova Express.* New York: Grove, 1964.

———. *Painting and Guns.* New York: Hanuman, 1992.

———. *The Place of Dead Roads.* New York: Holt, 1983.

———. *Queer.* New York: Viking, 1985.

———. *The Soft Machine.* Paris: Olympia, 1961. 2nd ed. New York: Grove, 1966. 3rd ed. London: Calder, 1968.

———. *The Ticket That Exploded.* Paris: Olympia, 1962. 2nd ed. New York: Grove, 1967.

———. "'Voices in Your Head.'" Introduction. *You Got to Burn to Shine.* By John Giorno. London: Serpent's Tail, 1994. 1–6.

———. *The Western Lands.* New York: Viking Penguin, 1987.

———. *Word Virus: The William S. Burroughs Reader.* Ed. James Grauerholz and Ira Silverberg. New York: Grove, 1998.

———. *The Yage Letters.* San Francisco: City Lights, 1963. 2nd ed., 1975. 3rd ed., 1990.

Burroughs, William S., and Brion Gysin. *The Third Mind.* New York: Viking, 1978.

Burroughs, William S., Brion Gysin, Sinclair Beiles, and Gregory Corso. *Minutes to Go.* Paris: Two Cities Editions, 1960.

Butler, Judith. *Bodies That Matter: On the Discursive Limits of "Sex."* New York: Routledge, 1993.

Cage, John. *Silence: Lectures and Writings.* London: Marion Boyars, 1971.

Carroll, Lewis. *Alice's Adventures in Wonderland and Through the Looking-Glass.* Oxford: Oxford UP, 1975.

Caserio, Robert L. "Queer Passions, Queer Citizenship: Some Novels about the State of the American Nation, 1946–1954." *Modern Fiction Studies* 43.1 (Spring 1997): 170–205.

Caute, David. *The Great Fear: The Anti-Communist Purge under Truman and Eisenhower.* London: Secker, 1978.

Caveney, Graham. *The "Priest" They Called Him: The Life and Legacy of William S. Burroughs.* London: Bloomsbury, 1998.

Chambers, Ross. *Story and Situation: Narrative Seduction and the Power of Fiction.* Manchester: Manchester UP, 1984.

Charters, Ann. *Kerouac: A Biography.* London: Andre Deutsch, 1974.

———, ed. *The Portable Beat Reader.* New York: Viking, 1992.

Christie, Agatha. *The ABC Murders.* 1936. London: Fontana, 1962.

Clark, Suzanne. *Cold Warriors: Manliness on Trial in the Rhetoric of the West.* Carbondale: Southern Illinois UP, 2000.

Connolly, William E. *Identity/Difference: Democratic Negotiations of Political Paradox.* Ithaca: Cornell UP, 1991.

———. *Political Theory and Modernity.* Oxford: Oxford UP, 1982.

———. *Politics and Ambiguity.* Madison: U of Wisconsin P, 1987.

Connor, Steven. *Dumbstruck: A Cultural History of Ventriloquism.* Oxford: Oxford UP, 2000.

———. "Fascination, Skin and the Screen." *Critical Quarterly* 40.1 (1998): 9–24.

Conrad, Peter. *The Hitchcock Murders.* London: Faber, 2001.

Cook, Bruce. *The Beat Generation.* 1971. New York: Morrow, 1994.

Cook, David A. *A History of Narrative Film.* New York: Norton, 1996.

Cooper, Dennis. "Shotgun: The Paintings of William Burroughs." *Artscribe International* (Summer 1988): 70–71.

Corber, Robert J. *Homosexuality in Cold War America: Resistance and the Crisis of Masculinity.* Durham: Duke UP, 1997.

————. *In the Name of National Security: Hitchcock, Homophobia, and the Political Construction of Gender in Postwar America.* Durham: Duke UP, 1993.

Corso, Gregory. *The American Express.* Paris: Olympia, 1961.

Cousineau, Diane. *Letters and Labyrinths: Women Writing/Cultural Codes.* Newark: U of Delaware P, 1997.

Dawkins, Richard. *Climbing Mount Improbable.* New York: Viking, 1996.

————. *The Selfish Gene.* London: Granada, 1978.

Debord, Guy. *Comments on the Society of the Spectacle.* Trans. Malcolm Imrie. 1988. London: Verso, 1998.

————. *La Société du Spectacle.* 1967. Paris: Gallimard, 1992.

Decker, William Merrill. *Epistolary Practices: Letter Writing in America Before Telecommunications.* Chapel Hill: U of North Carolina P, 1998.

Deleuze, Gilles, and Félix Guattari. *Anti-Oedipus: Capitalism and Schizophrenia.* Trans. Robert Hurley, Mark Seem, and Helen R. Lane. New York: Viking, 1983.

————. *Kafka: Pour une littérature mineure.* Paris: Minuit, 1975.

————. "Kafka: Toward a Minor Literature: The Components of Expression." Trans. Marie Maclean. *New Literary History* 16.3 (Spring 1985): 591–608.

Dellamora, Richard. "Queer Apocalypse: Framing William Burroughs." *Postmodern Apocalypse: Theory and Cultural Practice at the End.* Ed. Dellamora. Philadelphia: U of Pennsylvania P, 1995. 136–67.

D'Emilio, John. *Sexual Politics, Sexual Communities: The Making of a Homosexual Minority in the United States, 1940–1970.* Chicago: Chicago UP, 1983.

Derrida, Jacques. *The Post Card: From Socrates to Freud and Beyond.* Trans. Alan Bass. 1980. Chicago: U of Chicago P, 1987.

Dillon, Millicent. *A Little Original Sin: The Life and Work of Jane Bowles.* London: Virago, 1988.

Dolar, Mladen. "At First Sight." Salecl and Žižek 129–53.

————. "'I Shall Be with You on Your Wedding Night': Lacan and the Uncanny." *October* 58 (Fall 1991): 5–23.

Dollimore, Jonathan. "Sex and Death." *Textual Practice* 9.1 (1995): 27–53.

————. *Sexual Dissidence: Augustine to Wilde, Freud to Foucault.* Oxford: Clarendon, 1991.

Douglas, Ann. "Punching a Hole in the Big Lie." Introduction. Burroughs, *Word Virus* xv–xxix.

————. "Telepathic Shock and Meaning Excitement: Kerouac's Poetics of Intimacy." *College Literature* 27. 1 (Winter 2000): 8–21.

Douglass, Mary. *Purity and Danger: An Analysis of Concepts of Pollution and Taboo.* London: Routledge, 1966.

Dowling, William C. *The Epistolary Moment: The Poetics of the Eighteenth Century Verse Epistle.* Princeton: Princeton UP, 1991.

Dunlop, Ian. *Van Gogh.* London: Weidenfeld, 1974.

Eagleton, Terry. *Literary Theory: An Introduction.* Oxford: Blackwell, 1983.

Eburne, Jonathan Paul. "Trafficking in the Void: Burroughs, Kerouac, and the Consumption of Otherness." *Modern Fiction Studies* 43.1 (Spring 1997): 53–92.

Edwards, Paul N. *The Closed World: Computers and the Politics of Discourse in Cold War America.* Cambridge: MIT P, 1996.

Ehrenreich, Barbara. Foreword. Theweleit 1: ix–xvii.

Ewen, Stewart. *Captains of Consciousness: Advertising and the Social Roots of the Consumer Culture.* New York: McGraw, 1977.

Farber, I. E., Harry F. Harlow, and Louis Jolyon West. "Brainwashing, Conditioning and DDD." *Sociometry* 20.4 (Dec. 1957): 271–85.

Ferrer, Daniel. "Clementis's Cap: Retroaction and Persistence in the Genetic Process." Trans. Marlena G. Corcoran. *Yale French Studies* 89 (1996): 223–36.

Fink, Bruce. *The Lacanian Subject: Between Language and Jouissance.* Princeton: Princeton UP, 1995.

Finlayson, Ian. *Tangier: City of the Dream.* London: Harper, 1992.

Fitzgerald, F. Scott. *Bernice Bobs Her Hair and Other Stories.* Harmondsworth: Penguin, 1968.

Fletcher, Angus. *Allegory: The Theory of a Symbolic Mode.* Ithaca: Cornell UP, 1964.

Ford, Ford Maddox. *Parade's End.* Harmondsworth: Penguin, 1982.

Foster, Dennis A. *Confession and Complicity in Narrative.* Cambridge: Cambridge UP, 1987.

———. *Sublime Enjoyment: On the Perverse Motive in American Literature.* Cambridge: Cambridge UP, 1997.

Foster, Edward Halsey. *Understanding the Beats.* Columbia: U of South Carolina P, 1992.

Foster, Hal. "Armour Fou." *October* 56 (Spring 1991): 65–98.

———. "Death in America." *October* 75 (Winter 1996): 37–59.

Foucault, Michel. Preface. Deleuze and Guattari, *Anti-Oedipus* xi–xiv.

Freud, Sigmund. *Art and Literature.* Trans. James Strachey. Pelican Freud Lib. 14. Harmondsworth: Penguin, 1985.

———. *Introductory Lectures on Psycho-Analysis.* Trans. James Strachey. Vol. 15 (1915–16) of *The Standard Edition of the Complete Psychological Works.* London: Hogarth, 1961.

———. *Two Case Histories.* Trans. James Strachey. Vol. 10 (1909) of *The Standard Edition of the Complete Psychological Works.* London: Hogarth, 1955.

García-Robles, Jorge. *La Bala Perdida: William S. Burroughs en Mexico (1949–1952).* Mexico: Ediciones del Milenio, 1995.

Geduld, Harry. *The Birth of the Talkies: From Edison to Jolson.* Bloomington: Indiana UP, 1975.

George, Paul S., and Jerold M. Starr. "Beat Politics: New Left and Hippie Beginnings in the Postwar Counterculture." *Cultural Politics: Radical Movements in Modern History.* Ed. Starr. New York: Praeger, 1985. 189–233.

George-Warren, Holly, ed. *The Rolling Stone Book of the Beats: The Beat Generation and American Culture.* New York: Hyperion, 1999.

Gifford, Barry, and Lawrence Lee. *Jack's Book: An Oral Biography of Jack Kerouac.* Harmondsworth: Penguin, 1979.

Gifford, Eric. "People and Places." *Tangier Gazette* 2 Mar. 1956: 7.

Ginsberg, Allen. *Collected Poems 1947–1980.* New York: Viking, 1985.

———. "Exorcising Burroughs." *Observer* 26 Apr. 1992: 26–30.

———. Interview with Thomas Clark (1965). *The Paris Review Interviews.* 3rd ser. Ed. George Plimpton. New York: Viking, 1967. 279–320.

———. *Journals: Early 50s/60s.* Ed. Gordon Ball. New York: Grove, 1977.

———. *Journals Mid-Fifties, 1954–1958.* Ed. Gordon Ball. London: Penguin, 1996.

——. "Notes for *Howl and Other Poems*" (1959). Allen and Tallman 318–21.

——. *Photographs*. Altadena: Twelvetrees, 1990.

——. "When the Mode of the Music Changes the Walls of the City Shake" (1961). Allen and Tallman 324–30.

Ginsberg, Allen, and Neal Cassady. *As Ever: The Collected Correspondence of Allen Ginsberg and Neal Cassady.* Ed. Barry Gifford. Berkeley: Creative Arts, 1977.

Ginsberg, Allen, and Gregory Corso. "The Literary Revolution in America." *Litterair Paspoort* (Amsterdam) Nov. 1957. Rpt. in Miles, *Howl* 166.

Girard, René. *Deceit, Desire, and the Novel: Self and Other in Literary Structure.* Trans. Yvonne Freccero. 1961. Baltimore: Johns Hopkins UP, 1965.

Glazer, Nathan. "The Method of Senator McCarthy." *Commentary* 15:3 (Mar. 1953): 244–56.

Godbout, Jacques T., and Alain Caillé. *The World of the Gift.* Trans. Donald Winkler. Montreal: McGill-Queen's UP, 1998.

Goldberg, Jonathan, ed. *Reclaiming Sodom.* New York: Routledge, 1994.

Gresset, Michel. *Fascination: Faulkner's Fiction, 1919–1936.* Durham: Duke UP, 1989.

Grunberg, Serge. *"A la recherche d'un corps": Langage et silence dans l'oeuvre de William S. Burroughs.* Paris: Éditions du Seuil, 1979.

Guillen, Claudio. "On the Edge of Literariness: The Writing of Letters." *Comparative Literature Studies* 31.1 (1994): 1–24.

Gunn, Drewey Wayne. *American and British Writers in Mexico, 1556–1973.* Austin: U of Texas P, 1974.

Guzlowski, John Z. Review of *Letters to Allen Ginsberg. Modern Fiction Studies* 29 (Winter 1983): 741.

Halberstam, David. *The Fifties.* New York: Villard, 1993.

Halberstam, Judith, and Ira Livingston, eds. *Posthuman Bodies.* Bloomington: Indiana UP, 1995.

Hansson, Ellis. "The Telephone and Its Queerness." *Cruising the Performative: Interventions into the Representation of Ethnicity, Nationality, and Sexuality.* Ed. Sue-Ellen Case, Philip Brett, and Susan Leigh Foster. Bloomington: Indiana UP, 1995. 34–58.

Hardack, Richard. "Bodies in Pieces, Texts Entwined: Correspondence and Intertextuality in Melville and Hawthorne." *Epistolary Histories: Letters, Fiction, Culture.* Ed. Amanda Gilroy and W. M. Verhoeven. Charlottesville: UP of Virginia, 2000. 126–51.

Harner, Michael J. "Common Themes in American Yagé Experiences." *Hallucinogens and Shamanism.* Ed. Harner. Oxford: Oxford UP, 1973. 155–75.

Harris, Oliver. "Beating the Academy." *College Literature* 27.1 (Winter 2000): 213–31.

——. "Cold War Correspondents: Ginsberg, Kerouac, and Cassady and the Political Economy of Beat Letters." *Twentieth Century Literature* 46.2 (Summer 2000): 171–92.

——. Introduction. Burroughs, *Letters 1945–1959* xv–xl.

——. "'It's No Calligraphy for School Children': A Response to John Watters, 'The Control Machine: Myth in *The Soft Machine* of William S. Burroughs.'" *Connotations: A Journal for Critical Debate* 6.3 (1996/1997): 337–53.

——. "Out of Epistolary Practice: E-Mail from Emerson, Post-Cards to Pynchon." *American Literary History* 13.1 (Spring 2001): 158–68.

——. "Queer Shoulders, Queer Wheel: Homosexuality and Beat Textual Politics."

Beat Culture: The 1950s and Beyond. Ed. Cornelis van Minnen et al. Amsterdam: VU, 1999. 221–40.

Harter, Deborah A. *Bodies in Pieces: Fantastic Narrative and the Poetics of the Fragment.* Stanford: Stanford UP, 1996.

Haut, Woody. *Pulp Culture: Hardboiled Fiction and the Cold War.* London: Serpent's Tail, 1995.

Hawkes, Terence. *Structuralism and Semiotics.* London: Methuen, 1977.

Hayman, Ronald. *Artaud and After.* Oxford: Oxford UP, 1977.

Hayter, Alathea. Introduction. *Confessions of an English Opium Eater.* By Thomas De Quincey. Ed. Hayter. Harmondsworth: Penguin, 1971. 7–24.

Hibbard, Allen, ed. *Conversations with William S. Burroughs.* Jackson: UP of Mississippi, 1999.

Hilfer, Anthony Channel. "Mariner and Wedding Guest in William Burroughs' *Naked Lunch.*" *Criticism* 22 (Summer 1980): 252–65.

Hocquenghem, Guy. "Towards an Irrecuperable Pederasty." Goldberg 233–46.

Hodges, Andrew. *Alan Turing: The Enigma.* London: Burnett, 1983.

Holton, Robert. "Kerouac among the Fellahin: *On the Road* to the Postmodern." *Modern Fiction Studies* 41.2 (Summer 1995): 265–83.

Horney, Karen. *The Neurotic Personality in Our Time.* New York: Norton, 1937.

Hummel, William. "Original Chaos Restored: Paternal Fictions in William S. Burroughs." *Naming the Father: Legacies, Genealogies, and Explorations of Fatherhood in Modern and Contemporary Literature.* Ed. Eva Paulino Bueno, Terry Caesar, and William Hummel. Lanham: Lexington Books, 2000. 288–310.

Huncke, Herbert. *The Herbert Huncke Reader.* Ed. Benjamin G. Schafer. 1997. London: Bloomsbury, 1998.

Hurley, James S. "Real Virtuality: Slavoj Žižek and 'Post-Ideological' Ideology." *Postmodern Culture* 9.1 (Sept. 1998). <http://jefferson.village.virginia.edu/pmc/text-only/issue.998/9.1.rhurley.txt>.

Husain, Aatif M. "Mimetic Smile." *Journal of Neurology, Neurosurgery, and Psychiatry* 63 (1997): 144.

Indiana, Gary. "Burroughs." Silverberg 121–25.

Ingram, David. "William Burroughs and Language." Lee 95–113.

Jameson, Fredric. *Signatures of the Visible.* London: Routledge, 1992.

Jardine, Alice A. *Gynesis: Configurations of Woman and Modernity.* Ithaca: Cornell UP, 1985.

Johnson, Barbara. *The Critical Difference: Essays in the Contemporary Rhetoric of Reading.* Baltimore: Johns Hopkins UP, 1980.

Johnson, Ronna C. "'You're Putting Me On': Jack Kerouac and the Postmodern Emergence." *College Literature* 27.1 (Winter 2000): 22–38.

Kafka, Franz. *The Collected Stories of Franz Kafka.* Ed. Nahum Glatzer. Harmondsworth: Penguin, 1988.

———. *Letters to Félice.* Ed. Erich Heller and Jurgen Born. Trans. James Stern and Elisabeth Duckworth. London: Minerva, 1992.

———. *Letters to Milena.* Ed. Willi Haas. Trans. Tania and James Stern. London: Secker, 1953.

Kahn, Douglas. *Noise, Water, Meat: A History of Sound in the Arts.* Cambridge: MIT P, 1999.

————. "Three Receivers (the Use of Radios and Sound by Author William Burroughs)." *TDR* 40.3 (Fall 1996): 80–88.

Kaplan, Amy. "'Left Alone with America': The Absence of Empire in the Study of American Culture." *Cultures of United States Imperialism*. Ed. Amy Kaplan and Donald E. Pease. Durham: Duke UP, 1993. 3–21.

Kaplan, Carla. "Undesirable Desire: Citizenship and Romance in Modern American Fiction." *Modern Fiction Studies* 43.1 (Spring 1997): 144–56.

Kauffman, Linda S. *Discourses of Desire: Gender, Genre, and Epistolary Fictions*. Ithaca: Cornell UP, 1986.

————. *Special Delivery: Epistolary Modes in Modern Fiction*. Chicago: U of Chicago P, 1992.

Kaufmann, Vincent. "Life by the Letter." Trans. Caren Litherland. *October* 64 (Spring 1993): 91–105.

————. *Post Scripts: The Writer's Workshop*. Trans. Deborah Treisman. 1990. Cambridge: Harvard UP, 1994.

————. "Valéry's Garbage Can." Trans. Deborah Treisman. *Yale French Studies* 89 (1996): 67–81.

Kazin, Alfred. *The Bright Book of Life: American Novelists and Storytellers from Hemingway to Mailer*. London: Secker, 1974.

Kennedy, John G. "Cultural Psychiatry." In *Handbook of Social and Cultural Anthropology*. Ed. John J. Honigmann. Chicago: Rand McNally, 1973. 1119–98.

Kenner, Hugh. *The Mechanic Muse*. New York: Oxford UP, 1987.

Kerouac, Jack. *Doctor Sax: Faust Part Three*. 1959. London: Panther, 1980.

————. *On the Road*. 1957. Harmondsworth: Penguin, 2000.

————. *Selected Letters, 1940–1956*. Ed. Ann Charters. New York: Viking, 1995.

————. *Selected Letters, 1957–1969*. Ed. Ann Charters. New York: Viking, 1999.

————. *The Town and the City*. 1950. London: Quartet, 1973.

————. *Visions of Cody*. 1972. New York: Penguin, 1993.

Klein, Marcus. "John Hawkes' Experimental Compositions." *Surfiction: Fiction Now . . . and Tomorrow*. Ed. Raymond Federman. Chicago: Swallow, 1975. 203–14.

Knickerbocker, Conrad. "Interview with William Burroughs" (1965). *The Paris Review Interviews*. 3rd ser. Ed. George Plimpton. New York: Viking, 1967. 143–74.

Koestenbaum, Wayne. *Double Talk: The Erotics of Male Literary Collaboration*. London: Routledge, 1989.

Korzybski, Alfred. *Science and Sanity: An Introduction to Non-Aristotelian Systems and General Semantics*. 1933. 2nd ed. Lancaster: Intl. Non-Aristotelian Lib., 1941.

Lacan, Jacques. *The Ego in Freud's Theory and in the Technique of Psychoanalysis*. Ed. Jacques Alain Miller. Trans. Sylvana Tomaselli. New York: Norton, 1991.

————. *The Ethics of Psychoanalysis, 1959–1960*. Ed. Jacques-Alain Miller. Trans. Dennis Porter. London: Routledge, 1992.

————. *The Four Fundamental Concepts of Psycho-Analysis*. Ed. Jacques-Alain Miller. Trans. Alan Sheridan. London: Vintage, 1998.

Langeteig, Kendra. "*Horror Autotoxicus* in the Red Night Trilogy: Ironic Fruits of Burroughs' Terminal Vision." *Configurations* 5 (1997): 135–69.

Laplanche, Jean. Interview with Martin Stanton. *Jean Laplanche: Seduction, Translation and the Drives*. Ed. John Fletcher and Martin Stanton. London: ICA, 1992. 3–18.

Lardas, John. *The Bop Apocalypse: The Religious Visions of Kerouac, Ginsberg, and Burroughs.* Urbana: U of Illinois P, 2001.

Lears, Jackson. "A Matter of Taste: Corporate Cultural Hegemony in a Mass-Consumption Society." *Recasting America: Culture and Politics in the Age of the Cold War.* Ed. Larry May. Chicago: U of Chicago P, 1989. 38–57.

Leddy, Michael. "'Departed Have Left No Address': Revelation/Concealment Presence/Absence in *Naked Lunch.*" *Review of Contemporary Fiction* 4.1 (1984): 33–40.

Lee, A. Robert, ed. *The Beat Generation Writers.* London: Pluto, 1996.

Lenson, David. *On Drugs.* Minneapolis: U of Minnesota P, 1995.

Levinson, Marjorie. *The Romantic Fragment Poem: A Critique of a Form.* Chapel Hill: U of North Carolina P, 1986.

Leyburn, Ellen Douglass. *Satiric Allegory: Mirror of Man.* New Haven: Yale UP, 1956.

Loewinsohn, Ron. "'Gentle Reader, I Fain Would Spare You This, but My Pen Hath Its Will like the Ancient Mariner': Narrator(s) and Audience in William S. Burroughs's *Naked Lunch.*" *Contemporary Literature* 39.4 (1998): 560–85.

Loranger, Carol. "'This Book Spill Off the Page in All Directions': What Is the Text of *Naked Lunch?*" *Postmodern Culture* 10.1 (Sept. 1999). <http://jefferson.village.edu/pmc/text-only/issue.999/10.1loranger.txt>.

Lotringer, Sylvère, ed. *Burroughs Live: The Collected Interviews of William S. Burroughs 1960–1997.* Los Angeles: Semiotext(e), 2001.

Luna, Luis Edwardo, and Steven White. *The Ayahuasca Reader: Encounters with the Amazon's Sacred Vine.* Santa Fe: Synergetic, 2000.

Lydenberg, Robin. "Sound Identity Fading Out: William Burroughs' Tape Experiments." *Wireless Imagination: Sound, Radio and the Avant-Garde.* Ed. Douglas Kahn and Gregory Whitehead. Cambridge: MIT P, 1992. 409–37.

———. *Word Cultures: Radical Theory and Practice in William S. Burroughs' Fiction.* Urbana: U of Illinois P, 1987.

Lyotard, Jean-François. *The Postmodern Condition: A Report on Knowledge.* 1979. Trans. Geoff Bennington and Brian Massumi. Minneapolis: U of Minnesota P, 1984.

MacArthur, Elizabeth. *Extravagant Narratives: Closure and Dynamics in the Epistolary Form.* Princeton: Princeton UP, 1990.

Malanga, Gerald. "An Interview with William Burroughs." *The Beat Book.* Ed. Arthur and Glee Knight. California: n.p., 1974. 90–112.

Manganotti, Donatella. "The Final Fix." *Kulchur* 4.15 (Autumn 1964): 76–87.

Marcus, Greil. "Undercover." *Rolling Stone* 19 May 1977. Rpt. in George-Warren 203–5.

Marks, John. *The Search for the 'Manchurian Candidate': The CIA and Mind Control.* London: Lane, 1970.

Martens, Lorna. *The Diary Novel.* Cambridge: Cambridge UP, 1985.

Martinez, Manuel Luis. "'With Imperious Eye': Kerouac, Burroughs, and Ginsberg on the Road in South America." *Aztlan* 23.1 (1998): 33–53.

McCarthy, Mary. "Burroughs' *Naked Lunch.*" *New York Review of Books* 1.1 (1963): 4–5. Rpt. in Skerl and Lydenberg 33–39.

McHale, Brian. *Constructing Postmodernism.* London: Routledge, 1992.

———. *Postmodernist Fiction.* New York: Methuen, 1987.

McKenna, Terrence. *Food of the Gods: A Radical History of Plants, Drugs and Human Evolution.* London: Random, 1992.

McNeill, Daniel. *The Face: A Guided Tour.* London: Hamilton, 1999.

McNicholas, Joseph. "William S. Burroughs and Corporate Public Relations." *Arizona Quarterly* 57.4 (Winter 2001): 121–49.

Meerloo, Joost A. M. *Mental Seduction and Menticide: A Psychology of Thought Control and Brainwashing.* London: Cape, 1957.

Melley, Timothy. *Empire of Conspiracy: The Culture of Paranoia in Postwar America.* Ithaca: Cornell UP, 2000.

Metz, Christian. *Psychoanalysis and Cinema: The Imaginary Signifier.* Trans. Celia Britton, Annwyl Williams, Ben Brewster, and Alfred Guzzetti. 1977. London: Macmillan, 1982.

Metzner, Ralph, ed. *Ayahuasca: Hallucinogens, Consciousness, and the Spirit of Nature.* New York: Thunder's Mouth, 1999.

Meyer, Adam. "'One of the Great Early Counsellors': The Influence of Franz Kafka on William S. Burroughs." *Comparative Literature Studies* 27.3 (1990): 211–19.

Michaud, Eric. "Van Gogh, or the Insufficiency of Sacrifice." *October* 49 (Summer 1989): 25–39.

Mikriammos, Philippe. *William S. Burroughs: la vie et l'oeuvre.* Paris: Seghers, 1975.

Miles, Barry. *Ginsberg: A Biography.* New York: Simon, 1989.

———, ed. *Howl: Original Draft Facsimile, Transcript and Variant Versions.* New York: Viking, 1986.

———. *William Burroughs: El Hombre Invisible.* London: Virgin, 1992.

Miller, Jane. *Seductions: Studies in Reading and Culture.* London: Virago, 1990.

Morgan, Ted. *Literary Outlaw: The Life and Times of William S. Burroughs.* New York: Holt, 1988.

Mottram, Eric. *William Burroughs: The Algebra of Need.* London: Boyars, 1977.

Muckle, John. "The Names: Allen Ginsberg's Writings." Lee 10–36.

Mulvey, Laura. *Fetishism and Curiosity.* London: BFI, 1996.

Murphy, Timothy S. "Intersection Points: Teaching William Burroughs' *Naked Lunch.*" *College Literature* 27.1 (Winter 2000): 84–102.

———. "William Burroughs: Between Indifference and Revalorization, Notes Towards a Political Reading." *Angelaki* 1.1 (1993): 113–24.

———. *Wising Up the Marks: The Amodern William Burroughs.* Berkeley: U of California P, 1997.

Nash, Christopher. *World Postmodern Fiction.* London: Longman, 1993.

Nathanson, Tenney. "Collage and Pulverization in Contemporary American Poetry: Charles Bernstein's *Controlling Interests.*" *Contemporary Literature* 33.2 (1992): 302–19.

Nealon, Jeffrey T. *Alterity Politics: Ethics and Performative Subjectivity.* Durham: Duke UP, 1998.

Nelson, Cary. "The End of the Body: Radical Space in Burroughs." *The Incarnate Word: Literature and Verbal Space.* Urbana: U of Illinois P, 1973. 208–29. Rpt. in Skerl and Lydenberg 119–32.

Neumann, John von, and Oskar Morgenstern. *Theory of Games and Economic Behavior.* Princeton: Princeton UP, 1944.

Newhouse, Thomas. *The Beat Generation and the Popular Novel in the United States, 1945–1970.* Jefferson: McFarland, 2000.

O'Brien, Geoffrey. *Hardboiled America: Lurid Paperbacks and the Masters of Noir.* 1981. Rev. ed. New York: De Capo, 1997.

O'Hara, John. *Appointment in Samarra.* 1935. London: Corgi, 1967.

Olson, Charles. *Call Me Ishmael: A Study of Melville.* San Francisco: City Lights, 1947.

Orvell, Miles. *The Real Thing: Imitation and Authenticity in American Culture, 1880–1940.* Chapel Hill: U of North Carolina P, 1989.

Osteen, Mark. "The Big Secret: *Film Noir* and Nuclear Fear." *Journal of Popular Film and Television* 22.2 (Summer 1994): 79–91.

Oxenhandler, Neal. "Listening to Burroughs' Voice." *Surfiction: Fiction Now . . . and Tomorrow.* Ed. Raymond Federman. Chicago: Swallow, 1975. 181–201. Rpt. in Skerl and Lydenberg 133–47.

Packard, Vance. *The Hidden Persuaders.* 1957. Harmondsworth: Penguin, 1960.

Palmer, Robert. "Interview with William Burroughs." *Rolling Stone* 11 May 1972: 48–53.

Passaro, Vince. "The Forgotten Killer." *Harper's Magazine* Apr. 1998: 71–75.

Payne, Johnny. *Conquest of the New World: Experimental Fiction and Translation in the Americas.* Austin: U of Texas P, 1993.

Perry, Ruth. *Women, Letters, and the Novel.* New York: AMS, 1980.

Phillips, Adam. *Promises, Promises: Essays on Literature and Psychoanalysis.* London: Faber, 2000.

Phillips, Rod. *"Forest Beatniks" and "Urban Thoreaus": Gary Snyder, Jack Kerouac, Lew Welch, and Michael McClure.* New York: Lang, 2000.

Pinkard, Terry. *Hegel's Dialectic: The Explanation of Possibility.* Philadelphia: Temple UP, 1988.

Plant, Sadie. *Zeroes and Ones: Digital Women + the New Technoculture.* London: Fourth Estate, 1997.

Ploog, Jurgen. "A Burroughs Primer." *Review of Contemporary Fiction* 4.1 (1984): 135–40.

Poe, Edgar Allen. *Complete Tales and Poems.* New York: Vintage, 1975.

Poggi, Christine. *In Defiance of Painting: Cubism, Futurism, and the Invention of Collage.* New Haven: Yale UP, 1992.

Polan, Dana. *Power and Paranoia: History, Narrative and the American Cinema, 1940–1950.* New York: Columbia UP, 1986.

Polizzotti, Mark. "In Search of André Breton." *Agni* 40 (1994): 77–83.

Porush, David. *The Soft Machine: Cybernetic Fiction.* New York: Methuen, 1985.

Potter, David A. *People of Plenty: Economic Abundance and the American Character.* Chicago: U of Chicago P, 1954.

Pounds, Wayne. "A Postmodern Anus: Parody and Utopia in Two Recent Novels by William Burroughs." *Poetics Today* 8.3–4 (1987): 611–29. Rpt. in Skerl and Lydenberg 217–32.

Pulsifer, Gary, ed. *Paul Bowles by His Friends.* London: Owen, 1992.

Punday, David. "Narrative after Deconstruction: Structure and the Negative Poetics of William Burroughs's *Cities of the Red Night.*" *Style* 1 (1995): 36–55.

Rader, Melvin. *Wordsworth: A Philosophical Approach.* Oxford: Oxford UP, 1967.

Ragland, Ellie. *Essays on the Pleasures of Death: From Freud to Lacan.* New York: Routledge, 1995.

Rajan, Balachandra. *The Form of the Unfinished: English Poetics from Spenser to Pound.* Princeton: Princeton UP, 1985.

Redding, Arthur F. *Raids on Human Consciousness: Writing, Anarchism, and Violence.* Columbia: U of South Carolina P, 1998.

Reich, Wilhelm. *The Mass Psychology of Fascism.* Trans. Vincent R. Carfango. 1933. Harmondsworth: Penguin, 1975.

Reid, Ian. *Narrative Exchanges.* London: RKP, 1992.

Rimbaud, Arthur. *Complete Works, Selected Letters.* Trans. Wallace Fowlie. Chicago: U of Chicago P, 1966.

Rodden, John. *The Politics of Literary Reputation: the Making and Claiming of St. George Orwell.* Oxford: Oxford UP, 1989.

Rodley, Chris, ed. *Cronenberg on Cronenberg.* London: Faber, 1993.

———. "So Deep in My Heart That You're Really a Part of Me." Silverberg 111–18.

Rogin, Michael Paul. *Ronald Reagan, the Movie and Other Episodes in Political Demonology.* Berkeley: U of California P, 1987.

Rondeau, Daniel. *Tanger.* Paris: Quai Voltaire, 1987.

Ronell, Avital. "Our Narcotic Modernity." *Rethinking Technologies.* Ed. Verena Andermatt Conley. Minneapolis: U of Minnesota P, 1993. 59–73.

———. *The Telephone Book: Technology, Schizophrenia, Electric Speech.* Lincoln: U of Nebraska P, 1989.

Rose, Jacqueline. *The Haunting of Sylvia Plath.* London: Virago, 1991.

Ross, Andrew. *No Respect: Intellectuals and Popular Culture.* New York: Routledge, 1989.

Ross, Daniel W. "Seeking a Way Home: The Uncanny in Wordsworth's 'Immortality Ode.'" *Studies in English Literature 1500–1900* 32.4 (Autumn 1992): 625–43.

Russell, Jamie. *Queer Burroughs.* New York: Palgrave, 2001.

Salecl, Renata, and Slavoj Žižek, eds. *Gaze and Voice as Love Objects.* Durham: Duke UP, 1996.

Savran, David. *Communists, Cowboys, and Queers: The Politics of Masculinity in the Work of Arthur Miller and Tennessee Williams.* Minneapolis: U of Minnesota P, 1992.

———. *Taking It like a Man: White Masculinity, Masochism and Contemporary American Culture.* Princeton: Princeton UP, 1998.

Schneider, Pierre. "The Moroccan Hinge." *Matisse in Morocco: The Paintings and Drawings, 1912–1913.* Ed. Jack Cowart and Pierre Schneider. London: Thames, 1990. 17–56.

Schultes, Richard Evans. *Vine of the Soul: Medicine Men, Their Plants and Rituals in the Colombian Amazonia.* Santa Fe: Synergetic, 1992.

Seed, David. "Mankind vs Machines: The Technological Dystopia in Kurt Vonnegut's *Player Piano.*" *Impossibility Fiction: Alternativity, Extrapolation, Speculation.* Ed. Derek Littlewood and Peter Stockwell. Amsterdam: Rodopi, 1996. 11–23.

Seem, Mark. Introduction. Deleuze and Guattari, *Anti-Oedipus* xv–xxiv.

Self, Will. Review of *Junky. Sunday Times* (London) 2 May 1993: 6.

Seltzer, Alvin J. *Chaos in the Novel, the Novel in Chaos.* New York: Schochen, 1974.

Server, Lee. *Over My Dead Body: The Sensational Age of the American Paperback: 1945–1955.* San Francisco: Chronicle, 1994.

Shaftesbury, Edmund [Webster Edgerly]. *Instantaneous Personal Magnetism.* 36th ed. Marple, England: Psychology Publishing, 1961.

Shaviro, Steven. *The Cinematic Body.* Minneapolis: U of Minnesota P, 1993.

———. *Passion and Excess: Blanchot, Bataille, and Literary Theory.* Tallahassee: Florida State UP, 1990.

———. "Two Lessons from Burroughs." Halberstam and Livingston 38–54.

Shiva, Vandana. *Biopiracy: The Plunder of Nature and Knowledge.* Totnes: Green, 1998.

Shklovsky, Viktor. *Zoo: or, Letters Not about Love.* Ed. and trans. Richard Sheldon. 1923. Ithaca: Cornell UP, 1971.

Silverberg, Ira, ed. *Everything Is Permitted: The Making of "Naked Lunch."* London: Harper, 1992.

Silverman, Kaja. *Male Subjectivity at the Margins.* New York: Routledge, 1992.

Simmell, George. *The Sociology of George Simmell.* Ed. and trans. Kurt H. Wolff. New York: Free, 1950.

Sinfield, Alan. "Diaspora and Hybridity: Queer Identities and the Ethnicity Model." *Textual Practice* 10.2 (1996): 271–93.

Skerl, Jennie. *William S. Burroughs.* Boston: Twayne, 1985.

Skerl, Jennie, and Robin Lydenberg, eds. *William S. Burroughs at the Front: Critical Reception, 1959–1989.* Carbondale: Southern Illinois UP, 1991.

Sobieszek, Robert. *Ports of Entry: William S. Burroughs and the Arts.* London: Thames, 1996.

Stephenson, Gregory. *The Daybreak Boys: Essays on the Literature of the Beat Generation.* Carbondale: Southern Illinois UP, 1990.

Stull, William L. "The Quest and the Question: Cosmology and Myth in the Work of William S. Burroughs, 1953–1960." *The Beats: Essays in Criticism.* Ed. Lee Bartlett. Jefferson: McFarland, 1981. 14–29.

Sugars, Cynthia. "Sylvia Plath as Fantasy Space: Or, the Return of the Living Dead." *Literature and Psychology* 45.3 (1999): 1–28.

Sukenick, Ron. *Down and In: Life in the Underground.* New York: Morrow, 1987.

Sussman, Mark. "Performing the Intelligent Machine." *TDR* 43.3 (Fall 1999): 81–96.

Tanner, Tony. *City of Words: American Fiction, 1950–1970.* London: Cape, 1971.

Taussig, Michael. *Defacement: Public Secrecy and the Labor of the Negative.* Stanford: Stanford UP, 1999.

———. *Mimesis and Alterity: A Particular History of the Senses.* London and New York: Routledge, 1993.

———. *Shamanism, Colonialism, and the Wild Man: A Study in Terror and Healing.* Chicago: U of Chicago P, 1987.

Telotte, J. P. *Voices in the Dark: Narrative Patterns in Film Noir.* Urbana: U of Illinois P, 1989.

Terry, Jennifer. "Anxious Slippages Between 'Us' and 'Them': A Brief History of the Scientific Search for Homosexual Bodies." *Deviant Bodies: Critical Perspectives on Difference in Science and Popular Culture.* Ed. Terry and Jacqueline Urla. Bloomington: Indiana UP, 1996. 129–69.

———. "The Seductive Power of Science in the Making of Deviant Subjectivity." Halberstam and Livingston 135–61.

Theweleit, Klaus. *Male Fantasies.* Trans. Stephen Conway, Erica Carter, and Chris Turner. 2 vols. Cambridge: Polity, 1987–89.

Thoreau, Henry David. *Walden and Resistance to Civil Government.* Ed. William Rossi. New York: Norton, 1992.

Tietchen, Todd. "Language out of Language: Excavating the Roots of Culture Jamming and Postmodern Activism from William S. Burroughs' *Nova* Trilogy." *Discourse* 23.3 (Fall 2001): 107–29.

Tytell, John. "John Tytell Talks with Carl Solomon" (1974). *The Beat Vision: A Primary Sourcebook.* Ed. Arthur and Kit Knight. New York: Paragon, 1987. 241–58.

———. *Naked Angels: The Lives and Literature of the Beat Generation.* 1976. New York: Grove, 1991.

———. *Paradise Outlaws: Remembering the Beats.* New York: Morrow, 1999.

Vernon, John. *The Garden and the Map: Schizophrenia in Twentieth Century Literature and Culture.* Urbana: U of Illinois P, 1973.

Vila, Christian. *William S. Burroughs: le genie empoisonne.* Paris: Editions du Rocher, 1992.

Ward, Geoff. "The Mutations of William Burroughs." *An Introduction to Contemporary Fiction: International Writing in English since 1970.* Ed. Rod Mengham. Cambridge: Polity, 1999. 110–22.

———. "William Burroughs: A Literary Outlaw?" *Cambridge Quarterly* 22.4 (1993): 339–54.

Watson, Steven. *The Birth of the Beat Generation: Visionaries, Rebels, and Hipsters, 1944–1960.* New York: Pantheon, 1995.

Weinreich, Regina. "Queer." Lotringer 613–19.

Weinstein, Arnold. "Freedom and Control in the Erotic Novel: The Classical *Liaisons dangereuses* Versus the Surrealist *Naked Lunch.*" *Dada/Surrealism* 10/11 (1982): 29–38.

———. "Kafka's Writing Machine: Metamorphosis in the Penal Colony." *Critical Essays on Franz Kafka.* Ed. Ruth V. Gross. Boston: Hall, 1990. 120–30.

Weiss, Allen S. "An Eye for an I: On the Art of Fascination." *SubStance* 51 (1986): 87–95.

———. *Phantasmic Radio.* Durham: Duke UP, 1995.

Whitfield, Stephen J. *The Culture of the Cold War.* Baltimore: John Hopkins UP, 1991.

Whitman, Walt. *The Complete Poems.* Harmondsworth: Penguin, 1975.

Wiener, Norbert. *Cybernetics, or Control and Communication in the Animal and the Machine.* 1948. 2nd ed. New York: MIT P, 1961.

———. *The Human Use of Human Beings: Cybernetics and Society.* London: Eyre, 1950.

Willett, John. "UGH . . ." *Times Literary Supplement* 14 Nov. 1963: 919. Rpt. in Skerl and Lydenberg 41–44.

Young, Elizabeth, and Graham Caveney. *Shopping in Space: Essays on American "Blank Generation" Fiction.* London: Serpent's Tail, 1992.

Ziegesar, Peter Von. "Mapping the Cosmic Currents: An Interview with William Burroughs." Hibbard 160–70.

Žižek, Slavoj. *Enjoy Your Symptom! Jacques Lacan in Hollywood and Out.* London: Routledge, 1992.

———. *For They Know Not What They Do: Enjoyment as a Political Factor.* London: Verso: 1991.

———. "I Hear You with My Eyes." Salecl and Žižek 90–126.

———. *The Indivisible Remainder: An Essay on Schelling and Related Matters.* London: Verso, 1996.

———. *Looking Awry: An Introduction to Jacques Lacan Through Popular Culture.* Cambridge: MIT P, 1992.

————. *The Metastases of Enjoyment: Six Essays on Woman and Causality.* London: Verso: 1994.

————. *The Plague of Fantasies.* London: Verso, 1997.

————. *The Sublime Object of Ideology.* London: Verso, 1989.

————. "'The Thing That Thinks': The Kantian Background of the Noir Subject." *Shades of Noir: A Reader.* Ed. Joan Copjec. London: Verso, 1993. 199–226.

Index

Decker, William, 255n. 10

Deleuze, Gilles, 90, 159, 195, 199–200, 202, 229

Dellamora, Richard, 85, 120, 148, 259n. 11

"Deposition: Testimony Concerning a Sickness" (Burroughs), 4, 39, 40, 76; as false preface, 187–88; and reception of *Naked Lunch*, 184, 185–87, 201, 205, 216

De Quincey, Thomas, 71, 184

Derrida, Jacques, 148

Dickinson, Emily, 145

Didion, Joan, 30

Doctor Sax (Kerouac), 35, 96

Dolar, Mladen, 98, 210

Dollimore, Jonathan, 87

Double Talk: The Erotics of Male Literary Collaboration (Koestenbaum), 195

Douglas, Ann, 31–32, 44, 59

Douglass, Mary, 94, 211

"Dream of the Penal Colony" (Burroughs), 152–54, 183

"Driving Lesson" (Burroughs), 152–55, 173, 213, 257n. 29

Dutoit, Ulysse, 10, 19

Early Routines (Burroughs): editing of, 208, 259n. 18. *See also* "Lee's Journals [and Letters]"

Eburne, Jonathan Paul, 168

Edwards, Paul, 121–22

Ehrenreich, Barbara, 106

Elvins, Kells, 69

Emerson, Ralph Waldo, 60, 145

epistolarity: Beat, 145; Burroughs', 145; defined, 135. *See also under* "In Search of Yage"; *Queer*

epistolary (general): absence and presence in, 136, 138–44, 172–76; address in, 136, 138, 140–42, 174–77, 238–39; as archaic, 60, 135, 202, 256n. 18; authenticity and, 158, 191, 198; as biographical resource, 44, 57, 135, 191; as critical and creative context for Burroughs, 43, 135, 159–60, 189, 202; criticism, 135, 204; demonic secret

side of, 199, 258n. 13; ethics of scholarship on, 192; as fictional genre, 158, 159; genetic role of, 43, 135–36, 197, 204; intersubjective economy in, 136, 141–42, 147, 192, 198–99, 218, 242; and journal form, 176, 205–9; and letter-writing as left-handed labor, 151, 185, 190, 192, 204; and literature, 158–59, 191, 192, 204, 210; power relationships in, 192, 194–96, 200–203; and speech, 141, 175; as technology of writing, 136, 143–44, 201–2; unity of desire and writing in, 141–42, 191–93, 196–97; utopian theme in, 58, 60, 145, 195. *See also under* Beat Generation; Burroughs, William S., and Ginsberg; Burroughs, William S., works of; epistolarity; Ginsberg, Allen; *individual works;* Kerouac, Jack; Marker, Lewis; master-slave dialectic; routine form; textual politics; vampirism

epistolary relationship between Burroughs and Ginsberg, 43–44, 54–55, 189, 190–96, 200–201, 218, 231–32, 237–39, 242; as analytic encounter, 198, 242; compared to epistolary relationship with Marker, 192–94, 196, 198–99, 200; exploitation of, 205–6, 238–39; one-sidedness of, 194–96, 198, 202, 238; and sign-off phrase of Burroughs, 245, 260n. 15. *See also under* Ginsberg, Allen; *Naked Lunch*, writing of

Everything Is Permitted: The Making of Naked Lunch (Silverberg), 234

Ewen, Stewart, 225

Exterminator! (Burroughs), 30, 249n. 9

fantasmatic, defined, 252n. 10. *See also under Queer*

fascination: attraction-repulsion in, 15, 17; of biographical pursuit, 10–12; of Burroughs, 1, 9–12, 13–17, 30–32, 181–82, 245; and desire, 10–11, 20–25; as fantasy, 25; as infectious, 2, 16, 29, 32–33, 251n. 12; lesson of, 217; and meaning, 6, 10, 13, 17, 26, 28, 30–31, 210–11, 221–22, 245; as problem for

Oliver Harris began his work on William Burroughs in 1984 at Christ Church, Oxford. In 1988, he was invited to edit *The Letters of William S. Burroughs, 1945–1959* and undertook extensive manuscript research, aided by Burroughs himself. Since then, as a professor in the School of American Studies at Keele University, he has published articles on Burroughs, the Beat Generation, film noir, and the epistolary in numerous journals and critical volumes. He is currently completing a restored, fiftieth-anniversary edition of Burroughs' first novel, *Junky*.